TWO ASIAS
The Emerging Postcrisis Divide

TWO ASIAS
The Emerging Postcrisis Divide

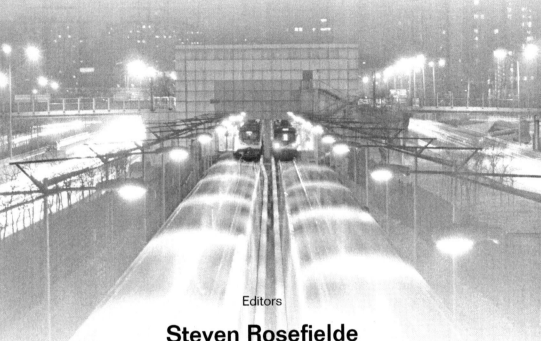

Editors

Steven Rosefielde
The University of North Carolina, USA

Masaaki Kuboniwa
Hitotsubashi University, Japan

Satoshi Mizobata
Kyoto University, Japan

NEW JERSEY · LONDON · SINGAPORE · BEIJING · SHANGHAI · HONG KONG · TAIPEI · CHENNAI

Published by

World Scientific Publishing Co. Pte. Ltd.
5 Toh Tuck Link, Singapore 596224
USA office: 27 Warren Street, Suite 401-402, Hackensack, NJ 07601
UK office: 57 Shelton Street, Covent Garden, London WC2H 9HE

British Library Cataloguing-in-Publication Data
A catalogue record for this book is available from the British Library.

TWO ASIAS
The Emerging Postcrisis Divide

Copyright © 2012 by World Scientific Publishing Co. Pte. Ltd.

All rights reserved. This book, or parts thereof, may not be reproduced in any form or by any means, electronic or mechanical, including photocopying, recording or any information storage and retrieval system now known or to be invented, without written permission from the Publisher.

For photocopying of material in this volume, please pay a copying fee through the Copyright Clearance Center, Inc., 222 Rosewood Drive, Danvers, MA 01923, USA. In this case permission to photocopy is not required from the publisher.

ISBN-13 978-981-4366-26-7
ISBN-10 981-4366-26-9

In-house Editor: Dan Jun

Typeset by Stallion Press
Email: enquiries@stallionpress.com

Printed in Singapore.

Dedication

For David Rosefielde

PREFACE

This compendium is based on a series of symposia devoted to the 2008 global financial crisis and its impact on Asia, held at Kyoto and Hitotsubashi universities in 2009 and 2010, funded by the Japan Foundation's Center for Global Partnership. Steven Rosefielde, Masaaki Kuboniwa, and Satoshi Mizobata, the project directors, coordinated a large team of experts across the globe with the participation of the institutes of economic research of Kyoto and Hitosubashi universities, the University of North Carolina, Institute of Transition Economics (Stockholm School of Economics), the Economies in Transition department of the Bank of Finland, and the University of Trento. The project's title was "Global Shock Wave: Rethinking Asia's Future in Light of the Worldwide Financial Crisis and Depression 2008–2010."

The symposia were designed to illuminate the character, complexities and implications of the crisis and its aftermath as a benchmark for gauging Asia's futures. This conference volume adheres to that format and has been structured more like a monograph than a compendium to highlight the project's central mission. Readers can trace the thread of the *Two Asias* hypothesis chapter by chapter, and/or tarry over sub-issues like the 2008 financial crisis's causes probed in great depth by various authors.

The volume's principal finding is that while the crisis affected Asian countries diversely, it did not cause epochal changes. Core tendencies evident during the last two decades seem destined to persist in a gradually deteriorating global economic environment, characterized by decelerating aggregate economic growth, and perhaps increased financial and international commercial disorder. Asia as a whole may continue to converge to the West's high frontier, but will remain highly stratified. The most problematic issues seem to be whether Japan will suffer a third "lost decade" and/or its paralysis will spread to Taiwan's and South Korea's filial systems.

ACKNOWLEDGMENTS

The editors wish to express their gratitude for the invaluable assistance of many institutions and individuals who made the project possible. First and foremost, our greatest debt is to the Japan Foundation's Center for Global Partnership which generously funded two brainstorming conferences and two symposia at Kyoto and Hitotsubashi universities critical for grappling with the manifold aspects of the 2008 financial crisis and its aftermath. The Kyoto Institute for Economic Research, the Hitotsubashi Institute for Economic Research, University of North Carolina, the Institute of Transition Economics (SITE, Stockholm School of Economics), the Economies in Transition department of the Bank of Finland (BOFIT), and the School on Local Development at the University of Trento all provided precious support. We also wish to thank the conference and symposia participants, both attendees and those contributing from afar, as well as Emiko Horibe (KIER), Nancy Kocher (UNC), and Huan Zhou who coordinated meetings, typed manuscripts and compiled this volume. We acknowledge all these contributions with our deepest appreciation.

CONTENTS

Preface		vii
Acknowledgments		ix
List of Tables and Figures		xiii
List of Contributors		xxi

Introduction		1

Part I	**Asia's Rebirth**	**7**
Chapter 1	Asian Economic Performance 1500–2010 *Steven Rosefielde and Huan Zhou*	9

Part II	**The 2008 Financial Crisis and Its Global Aftermath**	**67**
Chapter 2	Global Financial Crisis *Assaf Razin and Steven Rosefielde*	69
Chapter 3	Global Bust *Iikka Korhonen and Aaron Mehrotra*	81

Part III	**Asian Repercussions**	**103**
Chapter 4	Pan Asian Shock Wave *Takeo Hidai*	105
Chapter 5	Policy Response *Takuji Kinkyo*	155
Chapter 6	Japan *Satoshi Mizobata*	177
Chapter 7	China *Kai Kajitani*	199

xii *Contents*

Chapter 8	Russia *Eric Brunat*	209
Part IV	**Export-Led Modernization and Decoupling**	**249**
Chapter 9	Export-Led Development and Dollar Reserve Hoarding *Steven Rosefielde*	251
Chapter 10	Chinese Overtrading *Jonathan Leightner*	267
Chapter 11	Counter-Crisis Trade Expansion *Mia Mikic*	295
Chapter 12	Collapse, Consequences, and Prospects of Japan's Trade *Ryuhei Wakasugi*	327
Chapter 13	Business Cycle Decoupling *Iikka Korhonen, Jarko Fidrmuc and Ivana Bátorová*	345
Part V	**Petro Shock**	**359**
Chapter 14	Lessons From BRICs *Masaaki Kuboniwa*	361
Part VI	**Western Economic Fatigue**	**377**
Chapter 15	Eurozone and Global Financial Imbalances *Bruno Dallago and Chiara Guglielmetti*	379
Part VII	**Two Asias**	**419**
Chapter 16	East-West Convergence and Intra-Asian Stratification *Steven Rosefielde, Masaaki Kuboniwa and Satoshi Mizobata*	421
Conclusion		439
Index		441

LIST OF TABLES AND FIGURES

Tables

Table 1.1	Per capita GDP AD 1–2001	10
Table 1.2	Population growth (1–2001 AD)	12
Table 1.3	Communist per capita GDP growth 1985–2001	12
Table A1.1a	Per capita GDP in 12 East Asian countries, 1820–2001 (1990 international Geary-Khamis dollars)	21
TableA1.1b	Per capita GDP in four East Asian countries, 1820–2001 (1990 international Geary-Khamis dollars)	28
Table A1.2a	Population growth in 13 East Asian countries, 1820–2001	33
Table A1.2b	Population growth in four East Asian countries, 1820–2001	42
Table A1.3a	GDP in 13 East Asian countries, 1820–2001 (1990 international Geary-Khamis dollars)	47
Table A1.3b	GDP in four East Asian countries, 1820–2001 (1990 international Geary-Khamis dollars)	56
Table 3.1	General government debt, percentage of GDP, 2005–2009	90
Table 5.1	Year-on-year GDP growth rates	157
Table 5.2	The share of goods by stages of process in trade	159
Table 5.3	The ratio of foreign reserves to short-term external debt	160
Table 5.4	Prudential indicators of Asian banks	162
Table 5.5	Unit root tests	164

xiii

xiv *List of Tables and Figures*

Table 5.6	Contribution and borrowing limits of CMIM	170
Table 6.1	Number of bankrupt banks	179
Table 6.2	Employment protection of core workers (late 1990s)	187
Table 6.3	Employment protection in OECD countries, 2008	187
Table 6.4	Irregularly employed workers in Japan (%)	189
Table 6.5	Changes in employment (thousands, %)	189
Table 6.6	Length of service in Japan (%)	190
Table 8.1	Traditional Russian values and principal consequences	210
Table 8.2	Annual percentage variation in Russian GDP	214
Table 8.3	Principal macroeconomic indicators 2006–2009	219
Table 8.4	Structure of Russian imports and exports in percentage 2008	226
Table 8.5	Comparison of the knowledge economy index of several nations. Indexes recomposed by the World Bank from 0 to 10	234
Table 8.6	Comparison between the data for 2005–2006 and the 2020 objectives of the ministry of economic development and trade of the Russian federation (in %) — MEDT	235
Table 8.7	Russia's commercial partners as percentage of total in 2005	238
Table 8.8	Direct foreign investments — DFI: Comparison of Russia, Ukraine, and Poland	241
Table 10.1	The normalized GDP data	279
Table 10.2	The normalized government spending data	280
Table 10.3	$\partial GDP/\partial G$ BD-RTPLS estimates	281
Table 11.1	Advantages and disadvantages of export-led growth	297
Table 11.2	Geographical reorientation of Asia Pacific exports, 1995–2007	304
Table 11.3	Export dependence of ESCAP countries, 1995–2007, percentage point difference	306
Table 11.4	Who are the major players in the Asia-Pacific intraregional trade? (%)	315

List of Tables and Figures   xv

Table 12.1	Growth rates of GDP	328
Table 12.2	Changing rates of the US imports by country and product	331
Table 12.3	Changes of Japanese export by country and goods	332
Table 12.4	Shifting sources of US imports	333
Table 12.5	Shifting destination of Japanese export (%)	334
Table 12.6	Estimation of extensive and intensive margins: export to the US	338
Table 12.7	Estimation of extensive and intensive margins: export to China	339
Table 12.8	Extensive and intensive margins of Japanese exports to the US	340
Table 12.9	Extensive and intensive margins of Japanese exports to China	341
Table 12.10	Growth of middle-income countries	343
Table 13.1	Correlation of Chinese and Indian stock market returns	351
Table 13.A1	Stock indices used	356
Table 14.1	Foreign trade data of China	370
Table 14.2	Average growth of GDP and trading gains in the BRICs: 1995–2010	374
Table 15.1	EU trade with the US	387
Table 15.2	The Economist house-price indicators (% change)	389
Table 15.3	Households' net saving rate (1995, 2000, and 2008)	391
Table 15.4	Eurozone banking exposure, eurozone core bank's holding of PIGS, UK, and US Debts (millions of US$)	392
Table 15.5	Intra-eurozone banking exposure, EZ core banks' holding of PIGS Debt	393
Table 15.6	European banks' leverage ratio	393
Table 15.7	Interventions (governments and central banks) in favor of the banking system in Europe during the current crisis (billions of euros)	395
Table 15.8	Deficit, current account, inflation, and growth in the EZ: 2000–2007	402
Table 15.9	Intra EZ export (% of total export)	404

xvi *List of Tables and Figures*

Figures

Figure 1.1	Chinese–EU divergence and convergence 1500–2010 per capita GDP (Western Europe = 100)	15
Figure 1.2	Japanese–EU divergence and convergence 1500–2010 per capita GDP (Western Europe = 100)	16
Figure 1.3	Taiwanese–EU divergence and convergence 1820–2010 per capita GDP (Western Europe = 100)	16
Figure 1.4	Thai–EU divergence and convergence 1820–2010 per capita GDP (Western Europe = 100)	17
Figure 1.5	Myanmar–EU divergence and convergence 1820–2010 per capita GDP (Western Europe = 100)	18
Figure 1.6	Vietnam–EU divergence and convergence 1820–2010 per capita GDP (Western Europe = 100)	19
Figure 1.7	North and South Korean divergence and convergence 1820–2010 per capita GDP (Western Europe = 100)	20
Figure A1.1	Singaporean–EU divergence and convergence 1820–2010 per capita GDP (Western Europe = 100)	61
Figure A1.2	Hong Kong–EU divergence and convergence 1820–2010 per capita GDP (Western Europe = 100)	61
Figure A1.3	Cambodian–EU divergence and convergence 1820–2010 per capita GDP (Western Europe = 100)	62
Figure A1.4	Laotian–EU divergence and convergence 1820–2010 per capita GDP (Western Europe = 100)	62
Figure A1.5	Indian–EU divergence and convergence 1500–2010 per capita GDP (Western Europe = 100)	63

List of Tables and Figures xvii

Figure A1.6	Russian–EU per capita GDP: comparative size 1820–2010 (West European = 100)	63
Figure A1.7	USSR–EU territorial per capita GDP: comparative size 1500–2010 (West European = 100)	64
Figure A1.8	Malaysia–EU per capita GDP: divergence and convergence 1820–2010	64
Figure A1.9	Indonesia–EU per capita GDP: divergence and convergence 1820–2010	65
Figure A1.10	Philippines–EU per capita GDP: divergence and convergence 1820–2010	65
Figure 2.1	Employment declines in various US crises	72
Figure 2.2	World industrial production	76
Figure 3.1	GDP growth rates (%) in major regions, 2000–2011	82
Figure 3.2	Domestic credit to private sector, percentage of GDP	83
Figure 3.3	Net new bank lending to nongovernment sector in the euro area, January 1999 — November 2010, billion euros	85
Figure 3.4	Volume of world trade (seasonally adjusted), 2000 = 100, January 1991–October 2010	86
Figure 3.5	GDP growth in the US, first quarter of 2007 — third quarter of 2010	87
Figure 3.6	USD nominal effective exchange rate (upward movement signifies appreciation), January 2006–October 2010	96
Figure 3.7	USD/EUR exchange rate, January 2, 1999 to December 31, 2010	97
Figure 3.8	Growth contributions of Chinese GDP components	99
Figure 5.1	Year-on-year growth rates of exports	158
Figure 5.2a	Korea: accumulated structural shocks	165
Figure 5.2b	Thailand: accumulated structural shocks	166
Figure 6.1	GDP and economic growth in Japan	178
Figure 6.2	Income and consumption	180

xviii *List of Tables and Figures*

Figure 6.3	Labor market in Japan	182
Figure 6.4	Type of shareholder	184
Figure 6.5	Shareholders composition	186
Figure 6.6	Labor share	188
Figure 6.7	Unemployment and irregularly employed	189
Figure 6.8	Earnings and hours worked	191
Figure 6.9	Corporate governance of J firms	192
Figure 7.1	Financial policy of China	200
Figure 7.2	Annual growth rate of financial figures	200
Figure 7.3	Annual growth rate of import and export	201
Figure 7.4	Mechanism of "loan platform"	201
Figure 7.5	Dollar-RMB rate and foreign exchange reserve of China	202
Figure 7.6	Long-term real interest rate in China and US	203
Figure 7.7	US's current account deficit and China's and Japan's surpluses	204
Figure 7.8	Low capital returns in the emerging countries and global imbalances	205
Figure 8.1	Movement in capitalisation of Russian securities market (in % of GDP) and Urals oil price	224
Figure 8.2	Internal expenditure on R&D in different countries (in % of GDP) — scale on left. Volume of personnel engaged in R&D — researchers and other personnel — per 10,000 employees, red curve, and scale on right (for year 2004 and following years where data available) Global internal expenditure on R&D column on right, public internal expenditure R&D column on left	226
Figure 8.3	Structure of the wealth of nations in percentage	229
Figure 10.1	China's data and results	283
Figure 10.2	$\partial GDP / \partial G$ for big spenders in 2008–2009	284
Figure 10.3	$\partial GDP / \partial G$ for more steady spenders in 2008–2009	285
Figure 10.4	$\partial GDP / \partial G$ for neither big nor steady spenders	287

Figure 11.1	Trends in exports of selected Asian economies, February 1996–June 2009	302
Figure 11.2	Trends in imports of selected Asian economies, February 1996–June 2009	303
Figure 11.3	Export to US, EU, and Japan in total exports (percentage point differences, 1995–2007)	304
Figure 11.4	Export to China, India, and ASEAN in total exports (percentage point differences, 1995–2007)	305
Figure 11.5	Export dependence on US and Chinese markets, 1995–2007, percentage point differences	307
Figure 11.6	Export dependence on Japanese and the EU markets, 1995–2007, percentage point differences	308
Figure 11.7	Direct and total export exposure changes (1995–2007) in US and EU markets	309
Figure 11.8	Breakdown of emerging Asian exports	311
Figure 11.9	Change in sourcing of Chinese imports, 1995–2007 (percentage point differences)	312
Figure 11.10	Are Chinese exports to US and Asian exports to China associated?	313
Figure 11.11	Growth of total and intraregional trade of developing Asia Pacific economies	313
Figure 11.12	Intraregional exports and imports as share in total exports and imports of ASEAN + 3 (monthly)	315
Figure 11.13	Selected stimulus packages as share in economy's GDP	317
Figure 11.14	Stimulus breakdown by use	318
Figure 11.15	Difference between applied and bound tariffs	319
Figure 11.16	Trade measures enacted by Asia Pacific countries from October 2008 to June 2009	320
Figure 11.17	Regional currencies movements against US$	322
Figure 11.18	Regional currencies movements against the euro	322
Figure 12.1	Changing US imports by country and region	330
Figure 12.2	Japan's export to US by commodity (2008)	331

xx List of Tables and Figures

Figure 12.3	Shifting sources of US imports: China's rise and decline of Japan and other East Asia	333
Figure 12.4	Destination of offshoring	335
Figure 12.5	Current balance of major countries	342
Figure 13.1	Log difference of shanghai composite index	348
Figure 13.2	Moving correlation of Chinese stock market (one-year window)	349
Figure 13.3	Moving correlation of Indian stock market (one-year window)	350
Figure 13.4	Dynamic correlation of stock market returns between China and selected countries	353
Figure 13.5	Dynamic correlation of stock market returns between India and selected countries	354
Figure 14.1	GDP growth in BRICs in the 2000s	363
Figure 14.2	GDP growth in BRICs for 1990–2010	364
Figure 14.3	GDP at a current US$ basis in BRICs and Japan (in billions)	365
Figure 14.4	GDP, manufacturing and oil prices in Russia.	366
Figure 14.5	GDP and GDI (Command-Basis GDP) in the BRICs	371
Figure 15.1	Top 0.1% income share in English speaking countries (1908–2010)	381
Figure 15.2	Residential property price index, EU 16 (new and existing dwelling)	388
Figure 15.3	Private and government liabilities in the EZ (% GDP)	391
Figure 15.4	Labor productivity per hour worked (EU–27 = 100)	400
Figure 15.5	Gini index	401
Figure 15.6	Current account balance (% GDP)	404
Figure 15.7	Average government debt as a percentage of GDP in the Eurozone	408
Figure 15.8	Average government deficit as a percentage of GDP in the Eurozone	408
Figure 15.9	Interest rates spread in Europe	409

LIST OF CONTRIBUTORS

Steven Rosefielde
Steven Rosefielde is a professor of economics at the University of North Carolina, Chapel Hill and a co-director of the Japan Foundation's Center for Global Partnership project on *Two Asias: The Emerging Postcrisis Divide*. He received his PhD in Economics from Harvard University and is a member of the Russian Academy of Natural Sciences (RAEN). He has taught in Russia, China, Japan, and Thailand. Most recently, he published the following: *Russia in the 21st Century: The Prodigal Superpower*, Cambridge University Press, 2005; *Masters of Illusion*, Cambridge University Press, 2007 (with Quinn Mills); *Russia Since 1980*, Cambridge University Press, 2008 (with Stefan Hedlund); *Rising Nations*, Amazon, 2009 (with Quinn Mills); *Red Holocaust*, Routledge, 2010; *Democracy and its Elected Enemies*, Cambridge University Press, 2012. He is at present completing *Asian Economic System* with the following book: *Prevention and Crisis Management: Lessons for Asia from the 2008 Crisis* (co-edited with Masaaki Kuboniwa and Satoshi Mizobata, 2012.

Huan Zhou
Huan Zhou is a PhD candidate in the Economics Department, University of North Carolina, Chapel Hill. Her research fields are Macroeconomics and International Economics. Her current research focuses on global imbalances.

Assaf Razin
Assaf Razin is the Friedman professor of International Economics at Cornell University, professor emeritus at Tel Aviv University, and research associate in the NBER, CEPR, and Cesifo. Assaf Razin's recent books include the following: *Labor, Capital, and Finance: International*

Flows, Cambridge University Press, September 2001(with Efraim Sadka); *The Decline of the Welfare State: Political Economics of Demography and Globalization*, 2005, MIT Press (with Efraim Sadka); *Foreign Direct Investment: Analysis of Aggregate Flows*, Princeton University Press, November 2007 (with Efraim Sadka); *Migration and the Welfare State: Political-Economy Policy Formation*, MIT Press,June 2011 (with Efraim Sadka and Benjarong Suwankiri).

Iikka Korhonen
Dr Iikka Korhonen has worked at the Bank of Finland since July 1995 when he joined the Institute for Economies in Transition (BOFIT). At the BOFIT he has followed, among other things, the banking and financial systems of the Baltic States and Russia. His past duties include working as BOFIT's research supervisor, and since October 1, 2009, he has been the Head of BOFIT. His research interests include exchange rates and inflation in transition as well as emerging market countries. In addition, he has published widely for example, on the correlation of economic activity between different countries, as well as on the effects of oil prices on economic activities.

Aaron Mehrotra
Aaron Mehrotra is an adviser at the Bank of Finland Institute for Economies in Transition (BOFIT). His areas of expertise include the Chinese economy and economic policy, and also monetary policy in transition economies. Mr Mehrotra's research has been published in academic journals including the *Journal of Comparative Economics, Economics of Transition,* and *China Economic Review*. Aaron Mehrotra is also adjunct professor at the Aalto University School of Economics. He holds a PhD from the European University Institute in Florence, Italy.

Takeo Hidai
Takeo Hidai was born on July 1, 1973 in Yokohama city, Japan. He was educated at Faculty of Economics, University of Tokyo (BA in Economics), Graduate School of Economics, University of Tokyo (MA in Economics). He has worked as Economist (CIS countries), Japan Center for International Finance (2003–2004), Attaché (Economic Affairs),

Embassy of Japan in Moscow (2005–2007), Guest Analyst (CIS countries), Ministry of Foreign Affairs, Japan (2007–2008), Economist (CIS countries), Japan Center for International Finance (2007–2009), Research Associate, Institute of Economic Research, Hitotsubashi University (2009) and from 2010 as a Lecturer (part-time), Ferris University. He has academic interests in political economy of Russia (especially economic policy of Putin–Medvedev administration) and economic history of Soviet Union (especially kolkhoz in 1930s).

Takuji Kinkyo

Takuji Kinkyo is a professor of economics at Graduate School of Economics, Kobe University. He previously worked as Director, International Department at Ministry of Finance Japan and was a visiting lecturer at School of Oriental and African Studies, University of London. He was educated at Kyoto University (BA) and University of London (PhD). His research interests include the following: emerging market financial crises; Asian economic integration; the choice of exchange rate regimes; finance and development; and international financial architecture. His work has been published in leading academic journals, including *Cambriage Journal of Economics and Wolrd Developemnt*.

Satoshi Mizobata

Satoshi Mizobata is a professor and vice-director at the University of Kyoto, Kyoto Institute of Economic Research. His research areas are comparative studies in economic systems, corporate governance and business organization and the Russian and East European economies, focusing on the enterprises and market structure. He is the editor of *The Journal of Comparative Economic Studies* in Japan and Executive Committee member of European Association for Comparative Economic Studies. His recent works include the following: *Melting Boundaries: Institutional Transformation in the Wider Europe* (co-edited with K. Yagi), Kyoto: Kyoto University Press, 2008; "Diverging and Harmonizing Corporate Governance in Russia," in John Pickles (ed.) *State and Society in Post-socialist Economies*, New York: Palgrave Macmillan, 2008; and *Varieties of Capitalisms and Transformation*, Kyoto: Bunrikaku, 2008, and others.

Kai Kajitani

Kai Kajitani is an associate professor of Economics at Kobe University. *Kajitani* has been mainly focusing on the analysis about following two kinds of topics.

(1) The central–local relationship in China and its influence to the financial policy or macro-control by the central government.
(2) The China's contribution to the phenomenon known as "Global Imbalance" and its influence to domestic financial policy in China.

Kajitani has got a PhD in Economics from Kobe University and has published many papers about modern and contemporary Chinese economy.

Eric Brunat

Eric Brunat was vice-president of the University of Savoie (France) from 1999 through 2002 and from 2008 until now; PhD, Professor of ecomomics (accreditation to supervise research); Honorary doctorate (*"honoris causa"*) received from the State University of Sochi (Russia) on October 18, 2010; Insigna of the Order of socioeconomic and cooperative development of the Russian Federation (Order signed by the President of the Federal Central Union, V.F. Ermakov, on March 5, 2007, Kaliningrad (Russia); former UNDP senior economist-advisor and Deputy Resident Representative (Moldova, Belarus, Russia); former scientific and executive director of the Russian European Center for Economic Policy in Moscow (European Union); more than 25 years of research, focusing on the Soviet-type economies and then on the conditions for the transformation and the modernization of the Russian Federation, emphasizing the importance of specific Russian institutional and territorial factors; conferences and visiting professor in many countries; 134 publications, conferences, and reports published from October 1984 to February 2011 (in French, English, Russian, Ukrainian, or Spanish).

Jonathan Leightner

Jonathan E. Leightner is a professor of economics at Augusta State University. He has taught courses on China's economy at the Johns Hopkins University–Nanjing University Center for American and Chinese

Studies (in Nanjing, China) and at Chulalongkorn University (in Bangkok, Thailand). His research focuses on Asia, especially China, Japan, and Thailand. He is the creator of Bi-Directional Reiterative Truncated Least Squares, a new regression technique that accounts for the influence of omitted variables without knowing, modeling, or finding proxies for them.

Mia Mikic

Mia Mikic is an economist in the Trade and Investment Division of the UN Economic and Social Commission for Asia and the Pacific and a coordinator of Asia-Pacific Research and Training Network on Trade. She has taught International Economics at the University of Zagreb and the University of Auckland and served as a head of the Department of Economic Theory and Director of the Economics and Business International Program at the University of Zagreb over 2002–2004. She is the author of International Trade (Macmillan, 1998), coauthor of Trade Statistics in Policy-Making (UN, 2009) and has contributed chapters to several edited volumes and published a number of journal articles and other papers. Her current work focuses on the impacts of preferential trade liberalization, services trade, and design of capacity-building programs for evidence-based trade policy-making. She obtained a PhD in Economics from the University of Zagreb.

Ryuhei Wakasugi

Ryuhei Wakasugi has been a professor of International Economics at the Institute of Economic Research, Kyoto University and research counselor of Research Institute of Economy, Trade, and Industry since 2006. Prior to working in Kyoto University, he was professor at Keio University and Yokohama National University and had done his PhD in economics from Tokyo University and his MA in economics from Yale University. He also has taught at Waseda University, Hokkaido University, and National University of Mongolia. His research interests include trade, FDI, technology transfer, and innovation. He is the author of numerous books and articles on these fields. He is advisory editor of Research Policy and was the editor-in-chief of *The International Economies*. He received the Kojima Kiyoshi Prize and an award from *Japan Academy of International Business Studies*.

Jarko Fidrmuc

Jarko Fidrmuc is a professor of International Economics at the Zeppelin University in Friedrichshafen, Germany. He is also a research fellow at the CESifo Institute in Munich and Institute of Eastern European Studies in Regensburg. He was a visiting researcher at several universities and institutions including China Foreign Affairs University in Beijing, National Institute for Public Finance and Policy in Delhi, Japanese Association of European Studies in Tokyo, University of Jerusalem, and Comenius University in Bratislava. His research focuses on international economics and finance especially with focus on Asian and Eastern European emerging economies.

Ivana Bátorová

Ivana Bátorová is a PhD student in the Department of Applied Mathematics and Statistics, Faculty of Mathematics, Physics, and Informatics, Comenius University in Bratislava, Slovakia. Her research focuses on spectral tools and their applications in econometrics.

Masaaki Kuboniwa

Masaaki Kuboniwa is a professor at Institute of Economic Research, Hitotsubashi University in Tokyo. He is appointed the president of the Japanese Association for Comparative Economic Studies for 2011–2013. He received the degree of honorable doctor from Central Economics and Mathematics Institute of the Russian Academy of Sciences in 2003 and was named a Leontief Medal laureate by the Russian Academy of Natural Sciences in 2004. He has published numerous articles in Japanese, English, and Russian economic journals and is the author of the following: *Quantitative Economics of Socialism* (Oxford University Press, 1989); *Development of Capitalism in Russia* (with Evgeny Gavrilenkov, Maruzen, 1997); and *Economics of Intergenerational Equity in Transition Economies* (with Yoshiaki Nishimura, Maruzen, 2006).

Bruno Dallago

Bruno Dallago, PhD, is a professor of economics at the University of Trento, Italy. He is the dean of the Faculty of Sociology and director of the School on Local Development at the University of Trento and academic director of the Erasmus Mundus Joint European Master in

Comparative Local Development. He was president of the European Association for Comparative Economic Studies and visiting professor at the following universities: the University of California at Berkeley, USA; Hitotsubashi University, Tokyo, Japan; and Tshwane University of Technology, Pretoria, South Africa. He is the author and editor of several scholarly books and journal articles. He has acted as a consultant to various international organizations, including the World Bank and the OECD. His research interests include comparative economics, the transforming economies of Central and East Europe, SMEs and entrepreneurship, local development.

Chiara Guglielmetti

Chiara Guglielmetti is a postdoctoral research fellow at the Department of Sociology and Social Research of the University of Trento, Italy and holds a PhD in Law and Economics from the University of Bologna, Italy.

She has been a visiting scholar at the University of North Carolina (UNC) at Chapel Hill (USA) and Erasmus Mundus research scholar at the University of Belgrade, Serbia. Her research interests include transition in Eastern Europe, SMEs and entrepreneurship, inequality and social policies.

INTRODUCTION

The global recession depression (2008–2010) has been the severest postwar decline on record.[1] It began symbolically with the collapse of Lehman Brothers on September 15, 2008 and may not have fully run its course, although the NBER "officially" declared that America's recession was over in June 2010.[2]

The financial crisis spread with extraordinarily rapidity around the world, but Asia was spared cascading bank failures because in the aftermath of its own 1997 financial crisis, banks shunned speculative practices, and governments accumulated hefty foreign currency reserves.

Asia did not go unscathed. Its exports to America and the European Union plunged, depressing regional aggregate economic activity. Western outsourcing, foreign direct investment, and technology transfer likewise slowed.

Other things being equal therefore, it might be surmised that the status *quo ante* will be swiftly restored in 2011, assuming that western financial practices are righted,[3] related problems like petro bubbles and trade imbalances resolved, and excess debt burdens and government over-regulation eliminated. Fulfillment of these conditions however is

---

[1] Korhonen, I and A Mehrotra. "Global Bust" in Chapter 3.

[2] The National Bureau of Economic Research (NBER), the conventional arbiter of business cycle dating, announced on September 20, 2010 that America's recession began in December 2007 and ended in June 2009. This does not mean that the committee judged recovery complete; only that the recession's trough was set, and that recovery is in progress. The 2007–2009 recession is the longest on postwar record. GDP remains 1.3% below its previous peak. See *Wall Street Journal blogs* dated September 20, 2010.

[3] Blinder A and M Zandi (2010). "How the Great Recession Was Brought to an End." http:\\ www.economy.com/mark-zandi/documents/End-of-Great.

2 Introduction

problematic, and may be especially harmful in Asia when noncyclical factors like diminishing catch-up effects, bounded systems potential, and decoupling are added to the mix.

The East is more likely to experience a significant reconfiguration of wealth and power due to epochal and aberrant cyclical factors. Will the aftershocks of the "Great Recession" contribute to a third Japanese "lost decade," while China effortlessly bolts ahead? Will the "tigers" succumb to a climateric like Japan? What is in store for Asian communist and Theravada Buddhist nations?

Two Asias addresses all these issues through the prism of the shifting divide between the East's laggard and mature countries. It forecasts growth deceleration for the tigers (Singapore, Taiwan, and South Korea) and Japan, subpar performance in North Korea and Myanmar, and decelerating rates of catch-up elsewhere for the next decade. Thereafter, when all Asian regimes have exhausted the advantages of relative backwardness, their static and dynamic performance will be governed by their systems potentials. The intermediate term prediction assumes coupling (verified in Chapter 11, 12, and 13) and the comparatively slow pace of growth suggested in Chapters 3, 5, 6, 8, 9, 11, and 15. It also rejects convergence in two senses. Some countries like North Korea and Myanmar are apt to diverge increasingly from the EU high per capita income frontier; others find themselves asymptotically bounded from above by their systemic limitations.

Judgments of these sorts require a sound grasp of cultures and systems of all Asian societies that exceed the authors' collective expertise. Accordingly, throughout most of the text, Asia is narrowly defined as East and Southeast Asia, excluding the Muslim, Hindu, and Christian Orient. Russia, India, Malaysia, and Indonesia will be discussed occasionally; however, the Asian states of primary concern will be Japan, market communist China, Vietnam, Laos, and Cambodia, command communist North Korea, command socialist Myanmar, and Asian tigers South Korea, Taiwan, and Singapore (Hong Kong and Macao are treated as administrative units of China).

The theory and evidence behind this parsing of the shape of things to come are eclectic. The foundation is neoclassical microeconomics including growth theory, rooted in the concept of unfettered, competitive utility and profit-seeking at home and abroad. Under a set of well-known assumptions, perfect competition (and perfect planning) automatically allocates factors (including finance and technology) to best use. The goods and services produced with optimal technologies, finance, and variable factors are then distributed in accordance with the full value-added earnings of workers and asset holders. This allows individuals to maximize their utility and for those, starting in an inferior position, to learn and take action to completely realize their potentials over time. Natural endowments aside, competitive utility-seeking should bring about a close merging of living standards across the globe. Although it is broadly recognized that this line of reasoning is utopian, many microtheorists nonetheless claim that competitive utility and profit-seeking nudge results in the right outcomes, reinforced by globalization.

The path forward however is never smooth. Business activity oscillates for technical and speculative reasons. Nassim Taleb metaphorically calls fluctuations around the technology growth trend "White Swans."[4] Governments strive to modulate ebbs and flows with monetary and fiscal policy. When they succeed short and long-term factors are easily distinguished. However, economies occasionally are beset by more serious disequilibria, resulting in "Black Swans": extreme V-shaped depressions, multiple dips (W-shaped declines), and prolonged recoveries.

Epochal changes complicate matters and are best understood for our purposes as shifts in underlying growth trajectories. Systems can accelerate, decelerate, stagnate, and decline for internal reasons or due to exogenous shocks including "Black Swan" cyclical aberrations. The Great Depression, postwar acceleration, post-1975 deceleration, and post-command communist global growth surge all are examples of epochal shifts caused by profound changes in internal states, cyclical conjunctures, and the external environment.

Inconsistencies between micro and macroeconomic concepts and statistics also cloud causal discourse. Microeconomic notions of growth filter out business cycles and policy effects, focusing instead on intermediate

---

[4] Taleb N (2007). *Black Swan: The Impact of the Highly Improbable*. New York: Random House.

4   *Introduction*

and long-term sustainable improvements in aggregate productivity (Robert Solow's "golden age economic growth" hypothesis). Macrotheory by contrast, combines transitory with sustainable changes, often misconstruing disequilibrium surges with permanent, government-induced improvements in long-term economic performance (endogenous growth).

Macroeconomic statistical conventions furthermore blur causality. For example, where microtheorists might attribute recessions or depressions to weak export demand, macro theorists tend to impute the same downturns to diminished aggregate consumption and investment, because by statistical definition, if imports and exports fall in tandem GDP is unchanged or only mildly effected.[5] The correct policy response for microtheorists is stimulating exports; for macro theorists, it is stimulating domestic investment and consumption.[6] Similarly, purchasing power imbalances associated with oil, food, service prices, and tax shocks are airbrushed out of the macrostatistics.

These nuances bear directly on perceptions of the 2008 global financial crisis's impact on Asia. International trade and coupling appear to be the dominant causes of the East's plight from a microeconomic perspective but plays almost no role in the macro story which attributes Asian performance to changes in domestic aggregate investment and consumption (see Chapter 10).

Both interpretations are useful, highlighting as they do different aspects of the emerging postcrisis "Two Asias" story but cannot be completely integrated because economics as practiced is not a unified science (analogous to the conflict between the quantum mechanics of Neils Bohr and the general field theory in physics of Albert Einstein). Judgment is essential for cogent descriptive and policy purposes.

The critical forces shaping contemporary Asia, culled from the case studies in this compendium, are export-led development, prospective diminishing returns to technology transfer, and dollar reserve hoarding.

---

[5] The macroeconomic formulation of $GDP(Y) = C + I + G + (X - M)$, where C is aggregate consumption, I is aggregate Investment, G is government, X is exports, and M is imports). If X and M equal 100, a proportional decline in both leaves Y unchanged.

[6] Korhonen and Mehrotra, "Global Bust."

They collectively imply that Asia is coupled to the West in three decisive ways. First, various internal barriers make overexporting a better choice than the counterfactual and unattainable generally competitive ideal. Second, the static gains from Asian overexporting, achieved through foreign exchange rate undervaluation, are enhanced with outsourcing, foreign direct investment and technology, and also transfer-driven, export-led development. This linkage sparked rapid catch-up during 1990–2010, but diminishing returns are setting in, making the East more and more vulnerable to Western economic fatigue. Third, the Orient's post-1997 preference for holding excess dollar reserves (and hence underimporting), especially in China, dampens Western aggregate effective demand, and in times of full employment, intensifies cyclical and secular disequilibria, harmful to the East's long-term prospects.

Careful scrutiny of these forces suggest that Asia and the West are entering a new epoch of sluggish growth and cyclical instability that will harm today's hares (China and Vietnam) and set the stage for the resurgence later of at least one of its tortoises (Japan). "Two Asias" during the early phase of this new epoch will mean that Taiwan and South Korea will find it difficult to surpass the American living standard and like Japan could fall back, while the Chinese economic miracle fades. Vietnam and others in Southeast Asia should fare better, but eventually all will be limited by their systems potential. At the end of the day, when catch-up effects are exhausted, the living standards in Japan and the other Asian tiger countries will shine, but the pace of Asian advance will diminish toward historical global benchmark, in the vicinity of 1% to 2% per annum (reversion to the mean), The East–West living standard gap will persist, if the EU and America can reverse paralyzing aspects of government misregulation and deficit spending (see Chapter 15).

It is premature to forecast the specific regional impacts of future financial crises and depressions, but China may fare especially poorly if it continues its dollar reserve hoarding. The partitioning of Asia into two parts, one with high, the other with much lower potentials thus not only offers a vision of long-term comparative merit (Box I.1) but hints at the possibility of complex and hostile intra-regional conflicts.

6 Introduction

Box I.1. Timeline.

Asian economic backwardness in historical perspective (comparative per capita GDP).

1500–1870: Asia declines.

1870–1942: Japan, South Korea, Taiwan rise while China and Indochina decline.

1945–1950: Asia declines.

1950–1990: Japan and tigers surge.

1990–2010: Market communist Asia surges, command communist Asia declines, Japan flags.

2010–2020: Market communist moment, waning regional vitality.

2020– : Limits of modernization.

The basis for these prognostications is laid out in the sections that follow. Part I documents Asia's 450-year plunge into comparative poverty during AD 1500 to AD 1950, and its staggered resurgence, highlighting the epochal shift that occurred after the Tiananmen Square massacre (Chapter 1, Rosefielde and Zhou). This provides context for investigating the forces molding Asia's future. The impact of the 2008 financial crisis and its global aftermath are examined in Part II, Chapter 2 (Razin and Rosefielde) and Chapter 3 (Korhonen and Mehrotra). Part III scrutinizes broad regional impacts in Asia in Chapter 4 (Hitotsubashi) and Chapter 5 (Kinkyo), supplemented with case studies of Japan and China, Chapter 6 (Mizobata), Chapter 7 (Kajitani), and Russia, Chapter 8 (Brunat). Part IV shifts from description to causal analysis by probing the twin phenomena of export-led development and decoupling, with the modalities plumbed in Chapter 9 (Rosefielde), Chapter 10 (Leightner), Chapter 11 (Mikic), Chapter 12 (Wakasugi), and Chapter 13 (Korhonen, Fidrmuc, and Batorova). Part V appraises the role of petroleum in the Asian drama; Chapter 14 (Kuboniwa) and Part VI studies adverse epochal changes in the EU that augur waning Western demand for the East's products (Chapter 15, Dallago and Guglielmetti). Finally, Part VII, Chapter 16 (Rosefielde) consolidates the volume's findings by parsing prospects for East–West convergence and the realignment of intra-Asian wealth and power.

PART I

ASIA'S REBIRTH

CHAPTER 1

ASIAN ECONOMIC PERFORMANCE 1500–2010

STEVEN ROSEFIELDE AND HUAN ZHOU
University of North Carolina, Chapel Hill

Living standards of the East and West were broadly similar a millennium ago and remained that way for 500 years before the East swooned into a protracted decline. Asian per capita GDP fell relative to the EU benchmark for nearly 400 years, before Japan began closing the East–West gap in the late 19th century. Taiwan and South Korea followed suit after being annexed by Japan and then continued their advance independently after the Second World War. China, Vietnam, Laos, and Cambodia joined the bandwagon in the 1980s after shifting from siege-mobilized terror-command to market communism. Thailand also has progressed, but North Korea and perhaps Myanmar continue to languish. There was a time when Asia's ascent seemed unstoppable. Many confidently predicted that Japan and the tigers would overtake the West and just keep progressing. Similar claims are now being made for China and Vietnam, but this should not be taken seriously until the sources of their purported institutional superiority are convincingly elaborated. Asian economic systems have virtues, but their cultures constrain competitive utility-seeking, judged from the neoclassical perspective, rendering them underproductive and inefficient. Although, this clouds Asia's prospects, it does not settle the issue of comparative merit because the West violates its own ideal.

1.1. Introduction

Nobel Prize winner Gunnar Myrdal argued as late as 1968 that Asia not only was economically backward, but might remain permanently so unless

10   Steven Rosefielde and Huan Zhou

it discovered an effective social mobilization strategy.[1] It might seem to follow that Asian underdevelopment was endemic. Unless Asia westernized in a liberal or Marxist fashion, it would always remain impoverished.

Myrdal's concern was widely shared, but misleading in two senses. Asia's economic performance was not always laggard, and modernization was not tantamount to complete westernization. Asian economic growth paced the global mean for the first 1,500 years of the common era; and although the East fell behind during the ensuing centuries, Japan began successfully modernizing almost immediately after being opened by Admiral Perry in 1853. Many Asian latecomers have followed suit, without abandoning their culture-governed economic systems. They are modernizing without cloning the West.

1.2. Historical Record

The historical record is clear on the growth issue. The data demonstrate that despite diverse cultural evolutions, the aggregate economic performance of Asia and the West was similar up to the European commercial revolution. Table 1.1 shows that in the first year of the Christian era,

Table 1.1. Per capita GDP AD 1–2001.

	1	1000	1500	1820	1870	1913	1950	1973	2001
United Kingdom	400	400	714	1706	3190	4921	6939	12025	20590
Western Europe (including UK)	599	425	797	1234	2080	3687	5005	12124	20235
Former USSR	400	400	499	688	943	1488	2841	6059	4750
United States	400	400	400	1257	2445	5301	9561	16689	28405
Japan	400	425	500	669	737	1387	1921	11434	20736
China	450	466	600	600	530	552	448	838	3759
World	467	453	566	666	870	1524	2111	4083	6132

Note: Western Europe includes the following: Austria, Belgium, Denmark, Finland, France, Switzerland, Germany, Italy, Netherlands, Norway, Sweden, and United Kingdom.
Source: http://www.ggdc.net/maddison/Historical_Statistics/horizontal-file_03-2009xls. Statistics on world population, GDP, and per capita GDP AD 1–2006. (last update: March 2009, horizontal file; copyright Angus Maddison).

---

[1] Myrdal, G (1968). *The Asian Drama: An Inquiry in the Poverty of Nations*, Vols. 3. Pantheon: New York.

AD 1, per capita GDP in Japan and China were close to the world norm, a position they maintained for the next 1,500 years.

After the 15th century, the situation changed dramatically. Living standards in the United Kingdom, Western Europe (including the UK), and United States steadily grew to twice the Japanese and Chinese levels, spurred by systemic change and engendered by rapidly expanding exploration, international commerce, the Renaissance, Reformation, and Enlightenment. This disparity widened throughout the industrial revolution from 1820 to 1950, when American per capita GDP exceeded that of China by a factor of 20. During the postwar years from 1950 to 1973, Japanese living standards miraculously surged to within hailing distance of the UK and Western Europe, but China continued languishing, despite Mao's claims of rapid advance. It was this wretched performance, together with anemic growth in Korea and Indochina from 1820 to 1950 that prompted Myrdal's misgivings about Asian economic prospects, despite Japan's exceptionalism and the successes of niche players like Singapore, Hong Kong, and Taiwan.

China should have done better. It was inventive[2] and commercially vibrant at home and abroad. It had ample opportunities to receive western technology through the silk route and sea trade with India and the Middle East. It was dynastically stable, a great regional power, and had undergone its own maritime revolution in 1433; yet, these advantages did not suffice. Nor can blame be laid at Malthus's door. Table 1.2 reveals that the British and EU populations grew more rapidly than the Chinese until 1950. Similar arguments hold for Korea and Southeast Asia. Were these national cultures fatally flawed despite the innate talents of their people?

1.3. Communist Growth

Perhaps, but not irreparably! Although, communist national income statistics are suspect, there seems little reason to doubt that China made

---

[2] China is famous for four major innovations: (1) papermaking: Cai Lun (AD 50–121); (2) printing: woodblock (circa 650) movable type; bookbinding: Shen Kuo (1031–1095) Song dynasty; (3) gunpowder: Five Dynasties and Ten Kingdoms period (907–960); and (4) magnetic compass: Han Dynasty (circa first century AD). These contributions are only the tip of the iceberg.

12 Steven Rosefielde and Huan Zhou

Table 1.2. Population growth (1–2001 AD).

	1–1000	1000–1500	1500–1820	1820–1870	1870–1913	1913–1950	1950–1973	1973–2001
United Kingdom			0.27	1.26	1.01	0.93	2.42	1.86
12 countries average			0.14	1.04	1.33	0.84	3.92	1.80
Former USSR	0.00	0.04	0.1	0.63	1.06	1.76	3.35	−0.96
United States			0.36	1.34	1.82	1.61	2.45	1.86
Japan	0.01	0.03	0.09	0.19	1.48	0.88	8.06	2.14
China	0.00	0.06	0.00	−0.25	0.10	−0.62	2.86	5.32
World	0.00	0.05	0.05	0.54	1.30	0.88	2.92	1.41

Source: Maddison (2003). *The World Economy: Historical Statistics*. OECD, p. 637.

Table 1.3. Communist per capita GDP growth 1985–2001.

	1985–1990	1990–1995	1995–2001
China	4.1	7.4	5.1
Vietnam	2.2	6.2	4.8
Cambodia	−2.0	1.8	2.4
Laos	0.2	3.0	1.8
North Korea	0.0	−11.8	−4.5

Source: http://www.ggdc.net/maddison/Historical_Statistics/horizontal-file_03-2009xls. Statistics on world population, GDP, and per capita GDP AD 1–2006. (last update: March 2009, horizontal file; copyright Angus Maddison).

progress under Mao Tsetung during 1950–1976, and that the entire Asian communist bloc (China, Vietnam, Cambodia, and Laos), with the exception of North Korea accelerated its advance after 1985 (see Table 1.3), when these nations began embracing the market reforms that define their contemporary systems. The Stalinist command models providing the foundation for Chinese and Vietnamese growth before 1985 enabled them to temporarily overcome their lethargy, albeit at immense human cost,[3] and eventually transition to a more powerful system. Cambodia and Laos were latecomers to communism, and North Korea is essentially an unreformed Stalinist command system that performed well enough during 1950–1991 and then collapsed after the Soviet Union disappeared, echoing the

---

[3] Rosefielde, S (2010). *Red Holocaust*. Routledge: Oxford.

postcommunist former Soviet Republics during 1991–2000, and significantly underperforming those countries thereafter.

1.4. Noncommunist Growth

The performance of noncommunist Asia during the post-war era has been more diverse, especially after 1985. The nationalist systems (South Korea, Taiwan, Hong Kong, and Singapore), often called the tigers, did well converging toward the global high frontier but exhibited unmistakable signs of fatigue. Theravada Buddhist Thailand, with its constitutional monarchy and open economy followed a similar trajectory, even though it was severely affected by the Asian financial crisis of 1997. Japanese experience also paralleled the Confucian nationalist systems, but its growth retardation was more pronounced converging toward stagnation ("the lost decade"). National socialist Myanmar by contrast ascended steeply with no signs yet of deceleration. It claims to be growing at double digit rates during the new millennium, despite being a closed command-style economy, but the data should be treated skeptically.

Thus, 40 years after Myrdal's alarm, it seems that his forebodings were mostly misplaced. China, Vietnam, South Korea, Taiwan, Singapore, Hong Kong, Thailand, and perhaps Laos, Cambodia, and Myanmar have found disparate modernization paths that have allowed them to narrow the East–West living standard gap. North Korea, the lone command communist system, however continues to falter, and Japan is losing ground to the United States and Western Europe, raising the possibility that Asian catch-up may never be permanently complete. Taiwan, South Korea, and Singapore having reached high levels of development, likewise seem to be flirting with the Japanese disease. After the initial benefits of relative economic backwardness are exhausted, in a postindustrial epoch, perhaps other Asian nations will swoon into relative decline because their systems lack staying power. Those who believe that catch-up is merely a matter of modernization, and that systems do not matter, harbor no doubts, but careful sifting of the evidence does not support such optimism.

1.5. New Problematic

This is the new problematic. Contemporary Asian modernization is being driven by six distinctive paradigms: (1) communalism [Japan]; (2) market

14 *Steven Rosefielde and Huan Zhou*

communism [China, Vietnam, Laos, and Cambodia]; (3) command communism [North Korea]; (4) Confucian nationalism [South Korea, Hong Kong, Taiwan, and Singapore]; (5) national socialism [Myanmar]; and (6) Theravada Buddhism [Thailand]. All are more authoritarian than American free enterprise and European social democracy and limit individual, political, and civic liberty. It seems likely that North Korean command communism is at a dead-end. However, this leaves ample room for the other systems to prove their mettle practically and be judged from the standpoint of the American and European ideals. All may thrive or merely survive, but some are apt to outperform others over the next few decades; and some may even surpass a West, stultified by overregulation (Eurosclerosis).

1.6. Country Comparisons

These findings are further illuminated below. Figure 1.1 compares living standards in China with 12 West European nations 1500–2006,[4] using Western Europe as the benchmark indexed to 100. It reveals that Chinese per capita GDP was 80% of the EU norm 500 years ago, gradually losing ground until 1820 when the divergence accelerated. The disparity in 1950 just after Mao Tsetung seized power was more than tenfold, with China's per capita GDP just 9% of the West European level. The gap widened slightly thereafter to 7%, before a reversal started in 1977. After 477 years, China began a great ascent to 28% of the West European benchmark: a convergent trend that shows no sign of fading. Judging by the Japanese (Figure 1.2), Taiwanese (Figure 1.3), Singaporean (Figure A1.1), and Hong Kong (Figure A1.2) precedents, China could catch up completely with the Western Europe in a few decades, eliminating the East–West divide, or making allowance for the intrinsic inferiority of market communist systems, full convergence may never be achieved. Either way, however, Beijing has successfully devised modernization strategies which have forestalled Myrdal's nightmare.

This inference holds even if substantial adjustments are made for the inferior quality of Chinese and Indochinese communist growth resulting

---

[4] Austria, Belgium, Denmark, Finland, France, Switzerland, Germany, Italy, Netherlands, Norway, Sweden, and United Kingdom.

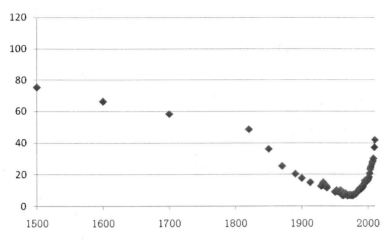

Figure 1.1. Chinese–EU divergence and convergence 1500–2010 per capita GDP (Western Europe = 100).

Source: Table A1.1.

from various types of forced substitution, especially in the domestic market. Likewise, using the United States instead of Western Europe as benchmark merely alters the scale, not East–West living standard trends (see Chapter 5). America's per capita GDP was 39.6% higher than that of Western Europe in 2001. The comparative sizes of China and other Asian economies using the American benchmark therefore are correspondingly lower, but the reality of catch-up remains intact.

It should also be noted that workdays in Asia during the catch-up years were longer than those in Europe, and the gap widened throughout. If Figure 1.1 were computed on a man-hour basis, instead of per capita GDP basis, the speed of Chinese and other Asian catch-up would be diminished.

The systemic dimension of catch-up, and perhaps *fall-back*, has two aspects: modernization and sustainability. Technology transfer provides a golden opportunity for less developed nations to increase productivity by adopting advanced technologies, skipping intermediate stages, and economizing research and development costs. Any nation can modernize in this sense without making significant concessions to western culture, but this does not mean that inferior systems will fully realize potential benefits. Moreover, even if it appears that Asian systems have boundless horizons

16 *Steven Rosefielde and Huan Zhou*

during the early catch-up phase, diminishing returns, fatigue, and social adaptation seem to slow, or even reverse their progress. The Japanese case is instructive. Although, Figure 1.2 documents its early vitality, this was partly accomplished by overwork and social arousal. There were more Japanese employed in the workforce, laboring longer hours more

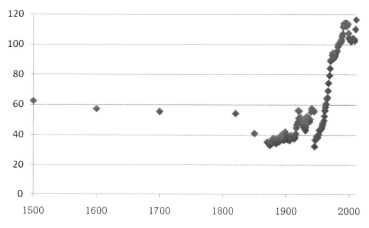

Figure 1.2. Japanese–EU divergence and convergence 1500–2010 per capita GDP (Western Europe = 100).

Source: Table A1.1.

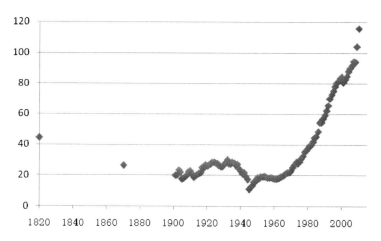

Figure 1.3. Taiwanese–EU divergence and convergence 1820–2010 per capita GDP (Western Europe = 100).

Source: Table A1.1.

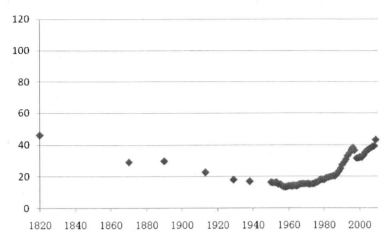

Figure 1.4. Thai–EU divergence and convergence 1820–2010 per capita GDP (Western Europe = 100).
Source: Table A1.1.

diligently than their West European counterparts throughout the 20th century, but recently the Japanese are reconsidering whether the material gain is worth the sacrifice in life quality. As social mobilization wanes, the demerits of its communalist system are becoming visible.

Taiwan was incorporated into Japan as a result of the First Sino–Japanese war during 1894–1895 and swiftly industrialized on the Japanese model until August 15, 1945 when Hirohito surrendered to the United States. This background may partly explain the parallel post-war catch-up patterns of the two nations, although the success also is a testament to positive aspects of the Chinese nationalist system. Like Japan, Taiwan's catch-up is flagging, particularly relative to the United States, and it will be interesting to learn whether its contemporary Confucian nationalist system has strong legs.

Thailand forms the middle ground (Figure 1.4). It has the same comparative size today *vis-à-vis* Western Europe that it had in 1820, after touching bottom in 1950. Its catch-up has been steady but less vigorous than the Confucian nationalist tigers. This reflects the world-denying aspects of Theravada Buddhist culture that make Thai society less productively aroused, but perhaps the slow and steady approach will prove superior in the long run.

Myanmar's prospects are less well defined (Figure 1.5). It fared worse than Thailand from 1820 to 1950, especially during World War II, and its

18 *Steven Rosefielde and Huan Zhou*

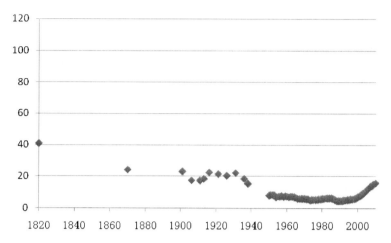

Figure 1.5. Myanmar–EU divergence and convergence 1820–2010 per capita GDP (Western Europe = 100).
Source: Table A1.1.

relative size continued shrinking uninterruptedly thereafter until 1990. Unlike its Confucian nationalist cousins, the military still rules with an iron fist, claiming to have achieved stupendous results with controls that have lost their appeal elsewhere in the region. Perhaps, it will succeed for a time, as North Korea did from 1950 to 1970, but without substantial liberalization, progress will fade.

Vietnam serves as a proxy for communist Indochina. Together with Cambodia and Laos, its post-war history was dominated by Mao's China, anticolonial wars of liberation, and conflict with the United States. The damage is vividly captured in Figure 1.6, which shows the nation's relative size diminishing when compared with Western Europe for 170 years. The switch from command to market communism has allowed recovery of some lost ground, but like Cambodia and Laos, living standards remain less than half what they were relative to the EU in 1820. Chinese progress under Mao offers hope for further market communist gains; however, it is premature to speculate about the model's sustainability.

Korea provides double insight into the Asian drama. Although, it has a shared Confucian and Buddhist tradition with China, and was annexed by Japan in 1910, its people are ethnically distinct and homogeneous. Reflecting this blend of cultural influences, Korea's comparative living standard fell steadily after 1820 from 40 to 20, but recovered part of that lost ground under

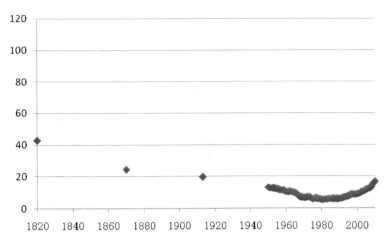

Figure 1.6. Vietnam–EU divergence and convergence 1820–2010 per capita GDP (Western Europe = 100).
Source: Table A1.1.

the Japanese yoke, only to lose the gain again toward the end of World War II when its relative backwardness was on a par with that of Thailand. This was the platform from which post-war Korea would try anew to overtake the West. However, the vagaries of the Cold War divided the nation into an industrialized communist north and agrarian Confucian nationalist south in 1947, providing an opportunity not only to test Myrdal's hypothesis, but to evaluate the comparative merit of Stalinist command communism and Confucian nationalist-managed markets under American tutelage. The results displayed in Figure 1.7 are startling. North Korea treaded water for 25 years *vis-à-vis* Western Europe and then tumbled into the abyss. Its per capita income today is the lowest in the region, and its fall the deepest from the 1820 benchmark. South Korea's performance was just the reverse. After a rocky start in the early 1960s, its trajectory skyrocketed, attributable in significant part to economic liberalization. Seoul recovered the 1820 parity by 1990 and is on a fast track to overtake Western Europe in the next few years, if the depression of 2008–2010 does not radically alter past trends.

Diversity, not homogeneity or convergence, is the defining characteristic of Asia's economy. There are 100 hybrid flowers blooming, under varied conditions (Tables A1.1a, A1.1b, A1.2a, A1.2b, A1.3a, A1.3b; Figures A1.1– A1.9, A1.20), giving the region a broad luster it lacked 40 years ago. However, we now know that some once promising experiments did not last.

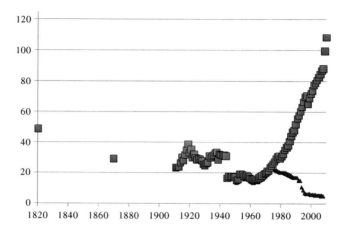

Figure 1.7. North and South Korean divergence and convergence 1820–2010 per capita GDP (Western Europe = 100).

Source: Table A1.1.

Command communism failed despite high expectations in many quarters, and the full story of Asian economic systems is only beginning to unfold.

1.7. Prospects

It is a story within a story because there is an outside context. The Orient is both culturally distinct and interdependent with the West. There are many internal Asian common denominators, but one of the most interesting is adversarial satisficing: a phenomenon where the powerful dominate the weak without either fully maximizing. Asians acquiesce to their station and play their roles rather than freely and competitively utility-maximizing. This occurs everywhere across the globe, but is more pronounced in the east, and constitutes a cultural barrier that could determine the long-term merit of two economic zones. For the moment, this factor is being masked by regional interdependence. China and much of Indochina are using disequilibrium exchange rate regimes to over-export and over-acquire foreign direct investment, turbocharging their growth; however, when the global system eventually adjusts through foreign devaluations and differential inflation, intrinsic systemic efficiencies will become more conspicuous. Micro and macroeconomic commonalities grab the headlines, but systemic factors tend to control global destinies.

Appendix

Table A1.1a. Per capita GDP in 12 East Asian countries, 1820–2001 (1990 international Geary-Khamis dollars).

	China	India	Japan	South Korea	Thailand	Taiwan	Myanmar	Singapore	Cambodia	Laos	North Korea	Vietnam	Former USSR	Russia	Western Europe Average
1820	600	533	669	600	646	499	504	615					687		1,242
1850	600														1,658
1870	530	533	737	604	712	550	504	682					943		2,087
1871			742												2,123
1872			746												2,191
1873			751												2,194
1874			756												2,290
1875			810												2,322
1876			785												2,264
1877			803												2,269
1878			794												2,280
1879			835												2,216
1880			863												2,297
1881			829												2,324
1882			844												2,391
1883			837												2,421
1884		551	836												2,424
1885		567	860												2,419
1886		548	916												2,444
1887		572	952												2,502

(Continued)

Table A1.1a. (*Continued*)

	China	India	Japan	South Korea	Thailand	Taiwan	Myanmar	Singapore	Cambodia	Laos	North Korea	Vietnam	Former USSR	Russia	Western Europe Average
1888		576	900												2,552
1889		559	933												2,599
1890	540	584	1,012		784										2,642
1891		529	956												2,633
1892		571	1,013												2,629
1893		584	1,008												2,670
1894		592	1,119												2,741
1895		577	1,123												2,788
1896		533	1,051												2,862
1897		630	1,062												2,866
1898		630	1,249												2,972
1899		580	1,143												3,057
1900	545	599	1,180										1,237		3,076
1901		608	1,206												3,043
1902		655	1,129												3,049
1903		660	1,193												3,093
1904		659	1,188												3,120
1905		643	1,157												3,179
1906		657	1,297												3,251
1907		614	1,325												3,352

(*Continued*)

Table A1.1a. (Continued)

	China	India	Japan	South Korea	Thailand	Taiwan	Myanmar	Singapore	Cambodia	Laos	North Korea	Vietnam	Former USSR	Russia	Western Europe Average
1908		619	1,318												3,307
1909		700	1,301												3,379
1910		697	1,304												3,379
1911		691	1,356	777											3,501
1912		689	1,384	782	722										3,604
1913	552	673	1,387	820	841	747	685	1,279					1,487		3,687
1914		709	1,327	862		747									3,439
1915		691	1,430	966		765									3,501
1916		710	1,630	969		963	823								3,632
1917		697	1,665	1,021		1,057									3,533
1918		607	1,668	1,087		925									3,430
1919		690	1,827	1,049		982									3,244
1920		635	1,696	1,009		959									3,304
1921		679	1,860	1,051		873	711								3,311
1922		701	1,831	1,018		980									3,580
1923		671	1,809	1,030		1,027									3,512
1924		697	1,836	1,025		1,025									3,769
1925		698	1,885	1,016		1,099									3,949
1926		713	1,872	1,038		1,028	814								3,973
1927		706	1,870	1,086		1,011									4,131

(Continued)

Table A1.1a. (Continued)

	China	India	Japan	South Korea	Thailand	Taiwan	Myanmar	Singapore	Cambodia	Laos	North Korea	Vietnam	Former USSR	Russia	Western Europe Average
1928		706	1,992	1,047		1,211							1,369		4,292
1929	562	728	2,026	1,014	793	1,146							1,385		4,385
1930	567	726	1,850	1,020		1,099							1,448		4,287
1931	569	711	1,837	990		1,066	902						1,461		4,040
1932	583	709	1,962	1,016		1,181							1,438		3,894
1933	578	700	2,122	1,145		1,059							1,493		4,021
1934	525	697	2,098	1,115		1,107							1,630		4,164
1935	565	680	2,120	1,242		1,295							1,863		4,324
1936	597	697	2,244	1,315		1,233	838						1,990		4,511
1937	580	676	2,315	1,482		1,263							2,155		4,715
1938	562	668	2,449	1,459	826	1,302	740						2,149		4,816
1939		674	2,816	1,297		1,390							2,236		5,070
1940		686	2,874	1,442		1,347							2,143		4,983
1941		691	2,873	1,441		1,439									5,049
1942		679	2,818	1,412		1,502									4,995
1943		698	2,822	1,411		998									4,993
1944		683	2,659	1,330		684									4,777
1945		664	1,346	616		742									4,153
1946		622	1,444	619		806							1,913		3,919
1947		618	1,541	648		904							2,125		4,133

(Continued)

	China	India	Japan	South Korea	Thailand	Taiwan	Myanmar	Singapore	Cambodia	Laos	North Korea	Vietnam	Former USSR	Russia	Western Europe Average
1948		617	1,725	692		931							2,401		4,387
1949		624	1,800	738		932							2,623		4,718
1950	439	619	1,921	770	817	924	396	2,219	518	613	770	658	2,841		5,004
1951	479	623	2,126	709	849	991	446	2,253	522	621	709	676	2,805		5,257
1952	537	629	2,336	753	869	1,063	449	2,280	542	628	753	694	2,936		5,412
1953	554	657	2,474	966	935	1,140	454	2,314	534	635	966	712	3,012		5,667
1954	558	672	2,582	1,013	898	1,193	419	2,320	582	642	1,013	732	3,106		5,941
1955	575	676	2,771	1,054	945	1,250	467	2,358	556	649	1,054	750	3,312		6,282
1956	619	701	2,948	1,036	930	1,270	490	2,333	614	655	1,036	764	3,566		6,514
1957	637	680	3,136	1,087	910	1,314	510	2,318	638	661	1,087	775	3,575		6,758
1958	693	716	3,289	1,112	914	1,382	488	2,295	653	667	1,112	785	3,777		6,864
1959	697	717	3,554	1,120	992	1,462	555	2,186	698	673	1,120	792	3,669		7,161
1960	673	753	3,986	1,105	1,078	1,492	564	2,310	720	679	1,105	799	3,945		7,581
1961	557	758	4,426	1,124	1,100	1,551	568	2,422	694	686	1,124	812	4,097		7,887
1962	553	758	4,777	1,122	1,149	1,632	606	2,520	719	692	1,122	885	4,140		8,162
1963	592	779	5,129	1,186	1,205	1,804	613	2,701	753	698	1,186	882	3,985		8,439
1964	648	821	5,668	1,253	1,249	1,977	613	2,541	713	705	1,253	895	4,438		8,854
1965	706	771	5,934	1,295	1,308	2,056	617	2,667	728	712	1,295	877	4,633		9,123
1966	753	762	6,506	1,415	1,412	2,205	580	2,891	742	719	1,415	859	4,803		9,369
1967	712	807	7,152	1,483	1,486	2,395	586	3,163	760	726	1,483	731	4,962		9,617

(*Continued*)

Table A1.1a. (Continued)

	China	India	Japan	South Korea	Thailand	Taiwan	Myanmar	Singapore	Cambodia	Laos	North Korea	Vietnam	Former USSR	Russia	Western Europe Average
1968	678	809	7,983	1,633	1,561	2,539	613	3,540	774	733	1,633	699	5,201		10,060
1969	722	845	8,874	1,839	1,636	2,706	626	3,965	765	740	1,839	739	5,225		10,543
1970	783	868	9,714	1,954	1,694	2,980	642	4,439	685	748	1,954	735	5,575		10,916
1971	799	856	10,040	2,522	1,725	3,324	650	4,904	648	755	2,522	754	5,667.245		11,173
1972	802	834	10,734	2,561	1,748	3,767	642	5,460	605	763	2,561	802	5,642.894		11,545
1973	839	853	11,434	2,841	1,874	4,091	628	5,977	813	770	2,841	836	6,059.251	6,581	12,109
1974	836	843	11,145	3,015	1,910	3,942	648	6,276	686	777	2,841	783	6,175.796		12,295
1975	874	897	11,344	3,162	1,959	3,958	663	6,430	604	784	2,841	710	6,134.713		12,180
1976	852	889	11,669	3,476	2,091	4,566	690	6,797	672	804	2,841	809	6,363.172		12,685
1977	895	937	12,064	3,775	2,249	5,020	718	7,224	751	821	2,841	818	6,454.464		13,007
1978	979	966	12,585	4,064	2,422	5,542	752	7,752	847	836	2,841	806	6,558.515		13,359
1979	1,040	895	13,163	4,294	2,496	5,831	773	8,362	869	856	2,841	795	6,472.338		13,839
1980	1,067	938	13,428	4,114	2,554	5,869	823	9,058	866	876	2,841	758	6,427.244		13,998
1981	1,103	977	13,754	4,302	2,653	6,229	854	9,460	849	891	2,841	768	6,432.64		13,987
1982	1,192	985	14,078	4,557	2,744	6,446	884	9,674	880	899	2,841	813	6,535.975		14,071
1983	1,265	1,043	14,307	5,007	2,847	7,036	907	10,330	906	904	2,841	840	6,687.238		14,318
1984	1,396	1,060	14,773	5,375	2,960	7,790	936	10,982	943	911	2,841	895	6,709.003		14,665
1985	1,522	1,079	15,331	5,670	3,049	8,113	947	10,764	982	918	2,841	929	6,708.457		15,012
1986	1,597	1,101	15,679	6,263	3,168	9,088	924	10,966	1,004	921	2,841	935	6,922.546		15,396

(Continued)

	China	India	Japan	South Korea	Thailand	Taiwan	Myanmar	Singapore	Cambodia	Laos	North Korea	Vietnam	Former USSR	Russia	Western Europe Average
1987	1,706	1,125	16,251	6,916	3,418	9,641	875	11,827	947	923	2,841	949	6,952.002		15,765
1988	1,816	1,216	17,185	7,621	3,817	9,623	766	12,821	934	925	2,841	985	7,042.584		16,313
1989	1,827	1,270	17,942	8,027	4,222	9,665	786	13,599	922	927	2,841	1,006	7,111.778		16,746
1990	1,858	1,309	18,789	8,704	4,629	9,886	800	14,365	888	929	2,841	1,035	6,894.108	7,778	16,792
1991	1,940	1,299	19,309	9,417	4,959	10,522	788	14,801	921	931	2,841	1,073	6,422.815	7,373	16,990
1992	2,098	1,341	19,430	9,814	5,290	11,128	860	15,537	942	953	2,578	1,144	5,473.315	6,300	17,120
1993	2,277	1,390	19,457	10,238	5,661	11,720	906	17,018	934	1,020	2,542	1,214	4,931.457	5,752	17,006
1994	2,475	1,463	19,602	10,965	6,094	12,430	957	18,404	937	1,054	1,849	1,297	4,251.697	5,020	17,429
1995	2,653	1,538	19,849	11,818	6,573	13,104	1,015	19,225	973	1,079	1,519	1,397	4,028.646	4,812	17,804
1996	2,820	1,630	20,494	12,495	6,877	13,796	1,070	19,963	1,003	1,077	1,251	1,503	3,914.798	4,644	18,041
1997	2,973	1,679	20,798	12,991	6,702	14,598	1,122	20,921	1,008	1,105	1,170	1,602	3,998.182	4,717	18,449
1998	3,117	1,760	20,534	12,016	5,930	15,134	1,178	20,198	1,001	1,110	1,171	1,672	3,910.685	4,475	18,853
1999	3,259	1,841	20,631	13,222	6,123	15,827	1,297	20,854	1,051	1,137	1,180	1,719	4,102.421	4,776	19,318
2000	3,425	1,910	21,069	14,343	6,336	16,642	1,353	22,207	1,087	1,173	1,169	1,790	4,459.612	5,277	19,993
2001	3,583	1,957	20,683	14,673	6,383	16,214	1,409	21,011	1,124	1,204	1,154	1,850	4,750.251	5,573	20,234

Source: Maddison, A (2003). *The World Economy: Historical Statistics*. OECD, pp. 558–563, 566.

28 Steven Rosefielde and Huan Zhou

Table A1.1b. Per capita GDP in four East Asian countries, 1820–2001 (1990 international Geary-Khamis dollars).

	Hong Kong	Malaysia	Indonesia	Philippines
1820	615	603	612	584
1821				
1822				
1823				
1824				
1825				
1826				
1827				
1828				
1829				
1830				
1831				
1832				
1833				
1834				
1835				
1836				
1837				
1838				
1839				
1840				
1841				
1842				
1843				
1844				
1845				
1846				
1847				
1848				
1849				
1850			637	
1851				
1852				
1853				
1854				
1855				

(*Continued*)

Asian Economic Performance 1500–2010

Table A1.1b. *(Continued)*

	Hong Kong	Malaysia	Indonesia	Philippines
1856				
1857				
1858				
1859				
1860				
1861				
1862				
1863				
1864				
1865				
1866				
1867				
1868				
1869				
1870	683	663	578	624
1871			575	
1872			574	
1873			583	
1874			592	
1875			595	
1876			605	
1877			607	
1878			593	
1879			598	
1880			601	
1881			635	
1882			602	
1883			590	
1884			644	
1885			646	
1886			635	
1887			636	
1888			635	
1889			631	
1890			612	
1891			619	

(Continued)

30 *Steven Rosefielde and Huan Zhou*

Table A1.1b. *(Continued)*

	Hong Kong	Malaysia	Indonesia	Philippines
1892			638	
1893			650	
1894			654	
1895			662	
1896			651	
1897			653	
1898			654	
1899			686	
1900			704	
1901			688	
1902		.	671	673
1903			701	804
1904			708	679
1905			711	709
1906			726	722
1907			736	747
1908			730	775
1909			761	775
1910			803	874
1911		801	839	913
1912		822	838	911
1913	1,279	900	874	988
1914		920	864	952
1915		938	866	875
1916		996	870	1,003
1917		1,034	864	1,148
1918		969	883	1,286
1919		1,158	944	1,212
1920		1,110	923	1,289
1921		1,075	921	1,235
1922		1,152	926	1,357
1923		1,110	930	1,250
1924		1,060	969	1,338
1925		1,201	991	1,323
1926		1,316	1,034	1,364
1927		1,251	1,092	1,366

(Continued)

Table A1.1b. (*Continued*)

	Hong Kong	Malaysia	Indonesia	Philippines
1928		1,389	1,130	1,392
1929		1,682	1,147	1,413
1930		1,636	1,141	1,382
1931		1,548	1,037	1,360
1932		1,397	1,007	1,388
1933		1,440	983	1,368
1934		1,540	971	1,348
1935		1,364	987	1,227
1936		1,478	1,039	1,364
1937		1,308	1,119	1,428
1938		1,361	1,120	1,440
1939		1,609	1,109	1,508
1940		1,278	1,165	1,507
1941		1,238	1,182	
1942		1,673		
1943				
1944				
1945				
1946				646
1947		1,069		875
1948		1,185		993
1949		1,531	763	1,025
1950	2,218	1,559	803	1,070
1951	2,295	1,440	851	1,151
1952	2,377	1,471	879	1,186
1953	2,460	1,440	910	1,254
1954	2,546	1,490	952	1,308
1955	2,636	1,460	964	1,358
1956	2,729	1,505	962	1,410
1957	2,825	1,455	1,012	1,442
1958	2,924	1,413	960	1,448
1959	3,027	1,467	985	1,501
1960	3,134	1,530	1,012	1,476
1961	3,244	1,592	1,060	1,512
1962	3,652	1,637	1,037	1,537
1963	4,083	1,669	977	1,595
1964	4,327	1,728	993	1,600

(*Continued*)

32 Steven Rosefielde and Huan Zhou

Table A1.1b. (*Continued*)

	Hong Kong	Malaysia	Indonesia	Philippines
1965	4,825	1,804	983	1,633
1966	4,865	1,846	963	1,654
1967	4,824	1,830	922	1,690
1968	4,880	1,942	991	1,722
1969	5,345	2,005	1,091	1,750
1970	5,695	2,079	1,181	1,764
1971	5,968	2,180	1,221	1,808
1972	6,473	2,289	1,328	1,853
1973	7,105	2,560	1,490	1,964
1974	7,091	2,688	1,530	1,979
1975	6,991	2,648	1,497	2,033
1976	7,906	2,910	1,591	2,152
1977	8,707	3,076	1,675	2,211
1978	9,277	3,271	1,711	2,262
1979	9,796	3,457	1,763	2,323
1980	10,503	3,657	1,870	2,376
1981	11,202	3,824	1,957	2,396
1982	11,333	3,954	1,845	2,421
1983	11,797	4,096	1,878	2,407
1984	12,846	4,308	1,966	2,176
1985	12,763	4,157	1,972	1,967
1986	13,960	4,105	2,051	1,983
1987	15,597	4,218	2,114	2,019
1988	16,716	4,482	2,196	2,105
1989	17,043	4,789	2,351	2,184
1990	17,541	5,131	2,514	2,197
1991	18,323	5,494	2,602	2,136
1992	19,270	5,847	2,840	2,099
1993	20,131	6,278	2,994	2,099
1994	20,770	6,702	3,169	2,144
1995	21,029	7,199	3,369	2,194
1996	21,364	7,747	3,584	2,267
1997	22,087	8,139	3,704	2,331
1998	20,834	7,383	3,172	2,267
1999	21,367	7,673	3,147	2,293
2000	23,328	8,162	3,276	2,377
2001	23,246	8,027	3,358	2,364

Source: Maddison, A (2003). *The World Economy: Historical Statistics*. OECD, pp. 558–563, 566.

Table A1.2a. Population growth in 13 East Asian countries, 1820–2001.

	China	India	Japan	South Korea	Thailand	Taiwan	Myanmar	Singapore	Cambodia	Laos	North Korea	Vietnam	Former USSR	Russia
1820	381,000	209,000	31,000	9,395	4,665	2,000	3,506	30	2,090	470	4,345	6,551	54,765	
1821	383,711	209,842	31,033											
1822	386,442	210,688	31,066											
1823	389,193	211,537	31,099											
1824	391,962	212,389	31,132											
1825	394,752	213,245	31,164											
1826	397,561	214,105	31,197											
1827	400,391	214,967	31,231											
1828	403,240	215,834	31,264											
1829	406,110	216,703	31,297											
1830	409,000	217,577	31,330											
1831	409,299	218,453	31,363											
1832	409,598	219,334	31,396											
1833	409,898	220,218	31,429											
1834	410,197	221,105	31,463											
1835	410,497	221,996	31,496											
1836	410,797	222,891	31,529											
1837	411,098	223,789	31,563											
1838	411,398	224,691	31,596											
1839	411,699	225,596	31,630											
1840	412,000	226,505	31,663											
1841	412,000	227,418	31,697											

(*Continued*)

Table A1.2a. (*Continued*)

	China	India	Japan	South Korea	Thailand	Taiwan	Myanmar	Singapore	Cambodia	Laos	North Korea	Vietnam	Former USSR	Russia
1842	412,000	228,334	31,730											
1843	412,000	229,254	31,764											
1844	412,000	230,178	31,797											
1845	412,000	231,106	31,831											
1846	412,000	232,037	31,865											
1847	412,000	232,972	31,899											
1848	412,000	233,911	31,932											
1849	412,000	234,854	31,966											
1850	412,000	235,800	32,000	9,545	5,230	2,200	3,932	56					73,750	
1851	408,359	236,632	32,118											
1852	404,749	237,466	32,236											
1853	401,172	238,303	32,354											
1854	397,626	239,144	32,473											
1855	394,112	239,987	32,593											
1856	390,628	240,833	32,712											
1857	387,176	241,683	32,833											
1858	383,754	242,535	32,953											
1859	380,362	243,390	33,075											
1860	377,000	244,249	33,196											
1861	375,055	245,110	33,318											
1862	373,121	245,974	33,441											

(*Continued*)

	China	India	Japan	South Korea	Thailand	Taiwan	Myanmar	Singapore	Cambodia	Laos	North Korea	Vietnam	Former USSR	Russia
1863	371,196	246,842	33,564											
1864	369,282	247,712	33,687											
1865	367,377	248,586	33,811											
1866	365,482	249,462	33,935											
1867	363,597	250,342	34,060											
1868	361,722	251,225	34,185											
1869	359,856	252,111	34,311											
1870	358,000	253,000	34,437	9,753	5,775	2,345	4,245	84	2,340	755	4,511	10,528	88,672	
1871	358,988	253,417	34,648											
1872	359,978	253,834	34,859											
1873	360,971	254,253	35,070											
1874	361,967	254,672	35,235											
1875	362,966	255,091	35,436											
1876	363,967	255,512	35,713											
1877	364,971	255,933	36,018											
1878	365,978	256,354	36,315											
1879	366,988	256,777	36,557											
1880	368,000	257,200	36,807											
1881	369,183	259,359	37,112											
1882	370,369	261,536	37,414											
1883	371,560	263,732	37,766											
1884	372,754	265,946	38,138											

(Continued)

Table A1.2a. (Continued)

	China	India	Japan	South Korea	Thailand	Taiwan	Myanmar	Singapore	Cambodia	Laos	North Korea	Vietnam	Former USSR	Russia
1885	373,952	268,179	38,427											
1886	375,154	270,430	38,622											
1887	376,359	272,700	38,866											
1888	377,569	274,990	39,251											
1889	378,783	277,298	39,688											
1890	380,000	279,626	40,077	9,848	6,670	2,500	7,489	157					110,664	
1891	381,979	280,110	40,380											
1892	383,969	280,594	40,684											
1893	385,969	281,079	41,001											
1894	387,979	281,565	41,350											
1895	390,000	282,052	41,775											
1896	391,980	282,540	42,196											
1897	393,970	283,029	42,643											
1898	395,970	283,518	43,145			2,690								
1899	397,980	284,009	43,626			2,759								
1900	400,000	284,500	44,103	9,896	7,320	2,794	10,174	215					124,500	
1901	402,243	286,200	44,662		7,413	2,877	10,490							
1902	404,498	288,000	45,255		7,507	2,949	10,642							
1903	406,766	289,700	45,841		7,602	2,974	10,796							
1904	409,047	291,500	46,378		7,699	3,023	10,953							

(Continued)

Asian Economic Performance 1500–2010   37

Table A1.2a. (*Continued*)

	China	India	Japan	South Korea	Thailand	Taiwan	Myanmar	Singapore	Cambodia	Laos	North Korea	Vietnam	Former USSR	Russia
1905	411,340	293,300	46,829		7,797	3,101	11,112							
1906	413,646	295,100	47,227		7,896	3,135	11,273							
1907	415,965	296,900	47,691		7,996	3,164	11,437							
1908	418,297	298,700	48,260		8,098	3,191	11,603							
1909	420,642	300,500	48,869		8,201	3,227	11,771							
1910	423,000	302,100	49,518	10,096	8,305	3,276	11,942							
1911	427,662	303,100	50,215	10,258	8,431	3,345	12,115							
1912	432,375	303,400	50,941	10,422	8,559	3,411	12,220							
1913	437,140	303,700	51,672	10,589	8,689	3,477	12,326	323	3,070	1,387	4,897	19,339	156,192	
1914	441,958	304,000	52,396	10,764	8,822	3,529	12,433	331						
1915	446,829	304,200	53,124	10,911	8,957	3,545	12,541	341						
1916	451,753	304,500	53,815	11,086	9,094	3,569	12,650	351						
1917	456,732	304,800	54,437	11,263	9,232	3,616	12,760	360						
1918	461,766	305,100	54,886	11,443	9,418	3,638	12,871	370						
1919	466,855	305,300	55,253	11,627	9,608	3,681	12,893	380						
1920	472,000	305,600	55,818	11,804	9,802	3,721	13,096	391					154,607	
1921	473,673	307,300	56,490	12,040	10,000	3,786	13,212	418					152,836	
1922	475,352	310,400	57,209	12,281	10,202	3,844	13,351	436					152,403	
1923	477,037	313,600	57,937	12,526	10,435	3,904	13,491	458					153,055	
1924	478,728	316,700	58,686	12,777	10,673	3,959	13,633	469					155,581	
1925	480,425	319,900	59,522	13,005	10,916	4,048	13,776	492					158,983	

(*Continued*)

Table A1.2a. (Continued)

	China	India	Japan	South Korea	Thailand	Taiwan	Myanmar	Singapore	Cambodia	Laos	North Korea	Vietnam	Former USSR	Russia
1926	482,128	323,200	60,490	13,179	11,165	4,140	13,921	511					162,621	
1927	483,837	326,400	61,430	13,356	11,419	4,232	14,067	532					166,117	
1928	485,552	329,700	62,361	13,535	11,734	4,330	14,215	553					169,269	
1929	487,273	333,100	63,244	13,716	12,058	4,437	14,364	575					172,017	
1930	489,000	336,400	64,203	13,900	12,392	4,563	14,515	596					174,212	
1931	492,640	341,000	65,205	14,117	12,735	4,684	14,667	563					175,987	
1932	496,307	345,800	66,189	14,338	13,087	4,806	14,870	580					176,807	
1933	500,000	350,700	67,182	14,562	13,399	4,932	15,075	515					177,401	
1934	502,639	355,600	68,090	14,789	13,718	5,063	15,283	525					178,453	
1935	505,292	360,600	69,238	15,020	14,045	5,179	15,494	572					179,636	
1936	507,959	365,700	70,171	15,139	14,379	5,297	15,708	603					181,502	
1937	510,640	370,900	71,278	15,260	14,721	5,432	15,925	651					184,626	
1938	513,336	376,100	71,879	15,381	14,980	5,552	16,145	710					188,498	
1939	516,046	381,400	72,364	15,504	15,244	5,680	16,368	728					192,379	
1940	518,770	386,800	72,967	15,627	15,513	5,837	16,594	751					195,970	
1941	521,508	391,700	74,005	15,859	15,787	6,002	16,824	769						
1942	524,261	396,300	75,029	16,094	16,060	6,174	16,727							
1943	527,028	400,900	76,005	16,332	16,462	6,325	16,908							
1944	529,810	405,600	77,178	16,574	16,868	6,266	17,090							
1945	532,607	410,400	76,224	17,917	17,284	6,140	17,272							
1946	535,418	415,200	77,199	19,369	17,710	6,014	17,454						173,900	

(Continued)

Table A1.2a. (Continued)

	China	India	Japan	South Korea	Thailand	Taiwan	Myanmar	Singapore	Cambodia	Laos	North Korea	Vietnam	Former USSR	Russia
1947	538,244	346,000	78,119	19,886	18,148	6,419	17,636	938					174,000	
1948	541,085	350,000	80,155	20,027	18,569	6,724	17,818	961					175,100	
1949	543,941	355,000	81,971	20,208	19,000	7,302	18,000	979					177,500	
1950	546,815	359,000	83,805	20,846	20,042	7,456	19,488	1,022	4,471	1,886	9,471	25,348	179,571	101,937
1951	557,480	365,000	85,164	20,876	20,653	7,771	19,788	1,068	4,581	1,921	9,162	25,794	182,677	103,507
1952	568,910	372,000	86,459	20,948	21,289	8,031	20,093	1,127	4,694	1,957	8,865	26,247	185,856	105,385
1953	581,390	379,000	87,655	21,060	21,964	8,326	20,403	1,192	4,809	1,995	8,580	26,724	188,961	107,303
1954	595,310	386,000	88,754	21,259	22,685	8,635	20,722	1,248	4,928	2,035	8,572	27,210	192,171	109,209
1955	608,655	393,000	89,815	21,552	23,451	8,992	21,050	1,306	5,049	2,077	8,839	27,738	195,613	111,125
1956	621,465	401,000	90,766	22,031	24,244	9,341	21,387	1,372	5,184	2,121	9,116	28,327	199,103	112,859
1957	637,408	409,000	91,563	22,612	25,042	9,662	21,734	1,446	5,323	2,166	9,411	28,999	202,604	114,555
1958	653,235	418,000	92,389	23,254	25,845	10,020	22,090	1,519	5,465	2,213	9,727	29,775	206,201	116,259
1959	666,005	426,000	93,297	23,981	26,667	10,468	22,459	1,587	5,611	2,261	10,054	30,683	209,928	117,957
1960	667,070	434,000	94,092	24,784	27,513	10,861	22,839	1,646	5,761	2,309	10,392	31,656	213,780	119,632
1961	660,330	444,000	94,943	25,614	28,376	11,235	23,232	1,702	5,919	2,359	10,651	32,701	217,618	121,324
1962	665,770	454,000	95,832	26,420	29,263	11,615	23,638	1,750	6,084	2,409	10,917	33,796	221,227	122,878
1963	682,335	464,000	96,812	27,211	30,174	11,999	24,057	1,795	6,254	2,460	11,210	34,932	224,585	124,277
1964	698,355	474,000	97,826	27,984	31,107	12,385	24,490	1,842	6,427	2,512	11,528	36,099	227,698	125,522
1965	715,185	485,000	98,883	28,705	32,062	12,766	24,937	1,887	6,602	2,565	11,869	37,258	230,513	126,541
1966	735,400	495,000	99,790	29,436	33,036	13,140	25,399	1,934	6,780	2,619	12,232	38,378	233,139	127,415
1967	754,550	506,000	100,825	30,131	34,024	13,460	25,876	1,978	6,961	2,674	12,617	39,464	235,630	128,184

(Continued)

Table A1.2a. (Continued)

	China	India	Japan	South Korea	Thailand	Taiwan	Myanmar	Singapore	Cambodia	Laos	North Korea	Vietnam	Former USSR	Russia
1968	774,510	518,000	101,961	30,838	35,028	13,918	26,368	2,012	7,143	2,730	13,024	40,512	237,983	128,876
1969	796,025	529,000	103,172	31,544	36,050	14,200	26,874	2,043	7,329	2,787	13,455	41,542	240,253	129,573
1970	818,315	541,000	104,345	32,241	37,091	14,532	27,393	2,075	7,396	2,845	13,912	42,577	242,478	130,245
1971	841,105	554,000	105,697	32,883	38,202	14,862	27,926	2,113	7,388	2,904	14,365	43,614	244,887	130,977
1972	862,030	567,000	107,188	33,505	39,276	15,168	28,474	2,152	7,452	2,964	14,781	44,655	247,343	131,769
1973	881,940	580,000	108,707	34,073	40,302	15,454	29,235	2,193	7,536	3,027	15,161	45,736	249,712	132,556
1974	900,350	593,000	110,162	34,692	41,306	15,752	29,799	2,230	7,610	3,092	15,501	46,902	252,111	133,379
1975	916,395	607,000	111,573	35,281	42,272	16,061	30,335	2,263	7,491	3,161	15,801	48,075	254,519	134,293
1976	930,685	620,000	112,775	35,860	43,221	16,435	30,872	2,293	7,227	3,176	16,069	49,273	256,883	135,269
1977	943,455	634,000	113,872	36,436	44,148	16,753	31,408	2,325	6,991	3,208	16,325	50,534	259,225	136,264
1978	956,165	648,000	114,913	37,019	45,057	17,090	31,863	2,354	6,767	3,248	16,580	51,663	261,525	137,246
1979	969,005	664,000	115,890	37,534	46,004	17,448	32,405	2,384	6,734	3,268	16,840	52,668	263,751	138,164
1980	981,235	679,000	116,807	38,124	47,026	17,788	33,061	2,414	6,888	3,293	17,114	53,715	265,926	139,039
1981	993,861	692,000	117,648	38,723	47,937	18,097	33,669	2,535	7,080	3,337	17,384	54,903	268,123	139,900
1982	1,000,281	708,000	118,455	39,326	48,827	18,399	34,306	2,652	7,294	3,411	17,648	56,142	270,390	140,822
1983	1,023,288	723,000	119,270	39,910	49,694	18,657	34,980	2,689	7,521	3,495	17,918	57,436	272,717	141,862
1984	1,036,825	739,000	120,035	40,406	50,534	18,918	35,671	2,743	7,676	3,577	18,196	58,762	275,330	142,922
1985	1,051,040	755,000	120,754	40,806	51,342	19,148	36,346	2,750	7,822	3,657	18,481	60,093	277,812	143,938

(Continued)

Table A1.2a. (*Continued*)

	China	India	Japan	South Korea	Thailand	Taiwan	Myanmar	Singapore	Cambodia	Laos	North Korea	Vietnam	Former USSR	Russia
1986	1,066,790	771,000	121,492	41,214	52,129	19,332	36,998	2,750	8,079	3,762	18,772	61,440	280,296	144,967
1987	1,084,035	788,000	122,091	41,622	52,910	19,536	37,625	2,795	8,380	3,869	19,068	62,826	282,718	145,959
1988	1,101,630	805,000	122,613	42,031	53,683	19,752	38,196	2,869	8,692	3,980	19,371	64,211	285,020	146,866
1989	1,118,650	822,000	123,108	42,449	54,446	19,943	38,721	2,958	9,014	4,094	19,688	65,868	286,462	147,352
1990	1,135,185	839,000	123,537	42,869	55,197	20,172	39,243	3,047	9,345	4,210	20,019	67,283	288,361	147,973
1991	1,150,780	853,724	123,946	43,340	55,930	20,386	39,742	3,145	9,686	4,331	20,361	68,640	289,949	148,299
1992	1,164,970	869,090	124,329	43,837	56,667	20,591	40,133	3,236	10,123	4,454	20,711	69,941	290,950	148,400
1993	1,178,440	884,943	124,668	44,307	57,401	20,792	40,568	3,328	10,607	4,581	21,073	71,244	291,212	148,390
1994	1,191,835	901,176	125,014	44,719	58,129	20,984	41,158	3,428	10,963	4,712	21,329	72,539	291,052	148,442
1995	1,204,855	917,772	125,341	45,105	58,856	21,171	41,753	3,543	11,228	4,846	21,534	73,772	290,855	148,490
1996	1,217,550	934,692	125,645	45,468	59,559	21,347	42,308	3,672	11,481	4,971	21,606	74,941	290,625	148,312
1997	1,230,075	951,861	125,956	45,808	60,217	21,571	42,831	3,802	11,718	5,099	21,470	76,049	290,281	148,067
1998	1,241,935	969,153	126,246	46,152	60,846	21,769	43,338	3,905	11,946	5,229	21,205	77,092	289,919	147,813
1999	1,252,735	986,477	126,494	46,485	61,395	21,941	43,829	3,968	12,171	5,362	21,102	78,090	289,400	147,352
2000	1,262,645	1,004,124	126,729	46,839	61,863	22,133	44,301	4,037	12,396	5,498	21,263	79,060	288,719	146,710
2001	1,271,850	1,021,967	126,972	47,178	62,334	22,336	44,753	4,120	12,622	5,636	21,495	79,999	287,980	145,990

Source: Maddison, A (2003), *The World Economy: Historical Statistics*. OECD, pp. 558–563, 566.

42 Steven Rosefielde and Huan Zhou

Table A1.2b. Population growth in four East Asian countries, 1820–2001.

	Hong Kong	Malaysia	Indonesia	Philippines
1820	20	287	17,927	2,176
1821			18,076	
1822			18,226	
1823			18,377	
1824			18,530	
1825			18,684	
1826			18,839	
1827			18,996	
1828			19,154	
1829			19,313	
1830			19,473	
1831			19,635	
1832			19,798	
1833			19,962	
1834			20,128	
1835			20,296	
1836			20,464	
1837			20,634	
1838			20,806	
1839			20,978	
1840			21,153	
1841			21,328	
1842			21,506	
1843			21,684	
1844			21,864	
1845			22,046	
1846			22,229	
1847			22,414	
1848			22,600	
1849			22,788	
1850	33	530	22,977	3,612
1851			23,243	
1852			23,512	
1853			23,784	
1854			24,059	
1855			24,338	
1856			24,619	

(*Continued*)

Table A1.2b. (Continued)

	Hong Kong	Malaysia	Indonesia	Philippines
1857			24,904	
1858			25,192	
1859			25,484	
1860			25,779	
1861			26,077	
1862			26,379	
1863			26,684	
1864			26,993	
1865			27,305	
1866			27,621	
1867			27,941	
1868			28,264	
1869			28,591	
1870	123	800	32,743	5,063
1871			33,068	
1872			33,397	
1873			33,731	
1874			34,069	
1875			34,412	
1876			34,760	
1877			35,113	
1878			35,471	
1879			35,834	
1880			36,203	
1881			36,577	
1882			37,259	
1883			37,646	
1884			38,039	
1885			38,439	
1886			38,844	
1887			39,257	
1888			39,675	
1889			40,100	
1890	214	1,585	40,532	6,476
1891			40,955	
1892			41,384	

(*Continued*)

Table A1.2b. (Continued)

	Hong Kong	Malaysia	Indonesia	Philippines
1893			41,820	
1894			42,262	
1895			42,710	
1896			43,174	
1897			43,645	
1898			44,121	
1899			44,607	
1900	306	2,232	45,100	7,324
1901		2,288	45,575	7,465
1902		2,345	46,060	7,609
1903		2,404	46,552	7,755
1904		2,467	47,051	7,904
1905		2,532	47,559	8,056
1906		2,601	48,036	8,211
1907		2,672	48,520	8,369
1908		2,745	49,014	8,530
1909		2,821	49,518	8,694
1910		2,893	50,034	8,861
1911		2,967	50,563	9,032
1912		3,025	51,106	9,206
1913	487	3,084	51,637	9,384
1914	507	3,144	52,178	9,565
1915	528	3,207	52,729	9,749
1916	550	3,271	53,290	9,937
1917	573	3,337	53,856	10,128
1918	597	3,404	53,910	10,323
1919	622	3,473	54,438	10,522
1920	648	3,545	54,993	10,725
1921	625	3,618	55,601	10,932
1922	638	3,698	56,220	11,143
1923	668	3,779	56,847	11,358
1924	696	3,863	57,486	11,577
1925	725	3,949	58,135	11,800
1926	710	4,038	58,807	12,026
1927	725	4,128	59,501	12,305
1928	753	4,221	60,250	12,543
1929	785	4,316	61,019	12,890
1930	821	4,413	61,805	13,194

(Continued)

Asian Economic Performance 1500–2010   45

Table A1.2b.   (*Continued*)

	Hong Kong	**Malaysia**	**Indonesia**	**Philippines**
1931	840	4,513	62,878	13,507
1932	901	4,604	63,986	13,829
1933	923	4,697	65,131	14,158
1934	944	4,793	66,314	14,497
1935	966	4,890	67,538	14,843
1936	988	4,993	68,807	15,199
1937	1,282	5,099	70,121	15,563
1938	1,479	5,207	71,484	15,934
1939	1,750	5,317	72,903	16,275
1940	1,786	5,434	74,376	16,585
1941	1,639	5,554	75,588	16,902
1942		5,592	76,785	17,169
1943		5,630	77,615	17,552
1944		5,668	77,646	17,887
1945		5,707	77,545	18,228
1946	1,550	5,746	78,050	18,775
1947	1,750	5,786	78,880	19,338
1948	1,800	5,922	79,856	19,918
1949	1,857	6,061	81,120	20,516
1950	2,237	6,434	82,612	21,131
1951	2,015	6,582	83,773	21,775
1952	2,126	6,748	84,946	22,439
1953	2,242	6,929	86,167	23,122
1954	2,365	7,118	87,441	23,827
1955	2,490	7,312	88,766	24,553
1956	2,615	7,520	90,136	25,301
1957	2,736	7,739	91,559	26,072
1958	2,854	7,966	93,014	26,867
1959	2,967	8,196	94,506	27,685
1960	3,075	8,428	95,961	28,529
1961	3,168	8,663	97,610	29,410
1962	3,305	8,906	99,620	30,325
1963	3,421	9,148	101,674	31,273
1964	3,505	9,397	103,772	32,254
1965	3,598	9,648	105,913	33,268
1966	3,630	9,900	108,103	34,304
1967	3,723	10,155	110,339	35,357
1968	3,803	10,409	112,623	36,424

(*Continued*)

46 *Steven Rosefielde and Huan Zhou*

Table A1.2b. *(Continued)*

	Hong Kong	Malaysia	Indonesia	Philippines
1969	3,864	10,662	114,956	37,507
1970	3,959	10,910	117,338	38,604
1971	4,045	11,171	119,767	39,718
1972	4,116	11,441	122,565	40,850
1973	4,213	11,712	125,432	41,998
1974	4,320	11,986	128,369	43,162
1975	4,396	12,267	131,219	44,337
1976	4,518	12,554	134,314	45,574
1977	4,584	12,845	137,487	46,851
1978	4,668	13,139	140,739	48,172
1979	4,930	13,444	144,073	49,537
1980	5,063	13,764	147,490	50,940
1981	5,183	14,096	150,657	52,228
1982	5,265	14,441	153,895	53,557
1983	5,345	14,793	157,208	54,885
1984	5,398	15,157	160,595	56,258
1985	5,456	15,545	164,061	57,706
1986	5,525	15,942	166,997	59,186
1987	5,585	16,333	169,990	60,648
1988	5,628	16,731	173,041	62,081
1989	5,661	17,121	176,152	63,555
1990	5,688	17,507	179,323	65,088
1991	5,752	17,911	182,298	66,572
1992	5,830	18,325	185,327	67,978
1993	5,935	18,754	188,413	69,417
1994	6,067	19,187	191,554	70,945
1995	6,225	19,619	194,755	72,597
1996	6,392	20,053	196,962	74,336
1997	6,496	20,485	199,198	76,057
1998	6,545	20,921	201,461	77,741
1999	6,599	21,365	203,754	79,448
2000	6,659	21,804	205,132	81,222
2001	6,713	22,240	207,801	83,095

Source: Maddison, A (2003). *The World Economy: Historical Statistics.* OECD, pp. 538–543, 546.

Table A1.3a. GDP in 13 East Asian countries, 1820–2001 (1990 international Geary-Khamis dollars).

	China	India	Japan	South Korea	Thailand	Taiwan	Myanmar	Singapore	Cambodia	Laos	North Korea	Vietnam	F. USSR	Russia	Western Europe
1820	228,600	111,417	20,739	5,637	2,659	1,100	1,767	3			2,607	3,453	37,678		141,408
1821															
1822															
1823															
1824															
1825															
1826															
1827															
1828															
1829															
1830															
1831															
1832															
1833															
1834															
1835															
1836															
1837															
1838															
1839															
1840															

(Continued)

Table A1.3a. (*Continued*)

	China	India	Japan	South Korea	Thailand	Taiwan	Myanmar	Singapore	Cambodia	Laos	Vietnam	North Korea	F. USSR	Russia	Western Europe
1841															
1842															
1843															
1844															
1845															
1846															
1847															
1848															
1849															
1850	247,200	125,681	21,732												237,190
1851															
1852															
1853															
1854															
1855															
1856															
1857															
1858															
1859															
1860															

(*Continued*)

Table A1.3a. (Continued)

	China	India	Japan	South Korea	Thailand	Taiwan	Myanmar	Singapore	Cambodia	Laos	North Korea	Vietnam	F. USSR	Russia	Western Europe
1861															
1862															
1863															
1864															
1865															
1866															
1867															
1868															
1869															
1870	189,740	134,882	25,393	5,891	3,511	1,290	2,139	57			2,725	5,321	83,646		337,710
1871			25,709												343,991
1872			26,005												356,715
1873			26,338												359,269
1874			26,644												377,887
1875			28,698												386,615
1876			28,019												380,531
1877			28,910												385,242
1878			28,825												390,215
1879			30,540												383,340
1880			31,779												399,789
1881			30,777												407,435

(Continued)

	China	India	Japan	South Korea	Thailand	Taiwan	Myanmar	Singapore	Cambodia	Laos	North Korea	Vietnam	F. USSR	Russia	Western Europe
1882			31,584												421,409
1883			31,618												429,878
1884		146,409	31,872												433,294
1885		151,985	33,052												435,886
1886		148,134	35,395												443,723
1887		155,899	36,982												457,216
1888		158,358	35,310												469,759
1889		155,063	37,016												481,810
1890	205,379	163,341	40,556		5,229										493,244
1891		148,317	38,621												495,105
1892		160,224	41,200												497,653
1893		164,280	41,344												509,141
1894		166,799	46,288												526,945
1895		162,696	46,933												540,209
1896		150,699	44,353												559,505
1897		178,236	45,285												565,859
1898		178,599	53,883												592,644
1899		164,690	49,870												615,561
1900	218,154	170,466	52,020										154,049		624,220
1901		173,957	53,883			1,766	7,332								623,627
1902		188,504	51,089			1,810									630,990

(*Continued*)

Table A1.3a. *(Continued)*

	China	India	Japan	South Korea	Thailand	Taiwan	Myanmar	Singapore	Cambodia	Laos	North Korea	Vietnam	F. USSR	Russia	Western Europe
1903		191,141	54,671			2,164									645,501
1904		192,060	55,101			2,094									657,608
1905		188,587	54,170			1,738									675,665
1906		193,979	61,263			1,852	6,385								697,550
1907		182,234	63,198			2,069									726,429
1908		184,844	63,628			2,153									723,088
1909		210,241	63,556			2,430									746,002
1910		210,439	64,559			2,509									752,721
1911		209,354	68,070	8,361		2,395	7,348								787,286
1912		208,946	70,507	8,789		2,297									815,742
1913	241,431	204,242	71,653	9,206	7,304	2,545	8,445	413			4,257	14,062	232,351		840,482
1914		215,400	69,503	9,709		2,491									791,531
1915		210,110	75,952	11,433		2,605									806,661
1916		216,245	87,703	11,286		2,827	10,405								837,479
1917		212,341	90,641	12,596		3,212									812,667
1918		185,202	91,573	13,689		3,087									782,318
1919		210,730	100,959	14,705		3,210									723,553
1920		194,051	94,654	12,889		3,202									741,118
1921		208,785	105,043	14,069		3,361	9,392								737,524

(Continued)

Table A1.3a. *(Continued)*

	China	India	Japan	South Korea	Thailand	Taiwan	Myanmar	Singapore	Cambodia	Laos	North Korea	Vietnam	F. USSR	Russia	Western Europe
1922		217,594	104,757	13,075		3,779									803,105
1923		210,511	104,828	14,165		3,908									794,100
1924		220,763	107,766	14,420		4,254									859,604
1925		223,375	112,209	14,557		4,513									906,250
1926		230,410	113,212	15,177		4,604	11,326								918,230
1927		230,426	114,860	15,913		4,620									959,925
1928		232,745	124,246	16,105		4,762							231,886		1,002,663
1929	274,090	242,409	128,116	15,328	9,568	5,028							238,392		1,029,947
1930	277,567	244,097	118,801	14,583		5,247							252,333		1,014,063
1931	280,393	242,489	119,804	14,767		5,321	13,235						257,213		962,124
1932	289,304	245,209	129,835	14,899		5,649							254,424		931,870
1933	289,304	245,433	142,589	18,156		5,494							264,880		967,170
1934	264,091	247,712	142,876	18,275		5,795							290,903		1,006,850
1935	285,403	245,361	146,817	20,084		6,395							334,818		1,050,586
1936	303,433	254,896	157,493	21,753		6,769	13,167						361,306		1,100,979
1937	296,043	250,768	165,017	23,827		6,836							398,017		1,156,686
1938	288,653	251,375	176,051	24,895	12,380	7,252	11,942						405,220		1,189,457
1939		256,924	203,781	22,315		7,107							430,314		1,261,104

(Continued)

	China	India	Japan	South Korea	Thailand	Taiwan	Myanmar	Singapore	Cambodia	Laos	North Korea	Vietnam	F. USSR	Russia	Western Europe
1940		265,455	209,728	25,001		6,618							420,091		1,240,067
1941		270,531	212,594	25,347		6,356							333,656		1,253,151
1942		269,278	211,448	25,203		6,667							333,656		1,244,058
1943		279,898	214,457	25,569		6,177							333,656		1,243,487
1944		276,954	205,214	24,462		5,207							333,656		1,189,733
1945		272,503	102,607	12,236		2,782							333,656		1,027,872
1946		258,164	111,492	13,295		2,940							332,727		967,157
1947		213,680	120,377	14,295		3,604							369,903		1,034,018
1948		215,927	138,290	15,383		4,668							420,555		1,110,228
1949		221,631	147,534	16,548		5,628							465,631		1,204,137
1950	244,985	222,222	160,966	17,800	16,375	6,828	7,711	2,268	2,155	1,156	8,087	16,681	510,243		1,286,643
1951	273,733	227,362	181,025	16,430	17,532	7,375	8,834	2,406	2,228	1,192	6,496	17,445	512,566		1,360,880
1952	305,854	234,148	202,005	17,497	18,503	8,258	9,028	2,569	2,368	1,229	6,675	18,209	545,792		1,408,010
1953	321,030	248,963	216,889	22,570	20,542	9,029	9,265	2,758	2,392	1,267	8,288	19,034	569,260		1,482,446
1954	331,550	259,262	229,151	23,894	20,381	9,890	8,690	2,896	2,670	1,306	8,683	19,920	596,910		1,563,766
1955	350,908	265,527	248,855	25,191	22,162	10,692	9,822	3,078	2,614	1,347	9,316	20,806	648,027		1,663,674
1956	382,892	280,978	267,567	25,311	22,540	11,280	10,472	3,200	2,963	1,388	9,444	21,631	710,065		1,736,764
1957	405,386	277,924	287,130	27,262	22,792	12,110	11,089	3,352	3,163	1,431	10,230	22,486	724,470		1,813,652
1958	450,977	299,137	303,857	28,691	23,616	12,923	10,785	3,485	3,322	1,476	10,816	23,372	778,840		1,856,687
1959	457,139	305,499	331,570	29,803	26,457	13,912	12,457	3,470	3,646	1,521	11,260	24,289	770,244		1,952,580
1960	441,694	326,910	375,090	30,395	29,665	14,697	12,871	3,803	3,863	1,568	11,483	25,297	843,434		2,083,673

(*Continued*)

Table A1.3a. *(Continued)*

	China	India	Japan	South Korea	Thailand	Taiwan	Myanmar	Singapore	Cambodia	Laos	North Korea	Vietnam	F. USSR	Russia	Western Europe
1961	365,092	336,744	420,246	31,930	31,210	15,708	13,183	4,123	3,827	1,617	11,972	26,554	891,763		2,186,942
1962	366,465	344,204	457,742	32,898	33,636	16,949	14,332	4,411	4,139	1,667	12,249	29,917	915,928		2,287,608
1963	402,776	361,442	496,514	35,797	36,360	18,534	14,737	4,848	4,451	1,718	13,295	30,821	895,016		2,386,210
1964	450,312	389,262	554,449	38,888	38,841	20,796	14,999	4,680	4,331	1,772	14,445	32,322			2,525,407
1965	501,769	373,814	586,744	41,230	41,933	23,111	15,379	5,033	4,538	1,826	15,370	32,666			2,624,898
1966	548,841	377,207	649,189	46,195	46,654	25,171	14,737	5,593	4,744	1,883	17,308	32,975			2,716,726
1967	533,407	408,349	721,132	49,555	50,552	27,867	15,151	6,255	4,988	1,941	18,711	28,829			2,805,157
1968	522,728	418,907	813,984	55,880	54,695	30,423	16,148	7,123	5,214	2,001	21,268	28,329			2,950,544
1969	567,545	446,872	915,556	64,350	58,980	33,145	16,815	8,098	5,292	2,063	24,743	30,702			3,112,703
1970	636,937	469,584		69,877	62,842	36,868	17,575	9,209	4,785	2,127	27,184	31,295			3,243,118
1971	668,646	474,338		76,695	65,886	41,674	18,149	10,362	4,546	2,193	36,229	32,889			3,344,676
1972	688,186	472,766		82,304	68,666	47,224	18,284	11,752	4,301	2,261	37,854	35,815			3,476,249
1973	739,414	494,832		96,231	75,511	53,284	18,352	13,108	5,858	2,331	42,819	38,238		872,466	3,664,831
1974	751,924	500,146			78,894	53,903	19,323	13,994	5,007	2,403	44,038	36,744			3,734,794
1975	798,346	544,683			82,799	56,560	20,125	14,549	4,342	2,477	44,891	34,130			3,703,845
1976	793,568	551,402			90,391	64,399	21,350	15,588	4,650	2,554	45,652	39,879			3,861,124
1977	843,097	593,834			99,304	70,962	22,625	16,797	5,016	2,633	46,379	41,343			3,964,829
1978	935,083	625,695			109,112	80,608	24,086	18,245	5,484	2,714	47,104	41,622			4,076,084
1979		594,510			114,828	87,197	25,222	19,932	5,593	2,798	47,842	41,873			4,230,093
1980		637,202			120,116	93,563	27,381	21,865	5,705	2,885	48,621	40,671			4,289,883
1981		675,882			127,211	99,329	28,930	23,960	5,774	2,974	49,388	42,103			4,295,711

(Continued)

Table A1.3a. *(Continued)*

	China	India	Japan	South Korea	Thailand	Taiwan	Myanmar	Singapore	Cambodia	Laos	North Korea	Vietnam	F. USSR	Russia	Western Europe
1982		697,705			134,020	102,857	30,499	25,601	6,218	3,066	50,138	45,526			4,327,231
1983		753,942			141,504	111,545	31,827	27,695	6,660	3,161	50,905	48,042			4,407,012
1984		783,042			149,644	123,368	33,397	30,006	7,106	3,258	51,695	52,355			4,517,280
1985		814,344			156,598	129,478	34,349	29,451	7,554	3,359	52,505	55,481			4,630,348
1986		848,990			165,264	144,552	33,986	29,975	7,998	3,463	53,331	57,056			4,759,311
1987		886,154			180,996	167,970	32,624	32,817	7,839	3,570	54,172	59,127			4,884,240
1988		978,822			205,047	175,747	28,921	36,491	8,035	3,681	55,033	62,685			5,071,672
1989					230,043	190,217	29,989	39,857	8,233	3,795	55,934	65,615			5,235,115
1990					255,732	200,477	30,834	43,330	8,235	3,912	56,874	68,959			5,277,592
1991					277,618	215,620	30,634	46,259	8,860	4,031	57,846	72,965			5,366,507
1992					300,059	231,766	33,593	49,355	9,482	4,245	53,391	79,313		934,932	5,435,202
1993					325,215	248,023	35,622	55,404	9,870	4,674	53,552	85,720		853,593	5,426,318
1994					354,484	265,650	38,286	61,722	10,258	4,964	39,468	93,292		745,187	5,582,309
1995					387,097	282,715	40,946	66,685	10,940	5,230	32,758	102,192		714,634	5,721,433
1996					409,936	299,967	43,584	72,117	11,543	5,355	27,091	111,737		688,907	5,815,901
1997					404,197	319,997	46,088	78,283	11,846	5,636	25,249	120,845		698,552	5,964,849
1998					361,756	334,622	48,748	77,549	11,998	5,806	25,130	127,812		661,529	6,110,619
1999					377,846	352,772	54,084	82,869	13,294	6,257	25,310	133,913		703,867	6,278,174
2000					395,791	373,438	61,518	90,900	14,224	6,615	25,310	143,002		774,253	6,517,572
2001					404,369	365,281	68,470	89,169	15,035	6,992	25,310	152,862		813,740	6,618,129

Source: Maddison, A (2003). *World Economy: Historical Statistics*. OECD, pp. 548–553, 556.

56   *Steven Rosefielde and Huan Zhou*

Table A1.3b.   GDP in four East Asian countries, 1820–2001 (1990 international Geary-Khamis dollars).

	Hong Kong	Malaysia	Indonesia	Philippines
1820	12	173	10,970	1,271
1821				
1822				
1823				
1824				
1825				
1826				
1827				
1828				
1829				
1830				
1831				
1832				
1833				
1834				
1835				
1836				
1837				
1838				
1839				
1840				
1841				
1842				
1843				
1844				
1845				
1846				
1847				
1848				
1849				
1850			14,633	
1851				
1852				
1853				
1854				
1855				

(Continued)

Asian Economic Performance 1500–2010 57

Table A1.3b. (*Continued*)

	Hong Kong	Malaysia	Indonesia	Philippines
1856				
1857				
1858				
1859				
1860				
1861				
1862				
1863				
1864				
1865				
1866				
1867				
1868				
1869				
1870	84	530	18,929	3,159
1871			19,021	
1872			19,158	
1873			19,660	
1874			20,162	
1875			20,481	
1876			21,028	
1877			21,302	
1878			21,028	
1879			21,439	
1880			21,758	
1881			23,218	
1882			22,443	
1883			22,214	
1884			24,495	
1885			24,815	
1886			24,678	
1887			24,951	
1888			25,179	
1889			25,316	
1890			24,815	
1891			25,362	
1892			26,411	

(*Continued*)

58 Steven Rosefielde and Huan Zhou

Table A1.3b. *(Continued)*

	Hong Kong	Malaysia	Indonesia	Philippines
1893			27,187	
1894			27,643	
1895			28,281	
1896			28,099	
1897			28,509	
1898			28,874	
1899			30,608	
1900			31,748	
1901			31,352	
1902			30,904	5,119
1903			32,637	6,232
1904			33,314	5,367
1905			33,823	5,711
1906			34,869	5,932
1907			35,698	6,252
1908			35,800	6,610
1909			37,659	6,734
1910			40,180	7,747
1911		2,376	42,442	8,243
1912		2,486	42,818	8,390
1913	623	2,776	45,152	9,272
1914		2,893	45,076	9,103
1915		3,007	45,647	8,532
1916		3,258	46,350	9,966
1917		3,449	46,513	11,624
1918		3,300	47,597	13,272
1919		4,020	51,402	12,757
1920		3,936	50,779	13,826
1921		3,889	51,212	13,505
1922		4,259	52,033	15,124
1923		4,194	52,858	14,196
1924		4,095	55,683	15,495
1925		4,743	57,610	15,617
1926		5,316	60,781	16,399
1927		5,165	64,989	16,808
1928		5,865	68,099	17,458
1929		7,261	70,015	18,208

(Continued)

Asian Economic Performance 1500–2010 59

Table A1.3b. (*Continued*)

	Hong Kong	Malaysia	Indonesia	Philippines
1930		7,219	70,525	18,230
1931		6,988	65,218	18,372
1932		6,431	64,461	19,189
1933		6,762	64,035	19,370
1934		7,380	64,400	19,545
1935		6,672	66,674	18,218
1936		7,380	71,517	20,726
1937		6,672	78,485	22,219
1938		7,089	80,044	22,948
1939		8,557	80,861	24,548
1940		6,945	86,682	24,993
1941		6,878	89,316	
1942		9,354		
1943				
1944				
1945				
1946				12,131
1947		6,186		16,922
1948		7,017		19,772
1949		9,277	61,872	21,022
1950	4,962	10,032	66,358	22,616
1951	4,626	9,478	71,304	25,054
1952	5,054	9,930	74,679	26,609
1953	5,515	9,977	78,394	28,988
1954	6,021	10,607	83,283	31,168
1955	6,564	10,677	85,571	33,331
1956	7,136	11,320	86,700	35,670
1957	7,729	11,257	92,631	37,599
1958	8,345	11,256	89,293	38,900
1959	8,981	12,026	93,129	41,548
1960	9,637	12,899	97,082	42,114
1961	10,276	13,794	103,446	44,480
1962	12,072	14,578	103,332	46,603
1963	13,968	15,271	99,371	49,893
1964	15,165	16,235	103,043	51,613
1965	17,360	17,405	104,070	54,331

(*Continued*)

60 Steven Rosefielde and Huan Zhou

Table A1.3b. (*Continued*)

	Hong Kong	Malaysia	Indonesia	Philippines
1966	17,659	18,278	104,089	56,736
1967	17,959	18,587	101,739	59,756
1968	18,557	20,217	111,662	62,712
1969	20,652	21,382	125,408	65,632
1970	22,548	22,684	138,612	68,102
1971	24,144	24,359	146,200	71,799
1972	26,639	26,195	162,748	75,710
1973	29,931	29,982	186,900	82,464
1974	30,629	32,222	196,374	85,398
1975	30,729	32,489	196,374	90,150
1976	35,718	36,536	213,675	98,090
1977	39,908	39,513	230,338	103,585
1978	43,300	42,970	240,853	108,942
1979	48,289	46,469	253,961	115,086
1980	53,177	50,333	275,805	121,012
1981	58,066	53,901	294,768	125,154
1982	59,662	57,102	283,922	129,648
1983	63,055	60,588	295,296	132,115
1984	69,340	65,290	315,677	122,440
1985	69,639	64,617	323,451	113,493
1986	77,122	65,434	342,452	117,371
1987	87,099	68,898	359,323	122,432
1988	94,083	74,982	379,917	130,699
1989	96,478	81,996	414,090	138,809
1990	99,770	89,823	450,901	143,025
1991	105,395	98,397	474,421	142,191
1992	112,336	107,140	526,321	142,668
1993	119,466	117,741	564,053	145,704
1994	126,016	128,587	606,949	152,115
1995	130,912	141,226	656,101	159,264
1996	136,550	155,353	705,895	168,507
1997	143,476	166,729	737,760	177,264
1998	136,347	154,459	639,032	176,200
1999	141,006	163,939	641,286	182,192
2000	155,337	177,955	672,114	193,066
2001	156,057	178,532	697,849	196,439

Source: Maddison, A (2003). *World Economy: Historical Statistics*. OECD, pp. 548–553.

Asian Economic Performance 1500–2010   61

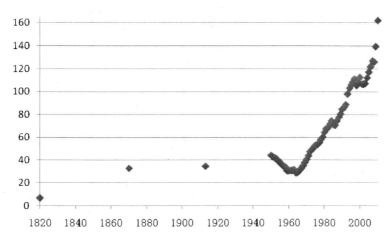

Figure A1.1.   Singaporean–EU divergence and convergence 1820–2010 per capita GDP (Western Europe = 100).

Source: Table A1.1.

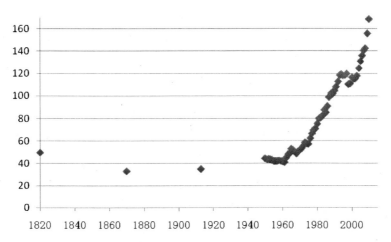

Figure A1.2.   Hong Kong–EU divergence and convergence 1820–2010 per capita GDP (Western Europe = 100).

Source: Table A1.1.

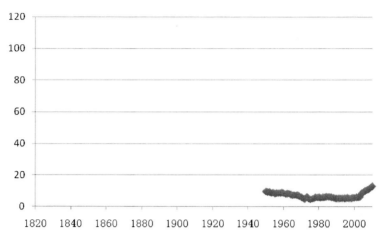

Figure A1.3. Cambodian–EU divergence and convergence 1820–2010 per capita GDP (Western Europe = 100).

Source: Table A1.1.

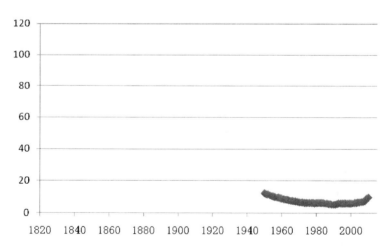

Figure A1.4. Laotian–EU divergence and convergence 1820–2010 per capita GDP (Western Europe = 100).

Source: Table A1.1.

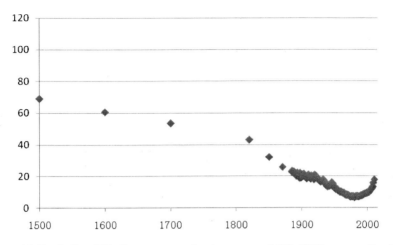

Figure A1.5. Indian–EU divergence and convergence 1500–2010 per capita GDP (Western Europe = 100).

Source: Table A1.1.

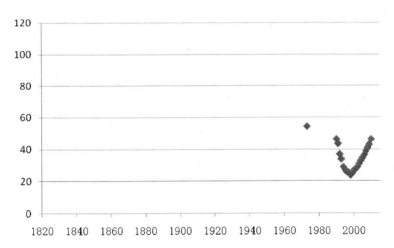

Figure A1.6. Russian–EU per capita GDP: comparative size 1820–2010 (West European = 100).

Source: http://www.ggdc.net/maddison/Historical_Statistics/horizontal-file_03-2009xls. (last updated: March 2009). West Europe includes Austria, Belgium, Denmark, Finland, France, Germany, Italy, Netherlands, Norway, Sweden, Switzerland, and the United Kingdom. GDP for West Europe and Russia is calculated in 1990 international Geary-Khamis dollars.

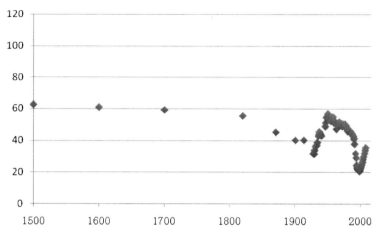

Figure A1.7. USSR–EU territorial per capita GDP: comparative size 1500–2010 (West European = 100).

Source: Table A1.1.

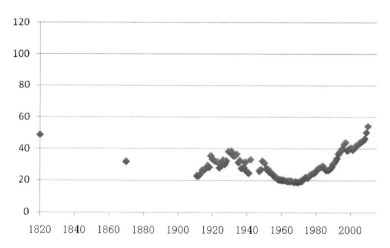

Figure A1.8. Malaysia–EU per capita GDP: divergence and convergence 1820–2010.

Source: Table 5.1.

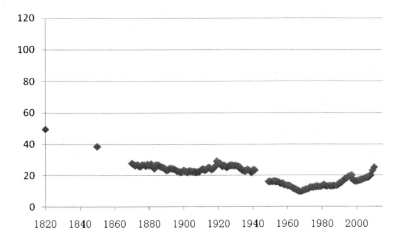

Figure A1.9. Indonesia–EU per capita GDP: divergence and convergence 1820–2010.
Source: Table 5.1.

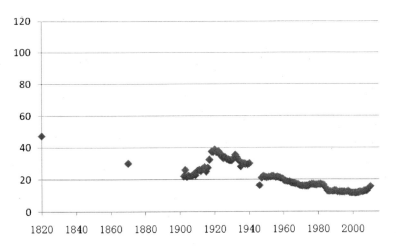

Figure A1.10. Philippines–EU per capita GDP: divergence and convergence 1820–2010.
Source: Table 5.1.

PART II

THE 2008 FINANCIAL CRISIS AND ITS GLOBAL AFTERMATH

CHAPTER 2

GLOBAL FINANCIAL CRISIS

ASSAF RAZIN
Cornell University, New York

STEVEN ROSEFIELDE
University of North Carolina, Chapel Hill

2.1. Introduction

The global financial crisis, which began with the subprime mortgage crisis and exploded in September 2008 with the collapse of Lehman Brothers Bank, took much of the macroeconomic professional by surprise, even though there were ample early warning signs. Theorists failed to adequately consider the destabilizing cumulative impacts of financial deregulation, hedge funds, electronic trading, shady financial entrepreneurship, moral hazard, regulatory laxness, regulatory hazard ("mark to market" FAS 157), structural deficits, the shift from Keynesian investment stimulus to general aggregate demand management, Phillip's Curve–justified perpetual monetary ease, subprime mortgages, derivatives, one-way-street speculation, "too big to fail" psychology, hard asset speculation (real estate, commodities, natural resources, precious metals, art, antiques, and jewelry), fiscal abuses, special interest transfers, and stealthy Chinese protectionism, beyond normal business cycle oscillations, because they had come to believe that policymakers had learned how to tame the beast. With the advantage of hindsight, two years after the mast,[1] both the strengths and weaknesses of the third millennium macroeconomic consensus can be discerned and appraised with an eye toward parsing the future.

---

[1] Allusion to Dana, RH, Jr (1840). *Two Years Before the Mast*. The Mast is quarters for ordinary sailors in the forecastle, and a metaphor for calamity and suffering.

70   Assaf Razin and Steven Rosefielde

It appears on reflection that the 2008 global financial crisis and the Great Recession[2] from 2007 to 2009 stunned the macroeconomic profession because a consensus had emerged that modern state regulatory mechanisms (including automatic stabilizers) had reduced business cycle oscillations in production and employment to a degree where fine tuning could be achieved merely by controlling short-term, and derivatively long-term, interest rates without fiscal assistance or fortified financial regulation. The headline therefore is that we now know better. This does not amount to a claim that we understand how to employ fiscal policy and supplementary monetary instruments to optimally recover, or prevent future recurrences, given the often destabilizing aspirations of the business, finance, and government communities. It only means that complacency is no longer tenable, and a reassessment of past output and employment stabilizing measures is in order. Let us therefore begin with a review of the third millennium macroeconomic consensus and recent refinements, and then proceed with a comparison of the 2008 global financial crisis and its predecessors, taking into account subsequent impacts on production and employment.

2.2. Pre-crisis Consensus

Conventional wisdom during 2000–2008 held that business cycle oscillations were primarily caused by productivity shocks that lasted until price- and wage-setters disentangled real from nominal effects.[3] These shocks sometimes generated inflation which it was believed was best addressed with monetary policy. Accordingly, central bankers were tasked with the mission of maintaining slow and stable inflation. Zero inflation and

---

[2] The National Bureau of Economic Research (NBER) declared on September 10, 2010 that the Great Recession's trough was reached in June 2009. The start date for the decline which lasted 18 months was set in December 2007, making it the longest postwar down draft. The 1973–1975 and 1981–1982 American recessions lasted 16 months. The Great Recession's end, according to NBER conventions, does not mean that there has been, or that there will be a full recovery. It only indicates that any subsequent decline will be classified as a separate recessionary event. The Great Recession now seems to have been a depression. The cumulative GDP decrease over the six quarters of the contraction is currently estimated at 5.1 percent, up from 4.1 percent. See Bureau of Economic Analysis, August 5, 2011

[3] Lucas, R, Jr (1975). An equilibrium model of the business cycle. *Journal of Political Economy*, 83, 1113–1144.

deflation were shunned because they purportedly were incompatible with full capacity employment.[4] Although central bankers were supposed to be less concerned with real economic activity, many came to believe that full employment and the two percent inflation could be sustained indefinitely by "divine coincidence." This miracle was said to be made all the better by the fact that real economic performance could be regulated with a single monetary instrument: the short-term interest rate. Therefore, arbitrage across time meant that central bankers could control all temporal interest rates, and arbitrage across asset classes implied that the Federal Reserve(Fed) could similarly influence risk-adjusted rates for diverse securities. Fiscal policy, which had ruled the roost under the influence of orthodox Keynesianism from 1950 to 1980, in this way, was relegated to a subsidiary role aided by theorists' beliefs in the empirical validity of Ricardian equivalence arguments and skepticism about lags and political priorities. The financial sector likewise was given short shrift (because it was perceived as a regulatory rather than a demand management issue), but this still left room for other kinds of nonmonetary intervention. The consensus view held that automatic stabilizers like unemployment insurance should be retained to share risks: that is, to assist in case there were any unpredictable shocks. Commercial bank credit similarly continued to be regulated, and federal deposit insurance preserved to deter bank runs, but otherwise finance was lightly supervised: especially "shadow banks," hedge funds, and derivatives.

The convergence of views among macroeconomists was based on post–World War II experience with business cycles. However, the current cycle is significantly different (see Figure 2.1).

2.3. New Dissensus

Needless to say, most theorists now concede that the monetarist consensus was mistaken, but for the moment, the profession has split into two contending camps. Both recognize that with the Federal funds rate near zero, the burden for stimulating recovery and growth depends on nonconventional monetary policies, such as quantitative and credit easing, and discretionary fiscal policy, but the agreement stops here. The

---

[4] Phillips, W (1958). The relationship between unemployment and the rate of change of money wages in the United Kingdom 1861–1957. *Economica*, 25(100), 283–299.

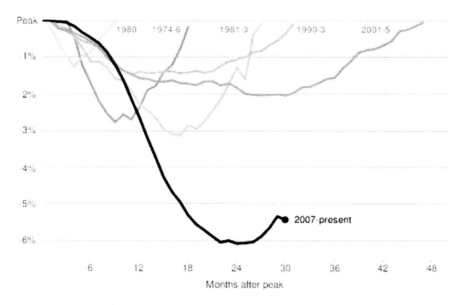

Figure 2.1. Employment declines in various US crises.
Source: Federal Reserve Board.

"Ricardian" faction contends that further over-budget spending with deficit to GDP ratios in many large nations like the United States, already above 10%, will drive up interest rates, crowd out private investment, and have negative stimulatory impact. This could easily cause a double-dip recession (depression) coupled with a bout of high inflation ("deflation"), due to excessive commercial bank liquidity. Similar arguments have been advanced for some EU members like Greece, Spain, and Italy, even though Eurozone debts until recently seemed more manageable.[5]

"Keynesian" fiscal bulls, however, see matters vice versa. They insist that deflation is the present danger (which via the Bernanke doctrine implies a Great Depression with rising real wages and excess savings)[6] and

---

[5] For a thorough discussion of the eurozone crisis, see Assaf Razin and Steven Rosefielde, *PIIGS*, in Steven Rosefielde, Masaaki Kuboniwa, and Satoshi Mizobata (eds.), *Prevention and Crisis Management: Lessons for Asia from the 2008 Crisis*, Singapore: World Scientific Publishers, 2012.

[6] Bernanke, B (1983). Nonmonetary effects of the financial crisis in the propagation of the great depression. *The American Economic Review*, 73, 257–276.

deduce avoiding disaster hinges on intensified deficit spending (Bush-era tax cut extension, December 2010), and continued central bank credit and quantitative easing. They are aware that this could have inflationary ramifications but brush the inflation peril aside by claiming that speculators will absorb most of the idle cash balances governments are prepared to print while inflationary expectations are on a downward trend. Moreover, they contend that excess credit can be quickly drained from the system, whenever banks decide to resume lending. Further, as an icing on the cake, they proclaim that large multiplier effects will not only restore full employment but provide the wherewithal to repay the government debt.

Insofar as communities believe one prognostication or the other, their speculative responses may spark inflation or deflation; increased or decreased long-term interest rates, productive recovery or decline, and rising or falling employment. And, if they are bewildered, behavior may become disoriented and perverse, including an "institutional" run on bank repurchase agreements (repos) not covered by the Federal Deposit Insurance Corporation (FDIC).

2.4. Omitted Variables

The bottom line, therefore, is that the pre-crisis faith in one monetary lever assured stability, and growth was wishful thinking. Macro dynamics depend on the rational, a-rational, and irrational expectations of erstwhile utility seekers in morally hazardous and incompletely mappable financial environments subject to sundry shocks and epochal changes such as falling populations, increasing per-worker social entitlement burdens, and diminishing returns to post-command communist economic catch-up. Policy management is correspondingly complex even when the goal is stable general competitive equilibrium and still more challenging in imperfect regulatory regimes where low inflation is targeted to assure full employment and rapid economic growth, susceptible to moral hazard and adverse selection — the unavoidable characteristics of any financial intermediation. Also, sight should not be lost of the financial sector. Wholesale funding is not fundamentally different from demand deposits and is subject to unexpected jolts. Fiscal policy too needs serious rethinking. The politically congenial notion that all deficit spending including tax rebates are equally efficacious is not valid, and a consensus needs to be forged on how governments attempting to resolve various conflicting economic and political interests can be disciplined to discharge their obligations responsibly, without squandering the benefits of deficit spending on special interests.

Macroeconomic policy management moreover is further complicated by external shocks and the complexities of international policy coordination. Ben Bernanke, Chairman of the Federal Reserve for one contends that a critical piece of the financial crisis and its perplexing aftermath is global imbalances, often called the global savings glut. This means that some nations like China underconsume and underimport, while other nations like the United States overconsume and overimport, devaluing the latter's currency and pressuring the Federal Reserve to keep interest rates too high for the purpose of stimulating recovery.[7] The contention is valid as far as it goes but fails to account for the related phenomenon of asset inflation in debtor nations. Asia's liquidity glut flooded into the wide-open, lightly regulated American shadow banking system (including mortgage institutions) and inundated many smaller countries like Iceland, Ireland, and Estonia sparking speculation and asset bubbles that soon burst with dramatic adverse effects on risk perceptions in the world's short-term interbank loanable funds market. The burst bubble reduced banks' worldwide lending ability: a problem compounded by tightened loan requirements limiting their access to emergency credit infusions. The international dimension, coupling the East and West, beyond the obvious trade linkages in this way was not only important for its restrictive impact on monetary policy. It was a key element in the larger planetary financial crisis. Perhaps, the most important lesson (re)learned from recent events therefore is that policymakers must take account of global leverage in addition to prices and interest rates.[8]

---

[7] Bernanke, BS (2005). "The Global Savings Glut and the US Current Account Deficit". Bernanke conjectured that China and other Asian nations amassed huge foreign currency reserves after 1998 to protect themselves against capital flight, causing them to become lenders to rest of the world. This hypothesis ignores the implicit import quota rationale used in Beijing to protect communist party insiders in the importables sector.

[8] Cf. Minsky, H (1982). *Can It Happen Again?: Essays on Instability and Finance.* New York: M. E. Sharpe. Tobin, J and S Golub (1998). *Money Credit and Capital.* New York: Irwin/McGraw Hill.

This is particularly important during recessions, when the potency of stimulus-induced, excess aggregate effective demand wanes, and the full consequences of China's underimporting come to the fore. Beijing's 2.6 trillion dollar reserve hoard is primarily a gambit to stealthily protect communist party insider-owned importable-companies from external competition. In ordinary times, this does not matter because monies are lent roundabout to third party importers. However, as Keynes emphasized in times of crisis, idle cash balances (such as hoarded dollar reserves) diminish aggregate effective demand dollar for dollar and inure mass involuntary unemployment. A two trillion dollar import order from China [larger and better targeted than America's one trillion dollar Troubled Asset Relief Program(TARP) and 600 billion dollar second round quantitative easing(QE2)], should provide a potent antidote. Complete macroeconomic theories and policy management schemes therefore must endogenize both domestic and foreign sources of disequilibrium, which in the present context requires taking full account of Chinese state-controlled trading and the danger posed to the global system by its stealthy beggar-thy-neighbor protectionism.

Consequently, the collapsed New-Keynesian-Perfect-Arbitrage consensus should serve as a clarion call for humility. There is no basis for persons to claim that they "know" how the new macro system will respond to various intervention strategies. Nor should persons believe that the past illuminates the present. The "White Swan" cyclical dynamics of yesterday may be irrelevant today due to the combined cumulative effects of structural deficits, quantitative easing, financial deregulation, destructive financial innovation, and the speculative fires they have fanned. Nonetheless, history does appear to provide some broad clues about trans-epochal regularities and the likely efficacy of countercyclical safeguards and policies.

2.5. Historical Benchmark

Carmen Reinhart and Kenneth Rogoff have discovered startling qualitative and quantitative parallels across a number of standard financial crisis indicators in 18 post-war banking crises.[9] They found that banking crises

---

[9] Reinhart, C and K Rogoff (2009). *This Time is Different: Eight Centuries of Financial Folly*. Princeton, NJ: Princeton University Press. Chancellor, E (2000). *Devil Take the Hindmost: A History of Financial Speculation*. New York: Plume.

were protracted (output declining on average for two years); asset prices fell steeply, with housing plunging 35% on average, and equity prices declining by 55% over 3.5 years. Unemployment rises by seven percentage points over four years, while output falls by 9%. Two important common denominators were reduced consumption, caused by diminished wealth effects, and impaired balance sheets, resistant to monetary expansion (liquidity trap). These regularities indicate that forecasts of a swift V-shaped recovery were never justified, and that it is premature to claim that the globe has averted a double-dip W-shaped recovery, or a catastrophic "Black Swan" event.[10] For the same reason, no definitive judgment is possible about liquidity traps at this juncture, even though the housing bubble, subprime mortgage crisis, financial sector toxic assets, and near-zero interest rates point to the possibility.

A careful mapping of plummeting GDP in the 2009 and 1929 (see Figure 2.2) suggests that this time around, humanity will be spared the

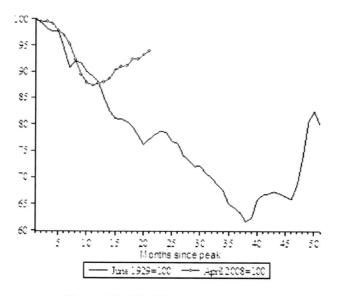

Figure 2.2. World industrial production.

Source: Eichengreen, B and K O'Rourke (2009). A Tale of Two Depressions. VoxEU.org (April 6, 2009).

---

[10] Taleb, N (2010). *Black Swan: The Impact of the Highly Improbable*. New York: Random House.

ravages of hyperdepression. The free fall and mass involuntary unemployment will be contained, even if conditions deteriorate further because the initial downward momentum has been blunted.[11] We shall not impute credit for this welcome outcome, but it is worth reviewing some important institutional changes that are likely to have forestalled a greater disaster.[12]

1. The intensity of deflationary expectations has been mitigated by abandoning the gold standard. People no longer have to fret that gold outflows will contract the supply of money and credit.
2. America and the West have become postindustrial societies less dependent on employment in the manufacturing sector. Direct and indirect federal and state employment today is vastly higher than in the 1920s, and on balance, has expanded during the crisis, thanks in part to the wage accommodative effects of furloughs.
3. Business has some, but still less, reason today to be fearful of an antibusiness, pro-labor, pro-state control, Roosevelt-style government, and revolutionary upheavals abroad than it did in the 1930s.[13]
4. Communities justifiably have more confidence today than yesterday that robust scientific and technological progress will ultimately boost productivity, profits, and employment, assuring eventual long-term recovery and golden-age growth.
5. The United States now has a generous unemployment insurance system that reduced the negative purchasing power (multiplier) effects of dismissals.
6. Bank deposit insurance, originally opposed by Franklin Roosevelt,[14] was nevertheless introduced by him into the American system in 1933. This appears to have greatly dampened the risk of small saver-driven bank runs compounding the repo-driven 2008 financial crisis.

---

[11] Unemployment in America in 1930 was 25%; now it is approaching 10%. America output peak-to-trough during 1929–1933 fell 25% compared with a 6.8% decline in 2009.

[12] Blinder, A and M Zandi (2010). How the Great Recession was brought to an end. http://www.economy.com/mark-zandi/documents/End-of-Great-Recession.pdf

[13] Rosefielde, S (2010). *Red Holocaust*. Oxford: Routledge.

[14] Pfouts, RW (2010). Economic Policy and the New Deal. Unpublished manuscript. Chandler, LV (1971). *American Monetary Policy 1928–41*, New York: Harper and Row.

7. Bank deposit insurance also forestalled financial bankruptcies preserving "informational capital" about creditworthiness essential for recovery.
8. The Federal Deposit Insurance Corporation not only guarantees household bank deposits; it shores up the system's integrity by seizing and auctioning insolvent banks.

Discretionary intervention policies likewise seem to have been constructive:

9. The global community (with the exception of China) responded cooperatively to the crisis and refrained from adopting "beggar-thy-neighbor" tariff and quota strategies that backfired during the 1930s.
10. Fiscal and monetary policy responses were swifter and more vigorous, including Geithner's controversial public–private scheme to buy toxic assets from banks.[15]
11. America's budgetary deficit during the crisis exceeded 10%: a striking change from Hoover's balanced federal budget, even though Blinder's and Zandi's data reveal that the real discretionary component of the American fiscal stimulus package was much smaller than that indicated by the headlines.[16]
12. Friedman and Schwartz claim that during the first three years of the Great Depression, the Fed tolerated and perhaps abetted a substantial shrinkage in the money base.[17] This time, the money base has doubled. The Great Depression and the Great Recession followed a similar track at the beginning, indicating a similar origin — a huge financial shock. But, because policy reactions to the shock were distinctly different, the paths diverge considerably after the first 12 months (see Figure 2.2).[18]

---

[15] For every dollar of toxic assets purchased from banks, the FDIC lent 85.7%, and the US treasury and private investors each lent 7.15%. If toxic assets fall in value below the FDIC loan, the FDIC will get stuck with the toxic asset. Benefits appear to be unconscionably great for private investors, including banks under the Geithner–Summers plan.

[16] Unemployment and medical assistance account for more than a quarter of the entire package. Federal transfers to states to forestall balanced budget mandated state program cuts were nearly as large. See Blinder and Zandi (2010).

[17] Friedman, M and A Schwartz (1963). *A Monetary History of the United States, 1867–1960*. Princeton, N.J.: Princeton University Press.

[18] Eichengreen, B and K O'Rourke (2009). A Tale of Two Depressions. VoxEU.org (April 6, 2009).

2.6. Prospects

We now know that the third millennium new-Keynesian-full-arbitrage consensus was wrong and that the macroeconomics profession is in disarray. We broadly know the particulars of the 2008 financial crisis and its aftermath, but understand very little about the underlying structural model determining aggregate outcomes. There are solid grounds for surmising that the fire this time will not be as dire as the one in 1929; nonetheless, it is essential to appreciate that macroeconomics is an insular discipline, largely purblind to political, financial, and epochal factors.[19]

The impact of disregarding the cumulative effects of structural deficits, quantitative easing, financial deregulation, and destructive speculation in the years ahead is likely to be negative. Ignoring omitted variables, likewise, will hamper macro-theory and hobble policymaking. Perhaps, financial variables will be endogenized in macro-theory in the near future, but the empirically verified explanation of how inflation, asset bubbles, and bursts are transformed into liquidity shortages, deleveraging, and output contractions is still on the drawing board.

Falling populations, shrinking labor forces, creeping state controls, increased political tolerance for speculative rent-seeking by government insiders, businessmen, and self-anointed activists, together with diminishing returns to technology transfers and outsourcing to post-command communist nations, suggest that effective countercyclical management tomorrow will be even more problematic than today.

---

[19] Reinhart, C and V Reinhart (2010). After the Fall. Unpublished manuscript.

CHAPTER 3

GLOBAL BUST

IIKKA KORHONEN
Institute for Economies in Transition, Bank of Finland (BOFIT)

AARON MEHROTRA
Aalto University School of Economics,
Institute for Economies in Transition, Bank of Finland (BOFIT)

3.1. Introduction

In 2008 and 2009, the global economy experienced a downturn that was worse than any other recession in the past 50 years. According to the International Monetary Fund (2010), global GDP (valued at market exchange rates) contracted by 2% in 2009.[1] The output losses were, however, very unevenly distributed. In many countries, GDP declined by more than 10 percentage points. Moreover, GDP declined clearly in the advanced economies, while many of the so-called emerging markets grew at a relatively rapid pace. Figure 3.1 shows GDP growth rates for the world's major regions. We can see that while growth rates have moved together, both before the global bust and during it, many emerging markets managed to grow also in 2009, while most of the OECD countries witnessed a contraction in economic activity.

In this chapter, we review the experiences of several economies during the crisis, although we will devote relatively more space to the emerging markets. Even though their economies were also affected by the crisis — especially in Central and Eastern Europe — it is now clear that many middle income countries have been able to grow also without a

---

[1] Using purchasing power parity-corrected exchange rates, the contraction was only 0.6%. For example, China and India have clearly undervalued currencies relative to the purchasing power standard.

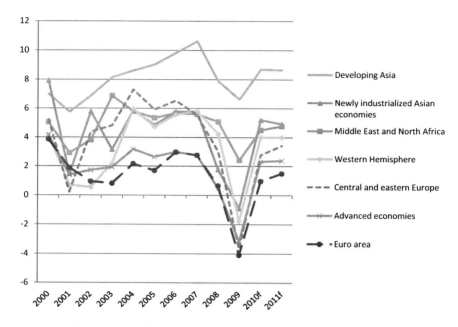

Figure 3.1. GDP growth rates (%) in major regions, 2000–2011.
Source: International Monetary Fund (2010).

significant demand for their exports in the more developed countries. Therefore, the global recovery is now proceeding at very different speeds.

3.2. Boom Before Bust

The period before the Great Recession was marked by rapid growth of both output and lending across the globe. Between 2000 and 2007, global output (measured at market exchange rates) expanded by 4% per annum on an average. Using purchasing power-adjusted exchange rates, the growth rate would have been even higher, as poorer countries grew at higher-than-average rates. This period of rapid growth was remarkable also because it was so widespread. Both advanced and developing countries grew at a rapid pace, and many large middle-income countries (e.g., China, India, and Russia) were able to catch up with the more advanced economies in terms of per capita income.

Strong economic growth was accompanied — and in many cases caused by — a rapid expansion in credit. Growth in bank lending also

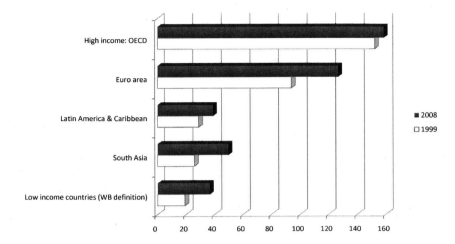

Figure 3.2. Domestic credit to private sector, percentage of GDP.
Source: World Bank Development Indicators.

caused housing market booms in many countries. Ahrend (2010) documents how relatively loose monetary policies in many OECD countries preceded significant increases in asset prices, which led to greater consumption and investment. Figure 3.2 shows the ratio of domestic credit to GDP in a number of regions and country groups around the world. It is obvious that even though economic growth was robust during this period, credit aggregates grew even faster. This was true even in high-income countries within the euro area. While in many poorer countries and regions the rapid increase in credit could be interpreted as a byproduct of economic progress and convergence, it is harder to make the same argument for high income countries.

Many commentators have connected this rapid increase in bank lending with the so-called global imbalances (see, e.g., Obsfeld and Rogoff, 2009). It is argued that inflows of foreign capital into the US due to the current account deficit helped to prolong the expansion of credit and, therefore, caused the subsequent crash. The idea is that countries with large current account surpluses (e.g., China and many oil-producers, but also Germany and Japan) had to invest their net export earnings somewhere, and the US was the only large and liquid market available to them. However, it is not obvious that global imbalances were the main reason for the rapid credit expansion. For example, China had an almost balanced current account until 2005, whereas credit expansion in the US and many European countries had by then been in progress for quite a while. Moreover, Lane and Milesi-Ferretti (2007) show that globalization had increased gross capital flows already in the mid-1990s, even though capital flows must have had an effect in many countries, especially in the formerly socialist countries in Central and Eastern Europe.

3.3. Financial System Goes Bust

In August 2007, problems emerged in the US subprime mortgage market. The price of credit risk started to rise, and interest rates on securities, collateralized by subprime loans, increased sharply (International Monetary Fund, 2007). Uncertainty about the eventual valuation losses rose. Moreover, nobody seemed to know how large the exposures of the individual financial institutions were. Given the uncertainty among financial institutions, the uncollateralized interbank interest rates strayed far from the collateralized rates. Central banks responded to the increase in short-term interest rates by injecting significant amounts of liquidity into the system. Interest rates on government securities started to fall as investors moved into safer securities. Corporations, relying on short-term money market-financing, experienced difficulties. The effects became visible also in the real economy. As financing became more expensive, investment and consumption started to suffer. Similarly, as stock prices fell, especially bank stocks, there was a negative wealth effect that began to weigh on consumption.

In March 2008, the investment bank Bear Sterns was not able to roll over its short-term financing and was about to declare bankruptcy. The US government came to the rescue and arranged the sale of Bear Sterns to JP Morgan Chase. It also provided guarantees on part of Bear Sterns' assets. On September 15, the investment bank Lehman Brothers, the largest company ever to fail in the US history, went bankrupt. As this bank was counterparty to countless financial transactions across the world, there were severe potential implications in the form of defaults of contracts across the globe. This bankruptcy was a turning point in that while the crisis had been in some parts of the world still limited to the financial sector and especially emerging markets had been quite well insulated, the world economy went into a freefall after the bankruptcy. After Lehman Brothers was allowed to fail, there was another financial giant on the brink — the American International Group (AIG). This is one of the largest insurance companies in the world. The fall of this giant would probably have led to even worse consequences than the fall of Lehman. Kos (2010) claims that European banks too were exposed in a significant way to AIG in addition to US banks. Therefore, the author argues that letting AIG fail was not an option. AIG was bailed out in the evening of September 16. Reis (2010) noted that this bailout signaled two things. First, the financial losses went far beyond banks, and second, there was uncertainty about how the government would react to possible large future bankruptcies.

After the fall of Lehman Brothers, the global financial system ground to a halt, as market participants were extremely cautious about extending credit to anyone. Counterparty risk was deemed too great. This freeze in lending affected all credit markets, not just the interbank market. As an example, Figure 3.3 shows the evolution of net new bank lending in the euro area from

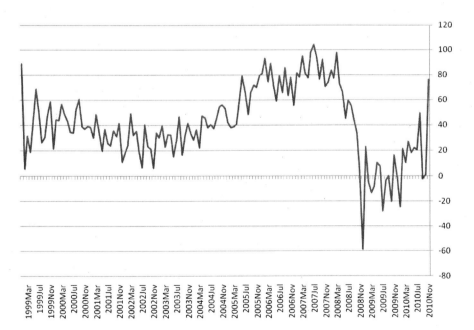

Figure 3.3. Net new bank lending to nongovernment sector in the euro area, January 1999 — November 2010, billion euros.

Source: European Central Bank.

1999 to 2010. We can see that in 2007 new bank lending averaged 85 billion euros per month, but in the final quarter of 2008 actually amounted to a negative 21 billion euros. Bank lending returned to its growth path only in 2010.

3.4. Global Trade Grinds to Halt and Inventories are Run Down

As the global financial system almost stopped working in late 2008, this had a clear and large effect on global trade. Figure 3.4 shows the evolution of the volume of global trade, and we can see how volumes dropped approximately 20% in just a few months; by October 2010, the trade volumes had not reached their pre-crisis peak. The drop in international trade naturally decreased exporters' revenues. However, from the point of view of national accounts, and more specifically GDP growth, the effect of the trade collapse was less pronounced. As exports declined, so did imports, and the net effect was often relatively small.

What was more significant in driving GDP developments in most major economies of the world was the drop in investment and downturn in

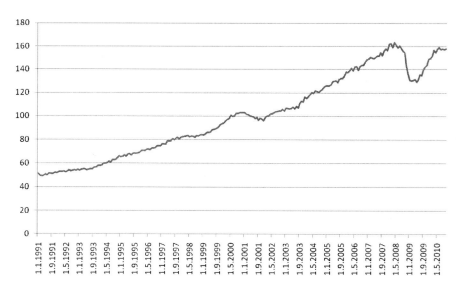

Figure 3.4. Volume of world trade (seasonally adjusted), 2000 = 100, January 1991–October 2010.

Source: Netherland Bureau for Economic Policy Analysis.

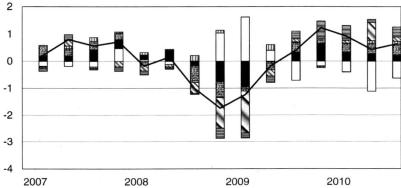

Figure 3.5. GDP growth in the US, first quarter of 2007 — third quarter of 2010.
Source: Bureau of Economic Analysis and Bank of Finland.

the inventory cycle. As financing became scarce and general uncertainty about the future increased, companies generally halted their investment projects. They also resorted to running down their inventories of both finished goods and raw materials. These two factors together explain much of the downturn in economic activity at the end of 2008 and the beginning of 2009. During the recovery phase in the latter half of 2009 and in 2010, the rebuilding of inventories was actually the single largest positive demand component in many countries. Figure 3.5 shows the growth contributions of the different demand components to headline GDP growth in the US. Developments were similar in many other countries, both developed and developing.

Therefore, the international propagation of the crisis occurred through several channels. In the global financial markets, risk perception increased very rapidly, and this affected the availability of financing everywhere. The contraction in global trade also had an effect, but the decline in investment activity was the single most important factor behind the GDP drop. Rose and Spiegel (2010) study the causes of the financial crisis, using a cross-country multiple indicator — multiple cause model. They consider interlinkages between countries and, in particular, the importance of a crisis epicenter. As a possible crisis epicenter, the United States is considered. In principle, when a country holds the epicenter's securities, it is affected by the finance channel, and a country exporting to this epicenter is hit through the trade channel. An interesting finding of these authors is that exposure to the United States has little impact on crisis incidence, and even the small impact may actually be positive. This result would suggest that international financial linkages are even more complex than previously envisaged.

3.5. Country Experiences

United States was truly at the heart of the crisis. After the collapse of Lehman came the worst of the quarters in terms of the real economy, as real GDP fell by 6.3% in the fourth quarter of 2008. As in other countries, financial markets were under heavy stress, credit was costly, employment prospects fell, and private consumption was dragged down. In a more positive vein, especially regarding the global imbalances, the US household savings rate finally started to increase, and with that the trade deficit started to shrink. However, the saving rate has again started to fall as the economy has recovered, and trade deficits are again increasing, especially *vis-à-vis* China. Housing prices fell, and the worsening labor market situation increased problems with loan repayments. At the time of writing (January 2011), the US unemployment rate still hovers between 9 and 10%. What is particularly worrisome is the fact that the duration of unemployment has clearly increased in contrast to previous downturns. This suggests that long-term unemployment may become a problem. During the recession, a total of eight million jobs were lost. Similarly, the housing market is still in a weak state, with no sign of improvement.

In the US, policy intervention was prompt both on the part of the Federal Reserve and the Treasury. Regarding monetary policy, the federal funds rate was lowered effectively to zero by the end of 2008. It was also signaled that the rates would be kept low for a considerable period in the future. Long-run yields were lowered by outright purchases of government bonds. The Federal Reserve also intervened in several markets, including those for the debt of government-sponsored enterprises, commercial paper, and mortgage-backed securities (International Monetary Fund, 2009b). Shortly after the fall of Lehman Brothers, the Troubled Asset Relief Program (TARP) was announced. At first, the TARP received a skeptical welcome both in Congress and by several commentators, and its purpose was later changed from buying toxic assets from banks' balance sheets to injecting liquidity (see Taylor, 2010). There were also counter-cyclical fiscal stimulus packages, in both 2008 and 2009.

Inside the euro area, the crisis had several serious consequences. As elsewhere, GDP declined with the contracting investment activity and running down of inventories. Authorities — both the European Central Bank (ECB) and national governments — were generally quick to embark on significantly more expansionary economic policies. And, as in the US, many financial institutions found themselves in a vulnerable position, and bank rescue operations had to be undertaken, e.g., in Ireland, Spain, and the Benelux countries. (Outside the euro area, the UK was the most affected of the larger European economies.) The ECB changed its operating procedures so that the banks were able to acquire practically any amount of liquidity they wanted, so long as they had sufficient collateral at hand. This restored some stability to the financial sector, which in turn enabled real sector growth. By the third quarter of 2009, euro area GDP was already growing quarter-on-quarter, although from a much lower base, of course. Growth even accelerated in the first half of 2010, especially in Germany and some other more export-oriented countries. However, the economic crisis revealed severe problems in many European countries, especially regarding government finances. Several euro area countries had high or very high debt levels before the crisis hit. Table 3.1 shows the government debt levels in 2005–2009, and we can see that even in 2007, after almost a decade of strong economic growth, general government debt was over 60% of GDP in eight of the 27 member countries. When the full costs of bank rescue packages became apparent, many countries' ability to service their debt came under scrutiny. Countries that had both high debt levels, entering the crisis, and vulnerable banking sectors saw the interest rates on their government bonds increase drastically. This effect was most serious for Ireland, Portugal, Spain, and especially Greece. In May 2010, Greece had to apply for a standby program from the IMF. In this connection, the European

90 *Iikka Korhonen and Aaron Mehrotra*

Table 3.1. General government debt, percentage of GDP, 2005–2009.

Column 1	2005	2006	2007	2008	2009
EU (27 countries)	62.8	61.4	58.8	61.6	73.6
Euro area (16 countries)	70.1	68.3	66	69.4	78.7
Belgium	92.1	88.1	84.2	89.8	96.7
Bulgaria	29.2	22.7	18.2	14.1	14.8
Czech Republic	29.7	29.4	29	30	35.4
Denmark	37.8	32.1	27.4	34.2	41.6
Germany	68	67.6	65	66	73.2
Estonia	4.6	4.5	3.8	4.6	7.2
Ireland	27.4	24.9	25	43.9	64
Greece	100	97.8	95.7	99.2	115.1
Spain	43	39.6	36.2	39.7	53.2
France	66.4	63.7	63.8	67.5	77.6
Italy	105.8	106.5	103.5	106.1	115.8
Cyprus	69.1	64.6	58.3	48.4	56.2
Latvia	12.4	10.7	9	19.5	36.1
Lithuania	18.4	18	16.9	15.6	29.3
Luxembourg	6.1	6.5	6.7	13.7	14.5
Hungary	61.8	65.6	65.9	72.9	78.3
Malta	70.1	63.7	61.9	63.7	69.1
Netherlands	51.8	47.4	45.5	58.2	60.9
Austria	63.9	62.2	59.5	62.6	66.5
Poland	47.1	47.7	45	47.2	51
Portugal	63.6	64.7	63.6	66.3	76.8
Romania	15.8	12.4	12.6	13.3	23.7
Slovenia	27	26.7	23.4	22.6	35.9
Slovakia	34.2	30.5	29.3	27.7	35.7
Finland	41.7	39.7	35.2	34.2	44
Sweden	50.8	45.7	40.8	38.3	42.3
United Kingdom	42.5	43.5	44.7	52	68.1

Source: Eurostat.

Commission and the other euro area member countries were also forced to extend credit to Greece, which seemed to calm the markets for a while. However, toward the end of the year, markets again became jittery, and Ireland especially was under pressure. The Irish banking sector had grown during the boom years, and in the crash the state had to rescue most of the large banks. This, in turn, placed severe strain on government finances, and in December 2010, Ireland also was forced to turn to the IMF, the European Commission, as well as other EU countries for rescue package.

Experience of the euro area illustrates how the economic crisis, which originated in the financial markets, spread to the real economy, and later had severe repercussions for public finances. In fact, the loose fiscal policies of 2009 and 2010 make fiscal adjustment necessary already in the near future. And the higher the debt level, the faster the needed adjustment. The coming fiscal adjustment will be a drag on economic growth in many countries.

Emerging Europe, like many other emerging markets, seemed to cope well with the global crisis until the last quarter of 2008. The region had little direct financial exposure to subprime assets. Nevertheless, there were some vulnerabilities, which, as pointed out by Gardó and Martin (2010), proved to be crucial when crisis hit. These included external vulnerabilities — current account deficits financed by capital inflows — and banking sector vulnerabilities. Regarding the latter, loan-to-deposit ratios were on the increase, and foreign funding was necessary in order to provide the countries with refinancing. Foreign liabilities increased, and in many countries, a significant part of household loans were denominated in foreign currencies. The importance of foreign currency liabilities varied from country to country, however; for example, in the Czech Republic and Poland, they were smaller than in many others. External debts were reaching high levels prior to the crisis, fuelled by strong domestic demand. As a large part of this was short-term debt, the region became vulnerable to sudden stoppages of capital flows.

Once the crisis hit, the countries were impacted to different extents. In general, countries in Central Eastern Europe were hit less hard than the Baltics. In particular, Poland was the only EU country that recorded positive growth in 2009. Gardó and Martin (2010) point out that those foreign direct investment inflows — very sizeable before the crisis — and intercompany lending helped to stabilize capital flows in the region. Although at first the presence of foreign banks — from advanced economies in need of capital themselves — was thought to worsen the impact of the crisis, in the end the presence of foreign banks was a stabilizing factor.

Only two countries in the region could benefit from membership in a large currency area and therefore more exchange rate stability: Slovenia and Slovakia. Indeed, Slovakia joined the Eurozone only at the last moment (January 2009) to escape the vulnerabilities induced by having a thin local currency market and therefore a potentially volatile currency. Slovenia had joined the common currency area already in 2007. Nevertheless, currency depreciations experienced by some of the countries in the region were also seen as beneficial, as they could support exports and hence aggregate output. However, it also seems fair to say that exchange rate stability in the Eurozone also benefited countries outside the currency union by supporting their exports.

The Baltic States had currency board arrangements *vis-à-vis* the euro (Latvia's arrangement is legally not a currency board, though), and instead of abandoning these arrangements along with the commitment to quickly join the euro area, they chose in many ways painful internal devaluations, bringing down wage levels, especially in the public sector. The aim of joining the euro area was indeed successfully achieved for Estonia, which became the 17th member of the Eurozone in January 2011.

An important part of stabilization efforts in the region was provided by the Vienna Initiative in early 2009. Here, EU-based parent banks promised to refinance and possibly recapitalize their subsidiaries in Emerging Europe. Assurances of policy support were also given by host-country governments and international financial institutions (Gardó and Martin, 2010). This pact was an important reason why foreign ownership of banks finally proved to be a stabilizing force in the region.

The experience of Russia during the crisis is illustrative for the problems faced by the Commonwealth of Independent States (CIS) more generally. Before the crisis intensified in autumn 2008, Russia, like Asia, was thought to be largely shielded from the financial crisis. Also it was true that the macroeconomic environment was very different from 1998, when Russia faced a largely domestically induced crisis. In the late 1990s, Russian fiscal policy was expansive, and foreign investors gradually lost confidence in the country's ability to service its debt. In the 2000s, in contrast, Russia conducted a very conservative fiscal policy, using its large current account surpluses to build up foreign exchange reserves and sovereign wealth funds. Similarly, the CIS countries were generally in better fiscal shape when the current crisis hit than when Russia defaulted on its debt in 1998.

However, once the crisis intensified, GDP in the CIS generally fell by more than in other emerging economies. A major reason for this is that numerous negative shocks were impacting Russia and the rest of CIS (International Monetary Fund, 2009a). As the demand for commodities in the advanced economies faded, oil and commodity prices fell, and export revenues and GDP suffered. The importance of commodities in revenue generation in the Russian case is highlighted by the fact that the share of oil and natural gas in total exports is more than 60%. Similarly, Kazakhstan is an important exporter of both oil and natural gas, but it also benefited from the high prices of copper and zinc in the years preceding the crisis. In the last quarter of 2008, the value of Russian export revenues dropped by almost 30% from the previous quarter. This fall in exports was accompanied by strong pressure for currency depreciation. Russia could use its foreign exchange reserves, accumulated in the 2000s, to support its currency. It allowed a stepwise devaluation in the value of the ruble. Similarly, Kazakhstan supported its currency, the tenge, with its foreign exchange reserves but was still forced to allow a one-time devaluation in January 2009. Nevertheless, and in line with the experience in Emerging Asia, the conservative policies prior to the crisis were largely vindicated, and foreign exchange reserves could be used to protect the national currencies.

Perhaps the aspect that was more difficult to anticipate was the crucial role of the financial sector. Especially, large Russian nonfinancial corporations were highly integrated into the global financial markets and heavily reliant on external refinancing. When the flight to safety began, this source of financing simply ceased to exist. Russia experienced capital flight of 130 USD billion in the final quarter of 2008. In addition to large nonfinancial firms, Russian banks also relied on foreign financing in order to accommodate the domestic demand for loans. This was particularly attractive prior to the crisis, as foreign interest rates were lower than domestic rates, and the ruble was appreciating due to strong commodity demand. Regarding other CIS countries, the Kazakhstan banking sector was also very open and had similarly suffered as foreign financing dried up. As in other economies, investments in Russia were hard hit by problems in the availability of funding. As real incomes began to shrink and unemployment increased — although the latter to a smaller extent than originally thought — domestic consumption fell. Also important was the reemergence of dollarization by households after many years of the reverse trend, as domestic currencies depreciated.

Regarding other countries in the region, Ukraine was one of the hardest hit by the crisis; GDP fell in early 2009 by close to 20%. The impact of the crisis was especially bad in the construction sector. Moreover, roughly half of the loans by the Ukrainian banking sector were in foreign currencies, and the depreciation of the gryvnia added to the problems of the banks. Many CIS countries were also heavily hit by the fall in remittances, especially from Russia. For many countries in the region migrant workers were a significant source of income, and many of them lost their jobs or simply had less money to send back home.

Wang and Whalley (2010) investigate the trade experience of the major Asian countries during the recent crisis. Their results highlight the important divergence of experiences of various countries. China saw a big decline in trade, whereas for Korea, the impact was milder and the rebound much quicker. Given China's somewhat unique position during this crisis, we shall look at it in more detail later. In Japan, the decline was notable, even though export growth was relatively sluggish going into the crisis, at least in comparison to many of its Asian peers. In India, imports were not much impacted. A similar finding is documented for commodity exporters, such as Malaysia. The relatively smaller impact of the global crisis on Asia is also highlighted by the fact that the Asian crisis led to a sharper decline in growth, but trade was much less affected, as the crisis was largely limited to the emerging economies.

Another major Asian economy, India, escaped the global crisis relatively unscathed. This was to some extent expected, given that the Indian economy has been relatively closed in terms of foreign trade, even though its trade-to-GDP ratio increased significantly in the 2000s. Nevertheless, growth in India did fall, to 7.3% in 2008 and 5.7% in 2009. In the previous three years, growth had exceeded 9%. The slowdown in growth was similar in size to that experienced in India during the bursting of the IT bubble in the early 2000s. In India, domestic consumption and investment took a beating as financing dried up. The Indian financial sector had been rapidly integrating into the world financial markets prior to the crisis, and the crisis reduced the supply of financing for both banks and nonfinancial corporations. However, growth in India resumed quickly; growth rates picked up significantly already in mid-2009. In particular, industrial production started to grow very rapidly after the peak of the crisis. In July 2010, the IMF forecasted growth of 9.4% for 2010, which by Indian standards represents an economy already growing above potential (International Monetary Fund, 2010). Despite its relatively large fiscal deficits — especially the combined deficits of central and state governments — India pursued a policy of fiscal expansion like many other economies. The fiscal measures were centered on improving public infrastructure and providing rural employment.

Even though GDP growth had been very slow in Japan for more than a decade before the crisis, the country was also heavily hit by the financial crisis. In 2009, GDP declined by 5.2%, as investments and net exports contracted. However, Japan was also relatively quick to recover from the effects of crisis, and during the latter half of 2009 and in early 2010, growth was already fairly robust, as net exports rose. Private consumption also returned to its previous (slow) growth trend. Going forward, it is now clear that net export growth is slowing down. As the Japanese public debt is already very high, fiscal policy needs to be tightened. This means that in all likelihood Japan will return to a period of very slow growth. Japan's problems are, of course, compounded by its demographic situation, as the labor force continues to shrink.

3.6. Exchange Rates During the Crisis

Prior to the crisis, there was a broad consensus that the unwinding of global imbalances, in particular the US current account deficit, would require a substantial depreciation of the US dollar. This would then support US exports by making them cheaper and so reduce its trade deficit. Obstfeld and Rogoff (2005) stated that to balance the US current account, the country would have to increase export revenue by almost 60% over 2004 levels. A plausible need for depreciation of the US dollar (in real effective terms) was 33%.

The interesting feature of the crisis was that during the crisis that originated in the United States, the US dollar actually appreciated against the currencies of both advanced and emerging economies. The movements in the USD nominal effective exchange rate are shown in Figure 3.6.

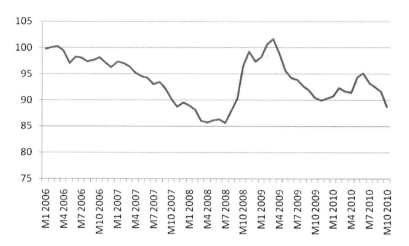

Figure 3.6. USD nominal effective exchange rate (upward movement signifies appreciation), January 2006–October 2010.
Source: International Financial Statistics.

Whereas the US dollar depreciated from the summer of 2007 to the summer of 2008, as the crisis intensified, there was a steep appreciation in the effective exchange rate of the dollar.

Fratzscher (2009) documents a striking finding in that during the crisis, negative news about the US macroeconomy actually led to a strengthening, rather than weakening, of the US dollar. He conjectures that this could happen because of repatriation of funds from other economies, or the expectation that bad news could bring about even worse outcomes for other economies. Fratzscher (2009) also finds those countries with small amounts of foreign exchange reserves, extensive financial exposure to the United States, and weak current accounts experienced larger depreciations than other economies.

The development of other major economies' exchange rates, the euro and yen, also show signs of a flight to safety in terms of capital flows. As regards the Chinese yuan, due to the reinstalled de facto US dollar peg in the summer of 2008, this currency also experienced an appreciation in its nominal effective exchange rate. In contrast, most emerging countries faced deep depreciations of their exchange rates, and foreign exchange reserves were used to defend their currencies.

Given the fall in demand for oil and other raw materials, the raw material exporters faced deep depreciations of their currencies at the onset of the crisis. Russia provides a good example. The price of Russian Urals oil reached its peak of 141 USD per barrel on July 4, 2008. Only some six months later, the price had fallen by about 70%. Depreciation pressure on the ruble started to build up in late summer of 2008. The value of the ruble is set against a basket comprised of the dollar (55% share) and the euro (45% share), and the value of the ruble against the basket fell by 25% between October 2008 and February 2009. Similar, although somewhat smaller, depreciations were experienced by the raw material exporters Australia, Canada, Kazakhstan, and Norway.

While the euro maintained its strength until the latter half of 2009 (see Figure 3.7), concerns about the sovereign debt of certain euro-area member states started to surface in the spring of 2010. In particular, the European Commission publicly condemned Greece for falsifying its data on public deficits, and subsequently Greece had to turn to the IMF and EU to finance its widening public sector deficit. After the initial skepticism concerning the future of the euro area and the external value of the euro, the European currency staged a comeback of sorts during the summer of 2010. Even with the fall in its value, the euro was

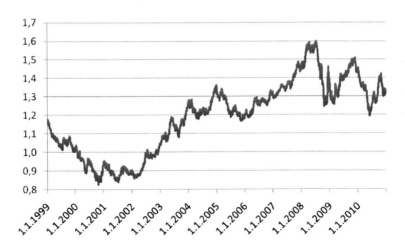

Figure 3.7. USD/EUR exchange rate, January 2, 1999 to December 31, 2010.
Source: Bank of Finland.

98 *Iikka Korhonen and Aaron Mehrotra*

still trading at roughly the estimated long-run equilibrium range against the USD.

3.7. The China Factor

An important element in supporting global growth during the crisis proved to be China. In part, this was expected given the country's robust growth already for three decades, which continued during the Asian crisis. However, there were also many reasons to expect that China would not be able to support global growth to a significant extent. While a large share of its exports go to Asia, some of these are intermediate goods and components whose final markets ultimately are in the advanced economies, most importantly the EU and US. Moreover, even if it were able to sustain growth due to its remaining catching-up potential, the important role of the export sector in Chinese manufacturing industries would mean that it would not be an easy task to replace its share in China's GDP. Finally, given the relatively small role of domestic demand in China's overall GDP, even rapid growth would probably not stimulate imports sufficiently to significantly support the trading partners' exports. It can be argued that China weathered the crisis much better than expected and was able to support global growth more than could be foreseen at the end of 2008, when the world economy was facing a significant downturn.

As in most other emerging economies, the global crisis impacted China through the collapse in international trade at the end of 2008. The financial linkages between China and the rest of the world were modest, as capital controls were still in place, especially for portfolio investment, and Chinese banks had only limited investments in toxic assets. In order to support growth, China's government in November 2008 announced a massive fiscal stimulus package totaling four trillion yuan (€460 billion). The package, only partly financed by the central government and much larger responsibility falling to local governments, was directed especially at infrastructure investment, that is, the building of roads, railroads, airports, and so on. The package necessitated massive support via lending by state-owned banks. The largest four banks increased their loan stock by 30% in 2009. The package could be put swiftly to operation, as many projects included in the package had already been planned in previous years

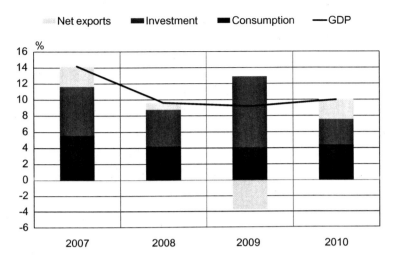

Figure 3.8. Growth contributions of Chinese GDP components.
Source: CEIC; BOFIT estimate for 2010.

but postponed due to economic overheating. China also supported domestic consumption demand by fiscal means. Rural workers could purchase household appliances such as televisions and refrigerators at a discount. Similarly, there were incentives to purchase automobiles, bringing China's car sales to par and above the level in the US in 2009. Figure 3.8 shows Chinese GDP growth and growth contributions of different expenditure categories. We can see that in 2009 the growth contribution of net exports turned significantly negative, but both investment and private consumption continued to expand rapidly.

The construction work related to the stimulus supported raw material markets worldwide, as China imported huge amounts of raw materials in the course of 2009. Whereas China's imports of iron ore were steadily increasing during the 2000s, there was a veritable surge in 2009. Similarly, 2009 saw significant increases in imports of copper and aluminum. As regards coal, China become a net importer in 2009 for the first time in at least 30 years, importing more coal in 2009 than during 2006–2008 combined. While some of the raw material imports were used for construction, part of it has been driven by the low world market prices and transportation costs. For raw material exporters that suffered from declining terms of trade during the crisis, China provided yuan-denominated lending in exchange for deals for long-term supplies of raw materials. Such oil-for-loans schemes were signed at least with Russia, Kazakhstan, Venezuela, and Brazil.

But China's ability to support world growth extended beyond its impact on raw material markets. Import demand in China has been especially important for its Asian neighbors, such as Korea and Japan. Similarly, Chinese imports from the EU remained strong throughout the crisis, with most EU member states' exports to China declining less than to other countries. There was hardly any change during the crisis in China's imports from Germany, the EU's largest exporter. The rapid increases in imports that China experienced in early 2010 actually drove its trade balance into a temporary deficit. This suggested that rapid growth was providing a boost to its trading partners' exports. In summer 2010, the value of China's trade, both imports and exports, had already exceeded pre-crisis levels.

As problems with some countries' sovereign debt started to emerge in spring 2010, China was again in the limelight as a possible engine for the world economy. As many G20 economies face the prospect of fiscal consolidation with the necessary increases in savings, China could perhaps be relied on to continue to support global consumption. In the spring and summer of 2010, the financial markets were nervously looking for any sign of a possible Chinese slowdown. This despite the fact that China's growth in the first quarter of 2010 indicated overheating (with a year-on-year GDP increase of 11.9%), and Chinese authorities were themselves trying to cool down the economy, especially the property market.

The massive fiscal stimulus in China was not without cost. As the central government's share in the fiscal stimulus amounted to less than one-third of the total, the majority of the state-owned banks and local governments had to be relied on for a large part of the stimulus. As local governments needed funds for investment, but are forbidden to run deficits, they used special vehicles to borrow money from the commercial banks. These liabilities do not show up in official budget figures and the numbers are not public, but their size is important. China's banking supervision authorities claimed that banks' loans to off-budget firms amounted to 7.4 trillion yuan (€750 billion; 22% of GDP) at the end of 2009, and they warned about the risks inherent in such lending. The authorities have also directly instructed the commercial banks to reduce their lending to these entities. Especially problematic are projects that do not create sufficient returns to pay back the interest and principal on the loans, even if the investments may be important in terms of supporting employment.

3.8. Concluding Remarks

The global crisis hit almost all the countries of the world. Some were better prepared than others, but all were affected. It seems that larger macroeconomic imbalances have been associated with larger output declines during the crisis, and as a region the Central and Eastern Europe has been especially adversely affected. Going forward, many emerging market countries are already growing rapidly, while richer countries face much more sluggish growth prospects. While large fiscal deficits were necessary during the crisis to prop up demand and — in some cases — rescue financial systems, fiscal policy needs to be tightened to prevent public debt from exploding. In some cases, this fiscal adjustment needs to be very large indeed. Most emerging market countries do not face this constraint on growth. Moreover, during the past decade or so, many emerging market countries have in fact had very tight fiscal policies, which helped them when the crisis hit.

This decoupling of rich and emerging market countries' growth trajectories means — paradoxically enough — faster economic convergence. In addition, the weight of Asia in the global economy will increase even faster than before.

References

Ahrend, R (2010). Monetary ease: A factor behind financial crises? Some Evidence from OECD countries. *Economics: The Open-Access, Open-Assessment E-Journal*, 4, 2010–2012.

Fratzscher, M (2009). What explains global exchange rate movements during the financial crisis? *Journal of International Money and Finance*, 28, 1390–1407.

Gardó, S and R Martin (2010). The impact of the global economic and financial crisis on Central, Eastern, and South-Eastern Europe. *ECB Occasional Paper*, No. 114.

International Monetary Fund (2007). *IMF World Economic Outlook*, October 2007. http://www.imf.org/external/pubs/ft/weo/2007/02/ [accessed on September 20, 2010].

International Monetary Fund (2009a). *IMF World Economic Outlook*, April 2009. http://www.imf.org/external/pubs/ft/weo/2009/01/ [accessed on September 20, 2010].

International Monetary Fund (2009b). *IMF World Economic Outlook*, October 2009. http://www.imf.org/external/pubs/ft/weo/2009/02/ [accessed on September 20, 2010].

International Monetary Fund (2010). *IMF World Economic Outlook Update*, July 2010. http://www.imf.org/external/pubs/ft/weo/2010/update/02/index.htm [accessed on August 25, 2010].

Kos, D (2010). The AIG Backdoor Bail — but a bailout of whom? *The International Economy*, Spring 2010, 50–53, 64.

Lane, PR and GM Milesi-Ferretti (2007). The external wealth of nations mark II: Revised and extended estimates of foreign assets and liabilities. *Journal of International Economics*, 73, 223–250.

Obstfeld, M and KS Rogoff (2005). Global current account imbalances and exchange rate adjustments. *Brookings Papers on Economic Activity*, 1, 67–123.

Obstfeld, M and KS Rogoff (2009). Global imbalances and the financial crisis: Products of common causes. In *Federal Reserve Bank of San Francisco Asia Economic Policy Conference*, October 18–20, 2009.

Reis, R (2010). Interpreting the unconventional U.S. monetary policy of 2007–2009. *NBER Working Paper*, 15662.

Rose, AK and MM Spiegel (2010). Cross-country causes and consequences of the 2008 crisis: International linkages and American exposure. *Pacific Economic Review*, 15(3), 340–363.

Taylor, JB (2010). Getting Back on Track: Macroeconomic policy lessons from the financial crisis. *Federal Reserve Bank of St. Louis Review*, May/June, 165–176.

Wang, J and J Whalley (2010). The trade performance of Asian economies during and following the 2008 financial crisis. *NBER Working Paper*, 16142.

PART III

ASIAN REPERCUSSIONS

CHAPTER 4

PAN ASIAN SHOCK WAVE

TAKEO HIDAI
Institute of Economic Research, Hitotsubashi University, Japan

The 2008 financial crisis's impact on Asia provided in Chapter 3 by Iikka Korhonen and Aaron Mehrotra is illuminated further with a battery of macro, fiscal, and monetary statistics for all Asian nations compiled by Takeo Hidai at the Institute of Economic Research, Hitotsubashi University. The macro indicators are GDP, new capital formation, industrial production, export and import activities, the current account (trade balance), and population. All are connected with the creation of value-added. They are complemented with fiscal indicators showing government revenues, expenditures and budgetary balances, and monetary indicators (money supply, wages, interest rates, reserves, and foreign exchange rates) essential for judging macroeconomic economic stimulus. Those wishing to evaluate the correlations between GDP trends and government stimulus country by country can do so by utilizing the following indicators.

Macroeconomic Indicators

	unit/note	2005	2006	2007	2008	2009
Bangladesh						
GDP growth rate	annual % change	7.0	6.8	9.1	8.9	5.4
GDP volume, Index Numbers	2005=100	100.0	106.8	116.5	126.9	133.7
GDP volume, current price	National currency, billion	3,707.07	4,157.28	4,724.77	5,458.22	6,147.95
GDP volume, current price	$ billion	57.628	60.309	68.599	79.568	89.050
GDP volume, PPP*	$ billion	173.643	190.999	209.019	226.314	241.269
GDP deflator, Index Numbers	2005=100	100	105.172	112.31	122.181	130.148
Gross Fixed Capital Formation	National currency, billion	909.2	1,024.8	1,155.9	1,321.3	1,488.4
Industrial production index	2005=100	100	108.531	114.494	n.a.	n.a.
Exports (Goods and Services)	$ million	10,551.5	12,887.5	14,091.1	17,497.7	17,010.9
Imports (Goods and Services)	$ million	−14,708.3	−16,783.9	−19,554.0	−25,170.3	−23,165.2
Current account	$ million	−176.2	1,196.1	856.9	926.2	3,344.9
Population	millions, Midyear Estimates	153.12	155.46	157.75	160.00	162.22

National currency: Taka

Source: IMF World Economic Outlook Database Oct. 2010 version.

Fiscal Indicators: General Government

		2005	2006	2007	2008	2009
Revenues*	National currency, billion	389.213	443.653	483.391	591.530	639.800
Expenditures*	National currency, billion	513.257	578.115	634.030	869.060	868.650
Balance (net lending/borrowing)*	National currency, billion	−124.044	−134.462	−150.639	−277.530	−228.850

Fiscal Year Ends June 30

Source: IMF World Economic Outlook Database Oct. 2010 version.

Monetary Indicators

		2005	2006	2007	2008	2009
Inflation (CPI)	annual average % change	7.05	6.77	9.11	8.90	5.42
M2 (period average)	National currency, millions	1,645,940	2,010,970	2,307,210	2,719,790	3,281,920
Average wages	Index numbers (2005=100): Period averages, monthly earnings	n.a.	n.a.	n.a.	n.a.	n.a.
Discount rate	%, end of period	5.00	5.00	5.00	5.00	5.00
Deposit interest rate	%	8.09	9.11	9.18	9.65	8.21
Lending interest rate	%	14.00	15.33	16.00	16.38	14.60
Forex reserves (excl. gold)	$ million	2,767	3,806	5,183	5,689	10,219
USD exchange rate	National currency per USD; period average	64.3275	68.9332	68.8749	68.5983	69.0391

Macroeconomic Indicators

	unit/note	2005	2006	2007	2008	2009
Cambodia						
GDP growth rate	annual % change	13.3	10.8	10.1	6.7*	−2.0*
GDP volume, Index Numbers	2005=100	100.00	110.77	122.00	n.a.	n.a.
GDP volume, current price	National currency, billion	25,755.5	29,849.1	35,002.2	45,582.8*	44,841.5*
GDP volume, current price	$ billion	6.293	7.275	8.629	11.277*	10.871*
GDP volume, PPP*	$ billion	20.143	23.040	26.140	28.499	28.197
GDP deflator, Index Numbers	2005=100	100.00	104.63	111.39	n.a.	n.a.
Gross Fixed Capital Formation	National currency, billion	4,864.24	5,774.65	6,720.68	n.a.	n.a.
Industrial production index	2005=100	n.a.	n.a.	n.a.	n.a.	n.a.
Exports (Goods and Services)	$ billion	4,028.38	4,988.69	5,636.02	6,353.13	5,926.70
Imports (Goods and Services)	$ billion	−4,560.77	−5,575.21	−6,354.28	−7,544.18	−6,898.15
Current account	$ billion	−306.70	−262.20	−487.68	−1,050.78	−865.55
Population	millions, Midyear estimates	13.87	14.09	14.32	14.56	14.81

National currency: Riel

Source: IMF World Economic Outlook Database Oct. 2010 version.

Fiscal Indicators: General Government

		2005	2006	2007	2008	2009
Revenues*	National currency, billion	3,204.09	4,192.22	4,929.19	6,867.49	7,007.39
Expenditures*	National currency, billion	3,172.83	4,063.31	4,944.58	6,403.62	8,508.21
Balance (net lending/borrowing)*	National currency, billion	31.26	128.91	−15.392	463.866	−1,500.82

Fiscal Year Ends December 31
Source: IMF World Economic Outlook Database Oct. 2010 version.

Monetary Indicators

		2005	2006	2007	2008	2009
Inflation (CPI)	annual average % change	6.35	6.14	7.67	25.00	−0.66
M2 (period average)	National currency, billions	4,962.54	6,974.65	11,287.50	11,902.30	16,137.40
Average wages	Index numbers (2005=100): Period averages, monthly earnings	n.a.	n.a.	n.a.	n.a.	n.a.
Discount rate	%, end of period	n.a.	n.a.	n.a.	n.a.	n.a.
Deposit interest rate	%	1.92	1.84	1.90	1.91	1.66
Lending interest rate	%	17.33	16.40	16.18	16.01	15.81
Forex reserves (excl. gold)	$ billion	952.98	1,157.25	1,806.91	2,291.55	2,851.13
USD exchange rate	National currency per USD; period average	4,092.50	4,103.25	4,056.17	4,054.17	4,139.33

Macroeconomic Indicators

	unit/note	2005	2006	2007	2008	2009
China, P.R., Hong Kong						
GDP growth rate	annual % change	7.1	7.0	6.4	2.2	−2.8
GDP volume, Index Numbers	2005=100	100.00	107.02	113.85	116.31	113.10
GDP volume, current price	National currency, billion	1,382.59	1,475.36	1,615.46	1,675.32	1,632.28
GDP volume, current price	$ billion	177.772	189.932	207.073	215.148	210.569
GDP volume, PPP*	$ billion	243.081	268.618	294.172	307.105	301.363
GDP deflator, Index Numbers	2005=100	100.00	99.71	102.63	104.18	104.38
Gross Fixed Capital Formation	National currency, billion	289.17	322.69	325.37	334.20	340.86
Manufactual production index	2005=100	100.00	102.16	100.75	93.99	86.18
Exports (Goods and Services)	$ million	353,288	390,335	430,685	457,351	408,142
Imports (Goods and Services)	$ million	−331,185	−368,694	−408,270	−435,415	−393,077
Current account	$ million	20,181	22,928	25,532	29,317	18,278
Population	millions, Midyear estimates	6.88	6.92	6.95	6.98	7.02

National currency: Hong Kong Dollar

Source: IMF World Economic Outlook Database Oct. 2010 version.

Fiscal Indicators: General Government

		2005	2006	2007	2008	2009
Revenues*	National currency, billion	247.035	288.014	358.465	316.562	318.442
Expenditures*	National currency, billion	233.071	226.863	234.814	315.112	292.525
Balance (net lending/borrowing)*	National currency, billion	13.964	61.152	123.650	1.450	25.917

Fiscal Year Ends 31 March

Source: IMF World Economic Outlook Database Oct. 2010 version.

Monetary Indicators

		2005	2006	2007	2008	2009
Inflation (CPI)	annual average % change	0.91	2.09	1.95	4.31	0.55
M2 (period average)	National currency, billions	4,379.06	5,054.48	6,106.35	6,268.06	6,602.31
Average wages	Index numbers (2005=100): Period averages, monthly earnings	100	103.279	106.114	111.23	108.851
Discount rate	%, end of period	5.75	6.75	5.75	0.5	0.5
Deposit interest rate	%	1.26	2.70	2.42	0.45	0.01
Lending interest rate	%	7.75	7.75	6.75	5.00	5.00
Forex reserves (excl. gold)	$ million	124,244.0	133,168.0	152,637.0	182,469.0	255,768.0
USD exchange rate	National currency per USD; period average	7.77733	7.76783	7.80142	7.78683	7.75175

Macroeconomic Indicators

	unit/note	2005	2006	2007	2008	2009
China, P.R., Mainland						
GDP growth rate	annual % change	11.3	12.7	14.2	9.6	9.1
GDP volume, Index Numbers	2005=100	100.00	112.68	128.63	141.03	153.88
GDP volume, current price	National currency, billion	18,713.1	22,224.0	26,583.4	31,490.1	34,502.4
GDP volume, current price	$ billion	2,283.67	2,787.25	3,494.35	4,531.83	5,050 55
GDP volume, PPP*	$ billion	5,364.26	6,242.02	7,337.64	8,217.40	9,046.99
GDP deflator, Index Numbers	2005=100	100.00	105.40	110.44	119.32	119.82
Gross Fixed Capital Formation	National currency, billion	7,423.29	8,795.41	10,394.90	12,808.40	15,668.00
Industrial production index	2005=100	15.90	15.39	n.a.	n.a.	n.a.
Exports (Goods and Services)	$ million	836,888	1,061,681	1,342,206	1,581,712	1,333,349
Imports (Goods and Services)	$ million	−712,091	−852,769	−1,034,729	−1,232,844	−1,113,234
Current account	$ million	160,818	253,268	371,833	436,107	297,142
Population	millions, Midyear estimates	1,312.25	1,320.72	1,329.09	1,337.41	1,345.75

National currency: Yuan

Source: IMF World Economic Outlook Database Oct. 2010 version.

Fiscal Indicators: General Government

		2005	2006	2007	2008	2009
Revenues*	National currency, billion	3,184.26	3,944.04	5,262.18	6,172.54	6,817.20
Expenditures*	National currency, billion	3,441.35	4,090.30	5,022.74	6,294.27	7,832.40
Balance (net lending/ borrowing)*	National currency, billion	−257.10	−146.25	239.44	−121.73	−1,015.20

Fiscal Year Ends December 31

Source: IMF World Economic Outlook Database Oct. 2010 version.

Monetary Indicators

		2005	2006	2007	2008	2009
Inflation (CPI)	annual average % change	1.82	1.46	4.75	5.86	−0.70
M2 (period average)	National currency, billions	29,875.6	34,557.8	40,340.1	47,516.7	60,622.5
Average wages, Index Numbers	2005=100, monthly earnings	n.a.	n.a.	n.a.	n.a.	n.a.
Discount rate*	%, end of period	3.33	3.33	3.33	2.79	2.79
Deposit interest rate	%	2.25	2.52	4.14	2.25	2.25
Lending interest rate	%	5.58	6.12	7.47	5.31	5.31
Forex reserves (excl. gold)	$ million	821,514	1,068,490	1,530,280	1,949,260	2,416,040
Exchange rate	National currency per USD; period average	8.19	7.97	7.61	6.95	6.83

*Bank rate

Macroeconomic Indicators

	unit/note	2005	2006	2007	2008	2009
India						
GDP growth rate	annual % change	9.5	9.7	9.2	6.7	7.4
GDP volume, Index Numbers	2005=100	100.00	109.71	119.83	127.88	137.39
GDP volume, current price	National currency, billion	37,064.7	42,839.8	49,478.6	55,744.5	62,311.7
GDP volume, current price	$ billion	840.47	945.54	1,196.62	1,281.33	1,287.29
GDP volume, PPP*	$ billion	2,434.37	2,756.43	3,118.09	3,390.00	3,615.33
GDP deflator, Index Numbers	2005=100	100.00	105.60	111.38	120.18	125.54
Gross Fixed Capital Formation	National currency, billion	11,269.20	13,470.60	16,305.10	18,385.00	20,189.20
Industrial production index	2005=100	100.00	110.33	121.66	126.77	135.14
Exports (Goods and Services)	$ million	154,702.3	193,498.1	240,712.9	302,813.0	258,821.4
Imports (Goods and Services)	$ million	−181,978.5	−225,268.1	−279,416.3	−379,220.3	−328,035.9
Current account	$ million	−10.3	−9.3	−8.1	−31.0	−26.6
Population	millions, Midyear estimates	1,130.62	1,147.75	1,164.67	1,181.41	1,198.00

National currency: Rupee

*Source: IMF World Economic Outlook Database Oct. 2010 version.

<h2>Fiscal Indicators: General Government</h2>

		2005	2006	2007	2008	2009
Revenues*	National currency, billion	6,812.0	8,311.0	10,380.5	10,989.7	11,781.3
Expenditures*	National currency, billion	9,195.4	10,565.5	12,371.3	15,139.0	17,780.2
Balance (net lending/borrowing)*	National currency, billion	−2,383.3	−2,254.5	−1,990.9	−4,149.3	−5,998.8

Fiscal Year Ends March 31
*Source: IMF World Economic Outlook Database Oct. 2010 version.

<h2>Monetary Indicators</h2>

		2005	2006	2007	2008	2009
Inflation (CPI)*	annual average % change	4.25	5.80	6.37	8.35	10.88
Quasi-Money	National currency, billions	16,595.0	20,361.1	25,517.9	31,634.4	37,351.3
Average wages	Index numbers (2005=100): Period averages, monthly earnings	n.a.	n.a.	n.a.	n.a.	n.a.
Discount rate**	%, end of period	6.0	6.0	6.0	6.0	6.0
Deposit interest rate	%	n.a.	n.a.	n.a.	n.a.	n.a.
Lending interest rate	%	10.75	11.19	13.02	13.31	12.19
Forex reserves (excl. gold)	$ million	131,924	170,738	266,988	247,419	265,182
USD exchange rate	period average	44.10	45.31	41.35	43.51	48.41

*Industrial workers, 50 centers
**Bank rate

Macroeconomic Indicators

	unit/note	2005	2006	2007	2008	2009
Indonesia						
GDP growth rate	annual % change	5.7	5.5	6.3	6.0	4.5
GDP volume, Index Numbers	2005=100	100.00	105.50	112.20	118.93	124.34
GDP volume, current price	National currency, billion	2,774,280	3,339,220	3,950,890	4,951,360	5,613,440
GDP volume, current price	$ billion	285.869	364.571	432.216	510.504	540.279
GDP volume, PPP*	$ billion	705.162	768.185	840.971	910.965	961.106
GDP deflator, Index Numbers	2005=100	100.00	114.09	126.93	150.06	162.73
Gross Fixed Capital Formation	National currency, billion	655,854	805,786	985,627	1,370,630	1,743,730
Industrial production index	2005=100	n.a.	n.a.	n.a.	n.a.	n.a.
Exports (Goods and Services)	$ million	99,921.8	115,048.0	130,501.5	154,852.5	133,258.8
Imports (Goods and Services)	$ million	−91,510.6	−95,261.7	−109,588.1	−144,935.0	−112,233.9
Current account	$ million	277.6	10,859.5	10,492.6	125.9	10,745.6
Population	millions, Midyear estimates	219.21	221.95	224.67	227.35	229.97

National currency: Rupiah

*Source: IMF World Economic Outlook Database Oct. 2010 version.

Pan Asian Shock Wave 117

Fiscal Indicators: General Government

		2005	2006	2007	2008	2009
Revenues*	National currency, billion	537,759	679,386	731,670	1,008,712	877,240
Expenditures*	National currency, billion	520,256	671,839	779,320	1,009,745	965,725
Balance (net lending/borrowing)*	National currency, billion	17,503	7,546	–47,650	–1,033	–88,485

Fiscal Year Ends December 31
Source: IMF World Economic Outlook Database Oct. 2010 version.

Monetary Indicators

		2005	2006	2007	2008	2009
Inflation (CPI)*	annual average % change	10.45	13.11	6.32	10.10	6.38
M2 (period average)	National currency, billions	1,202,760	1,382,490	1,649,660	1,895,840	2,141,380
Average wages	Index numbers (2005=100): Period averages, monthly earnings	n.a.	n.a.	n.a.	n.a.	n.a.
Discount rate	%, end of period	12.8	9.8	8.0	10.8	6.5
Deposit interest rate	%	8.1	11.4	8.0	8.5	9.3
Lending interest rate	%	14.1	16.0	13.9	13.6	14.5
Forex reserves (excl. gold)	$ million	33,140.5	41,103.1	54,976.4	49,596.7	63,563.3
USD exchange rate	period average	9,704.7	9,159.3	9,141.0	9,699.0	10,389.9

*17 capital cities

Macroeconomic Indicators

	unit/note	2005	2006	2007	2008	2009
Japan						
GDP growth rate	annual % change	1.9	2.0	2.3	−1.2	−6.3
GDP volume, Index Numbers	2005=100	100.00	102.04	104.40	103.11	97.70
GDP volume, current price	National currency, billion	501,734	507,365	515,520	505,114	474,219
GDP volume, current price	$ billion	4,552.20	4,362.59	4,377.94	4,886.99	5,068.06
GDP volume, PPP*	$ billion	3,872.84	4,080.55	4,299.91	4,341.07	4,152.30
GDP deflator, Index Numbers	2005=100	100.00	99.10	98.42	97.63	96.75
Gross Fixed Capital Formation	National currency, billion	116,885	118,467	118,237	117,755	97,643
Industrial production index	2005=100	100.0	104.4	107.3	103.8	81.7
Exports (Goods and Services)	$ million	677,782	733,111	807,207	895,228	673,615
Imports (Goods and Services)	$ million	−607,870	−670,065	−723,704	−877,886	−650,364
Current account	$ million	165,783	170,517	210,490	156,634	142,194
Population	millions, Midyear estimates	127.45	127.45	127.40	127.29	127.16

National currency: Yen

Source: IMF World Economic Outlook Database Oct. 2010 version.

Fiscal Indicators: General Government

		2005	2006	2007	2008	2009
Revenues*	National currency, billion	147,317	155,867	159,875	159,193	139,964
Expenditures*	National currency, billion	171,639	176,151	172,191	180,045	188,503
Balance (net lending/borrowing)*	National currency, billion	−24,322	−20,284	−12,316	−20,851	−48,539

Fiscal Year Ends in March 31

Source: IMF World Economic Outlook Database Oct. 2010 version.

Monetary Indicators

		2005	2006	2007	2008	2009
Inflation (CPI)*	annual average % change	−0.27	0.24	0.06	1.38	−1.35
M2 (period average)	National currency, trillions	701.374	708.427	719.577	734.583	754.462
Average wages	Index Numbers (2005=100): Periods averages, monthly earnings	100.00	100.60	102.27	101.44	98.89
Discount rate	%, end of period	0.10	0.40	0.75	0.30	0.30
Deposit interest rate	%	0.27	0.68	0.81	0.59	0.43
Lending interest rate	%	1.68	1.66	1.88	1.91	1.72
Forex reserves (excl. gold)	$ million	834,275	879,682	952,784	1,009,360	1,022,240
USD exchange rate	period average	110.22	116.30	117.75	103.36	93.57

*All Japan-485 items

Macroeconomic Indicators

	unit/note	2005	2006	2007	2008	2009
Kazakhstan						
GDP growth rate	annual % change	9.7	10.7	8.9	3.3	1.2
GDP volume, Index Numbers	2005=100	100.00	110.70	120.55	124.53	126.03
GDP volume, current price	National currency, billion	7,658.28	10,262.40	12,602.20	16,307.00	15,573.60
GDP volume, current price	$ billion	57.633	81.390	102.830	135.554	105.586
GDP volume, PPP*	$ billion	131.765	150.616	168.848	178.059	181.814
GDP deflator, Index Numbers	2005=100	100.00	132.79	165.77	226.13	220.44
Gross Fixed Capital Formation	National currency, billion	2,122.68	3,084.39	3,857.19	4,308.79	4,541.44
Industrial production index	2005=100	n.a.	n.a.	n.a.	n.a.	n.a.
Exports (Goods and Services)	$ million	28,446.60	38,908.10	48,497.10	72,116.80	44,107.10
Imports (Goods and Services)	$ million	−25,474.51	−32,880.79	−44,990.00	−49,571.20	−38,839.90
Current account	$ million	−1,055.84	−1,998.56	−8,321.92	6,279.49	−3,404.66
Population	millions, Midyear estimates	15.19	15.30	15.41	15.52	15.64

National currency: Tenge

Source: IMF World Economic Outlook Database Oct. 2010 version.

Fiscal Indicators: General Government

		2005	2006	2007	2008	2009
Revenues*	National currency, billion	2,131.72	2,803.92	3,705.75	4,542.24	3,765.85
Expenditures*	National currency, billion	1,694.58	2,067.44	3,105.76	4,368.96	4,002.29
Balance (net lending/borrowing)*	National currency, billion	437.14	736.47	599.99	173.28	−236.44

Fiscal Year Ends December 31

Source: IMF World Economic Outlook Database Oct. 2010 version.

Monetary Indicators

		2005	2006	2007	2008	2009
Inflation (CPI)	annual average % change	7.58	8.59	10.77	17.15	7.31
M2 (period average)	National currency, millions	1,515,970	2,814,550	3,553,640	4,619,520	5,335,200
Average wages	Index numbers (2005=100): Period averages, monthly earnings	100.00	120.45	154.34	179.32	n.a.
Discount rate*	%, end of period	8.00	9.00	11.00	10.50	7.00
Deposit interest rate	%	n.a.	n.a.	n.a.	n.a.	n.a.
Lending interest rate	%	n.a.	n.a.	n.a.	n.a.	n.a.
Forex reserves (excl. gold)	$ million	6,084	17,751	15,777	17,872	20,720
USD exchange rate	period average	132.88	126.09	122.55	120.30	147.50

*Refinancing rate

Macroeconomic Indicators

	unit/note	2005	2006	2007	2008	2009
Korea, Republic of						
GDP growth rate	annual % change	4.0	5.2	5.1	2.3	0.2
GDP volume, Index Numbers	2005=100	100.00	105.18	110.55	113.09	113.31
GDP volume, current price	National currency, billion	865,241	908,744	975,013	1,026,450	1,063,060
GDP volume, current price	$ billion	844.863	951.773	1,049.239	931.401	832.512
GDP volume, PPP*	$ billion	1,096.74	1,191.11	1,288.78	1,347.21	1,362.21
GDP deflator, Index Numbers	2005=100	100.00	99.86	101.93	104.90	108.43
Gross Fixed Capital Formation	National currency, billion	249,690	260,651	278,168	300,794	311,594
Industrial production index	2005=100	100.0	108.4	115.9	119.8	118.9
Exports (Goods and Services)	$ million	334,100.4	381,732.9	442,393.6	510,101.2	432,096.8
Imports (Goods and Services)	$ million	−315,075.6	−372,788.4	−433,993.2	−521,104.1	−393,172.5
Current account	$ million	14,980.9	5,385.3	5,876.0	−5,776.7	42,667.6
Population	millions, Midyear estimates	47.57	47.77	47.96	48.15	48.33

National currency: won

Source: IMF World Economic Outlook Database Oct. 2010 version.

Fiscal Indicators: General Government

		2005	2006	2007	2008	2009
Revenues*	National currency, billion	191,446	209,574	243,633	250,713	255,252
Expenditures*	National currency, billion	172,921	188,181	202,703	233,354	254,823
Balance (net lending/borrowing)*	National currency, billion	18,525	21,393	40,930	17,359	429

Fiscal Year Ends December 31
*Source: IMF World Economic Outlook Database Oct. 2010 version.

Monetary Indicators

		2005	2006	2007	2008	2009
Inflation (CPI)*	annual average % change	2.8	2.2	2.5	4.7	2.8
M2 (period average)	National currency, billions	1,021,450	1,149,260	1,273,610	1,425,890	1,566,850
Average wages	Index numbers (2005=100): Period averages, monthly earnings	100.00	105.65	114.49	115.55	114.45
Discount rate	%, end of period	2.00	2.75	3.25	1.75	1.25
Deposit interest rate	%	3.72	4.50	5.17	5.87	3.48
Lending interest rate	%	5.59	5.99	6.55	7.17	5.65
Forex reserves (excl. gold)	$ million	210,317	238,882	262,150	201,144	269,933
USD exchange rate	period average	1,024.12	954.79	929.26	1,102.05	1,276.93

*All cities

Macroeconomic Indicators

	unit/note	2005	2006	2007	2008	2009
Kyrgyz Republic						
GDP growth rate	annual % change	−0.2	3.1	8.5	8.4	2.3
GDP volume, Index Numbers	2005=100	100.00	103.12	111.87	121.31	124.07
GDP volume, current price	National currency, million	100,899	113,800	141,898	187,992	196,423
GDP volume, current price	$ billion	2.460	2.834	3.803	5.140	4.578
GDP volume, PPP*	$ billion	8.887	9.461	10.567	11.705	12.084
GDP deflator, Index Numbers	2005=100	100.00	109.38	125.72	153.59	156.91
Gross Fixed Capital Formation	National currency, billion	16,357.3	26,666.9	35,495.3	51,097.5	54,763.1
Industrial production index	2005=100	n.a.	n.a.	n.a.	n.a.	n.a.
Exports (Goods and Services)	$ million	946.25	1,284.72	2,022.61	2,770.44	2,560.24
Imports (Goods and Services)	$ million	−1,395.80	−2,252.14	−3,218.11	−4,746.38	−3,680.47
Current account	$ million	−62.07	−303.21	−261.27	−750.34	−300.19
Population	millions, Midyear estimates	5.22	5.28	5.35	5.41	5.48

National currency: Som

Source: IMF World Economic Outlook Database Oct. 2010 version.

Fiscal Indicators: General Government

		2005	2006	2007	2008	2009
Revenues*	National currency, billion	24.913	30.062	43.039	56.224	64.852
Expenditures*	National currency, billion	28.763	33.149	43.942	54.408	67.236
Balance (net lending/borrowing)*	National currency, billion	−3.850	−3.087	−0.903	1.816	−2.384

Fiscal Year Ends December 31

Source: IMF World Economic Outlook Database Oct. 2010 version.

Monetary Indicators

		2005	2006	2007	2008	2009
Inflation (CPI)	annual average % change	4.35	5.56	10.18	24.52	6.86
M2 (period average)	National currency, millions	15972.1	24121.1	34770.7	38152.5	44007.9
Average wages	Index numbers (2005=100): Period averages, monthly earnings	100.00	119.03	154.99	211.34	243.52
Discount rate*	%, end of period	6.20	5.94	8.29	15.11	9.07
Deposit interest rate	%	5.76	5.57	5.41	3.99	3.87
Lending interest rate	%	26.60	23.20	25.32	19.86	23.03
Forex reserves (excl. gold)	$ million	570	764	1,107	1,153	1,494
USD exchange rate	period average	41.01	40.15	37.32	36.57	42.90

*Lombard rate

Macroeconomic Indicators

	unit/note	2005	2006	2007	2008	2009
Lao People's Dem.Rep						
GDP growth rate	annual % change	7.3	8.3	7.5	7.8*	7.6*
GDP volume, Index Numbers	2005=100	100.00	108.28	116.39	n.a.	n.a.
GDP volume, current price	National currency, billion	30,594.1	35,407.3	39,284.2	46,214.7*	47,566.6*
GDP volume, current price	$ billion	2,871	3,485	4,091	5.313*	5.598*
GDP volume, PPP*	$ billion	9.687	10.867	12.055	13.271	14.447
GDP deflator, Index Numbers	2005=100	100.00	106.88	110.32	n.a.	n.a.
Gross Fixed Capital Formation	National currency, billion	n.a.	n.a.	n.a.	n.a.	n.a.
Industrial production index	2005=100	n.a.	n.a.	n.a.	n.a.	n.a.
Exports (Goods and Services)	$ million	757.31	1,105.46	1,200.83	1,493.54	1,444.16
Imports (Goods and Services)	$ million	−920.94	−1,097.63	−1,108.47	−1,488.47	−1,580.62
Current account	$ million	−173.79	75.31	139.41	115.49	9.26
Population	millions, Midyear estimates	5.88	5.98	6.09	6.21	6.32

National currency: Kip

Source: IMF World Economic Outlook Database Oct. 2010 version.

Fiscal Indicators: General Government

		2005	2006	2007	2008	2009
Revenues*	National currency, billion	4,155.15	5,255.30	6,383.99	7,374.93	8,370.29
Expenditures*	National currency, billion	5,164.04	6,328.57	7,413.38	9,124.16	11,579.00
Balance (net lending/borrowing)*	National currency, billion	−1,008.89	−1,073.27	−1,029.39	−1,749.24	−3,208.71

Fiscal Year Ends September 30
Source: IMF World Economic Outlook Database Oct. 2010 version.

Monetary Indicators

		2005	2006	2007	2008	2009
Inflation (CPI)	annual average % change	7.17	6.80	4.52	7.63	0.03
Quasi-Money (period average)	National currency, billions	4,001.43	5,047.80	6,709.51	7,848.62	n.a.
Average wages	Index numbers (2005=100): Period averages, monthly earnings	n.a.	n.a.	n.a.	n.a.	n.a.
Discount rate*	%, end of period	20.00	20.00	12.67	7.67	n.a.
Deposit interest rate	%	4.75	5.00	5.00	4.67	n.a.
Lending interest rate	%	26.83	30.00	28.50	24.00	n.a.
Forex reserves (excl. gold)	$ million	234.29	328.43	532.56	628.66	702.53
USD exchange rate	period average	10,655.20	10,159.90	9,603.16	8,744.06	8,516.04

*Bank rate

Macroeconomic Indicators

	unit/note	2005	2006	2007	2008	2009
Malaysia						
GDP growth rate	annual % change	5.3	5.8	6.5	4.7	−1.7
GDP volume, Index Numbers	2005=100	100.00	105.85	112.71	118.02	115.99
GDP volume, current price	National currency, million	522,445	574,441	642,049	740,907	679,687
GDP volume, current price	$ billion	137,954	156,601	186.774	222.106	192.846
GDP volume, PPP*	$ billion	301.306	329.318	360.979	386.234	383.095
GDP deflator, Index Numbers	2005=100	100.00	103.88	109.04	120.17	112.16
Gross Fixed Capital Formation	National currency, billion	107,185	119,213	138,393	144,634	136,824
Industrial production index	2005=100	100.00	105.01	107.28	108.08	99.75
Exports (Goods and Services)	$ million	161,383.7	182,597.4	205,682.1	230,054.2	186,424.0
Imports (Goods and Services)	$ million	−130,608.7	−147,125.0	−167,161.4	−178,741.8	−144,873.5
Current account	$ million	19,979.9	26,199.5	29,770.1	38,914.4	31,801.0
Population	millions, Midyear estimates	25.63	26.10	26.56	27.01	27.47

National currency: Ringgit

Source: IMF World Economic Outlook Database Oct. 2010 version.

Fiscal Indicators: General Government

		2005	2006	2007	2008	2009
Revenues*	National currency, billion	123.581	143.6	162.504	189.645	183.436
Expenditures*	National currency, billion	139.182	155.726	179.039	213.674	221.032
Balance (net lending/borrowing)*	National currency, billion	−15.601	−12.126	−16.535	−24.029	−37.596

Fiscal Year Ends December 31

Source: IMF World Economic Outlook Database Oct. 2010 version.

Monetary Indicators

		2005	2006	2007	2008	2009
Inflation (CPI)	annual average % change	2.96	3.61	2.03	5.44	0.58
M2 (period average)	National currency, millions	616,178	718,216	796,926	903,222	989,343
Average wages	Index numbers (2005=100): Period averages, monthly earnings	n.a.	n.a.	n.a.	n.a.	n.a.
Discount rate	%, end of period	n.a.	n.a.	n.a.	n.a.	1.00
Deposit interest rate	%	3.00	3.15	3.17	3.13	2.08
Lending interest rate	%	5.95	6.49	6.41	6.08	5.08
Forex reserves (excl. gold)	$ million	69,858.0	82,132.3	101,019.0	91,148.8	95,431.7
USD exchange rate	period average	3.79	3.67	3.44	3.34	3.52

Macroeconomic Indicators

	unit/note	2005	2006	2007	2008	2009
Mongolia						
GDP growth rate	annual % change	7.3	8.6	10.2	8.9	−1.6*
GDP volume, Index Numbers	2005=100	100.00	108.56	119.66	130.26	n.a.
GDP volume, current price	National currency, billion	2,815.21	3,778.57	4,807.79	5,430.21	6,055.79*
GDP volume, current price	$ billion	2.336	3.203	4.108	4.658	4.203*
GDP volume, PPP*	$ billion	6.662	7.468	8.474	9.432	9.365
GDP deflator, Index Numbers	2005=100	100.00	123.64	142.73	148.09	n.a.
Gross Fixed Capital Formation	National currency, billion	844,455	1,199,880	1,703,780	2,190,130	n.a.
Industrial production index	2005=100	n.a.	n.a.	n.a.	n.a.	n.a.
Exports (Goods and Services)	$ million	1,214.62	1,691.20	2,096.71	2,675.12	2,031.38
Imports (Goods and Services)	$ million	−1,097.42	−1,356.69	−2,003.10	−3,156.34	−2,074.16
Current account	$ million	−4.53	108.95	171.80	−690.11	−341.78
Population	millions, Midyear estimates	2.55	2.58	2.61	2.64	2.67

National currency: Togrog

Source: IMF World Economic Outlook Database Oct. 2010 version.

Fiscal Indicators: General Government

		2005	2006	2007	2008	2009
Revenues*	National currency, billion	837.86	1,360.41	1,880.49	2,170.38	1,992.99
Expenditures*	National currency, billion	764.60	1,054.92	1,749.70	2,466.77	2,321.60
Balance (net lending/borrowing)*	National currency, billion	73.26	305.49	130.79	−296.40	−328.61

Fiscal Year Ends December 31

*Source: IMF World Economic Outlook Database Oct. 2010 version.

Monetary Indicators

		2005	2006	2007	2008	2009
Inflation (CPI)	annual average % change	12.72	5.10	9.05	25.06	6.28
M2 (period average)	National currency, millions	1,140,140	1,536,490	2,401,250	2,270,000	2,880,030
Average wages	Index numbers (2005=100): Period averages, monthly earnings	100.00	n.a.	n.a.	n.a.	n.a.
Discount rate*	%, end of period	4.75	6.42	9.85	14.78	10.82
Deposit interest rate	%	13.00	13.01	13.46	11.39	13.28
Lending interest rate	%	30.57	26.93	21.83	20.58	21.67
Forex reserves (excl. gold)	$ million	333.15	583.40	801.75	561.48	1,294.47
USD exchange rate	period average	1,205.25	1,179.70	1,170.40	1,165.80	1,437.80

*Bank rate

Macroeconomic Indicators

	unit/note	2005	2006	2007	2008	2009
Pakistan						
GDP growth rate	annual % change	7.7	6.2	5.7	1.6	3.6
GDP volume, Index Numbers	2005=100	100.00	106.18	112.21	114.00	118.14
GDP volume, current price	National currency, billion	6,499.78	7,623.21	8,673.01	10,242.80	12,739.30
GDP volume, current price	$ billion	109.213	126,482	142.793	145.478	155.903
GDP volume, PPP*	$ billion	340.301	372.986	405.611	421.259	439.439
GDP deflator, Index Numbers	2005=100	100.00	110.46	118.91	138.23	165.90
Gross Fixed Capital Formation	National currency, billion	1,134.94	1,565.84	1,814.62	2,094.74	2,210.92
Manufactual production index	2005=100	100.00	111.21	117.00	116.82	110.53
Exports (Goods and Services)	$ million	19,111.0	20,555.0	21,955.1	25,476.5	22,220.0
Imports (Goods and Services)	$ million	−29,281.2	−35,114.5	−37,586.1	−47,933.0	−35,008.0
Current account	$ million	−3,606.2	−6,749.9	−8,286.0	−15,654.5	−3,583.0
Population	millions, Midyear estimates	165.82	169.47	173.18	176.95	180.81

National currency: Rupee

Source: IMF World Economic Outlook Database Oct. 2010 version.

Fiscal Indicators: General Government

		2005	2006	2007	2008	2009
Revenues*	National currency, billion	919.39	1,120.90	1,327.22	1,530.00	1,872.44
Expenditures*	National currency, billion	1,195.04	1,488.12	1,800.00	2,280.97	2,497.30
Balance (net lending/borrowing)*	National currency, billion	−275.65	−367.23	−472.78	−750.97	−624.85

Fiscal Year Ends June 30

Source: IMF World Economic Outlook Database Oct. 2010 version.

Monetary Indicators

		2005	2006	2007	2008	2009
Inflation (CPI)*	annual average % change	9.06	7.92	7.60	20.29	13.65
M2 (period average)	National currency, millions	3,201,680	3,665,540	4,387,940	4,637,790	5,321,730
Average wages	Index numbers (2005=100): Period averages, monthly earnings	n.a.	n.a.	n.a.	n.a.	n.a.
Discount rate	%, end of period	9.00	9.50	10.00	15.00	12.50
Deposit interest rate	%	n.a.	n.a.	n.a.	n.a.	n.a.
Lending interest rate	%	n.a.	n.a.	n.a.	n.a.	n.a.
Forex reserves (excl. gold)	$ million	10,033	11,543	14,044	7,194	11,318
USD exchange rate	period average	59.51	60.27	60.74	70.41	81.71

*12 major cities all included

Macroeconomic Indicators

	unit/note	2005	2006	2007	2008	2009
Philippines						
GDP growth rate	annual % change	5.4	5.4	7.5	6.4	4.0
GDP volume, Index Numbers	2005=100	100.00	105.40	113.34	120.54	125.37
GDP volume, current price	National currency, billion	5,444.04	6,031.16	6,648.62	7,409.37	7,678.92
GDP volume, current price	$ billion	98.829	117.534	144.070	167.166	161.052
GDP volume, PPP*	$ billion	250.24	272.191	300.067	317.946	324.263
GDP deflator, Index Numbers	2005=100	100.00	105.11	107.76	112.91	112.51
Gross Fixed Capital Formation	National currency, billion	783.40	846.65	978.28	1,090.51	1,130.07
Manufactual production index	2005=100	100.00	101.61	98.17	100.92	n.a.
Exports (Goods and Services)	$ million	44,788	52,970	59,278	57,968	47,611
Imports (Goods and Services)	$ million	−53,901	−59,565	−65,420	−69,695	−54,950
Current account	$ million	1.98	5.35	7.12	3.63	8.55
Population	millions, Midyear estimates	85.50	87.10	88.72	90.35	91.98

National currency: Peso

Source: IMF World Economic Outlook Database Oct. 2010 version.

Pan Asian Shock Wave 135

Fiscal Indicators: General Government

		2005	2006	2007	2008	2009
Revenues*	National currency, billion	815.63	975.42	1,047.48	1,172.69	1,121.87
Expenditures*	National currency, billion	976.75	1,057.54	1,148.71	1,267.35	1,424.50
Balance (net lending/borrowing)*	National currency, billion	−161.12	−82.12	−101.23	−94.66	−302.63

Fiscal Year Ends December 31

Source: IMF World Economic Outlook Database Oct. 2010 version.

Monetary Indicators

		2005	2006	2007	2008	2009
Inflation (CPI)*	annual average % change	7.63	6.24	2.83	9.31	3.23
Quasi-Money (period average)	National currency, billions	1,446.16	1,748.74	1,902.90	n.a.	n.a.
Average wages	Index numbers (2005=100): Period averages, monthly earnings	n.a.	n.a.	n.a.	n.a.	n.a.
Discount rate	%, end of period	5.70	5.04	4.28	6.00	3.50
Deposit interest rate**	%	5.56	5.29	3.70	4.49	2.74
Lending interest rate***	%	10.18	9.78	8.69	8.75	8.57
Forex reserves (excl. gold)	$ million	15,926.0	20,025.4	30,210.6	33,192.9	38,782.9
USD exchange rate	period average	55.09	51.31	46.15	44.32	47.68

*All Including House Holds-459 items

**Time (61–90 Days)

*** AVG COMM LEND RATE (ALL MATUR)

Macroeconomic Indicators

	unit/note	2005	2006	2007	2008	2009
Russian Federation						
GDP growth rate*	annual % change	6.4	8.2	8.5	5.2	−7.8
GDP volume, Index Numbers*	2005=100	100.00	108.15	117.38	123.52	113.83
GDP volume, current price*	National currency, billion	21,609.8	26,917.2	33,247.5	41,264.9	38,797.2
GDP volume, current price*	$ billion	764.018	989.930	1,299.705	1,660.366	1,222.329
GDP volume, PPP*	$ billion	1,696.7	1,894.9	2,117.1	2,276.8	2,116.1
GDP deflator, Index Numbers*	2005=100	100.0	115.2	131.1	154.6	157.7
Gross Fixed Capital Formation	National currency, billion	3,836.90	4,980.57	6,980.36	9,181.94	8,384.05
Industrial production index	2005=100	100.00	106.37	113.74	114.46	103.81
Exports (Goods and Services)	$ million	268,768.2	334,652.2	393,657.6	522,734.7	344,912.2
Imports (Goods and Services)	$ million	−164,179.0	−208,996.8	−281,630.9	−367,328.8	−253,090.0
Current account	$ million	84,602.2	94,686.4	77,768.3	103,661.0	49,432.6
Population	millions, Midyear estimates	143.17	142.53	141.94	141.39	140.87

National currency: Ruble

*Source: Rosstat website (http://www.gks.ru) as of February 1, 2011.

Fiscal Indicators: General Government

		2005	2006	2007	2008	2009
Revenues*	National currency, billion	8,851.3	10,625.8	13,250.7	16,003.5	13,420.7
Expenditures*	National currency, billion	7,088.8	8,384.0	11,005.7	14,229.2	15,847.3
Balance (net lending/borrowing)*	National currency, billion	1,762.5	2,241.8	2,245.0	1,774.2	−2,426.6

Fiscal Year Ends December 31
Source: IMF World Economic Outlook Database Oct. 2010 version.

Monetary Indicators

		2005	2006	2007	2008	2009
Inflation (CPI)	annual average % change	12.68	9.88	9.01	14.11	11.65
M2 (period average)	National currency, billions	6,044.7	8,995.8	13,272.1	13,493.2	15,697.7
Average wages	% change over previous period	22.01	19.24	24.24	21.97	7.15
Discount rate*	%, end of period	12.00	11.00	10.00	13.00	8.75
Deposit interest rate	%	3.99	4.08	5.14	5.76	8.58
Lending interest rate	%	10.68	10.43	10.03	12.23	15.31
Forex reserves (excl. gold)	$ million	175,891	295,568	466,750	411,750	416,649
USD exchange rate	period average	28.28	27.19	25.58	24.85	31.74

*Refinancing rate

Macroeconomic Indicators

	unit/note	2005	2006	2007	2008	2009
Singapore						
GDP growth rate	annual % change	7.6	8.6	8.5	1.8	−1.3
GDP volume, Index Numbers	2005=100	100.00	108.64	117.91	120.02	118.48
GDP volume, current price	National currency, billion	208,764	230,509	266,405	273,537	265,058
GDP volume, current price	$ billion	125,429.0	145,071.8	176,766.6	193,331.5	182,231.8
GDP volume, PPP*	$ billion	193.555	217.129	242.599	252.319	251.363
GDP deflator, Index Numbers	2005=100	100.00	101.63	108.22	109.18	107.17
Gross Fixed Capital Formation	National currency, billion	44,116.2	50,643.5	63,227.4	76,193.6	76,119.3
Manufacturing production index	2005=100	100.00	111.87	118.44	113.46	108.72
Exports (Goods and Services)	$ million	288,225.5	341,253.7	387,711.4	443,741.0	364,331.4
Imports (Goods and Services)	$ million	−251,397.1	−297,455.8	−331,606.3	−403,522.3	−325,605.4
Current account	$ million	26,665.9	35,125.7	47,084.1	36,010.9	32,628.1
Population	millions, Midyear estimates	4.27	4.36	4.49	4.62	4.74

National currency: Singapore Dollar

Source: IMF World Economic Outlook Database Oct. 2010 version.

Fiscal Indicators: General Government

		2005	2006	2007	2008	2009
Revenues*	National currency, billion	43.249	47.919	65.645	64.306	52.111
Expenditures*	National currency, billion	31.046	35.291	38.319	50.345	54.372
Balance (net lending/borrowing)*	National currency, billion	12.203	12.628	27.327	13.961	−2.261

Fiscal Year Ends March 31

Source: IMF World Economic Outlook Database Oct. 2010 version.

Monetary Indicators

		2005	2006	2007	2008	2009
Inflation (CPI)	annual average % change	0.43	1.02	2.09	6.52	0.60
M2 (period average)	National currency, millions	219,798	262,370	297,559	333,411	371,208
Average wages	Index numbers (2005=100): Period averages, monthly earnings	n.a.	n.a.	n.a.	n.a.	n.a.
SGS overnight repo rate	%, end of period	2.15	3.23	2.30	0.84	0.27
Deposit interest rate	%	0.44	0.57	0.53	0.42	0.29
Lending interest rate	%	5.30	5.31	5.33	5.38	5.38
Forex reserves (excl. gold)	$ million	116,172	136,260	162,957	174,193	187,803
USD exchange rate	period average	1.664	1.589	1.507	1.415	1.455

Macroeconomic Indicators

	unit/note	2005	2006	2007	2008	2009
Taiwan						
GDP growth rate	annual % change	4.7	5.4	6.0	0.7	−1.9
GDP volume, Index Numbers	2005=100	100.00	105.44	111.75	112.56	110.41
GDP volume, current price	National currency, billion	11,740.28	12,243.47	12,910.51	12,698.50	12,512.70
GDP volume, current price	$ billion	364,843	376,340	393,098	402,692	378,530
GDP volume, PPP*	$ billion	606.998	660.848	721.001	742.145	734.651
GDP deflator, Index Numbers	2005=100	100.00	98.91	98.41	96.09	96.50
Gross Fixed Capital Formation	National currency, billion	2,635.45	2,730.67	2,841.35	2,685.66	2,341.60
Industrial production index	2005=100	100.00	104.70	112.84	110.83	101.87
Exports (Goods and Services)	$ million	224,283	253,057	279,786	291,726	235,134
Imports (Goods and Services)	$ million	−211,480	−232,381	−250,981	−271,401	−202,666
Current account	$ million	17,578	26,322	35,154	27,505	42,916
Population	millions, Midyear estimates	22.77	22.88	22.96	23.04	23.12

National currency: NT dollar (New Taiwan dollar)

Source: National Statistics, Republic of China (http://eng.stat.gov.tw/mp.asp?mp=5)

Source: IMF World Economic Outlook Database Oct. 2010 version.

Fiscal Indicators: General Government

		2005	2006	2007	2008	2009
Revenues*	National currency, billion	2,502.35	2,425.59	2,568.16	2,510.37	2,286.99
Expenditures*	National currency, billion	2,713.54	2,623.29	2,749.81	2,817.40	3,011.38
Balance (net lending/borrowing)*	National currency, billion	−211.19	−197.70	−181.65	−307.03	−724.39

Fiscal Year Ends December 31

Source: IMF World Economic Outlook Database Oct. 2010 version.

Monetary Indicators

		2005	2006	2007	2008	2009
Inflation (CPI)	annual average % change	2.31	0.60	1.80	3.53	−0.87
M2 (period average)	National currency, millions	23,591	25,057	26,123	26,820	28,753
Average wages	Index numbers (2005=100): Period averages, monthly earnings	n.a.	n.a.	n.a.	n.a.	n.a.
Discount rate	%, end of period	2.25	2.75	3.38	2.00	1.25
Deposit interest rate (1 year)	%	1.99	2.20	2.62	1.42	0.89
Lending interest rate (Prime rate)	%	3.85	4.12	4.31	4.21	2.56
Forex reserves (excl. gold)	$ million	253,290	266,148	270,311	291,707	348,198
USD exchange rate	period average	32.18	32.53	32.84	31.53	33.06

Source: National Statistics, Republic of China (http://eng.stat.gov.tw/mp.asp?mp=5)

Macroeconomic Indicators

	unit/note	2005	2006	2007	2008	2009
Tajikistan						
GDP growth rate*	annual % change	6.7	7.0	7.8	7.9	3.4
GDP volume, Index Numbers	2005=100	n.a.	n.a.	n.a.	n.a.	n.a.
GDP volume, current price	National currency, million	7,206.6	9,335.2	12,804.4	17,706.9	20,622.8
GDP volume, current price	$ billion	2.312	2.830	3.720	5.161	4.978
GDP volume, PPP*	$ billion	9.674	10.689	11.862	13.078	13.647
GDP deflator, Index Numbers	2005=100	n.a.	n.a.	n.a.	n.a.	n.a.
Gross Fixed Capital Formation	National currency, billion	n.a.	n.a.	n.a.	n.a.	n.a.
Industrial production index	2005=100	n.a.	n.a.	n.a.	n.a.	n.a.
Exports (Goods and Services)	$ million	1,254.43	1,646.02	1,705.57	1,756.28	1,218.24
Imports (Goods and Services)	$ million	−1,682.45	−2,349.09	−3,707.09	−4,154.56	−3,061.67
Current account	$ million	−18.86	−21.40	−495.06	47.57	−179.86
Population	millions, Midyear estimates	6.54	6.63	6.73	6.84	6.95

National currency: Somoni

Source: IMF World Economic Outlook Database Oct. 2010 version.

Fiscal Indicators: General Government

		2005	2006	2007	2008	2009
Revenues*	National currency, billion	n.a.	n.a.	n.a.	n.a.	n.a.
Expenditures*	National currency, billion	n.a.	n.a.	n.a.	n.a.	n.a.
Balance (net lending/borrowing)*	National currency, billion	n.a.	n.a.	n.a.	n.a.	n.a.

Fiscal Year Ends December 31
*Source: IMF World Economic Outlook Database Oct. 2010 version.

Monetary Indicators

		2005	2006	2007	2008	2009
Inflation (CPI)	annual average % change	7.09	10.01	13.15	20.47	6.45
Quasi-Money (period average)	National currency, millions	304.54	556.98	962.98	811.91	n.a.
Average wages	Index numbers (2005=100): Period averages, monthly earnings	n.a.	n.a.	n.a.	n.a.	n.a.
Discount rate*	%, end of period	9.00	12.00	15.00	13.50	8.00
Deposit interest rate	%	9.75	9.09	8.43	7.35	5.80
Lending interest rate	%	23.27	24.37	22.87	23.70	22.91
Forex reserves (excl. gold)	$ million	168.22	175.12	n.a.	n.a.	n.a.
USD exchange rate	period average	3.12	3.30	3.44	3.43	4.14

*Refinancing rate

Macroeconomic Indicators

	unit/note	2005	2006	2007	2008	2009
Thailand						
GDP growth rate	annual % change	4.5	5.6	4.9	2.5	−2.2
GDP volume, Index Numbers	2005=100	100.00	105.57	110.78	113.50	110.95
GDP volume, current price	National currency, billion	7,102.96	7,850.19	8,529.84	9,075.49	9,050.72
GDP volume, current price	$ billion	176.602	207.227	247.111	272.428	263.979
GDP volume, PPP*	$ billion	445.196	483.353	522.114	546.663	539.273
GDP deflator, Index Numbers	2005=100	100.00	104.69	108.41	112.57	114.84
Gross Fixed Capital Formation	National currency, billion	2,057.02	2,203.97	2,249.94	2,488.94	2,208.40
Industrial production index	2005=100	n.a.	n.a.	n.a.	n.a.	n.a.
Exports (Goods and Services)	$ million	129,531.7	152,751.2	181,596.7	208,597.0	180,653.5
Imports (Goods and Services)	$ million	−133,008.1	−147,100.2	−162,904.3	−204,092.4	−155,777.5
Current account	$ million	−7,646.6	2,316.2	15,677.5	2,210.8	21,861.2
Population	millions, Midyear estimates	65.95	66.51	66.98	67.39	67.76

National currency: Bart

Source: IMF World Economic Outlook Database Oct. 2010 version.

Fiscal Indicators: General Government

		2005	2006	2007	2008	2009
Revenues*	National currency, billion	1,563.34	1,714.66	1,788.67	1,953.21	1,842.82
Expenditures*	National currency, billion	1,459.60	1,546.43	1,769.21	1,941.21	2,123.91
Balance (net lending/borrowing)*	National currency, billion	103.75	168.23	19.46	12.00	−281.09

Fiscal Year Ends September 30
*Source: IMF World Economic Outlook Database Oct. 2010 version.

Monetary Indicators

		2005	2006	2007	2008	2009
Inflation (CPI)*	annual average % change	4.54	4.64	2.24	5.47	−0.85
Broad Money (period average)	National currency, billions	7,927.97	8,574.50	9,110.64	9,945.50	10,618.30
Average wages	Index numbers (2005=100): Period averages, monthly earnings	n.a.	n.a.	n.a.	n.a.	n.a.
Discount rate	%, end of period	5.50	6.50	3.75	3.25	1.75
Deposit interest rate	%	1.88	4.44	2.88	2.48	1.04
Lending interest rate	%	5.79	7.35	7.05	7.04	5.96
Forex reserves (excl. gold)	$ million	50,690.7	65,291.4	85,221.3	108,661.0	135,483.0
USD exchange rate	period average	40.22	37.88	34.52	33.31	34.29

*Urban

Macroeconomic Indicators

	unit/note	2005	2006	2007	2008	2009
Turkmenistan						
GDP growth rate*	annual % change	13.0	11.4	11.6	10.5	6.1
GDP volume, Index Numbers	2005=100	n.a.	n.a.	n.a.	n.a.	n.a.
GDP volume, current price*	National currency (New Manat), billion	17.86	22.25	27.00	43.68	52.66
GDP volume, current price	National currency (Old Manat), billion	89,304.8	113,599.2	136,318.0	163,445.3	n.a.
GDP volume, current price*	$ billion	17.175	21.395	25.962	n.a.	n.a.
GDP volume, PPP*	$ billion	20.353	23.412	26.897	30.37	32.53
GDP deflator, Index Numbers*	2005=100	100.0	111.8	121.6	178.0	202.2
Gross Fixed Capital Formation	National currency (Old Manat), billion	20,468.3	27,033.5	31,703.4	38,123.0	n.a.
Industrial production index	2005=100	n.a.	n.a.	n.a.	n.a.	n.a.
Exports (Goods (fob))	$ million	4,944.1	7,155.5	9,114.0	11,786.0	14,500.0
Imports (Goods (fob))	$ million	−2,947.0	−2,557.7	−3,780.0	−5,363.0	−6,600.0
Current account	$ million	876.9	3,347.2	4,036.0	3,560.0	5,300.0
Population	million (as of 1 July)	4.84	4.91	4.98	5.04	5.11

National currency: Manat (In 01. Jan. 2009, denomination was held. 5000 Old Manat had been changed to 1 New Manat)

Source: ADB Statisticstical Database System (https://sdbs. adb.org/sdbs/index.jsp)

Source: IMF World Economic Outlook Database Oct. 2010 version.

Fiscal Indicators: General Government

		2005	2006	2007	2008	2009
Revenues*	National currency (New Manat), billion	3.657	4.495	4.684	10.323	11.807
Expenditures*	National currency(New Manat), billion	3.513	3.326	3.629	5.375	7.723
Balance (net lending/borrowing)*	National currency (New Manat), billion	0.144	1.169	1.055	4.948	4.084

Fiscal Year Ends December 31

Source: IMF World Economic Outlook Database Oct. 2010 version.

Monetary Indicators

		2005	2006	2007	2008	2009
Inflation (CPI)	annual average % change	10.7	10.5	8.6	12.0	5.5
M3	National currency (Old Manat), billion	9,404.9	10,411.2	20,447.6	18,893.6	n.a.
Average wages	Index numbers (2005=100): Period averages, monthly earnings	n.a.	n.a.	n.a.	n.a.	n.a.
Discount rate	%, end of period	n.a.	n.a.	n.a.	n.a.	n.a.
Deposit interest rate	%	n.a.	n.a.	n.a.	n.a.	n.a.
Lending interest rate	%	n.a.	n.a.	n.a.	n.a.	n.a.
Forex reserves (including gold)	$ million	4,457.0	8,059.2	13,221.5	n.a.	n.a.
USD exchange rate	period average	11,015.2	10,881.9	10,690.0	13,041.5	2.6*

†New Manat

Source: ADB Statisticstical Database System (https://sdbs.adb.org/sdbs/index.jsp)

Macroeconomic Indicators

	unit/note	2005	2006	2007	2008	2009
Uzbekistan						
GDP growth rate*	annual % change	7.0	7.5	9.5	9.0	8.1
GDP volume, Index Numbers	2005=100	n.a.	n.a.	n.a.	n.a.	n.a.
GDP volume, current price*	National currency, billion	15,923.4	20,759.3	28,186.2	37,746.7	48,097.0
GDP volume, current price*	$ billion	14.310	17.027	22.307	28.605	32.816
GDP volume, PPP*	$ billion	51.549	57.220	64.500	71.842	78.373
GDP deflator, Index Numbers	2005=100	n.a.	n.a.	n.a.	n.a.	n.a.
Gross Fixed Capital Formation	National currency, billion	3,518.4	3,838.3	5,987.3	7,080.4	12,531.9
Industrial production index	2005=100	n.a.	n.a.	n.a.	n.a.	n.a.
Exports (Goods)	$ million (fob)	5,408.8	6,389.8	8,991.5	11,572.9	11,771.3
Imports (Goods)	$ million (cif)	4,091.3	4,781.6	5,235.6	7,504.1	9,438.3
Current account	$ million	1,949.0	2,933.0	4,267.0	4,472.0	4,136.0
Population	millions, as of 1 July	26.2	26.5	26.9	27.3	27.8

National currency: Sum

Source: ADB Statisticstical Database System (https://sdbs. adb.org/sdbs/index.jsp)

Source: IMF World Economic Outlook Database Oct. 2010 version.

Fiscal Indicators: General Government

		2005	2006	2007	2008	2009
Revenues*	National currency, billion	4,900.0	7,139.9	10,030.3	15,357.3	18,009.7
Expenditures*	National currency, billion	4,701.0	6,057.2	8,547.9	11,325.5	16,469.8
Balance (net lending/borrowing)*	National currency, billion	199.0	1,082.7	1,482.4	4,031.8	1,539.9

Fiscal Year Ends December 31

Source: IMF World Economic Outlook Database Oct. 2010 version.

Monetary Indicators

		2005	2006	2007	2008	2009
Inflation (CPI)	previous year = 100, period average	107.8	106.8	106.8	107.8	108.4
M2 (period average)	National currency, trillions	2,299.0	3,146.0	4,598.0	6,088.0	n.a.
Average wages	Index numbers (2005=100): Period averages, monthly earnings	n.a.	n.a.	n.a.	n.a.	n.a.
Discount rate	%, end of period	n.a.	n.a.	n.a.	n.a.	n.a.
Deposit interest rate	%	n.a.	n.a.	n.a.	n.a.	n.a.
Lending interest rate	%	n.a.	n.a.	n.a.	n.a.	n.a.
Forex reserves (including gold)	$ million	2,895.0	4,459.0	7,413.0	10,145.0	n.a.
USD exchange rate	period average	1,106.1	1,215.6	1,260.8	1,314.2	1,465.6

Source: ADB Statisticstical Database System (https://sdbs. adb.org/sdbs/index.jsp)

Macroeconomic Indicators

	unit/note	2005	2006	2007	2008	2009
Vietnam						
GDP growth rate	annual % change	8.4	8.2	8.5	6.3	5.3
GDP volume, Index Numbers	2005=100	100.00	108.23	117.38	124.79	131.43
GDP volume, current price	National currency, billion	839,211	974,266	1,143,720	1,485,040	1,658,390
GDP volume, current price	$ billion	52.917	60.913	71.016	91.094	97.180
GDP volume, PPP*	$ billion	178.073	199.004	222.184	241.368	256.546
GDP deflator, Index Numbers	2005=100	100.00	107.27	116.10	141.81	150.35
Gross Fixed Capital Formation	National currency, billion	275,841	324,949	437,702	513,987	572,526
Industrial production index	2005=100	n.a.	n.a.	n.a.	n.a.	n.a.
Exports (Goods and Services)	$ million	36,623	44,926	54,591	69,726	62,862
Imports (Goods and Services)	$ million	−39,358	−47,710	−65,784	−83,423	−72,297
Current account	$ million	−560.19	−163.74	−6,953.10	−10,787.00	−7,440.32
Population	millions, Midyear estimates	84.07	85.10	86.11	87.10	88.07

National currency: Dong

*Source: IMF World Economic Outlook Database Oct. 2010 version.

Fiscal Indicators: General Government

		2005	2006	2007	2008	2009
Revenues*	National currency, billion	212,830	262,063	296,746	396,500	404,698
Expenditures*	National currency, billion	243,578	266,012	318,602	409,770	552,931
Balance (net lending/borrowing)*	National currency, billion	−30,748	−3,949	−21,857	−13,270	−148,233

Fiscal Year Ends December 31

Source: IMF World Economic Outlook Database Oct. 2010 version.

Monetary Indicators

		2005	2006	2007	2008	2009
Inflation (CPI)	annual average % change	8.28	7.39	8.30	23.12	7.05
Quasi-Money (period average)	National currency, billions	406,572	548,796	818,830	1,080,230	1,345,370
Average wages	Index numbers (2005=100): Period averages, monthly earnings	n.a.	n.a.	n.a.	n.a.	n.a.
Discount rate*	%, end of period	5.00	6.50	6.50	10.25	n.a.
Deposit interest rate	%	7.15	7.63	7.49	12.73	n.a.
Lending interest rate	%	11.03	11.18	11.18	15.78	n.a.
Forex reserves (excl. gold)	$ million	9,050.56	13,384.10	23,479.40	23,890.30	16,447.10
USD exchange rate	period average	15,858.9	15,994.3	16,105.1	16,302.3	17,065.1

*Refinancing rate

152 *Takeo Hidai*

4.1. Notes on "Two Asias" Selected Country/Regional Data

Twenty-three countries/regions are selected as follows:

Bangladesh, Cambodia, China (Mainland), China (Hong Kong), India, Indonesia, Japan, Kazakhstan, Korea (Republic of), Kyrgyz Republic, Lao People's Democratic Republic, Malaysia, Mongolia, Pakistan, Philippines, Russian Federation, Singapore, Taiwan, Tajikistan, Thailand, Turkmenistan, Uzbekistan, and Vietnam.

All country data is collected through IFS database except for Taiwan, Turkmenistan, and Uzbekistan, unless otherwise indicated.
Taiwan: National Statistics, Republic of China (http://eng.stat.gov. tw/mp.asp?mp=5). Turkmenistan and Uzbekistan: ADB Statistical Database System (https://sdbs.adb.org/sdbs/index.jsp).

Twenty-four indicators are selected as follows:

1. *Macroeconomic indicators*
   (1) *GDP growth rate, % (annual % change)
   (2) GDP volume, index numbers (2005 = 100)
   (3) **GDP volume, current price, National currency (billion)
   (4) **GDP volume, current price, $ (billion)
   (5) ***GDP volume, PPP, $ (billion)
   (6) GDP deflator, index numbers (2005 = 100)
   (7) Gross fixed capital formation, national currency (billion)
   (8) Industrial production index (2005 = 100; unadjusted)
   (9) Exports (goods and services), $ (million), <balance of payments base>
   (10) Imports (goods and services), $ (million), <balance of payments base>
   (11) Current account, $ (million)
   (12) Population, (millions; midyear estimates).

Cambodia (2008–2009), Laos (2008–2009), Mongolia (2009), Russia (2009), Tajikistan (2005–2009), Turkmenistan (2005–2009), Uzbekistan (2005–2009); Source = IMF World Economic Outlook Database October 2010 version.

***Cambodia (2008–09), Laos (2008–2009), Mongolia (2009), Turkmenistan (2005–2009), Uzbekistan (2005–2009); Source = IMF World Economic Outlook Database October 2010 version.*

***Source: IMF World Economic Outlook Database October 2010 version.

2. *Fiscal indicators:general government*

   (13) *Revenues, national currency (billion)
   (14) *Expenditures, national currency (billion)
   (15) *Balance (net lending/borrowing), national currency (billion)

*Source: IMF World Economic Outlook Database October 2010 version.

3. *Monetary indicators*

   (16) Inflation (CPI) (annual average % change)
   (17) M2 (period average), national currency (millions/billions/trillions)
   (18) Average wages, index numbers (2005 = 100; period averages; monthly earnings)
   (19) Discount rate, % percentage (end of period)
   (20) Deposit interest rate, %
   (21) Lending interest rate, %
   (22) Forex reserves (excluding gold), $ (million)
   (23) USD exchange rate (period averages).

CHAPTER 5
POLICY RESPONSE

TAKUJI KINKYO
Graduate School of Economics,
Kobe University, Japan

5.1. Introduction

The financial turmoil that was triggered in the US by the subprime mortgage crisis quickly spread across the globe and developed into the worst financial crisis since the Great Depression. It also had significant repercussions on the real economy. As a result, the world economy suffered a negative growth rate in 2009 for the first time since World War II.

The direct impact of the US financial turmoil on Asian banks was kept in check by the limited exposure of these banks to subprime mortgage securities. In spite of this, emerging economies in East Asia (hereafter referred to as "Asian economies") were hard hit by the global financial crisis because of the sharp disruption in foreign trade and external financing. However, Asian economies performed better than other emerging economies, particularly, those in Central and Eastern Europe. Moreover, the economic recessions experienced by the Asian economies during the global financial crisis were significantly less severe than the recessions they experienced during the Asian crisis of 1997–1998.

These observations raise several questions. Why were Asian economies able to perform better than other emerging economies during the recent global crisis? Did the structural and policy changes, undertaken after the Asian crisis, contribute to increased resilience against external shocks? What role did the Chiang Mai Initiative (CMI), a regional reserve arrangement, developed after the Asian crisis, play in Asia's response to the crisis? What are the policy challenges faced by the CMI and how they should be dealt with?

In the following sections, this chapter will seek to answer the above questions. Section 5.2 examines how Asian economies were affected by

155

156   *Takuji Kinkyo*

the global financial crisis and discusses why they performed better than other emerging economies. Section 5.3 uses a vector autoregression (VAR) model to examine the primary causes of the economic contractions experienced in Korea and Thailand during the global crisis. Section 5.4 discusses the policy challenges faced by the CMI and argues that they can be addressed by improving Asia's regional surveillance mechanism.

5.2. The Impact of the Global Financial Crisis on Asia

5.2.1. *Hard hit by the crisis*

Prior to the outbreak of the recent global crisis, it was expected that the global impact of the US economic downturn might be limited. The IMF (2007, p. 148), for example, observed the following: "most countries should be in a position to 'decouple' from the US economy and sustain strong growth if the US slowdown remains as moderate as expected." The main argument was that the US slowdown was being driven by US-specific developments related to housing market corrections and that the relatively small import content in the housing sector would help to mitigate the spillover effects in other countries.

The IMF provided evidence to suggest that the decoupling already mentioned might arise from the increasing divergence of business cycles among major economic regions. Specifically, it showed that the importance of common global factors, such as drivers of business cycle fluctuations, had declined, while the relative importance of regional factors among the highly integrated economies in North America, Western Europe, and emerging Asia had increased during the past two decades.

Despite their close intra-regional economic integration, Asian economies were unable to decouple from the US economy during the US-led economic downturn. As shown in Table 5.1, many Asian economies reported negative GDP growth rates beginning in the fourth quarter of 2008 through the second quarter of 2009. Although China, Indonesia, and Philippines maintained positive growth rates, their growth rates were substantially reduced.

These Asian economies were severely affected by the global crisis through two primary channels. The first channel was foreign trade. Asia's exports collapsed due to a sharp reduction in the "postponeable" demand for

Table 5.1. Year-on-year GDP growth rates.

								(%)
	China	Taiwan	Korea	Singapore	Thailand	Malaysia	Indonesia	Philippines
2007Q4	12.0	6.5	5.7	6.9	5.3	7.2	5.8	6.2
2008Q1	11.3	6.9	5.5	8.1	6.4	7.4	6.2	6.4
2008Q2	10.1	5.4	4.4	2.8	5.2	6.6	6.3	5.7
2008Q3	9.0	−0.8	3.3	0.1	2.9	4.8	6.2	6.5
2008Q4	6.8	−7.1	−3.3	−4.2	−4.2	0.1	5.3	6.8
2009Q1	6.2	−9.1	−4.3	−9.4	−7.1	−6.2	4.5	3.3
2009Q2	7.9	−6.9	−2.2	−3.1	−4.9	−3.9	4.1	4.4
2009Q3	9.1	−1.0	1.0	0.6	−2.7	−1.2	4.2	4.1
2009Q4	10.7	9.1	6.0	4.0	5.9	4.5	5.4	4.1
1997Q2	—	4.9	6.0	10.4	−0.6	8.4	—	5.6
1997Q3	—	5.8	5.1	11.5	−1.6	7.2	—	4.9
1997Q4	—	6.1	2.8	7.7	−4.2	6.1	—	4.7
1998Q1	—	4.0	−5.3	3.7	−7.1	−1.5	−3.3	1.1
1998Q2	—	3.4	−7.9	0.4	−13.9	−5.9	−14.5	−0.9
1998Q3	—	4.0	−8.1	−2.2	−13.9	−10.2	−16.2	−0.8
1998Q4	—	2.5	−6.0	−1.2	−7.2	−11.2	−17.6	−2.2
1999Q1	—	5.6	5.9	0.8	−0.2	−1.0	−7.3	1.7
1999Q2	—	6.5	9.7	6.6	3.4	4.8	3.2	3.7

Sources: ADB, ARIC Indicators System; IMF, International Financial Statistics.

consumer durable and investment goods at the epicenter of the crisis, particularly in the US (Baldwin, 2009). As shown in Figure 5.1, exports dropped particularly sharply in Korea, Malaysia, Singapore, Taiwan, and Thailand. This was due to the heavy reliance of these economies on US markets for the exports of automobiles, consumer electronics, and capital machinery.

Economic integration in East Asia has been led by foreign trade. A notable feature of the area's intra-regional trade is the high proportion of vertical intraindustry trade in intermediate goods (Fukao *et al.*, 2003; Wakasugi, 2007). This reflects the fragmentation of production processes and the expansion of vertically integrated supply chains across the region. However, the demand for the final goods made from these intermediate goods is heavily dependent on an extra-region, such as the US. As shown in Table 5.2, in Asian economies, the share of final goods is larger in extra-regional trade while the share of intermediate goods is larger in

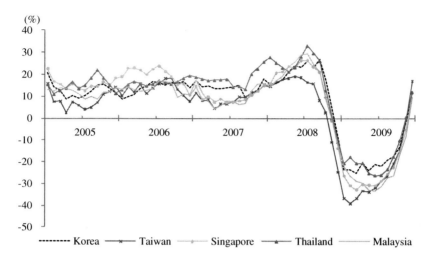

Figure 5.1. Year-on-year growth rates of exports.

Sources: ADB, ARIC Indicators System.

intra-regional trade. Accordingly, the global crisis caused not only a sharp reduction in Asia's exports of final goods to the US but also a contraction in the intra-regional trade of intermediate goods.

The second channel through which the global crisis was transmitted was that of financial transactions. The direct impact of the financial turmoil in the US on Asian banks was kept in check by the limited exposure of these banks to subprime mortgage securities. However, Asian firms' access to international capital markets was severely curtailed in the wake of the global liquidity squeeze that followed the "Lehman shock" in September 2008. The reduced availability of trade finance also contributed to the contraction of exports. In addition, a sharp reversal in international bank loans and portfolio investments put downward pressure on foreign reserves, exchange rates, and equity prices, which exercised a destabilizing effect on domestic financial systems (IMF, 2009, pp. 4–9).

5.2.2. Increased resilience against external shocks

Notwithstanding the fierce external shocks, Asian economies performed better than other emerging economies, particularly those in Central and Eastern Europe. Moreover, the economic recessions experienced by the

Table 5.2. The share of goods by stages of process in trade.

(%)

			Korea		Taiwan		Singapore	
			Intra-region	Extra-region	Intra-region	Extra-region	Intra-region	Extra-region
2005	Final	Capital Goods	17.7	31.8	17.6	25.8	14.9	28.6
		Consumer Goods	4.8	26.2	5.7	18.2	4.7	8.3
	Intermediate	Parts & Components	39.8	21.8	39.1	26.1	38.4	27.2
		Processed Goods	37.1	20.0	37.0	29.7	41.2	35.3
	Primary		0.6	0.2	0.6	0.2	0.8	0.6
2008	Final	Capital Goods	17.0	29.9	12.5	24.8	11.5	21.1
		Consumer Goods	3.3	19.4	4.8	13.4	3.3	9.4
	Intermediate	Parts & Components	35.6	24.2	43.2	23.1	38.5	16.1
		Processed Goods	43.3	26.1	38.8	38.4	45.2	52.3
	Primary		0.9	0.4	0.7	0.3	1.5	1.1
			Thailand		Malaysia		Indonesia	
			Intra-region	Extra-region	Intra-region	Extra-region	Intra-region	Extra-region
2005	Final	Capital Goods	19.0	27.5	12.8	35.4	6.8	10.3
	Intermediate	Consumer Goods	17.4	37.0	6.8	12.0	7.8	33.5
		Parts & Components	29.3	15.2	44.8	31.5	12.5	6.8
		Processed Goods	27.5	17.1	27.9	16.7	46.8	29.4
	Primary		6.8	3.2	7.6	4.4	26.1	20.0
2008	Final	Capital Goods	20.3	25.7	9.2	28.1	5.8	7.4
		Consumer Goods	16.9	34.9	5.4	13.3	7.1	29.3
	Intermediate	Parts & Components	25.5	14.6	35.7	24.1	8.6	6.5
		Processed Goods	28.8	20.3	41.3	25.3	44.5	33.8
	Primary		8.5	4.5	8.5	9.2	34.0	23.1

Source: Ministry of Economy, Trade and Industry, Japan, RIETI-TID 2009.

Asian economies during the global financial crisis was significantly less severe than the recessions they experienced during the Asian crisis of 1997–1998. Why did Asian economies suffer less form the global crisis? One answer lies in the noticeable structural and policy changes undertaken after the Asian crisis that made Asian economies more resilient to external shocks.

Asian economies accumulated a large stock of foreign reserves after the Asian crisis. This stock served as a buffer against sudden reversals in capital inflows. The accumulation of these reserves was partly the by-product of official interventions in the foreign exchange markets motivated by the desire to keep the exchange rate at a competitive level (Dooley *et al.*, 2003). There was also a deliberate attempt to accumulate foreign reserves as a precaution against a balance-of-payment crisis (Aizenman, 2009).

As shown in Table 5.3, the ratio of foreign reserves to short-term external debt was much higher on the eve of the recent global crisis than immediately before the Asian crisis. A sufficiently high level of foreign reserves seems to have exerted a stabilizing effect on market expectations, reducing the risk of panic-driven capital outflows.

Although Korea suffered large net capital outflows in the fourth quarter of 2008, in the first quarter of 2009, there was a V-shaped recovery in capital inflows. The temporary reduction of capital inflows reflects the difficulties experienced by Korean banks as they tried to roll over foreign currency loans. Korean banks relied heavily on wholesale markets to raise US dollar funds, which were used largely for forward covering of Korean firms' export deals (Tselichtchev and Debroux, 2009, p. 177). Korean banks' access to

Table 5.3. The ratio of foreign reserves to short-term external debt.

	End of 1996	End of 2006
Korea	0.4	2.1
Thailand	0.8	3.8
Malaysia	2.0	3.3
Indonesia	0.5	1.8
Philippines	1.1	1.8
China	3.3	13.3

Source: Joint BIS-IMF-OECD-WB External Debt Hub.

wholesale funding was severely disrupted after the Lehman shock. However, this disruption to external financing proved to be temporary, primarily because a currency swap agreement, signed with the US Federal Reserve in October 2008, had an immediate stabilizing effect on the market. This indicates that the temporary disruption in external financing was related more to the global liquidity squeeze than to the weakness of the Korean economy.

In addition to the accumulation of foreign reserves, the vulnerability of the domestic financial sector was reduced substantially by the domestic financial reforms made after the Asian crisis. Among these, the framework for financial regulations and supervision was improved in accordance with international standards. In addition, extensive restructuring and consolidation took place in the banking sector, and the share of foreign ownership in major domestic banks increased (Ghosh, 2006, pp. 63–65). These changes seem to have contributed to enhancing the soundness of banks' balance sheets. As shown in Table 5.4, Asian banks are now well-capitalized and more profitable. Their nonperforming loan (NPL) ratio is lower, and the provision coverage for nonperforming loans has increased. The increased resilience of the financial sector helped Asian economies to avoid a banking crisis and a resulting severe credit crunch during the global financial crisis, despite the severe tightening of external financing conditions.

In addition to financial reforms, a greater flexibility in exchange rates increased the scope of policy autonomy. Asian economies abandoned *de facto* dollar pegs in the wake of the Asian crisis and adopted more flexible exchange rate regimes, such as managed floating. Although the authorities continue to intervene in foreign exchange markets to stabilize the exchange rates, only a few have an explicit or rigid exchange rate targets. A notable example is China, which maintains a *de facto* adjustable peg against the US dollar.

As the proposition of the Impossible Trinity suggests, fixed exchange rates and autonomous monetary policy cannot coexist in a world of free capital movement. The greater exchange rate flexibility of Asian economies creates more room for proactive policies that safeguard against external shocks, despite these economies' high degree of integration with the global capital markets. In fact, Asian economies successfully counteracted the adverse impact of the global financial crisis by implementing fiscal and monetary stimulus measures.

162　*Takuji Kinkyo*

Table 5.4. Prudential indicators of Asian banks.

(%)

	Capital adequacy ratio			ROA			ROE			NPL ratio			Provisions to NPLs	
	2000–04 Average	2007	2008	2000–04 Average	2007	2008	2000–04 Average	2007	2008	2000–04 Average	2007	2008	2000	2008
China	−2.3	8.4	12.0	0.2	0.9	1.0	—	16.7	17.1	21.0	6.2	2.5	—	116.4
Taiwan	10.5	10.6	10.8	0.3	0.1	−0.1	4.1	2.6	−0.7	5.2	1.8	1.5	24.1	766.6
Korea	10.7	12.0	12.7	0.4	1.1	0.5	7.2	16.2	9.0	3.1	0.7	1.2	59.5	146.3
Singapore	17.7	13.5	14.7	1.1	1.3	1.0	9.6	12.9	10.7	5.3	1.5	1.4	—	109.1
Thailand	13.2	15.4	14.1	0.7	0.2	1.0	13.3	2.8	12.2	13.5	7.3	5.3	—	97.9
Malaysia	13.4	12.8	12.2	1.3	1.5	1.5	16.3	19.7	18.5	8.9	3.2	2.2	57.2	88.9
Indonesia	18.7	19.3	16.8	2.2	2.8	2.3	18.5	28.5	24.6	10.2	4.1	3.2	—	96.9
Philippines	17.0	15.9	15.7	0.8	1.4	0.8	5.9	11.8	7.2	14.8	4.4	3.5	43.7	86.0

Source: ADB (2009) Table 6~10.

These policies contrast sharply with the policy reactions to the Asian crisis. Thailand, Indonesia, and Korea initially tightened their fiscal and monetary policies in an attempt to stabilize capital flows and exchange rates in line with the IMF program. Critics of the IMF program argue that their contractionary policies further weakened domestic demand, exacerbating the economic downturn (Furman and Stiglitz, 1998).

In sum, the vulnerability of Asian economies was reduced substantially by the structural and policy changes undertaken after the Asian crisis. These changes seem to have made Asian economies more resilient to global financial shocks. In addition, their increased resilience seems to have helped stabilize market expectations, preventing panic-driven capital outflows during the global crisis.

5.3. Estimating Structural Shocks to Demand Components

This section uses a VAR model to determine the primary causes of the economic contractions experienced in Korea and Thailand during the global crisis. The structural shocks to the demand components of the countries' GDP were estimated following the methodology adopted by Blanchard (1993) and Ramaswamy and Rendu (2000). The VAR comprises six major demand components of real GDP: private consumption, government consumption, fixed capital investment, inventories, exports, and imports. The data were seasonally adjusted, and the sample period comprised 1990Q1 to 2009Q4 for Korea and 1993Q1 to 2009Q4 for Thailand.[1]

Table 5.5 shows the results of the unit root tests (augmented Dickey-Fuller tests). They indicate that the levels of the variables are nonstationary except in the case of inventories in both countries and exports in Thailand. Accordingly, all variables except inventories were log-differenced. The inventories were measured by the ratio to the trend real GDP. The unit root tests indicate that all of the log-differenced variables and the inventory ratio are stationary. A VAR was estimated using one lag for each variable. The lag length was selected using the Schwarz Bayesian criterion.

---

[1] The data sources include the Bank of Korea (http://www.bok.or.kr) and the Bank of Thailand (http://www.bot.or.th). The data for Thailand were seasonally adjusted using X-12-ARIMA.

164   *Takuji Kinkyo*

Table 5.5.   Unit root tests.

	Level		Log-difference
	No trend	**Trend**	**(# Ratio to trend GDP)**
Korea			
Private consumption	−0.96	−3.22	−5.98*
Government consumption	0.66	−1.42	−9.04*
Fixed capital investment	−1.51	−2.87	−5.44*
Inventories	−3.58*	−3.58*	−4.26*#
Exports	1.01	−2.09	−7.72*
Imports	−0.25	−2.90	−6.56*
Thailand			
Private consumption	−0.23	−1.77	−4.69*
Government consumption	1.15	−1.56	−8.88*
Fixed capital investment	−1.48	−2.21	−5.64*
Inventories	−6.82*	−6.77*	−6.69*#
Exports	−0.65	−3.65*	−5.67*
Imports	−1.07	−1.96	−6.66*

Note: * Indicates the significance at the 5% level.
Sources: Author's estimation as in text.

The residuals of each equation in the VAR are generally correlated to reflect their dependence on common shocks or their direct dependence on each other. To identify the structural shocks received by demand components, the following two identifying assumptions were adopted. First, it was assumed that feedback among the demand components of the GDP takes longer than one quarter to take effect, and the demand components therefore affect each other only through the GDP within each quarter. Thus, for example, the residuals of the private consumption equation (denoted by e_{pc}) depend only on the GDP residuals (denoted by e_y), not separately on the residuals of the equations of the other components.[2]

---

[2] The GDP residuals are the weighted average of the residuals of each equation. For simplicity, they are constructed using an auxiliary GDP equation: log-differenced real GDP is regressed on the set of right-hand-side variables of the VAR, and the residuals from this equation are used as proxies for GDP residuals. For further details, see Blanchard (1993, pp. 270–271).

Second, it was assumed that the residuals of the government consumption and exports equations (denoted by e_{gc} and e_x, respectively) were contemporaneously exogenous. Under these assumptions, e_{gc} and e_x can be used as instrumental variables to estimate the effects of e_y on the residuals of each demand component's equation.

The estimated structural shocks provide the basis for judging whether the behavior of a particular variable deviates significantly from its past pattern. That is, the presence of large structural shocks indicates a change in the behavior of a particular variable that is neither explained by its past pattern or by the patterns of other variables in the VAR. The estimated structural shocks to private consumption, fixed capital investment, inventories, and exports are shown in Figure 5.2. The observations represent the sum of accumulated shocks, each normalized by its respective standard deviation. Because each observation is an accumulated sum, a decline, for example, in value from one quarter to the next implies the presence of a negative shock in the latter quarter. The results yielded four notable points.

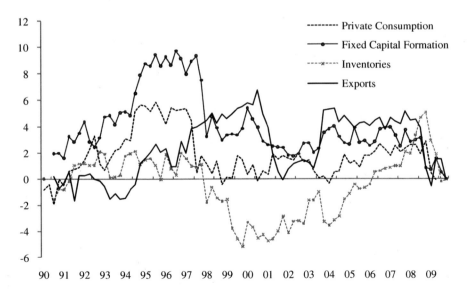

Figure 5.2a. Korea: accumulated structural shocks.
Sources: Author's estimation as in text.

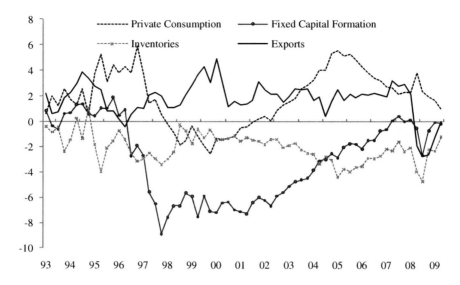

Figure 5.2b. Thailand: accumulated structural shocks.

Sources: Author's estimation as in text.

First, there was a large buildup of negative shocks to fixed capital investment during the Asian crisis in both countries. In parallel with these shocks, there were large negative shocks to private consumption. These results indicate that the severe economic contractions experienced during the Asian crisis were led by the collapse of domestic demand.

Second, these negative shocks to domestic demand were counterbalanced by a large accumulation of positive shocks to exports. The accumulation of positive export shocks continues until around the bursting of the so-called information technology (IT) bubble at the end of 2000, suggesting that economic recovery in Korea and Thailand after the Asian crisis was led by exports.

Third, even ten years after the Asian crisis, the sum of accumulated shocks to fixed capital investment has not returned to the pre-crisis level. Although there is a steady build up of positive investment shocks in Thailand, the sum of accumulated positive shocks is not large enough to offset the negative shocks that occurred during the Asian crisis. In Korea, even immediately before the eruption of the recent global crisis, the sum of accumulated investment shocks has remained far below the pre-Asian crisis peak. These results are consistent with the observed decline in the investment ratio after the Asian crisis. In the Thai and Korean economies, the level of investment, as a share of the GDP, remained substantially below that of the first half of the 1990s.

Fourth, in the recent global crisis there was a large buildup of negative shocks to exports. The size of the negative shock was particularly large in 2008Q4 and 2009Q1, presumably reflecting the adverse impact of the financial turmoil that intensified after the Lehman shock. In parallel with these shocks, there were large negative shocks to inventories. While there were also some negative shocks to fixed capital investment, they were much smaller in absolute terms than those that occurred during the Asian crisis. This seems to reflect the enhanced resilience of the financial sectors and the efficacy of the proactive policy responses, which helped to mitigate the adverse spillover effects through the financial channel. Overall these results indicate that the recent economic contractions were led primarily by a sharp contraction in exports and the associated reduction in inventories.

To sum up, the results of the VAR analysis suggest the following: in both Korea and Thailand, the primary causes of the economic contraction that occurred during the global crisis were adverse external demand shocks. This contrasts with the Asian crisis during which economic contractions were induced primarily by the sharp reduction in domestic demand, and particularly in the reduction of fixed capital investment. Economic recovery after the Asian crisis was led by exports while recovery to investment was slow. Their heavy reliance on exports might have made Asian economies vulnerable to the recent external demand shocks. However, the absence of severe shocks to domestic demand helped these economies to avoid the deep and prolonged recession observed during the Asian crisis.

5.4. Policy Challenges for the CMI

5.4.1. *Progress of the CMI*

The experience of Asian economies during the recent global crisis underscores the advantage of holding ample foreign reserves as self-insurance against balance-of-payment shocks. It should, however, be noted that reserve accumulation for self-insurance purpose is not without costs. As

168 *Takuji Kinkyo*

has been pointed out by Rodrik (2006), it entails a social cost equal to the spread between the opportunity cost of external borrowing and the yield on liquid reserve assets.[3]

One of the alternatives to costly reserve accumulation is the establishment of a regional reserve arrangement. A country can reduce the cost of balance-of-payment insurance by pooling part of their foreign reserves with those of regional neighbors. Following the Asian crisis, ASEAN+3 (China, Japan, and Korea) members agreed to establish a regional reserve arrangement known as the Chiang Mai Initiative (CMI). It was launched at the ASEAN+3 finance ministers' meeting in May 2000.

The CMI is primarily a network of bilateral currency swaps (BSAs) among ASEAN+3 members. When a member country is hit by balance-of-payment shocks, it may seek financial support by activating a swap. The activation, however, is not automatic because it requires the consent of the counterparty. Thus, the creditor country, which exchanges the US dollar for the partner's local currency, exercises their discretion over the financial support.

One of the prominent features of the CMI is its explicit link to create the IMF. To fully activate the swap, a borrowing country needs to negotiate an IMF program. To be precise, 20% of the swap can be activated without the program, but the remaining 80% requires an agreement or near-agreement with the IMF.[4] The IMF link is an indispensable element of the CMI primarily for the following two reasons:

First, it addresses a concern raised by an earlier Japanese proposal to the Asian Monetary Fund (AMF) (Kenen and Meade, 2008, p. 154). This AMF proposal was strongly opposed by the IMF and the US government because it could impair the ability of the IMF to influence the national policies of Asian countries by providing large amounts of funds with lax conditionality. The IMF link helps to allay such concerns by explicitly defining the supplementary role of the CMI for the IMF.

Second, the IMF link protects the interests of creditor countries by outsourcing the onerous task of negotiating policy conditionality to the IMF

---

[3] According to the estimates of Rodrik (2006), the social cost of excess reserves stands at close to 1% of developing countries' GDP.

[4] The ceiling on the IMF nonlink portion was raised from 10% to 20% in 2005.

(Nemoto, 2003, p. 23). In theory, the CMI members can develop their own policy conditionality for providing financial support. However, imposing strict conditionality would prove difficult because it could compromise the principle of noninterventionism that governs the decision-making process of the ASEAN. The IMF link allows members to adhere to this principle without undermining the interests of creditor countries.

Ten years after from the creation of the CMI, ASEAN+3 launched a new initiative called CMI multilateralization (CMIM). It introduces a single contractual agreement to govern all of the BSAs. This measure is expected to enhance the transparency of swap agreements and facilitate prompt and simultaneous activation of swaps by establishing a collective decision-making procedure.[5] The CMIM agreement came into effect in March 2010; the initiative's funds totaled 120 billion US dollars. Compared with the previous CMI, the CMIM is a more inclusive arrangement because all ASEAN+3 members participate in and financially contribute to it (see Table 5.6).

Notwithstanding a significant increase in the total size of available funds, the borrowing limit for each member remains small relative to the size of its foreign reserves. In addition, a member country retains the right to opt out of the collective decision to activate a swap. Most important, the IMF link and the 20% ceiling on the nonlink portion of the swap are still in place. In these important respects, the fundamental characteristics of the CMI have changed little.

5.4.2. *Enhancing the effectiveness of regional surveillance*

Despite the establishment of the CMI, Asian countries have failed to save the cost of balance-of-payment insurance by reducing their foreign reserves. Instead, they have accelerated the pace of reserve accumulation since the Asian crisis. This indicates that the CMI is not yet perceived as a serious alternative to costly self-insurance through reserve accumulation.

---

[5] For more details on the CMIM agreement, see the annex of the ASEAN+3 finance ministers' statement made on May 2, 2010 (available at: http://www.mof.go.jp)

170   *Takuji Kinkyo*

Table 5.6.   Contribution and borrowing limits of CMIM.

| | Financial contribution | | | Borrowing limit |
	USD (billions)	(%)	Multiple	USD (billions)
Plus 3	96.00	80.00		
Japan	38.40	32.00	0.5	19.20
China	38.40	32.00		
excl. HK	34.20	28.50	0.5	17.10
Hong Kong	4.20	3.50	2.5*	2.1
Korea	19.20	16.00	1	19.20
ASEAN	24.00	20.00		
Indonesia	4.552	3.793	2.5	11.38
Thailand	4.552	3.793	2.5	11.38
Malaysia	4.552	3.793	2.5	11.38
Singapore	4.552	3.793	2.5	11.38
Philippines	4.552	3.793	2.5	11.38
Vietnam	1.00	0.833	5	5.00
Cambodia	0.12	0.100	5	0.60
Myanmar	0.06	0.050	5	0.30
Brunei	0.03	0.025	5	0.15
Lao PDR	0.03	0.025	5	0.15
Total	120.00	100.00		

* Hong Kong's borrowing is limited to the IMF delinked portion because Hong Kong is not a member of the IMF.
Source: The Joint statement of the 13th ASEAN+3 Finance Ministers' Meeting (2 May 2010).

Furthermore, the CMI has never been activated even during the recent global crisis. As was already mentioned earlier, the Korean authorities arranged for a swap agreement with the US Federal Reserve and activated it during the crisis. However, they did not seek to activate the CMI.

Why has the CMI never been activated? It appears that ASEAN+3 members are reluctant to activate the CMI due to its explicit linkage to the IMF program. Asian countries have a deep distrust of IMF programs, as a result of their uncomfortable experience during the Asian crisis (Ito, 2007). Although the nonlink portion of the swap can be activated without the program, the available amount of funds would be insufficient to ameliorate a panic-driven liquidity crisis.

One possible solution to the nonuse of the CMI would be to raise the ceiling on the nonlink portion from the current 20%. By doing so, the CMI might become more accessible and thus a more reliable substitute for costly reserve accumulation. Alternatively, the framework of the CMI can be enlarged to introduce a new credit facility, which is similar to the Flexible Credit Line (FCL) recently established by the IMF. The FCL is designed to provide liquidity support for countries with strong fundamentals, policies, and track records of policy implementation. It assures those countries of large and upfront access to credit with no *ex post* conditions.

Developing an effective regional surveillance mechanism is a precondition for making the CMI more accessible either through raising the ceiling on the non-link portion or introducing a new credit facility. Effective surveillance is essential primarily for two reasons:

First, it will help distinguish whether illiquidity and insolvency is the cause of balance-of-payment difficulties. In principle, the nonlink portion of the swap should be activated to ameliorate a pure liquidity crisis arising from financial panic and deleveraging. In the case of insolvency, financial support requires conditionality for policy adjustment, and the IMF link is therefore indispensable.

Second, effective surveillance is necessary to guard against the risk of moral hazard arising from financial support. Regular economic monitoring and policy dialogue can help to detect vulnerabilities in the economy and encourage member countries to take remedial actions. By doing so, the moral hazard problem can be mitigated, contributing to crisis prevention.

One of the weaknesses of Asia's regional surveillance mechanism, known as the Economic Review and Policy Dialogue (ERPD), has been the absence of a permanent secretariat. Currently, the ERPD process is supported by the Asian Development Bank (ADB) and the ASEAN Secretariat. This weakness has been partially addressed by the recent establishment of an independent surveillance unit (ASEAN+3 Macroeconomic Research Office: AMRO) in Singapore. Although the ADB and ASEAN Secretariat will continue to assume a major role for the time being, the AMRO is expected to play a larger role in the expansion of surveillance capacity over time.

To further increase the effectiveness of Asia's regional surveillance, the following points should be addressed:

First, objective indicators should be used to evaluate the risk of a balance-of-payment crisis. This is an important step that will provide member countries with clear benchmarks and thus facilitate their policy adjustments. One of the key indicators necessary for identifying the risk of a balance-of-payment crisis is exchange rate misalignment, which is measured by the deviation from the estimated equilibrium exchange rate. Although the IMF uses this indicator in their regularly surveillance known as "Article IV consultations," limited availability of statistical data can be an obstacle. Asia's surveillance can complement that of the IMF by encouraging member countries to provide unpublished data for the purpose of regional surveillance. Moreover, when the data is not available due to a deficiency of statistics, technical assistance can be arranged and funded by the pooled reserves.

Second, the surveillance should also place a high priority on detecting vulnerabilities in the financial sector. As was demonstrated by the Asian crisis of 1997–1998, financial vulnerability makes an economy susceptible to the "twin crises": crises that involve both a balance-of-payment and a banking crisis in a mutually reinforcing way. The major source of vulnerability in the Asian financial sectors during the Asian crisis was the presence of extensive currency and maturity mismatches on the balance sheets of banks. These mismatches, which resulted from banks' imprudent overseas borrowing, made the balance sheets of banks vulnerable to sudden capital flow reversals and the associated sharp exchange rate depreciation. Drawing on these lessons, surveillance should pay careful attention to financial vulnerability arising in particular from double mismatches on the balance sheets.

Third, cross-border spillover effects should be adequately taken into account when crafting policy advice. This is particularly important for Asia where the degree of economic integration is high. For instance, a harmful competitive devaluation can be prevented by ensuring consistency in exchange rate policies across the region. Moreover, such an effort may pave the way for introducing a formal policy coordination mechanism in the future.

Policy Response 173

In a similar vein, the surveillance should address the adverse consequence of the unilateral imposition of capital controls. Supposing an entire region experienced a surge in capital inflows, unilateral imposition of capital controls in one country could accelerate capital inflows in others, putting undue upward pressures on their exchange rates. To avoid this, it will be necessary to develop a guideline for capital controls. The guidelines will help Asian countries to avoid the adverse impact of unilateral actions by outlining prerequisites and procedures for the imposition of capital controls. In addition, a set of guidelines should be developed for a wider range of financial regulations. Such comprehensive guidelines could serve to facilitate the harmonization of financial regulations, which would contribute to the reduction of distortion in cross-border capital flows and thus enhance efficiency and stability across regional financial systems.

5.5. Summary and Conclusions

Prior to the outbreak of the global financial crisis, there were optimistic expectations that Asia might be able to decouple from the US economy during the US-led economic downturn because of its close intra-regional economic integration. However, Asian economies were hard hit by the crisis because of the severe disruption in both foreign trade and in external financing. Those economies that rely heavily on the US market for the exports of durable consumer and investment goods were affected particularly severely.

The results of the VAR analysis on Korea and Thailand also suggest that the primary causes of the economic contraction during the global crisis were adverse external demand shocks. This contrasts with the Asian crisis during which economic contractions were induced primarily by the sharp reduction in domestic demand, particularly for investment.

Notwithstanding the fierce external shocks, Asian economies performed better than other emerging economies during the global crisis. Furthermore, the severity of the economic recessions experienced by Asian economies was significantly less than during the Asian crisis. There were important structural and policy changes undertaken after the Asian crisis that seem to have made Asian economies more resilient to external shocks. First, Asian economies accumulated a large stock of foreign reserves, which served as a buffer against capital flow reversals.

Second, the vulnerability of the domestic financial sector was reduced substantially by the domestic financial reforms made after the Asian crisis. Third, a greater flexibility in exchange rates increased the scope for policy autonomy, which allowed Asian economies to counteract adverse shocks effectively using fiscal and monetary stimulus measures.

Although a large holding of foreign reserves can serve as self-insurance against balance-of-payment crisis, it entails a social cost. Alternatively, a country can reduce the cost of balance-of-payment insurance by pooling part of their foreign reserves with those of regional neighbors. Following the Asian crisis, the ASEAN+3 members have developed such a regional reserve arrangement, which is known as the CMI.

Despite the significant progress that has been made over the past 10 years, the CMI seems not to be perceived as a serious alternative to costly self-insurance through reserve accumulation. This is indicated by the large accumulation of foreign reserves in member countries. Moreover, the CMI has never been activated even during the recent global crisis. The reason behind this seems to be the existence of an IMF link in the activation of swaps. Asian countries appear to have a deep distrust of IMF programs as a result of their uncomfortable experience during the Asian crisis.

One possible solution to the nonuse of the CMI would be to raise the ceiling on the IMF nonlink portion from the current 20%. By doing so, the CMI might become a more accessible and therefore a more reliable substitute for reserve accumulation. Alternatively, the framework of the CMI can be enlarged to introduce a new credit facility, which is similar to the Flexible Credit Line (FCL). A crucial precondition for these reforms is to develop an effective regional surveillance mechanism.

The weakness of the existing surveillance has been partially addressed by the establishment of an independent surveillance unit. To further enhance the effectiveness of Asia's surveillance, the following points should be addressed. First, objective indicators such as exchange rate misalignment should be used to evaluate the risk of a balance-of-payment crisis. Second, the surveillance should place a high priority on detecting financial vulnerability arising particularly from double mismatches on the balance sheets of banks. Third, cross-border spillover effects should be adequately taken into account when crafting policy advice. This is important, for example, to prevent harmful competitive devaluation within the region. Furthermore, regional guidelines should be developed for capital controls and other financial regulations, which will contribute to the reduction of distortion in cross-border capital flows and thus enhance efficiency and stability in regional financial systems.

References

Aizenman, J (2009). Reserves and the crisis: A reassessment. *Central Banking*, 19(3), 21–26.

Baldwin, R (2009). The great trade collapse: What caused it and what does it mean? In *The Great Trade Collapse: Causes, Consequences and Prospects*, Baldwin, R (ed.). Available at www.VoxEU.org, November 27.

Blanchard, O (1993). Consumption and the recession of 1990–1991. *American Economic Review*, 83(2), 270–274.

Dooley, MP, D Folkerts-Landau and P Garber (2003). An essay on the revived Bretton Woods System. *NBER Working Paper* No. 9971. Cambridge MA: National Bureau of Economic Research.

Fukao, K, H Ishido and K Ito (2003). Vertical intra-industry trade and foreign direct investment in East Asia. *Journal of the Japanese and International Economies*, 17(4), 468–506.

Furman, J and JE Stiglitz (1998). Economic crises: Evidence and insights from East Asia. *Brookings Papers on Economic Activity*, 2, 1–114.

Ghosh, SR (2006). *East Asian Finance: The Road to Robust Markets*. Washington, DC: World Bank.

IMF (2007). *World Economic Outlook*. Washington DC: IMF, April.

IMF (2009). *Regional Economic Outlook: Asia and Pacific*. Washington, DC: IMF, May.

Ito, T (2007). Asian currency crisis and the International Monetary Fund, 10 years later: Overview. *Asian Economic Policy Review*, 2, 16–49.

Kenen, BK and EE Meade (2008). *Regional Monetary Integration*. New York, NY: Cambridge University Press.

Nemoto, Y (2003). *An Unexpected Outcome of the Asian Financial Crisis: Is ASEAN+3 (China, Japan, and South Korea) a Promising Vehicle for East Asian Monetary Cooperation?* Princeton, NJ: Princeton University Institute for International and Regional Studies.

Ramaswamy, R and C Rendu (2000). Identifying the shocks: Japan's economic performance in the 1990s. In *Post-Bubble Blues: How Japan Responded to Asset Price Collapse*, Bayoumi, T and C Collyns (eds.). Washington DC: IMF.

Rodrik, D (2006). The social cost of foreign exchange reserve. *International Economic Journal*, 20(3), 253–266.

Tselichtchev, I and P Debroux (2009). *Asia's Turning Point*. Singapore: John Wiley & Sons (Asia).

Wakasugi (2007). Vertical-intra-industry trade and economic integration in East Asia. *Asian Economic Papers*, 6(1), 26–39.

CHAPTER 6
JAPAN*

SATOSHI MIZOBATA
University of Kyoto, Japan

6.1. Introduction

Japan's economy was hard hit by the financial crisis which rocked the world in 2008, but it soon recovered spurring hopes for long-term revival. Have the crisis and its aftermath fundamentally altered Japan's economic growth prospects or will the future be rosier than the recent past?

6.2. The "Lost Decade" and After

Japan's so-called "lost decade" occurred in the 1990s, after the collapse of the bubble economy. During this decade, a long-term recession hit Japan, and the country was unable to recover (Figure 6.1). Reduced investment and employment and the strong yen drove Japan to slump and asset prices to fall.

Japan's public finances showed a surplus until 1992.[1] However, due to a decline in tax revenues following the collapse of the bubble economy and an increase in the public expenditures needed for recovery, public finances worsened after 1993. Accumulated deficits reached 95% of GDP in 1996. Tax revenues have been declining since 1990 — in that year, ¥59 trillion were collected and, even in 2009, tax revenues remained low (¥46 trillion). State expenditures, however, have continued to increase, especially in the

---

* The original paper "The Japanese Economic System under the Global Crisis: Change and Continuity" was published in *Society and Economy*, Journal of the Corvinus University of Budapest, Akademiai Kiado, 33(2011)2, pp. 271–294.

[1] National government debts equal government bonds, borrowings, and financial bills. All the financial data are based on Ministry of Finance Japan (http://www.mof.go.jp) and Bank of Japan (http://www.boj.or.jp).

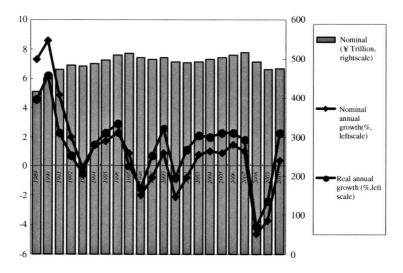

Figure 6.1. GDP and economic growth in Japan.

Note: Each year means fiscal year.
Source: Bank of Japan, *Financial and Economic Statistical Monthly*, August 17, 2011, http://www.boj.or.jp.

forms of social security and state bond payments; they have risen to ¥89 trillion. The government has been unable to improve the balance between revenues and expenditures, and accumulated state debts mounted to ¥973.2 trillion (203% of 2010 GDP) at the end of 2010. Around ¥5 trillion of fresh government-issued bonds were in circulation at the beginning of 1990s, but that number increased to ¥30 trillion in 1999 and ¥40 trillion in 2010 (Ministry of Finance Japan). If interest rates rise under these conditions, the national budget could easily collapse.

The second financial problem that plagued Japan during the 1990s was bad loans.[2] Land and stock prices showed sharp declines. Loans collateralized with these assets soared, forcing 180 banks to fail during 1993–2002 (Table 6.1). Nonbank financial institutions that were not as tightly regulated as financial institutions contributed to the bad-loan

---

[2] The bad loans were determined in the establishment of the *Financial Rehabilitation Law* in 1998: failed credit by self-assessment and failed risk credit.

Table 6.1. Number of bankrupt banks.

Year	1991–1997	1998	1999	2000	2001	2002–2005
Number	36	30	44	14	56	1

Sources: Fujii (2009, p.238).

debacle.[3] The nonbank institution Housing Finance Corporation collapsed in 1996; the Hokkaido-Takushoku Bank and Yamaichi Securities went bankrupt in 1997: the latter's debt reaching ¥3 trillion.

Under such circumstances, the Japanese government decided to reform its banking laws,[4] and nationalized some banks: the Japan Long-term Credit Bank and Japan Bond Credit Bank, in 1998, and the Ashikaga Bank in 2003. It took more than 15 years before bad loans were settled in March 2005 and financial organizations fully repaid ¥96 trillion in debts (Fujii, 2009, p. 215).

The traditional Japanese economic system also hindered economic recovery, prodding the Japanese toward Anglo-Saxon model.

Japan showed signs of emerging from the long-term crisis in 2003. During the period of "Great Moderation" in 2002–2007, Japan recorded 10.9% real GDP growth (annually 2.1%). Both domestic demand and exports contributed to the growth (Nakao, 2010, p. 24). Corporate profits and durable investment rose, and demand–supply gaps diminished. The labor supply improved; although most of the newly hired persons worked irregular hours or were seasonal. Stock prices increased, and the settlement of bad loans weakened deflationary pressures. The central bank cancelled both its "quantitative easing" and "zero-interest policies." Japan's Cabinet Office (Economy and Finance) correctly forecast a positive trend for 2002–2006. The country's corporate, household and external sectors advanced (Cabinet Office, 2006).

Private firms performed positively, with increased profits attributable to deflation, restructuring, loan repayments, and stock adjustments. The excessively weak yen-spurred exports helped but caused structural distortions.

---

[3] Nonbank financial institutions financed ¥98 trillion at the end of March 1991, accounting for 14.7% of all private loans. Most loans were directed to real estate and construction, and they took their mother banks' place (Fujii, 2009).

[4] The government injected ¥12.4 trillion, of which 74% was returned; ¥3.2 trillion remained unreturned as of 2008.

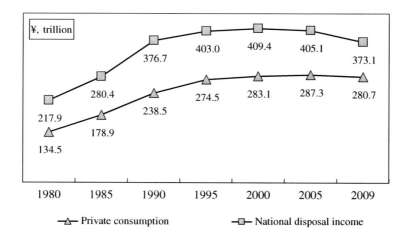

Figure 6.2. Income and consumption.

Source: SANA Statistics, Economic and Social Research Institute, Cabinet Office, Government of Japan (www.esri.cao.go.jp, February 20, 2011).

Three economic branches (electric machinery, automobiles, and business companies) accounted for 52% of the total profits. Five branches (the above three, plus machinery and steel) accounted for two-thirds of the gain (April 2, 2009, *Nihonkeizai newspaper*). External demand led Japan's growth, but also made it vulnerable to the global crisis.[5]

The 2002–2007 expansion differed from its predecessor. It was long-lasting, but weak. Adverse wage and employment trends impeded consumption growth. Figure 6.2 shows that national disposable income and private consumption stagnated in 2000s and declined in 2009. Firms were able to bolster profits by restructuring, but productivity gains were disappointing, underscoring the fragility of Japan's prospects.

6.3. The Global Crisis and Fragile Recovery

The long and weak growth during the period 2002–2007 was followed by a recession in October 2007. Private consumption and investment decreased, and domestic demand declined; the global crisis intensified this economic

---

[5] The export dependence rate of Japan in 2007 was 17.6%; this rate was considerably lower than those of Germany (46.9%), South Korea (46.4%), China (41.3%), France (26.9 %), and UK (25.8%). However, in Japan, the rate has generally doubled since 1990.

decline. After the bailout of the US investment bank Lehman Brothers in September 2008, stock prices fell sharply and the real sector shrank.

Although subprime loans did not severely affect Japanese banks and corporations directly, global monetary imbalances and loose credit took their toll. The global financial crisis caused Japan's GDP to plummet (Figure 6.1).

Real GDP growth fell more than 14% (annual base) in the last quarter of 2008 and the first quarter of 2009: worse than during the oil shock of 1974. All the indicators such as private consumption, residential investment, equipment investment, and exports showed sharp declines. Demand evaporated (Aoki, 2010). The weak US dollar shocked the Japanese export market. Japan's current account surplus fell 33% to ¥16.4 trillion in 2008. The surpluses in 2009 and 2010, respectively were ¥13.3 trillion and ¥17.1 trillion. A strong yen all but eliminated profit transfers from overseas companies.

Japan's export dependence is not as high as that of Korea, China, and Germany but is more sensitive to global oscillations because exports are concentrated in advanced manufacturing high-end products; the automobile, electric equipment, machinery, iron, and steel industries. Operating profits of the top five branches with the highest overseas sales (i.e., automobiles, precision machinery, machinery, shipbuilding and electronic machinery) declined from 50%–60% in March 2008 to 27% in the first half of 2009 (June 3, 2009, *Nihonkeizai newspaper*).

This caused a chain reaction. A decline in production aggravated employment and consumption, which in turn caused production to fall further. Figure 6.3 shows that as unemployment rates rose, and the job offers-to-seeker ratio fell, irregular employment increased. Some industrial regions like Aichi and Gunma were better off than others, but still were unable to re-attain the pre-crisis level (September 2008).

The International Monetary Fund (2009) says that, "In Japan, following a dismal first quarter, there are signs that output is stabilizing. Improved consumer confidence, progress in inventory adjustment, aggressive fiscal policies, and strong performance by some other Asian economies are expected to lift growth in the coming quarters." The recovery path, however, is proving to be long, winding, and rocky.[6] After a year

---

[6] Mr Masaaki Shirakawa, president of Bank of Japan, considered the recovery a "false dawn" on April 23, 2009.

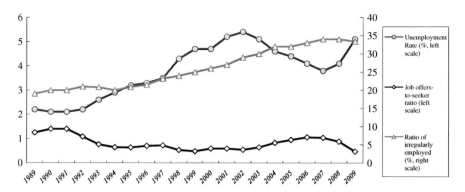

Figure 6.3. Labor market in Japan.

Source: Bank of Japan, *Financial and Economic Statistics Monthly*, February 15, 2010, http://www.boj.or.jp, Ministry of Health, Labor and Welfare, data of an employment agency (http://www.mhlw.go.jp, February 14, 2010).

of fragile and uneven recovery, growth of the world economy is now decelerating on a broad front, presaging weaker global growth (United Nations, 2011, p. 1).

Japan is recovering. Consumption has been stimulated by automobile and consumer durable subsidies and increased government investment. The Bank of Japan adopted an expansionary monetary policy, which reduced the interest rate to 0%–0.1%. It established a new fund for purchasing state bonds. Emerging market demand spurred Japan's export, GDP, and investment growth.[7] The recovery, however, is fragile.

Japan's Ministry of Internal Affairs and Communications is cautious.[8] The labor market is soft, especially for young males. The consumer price index also displays symptoms of a deflationary spiral. Some businesses have not fully recovered, and regional gaps are widening.

---

[7] The export recovery enhanced dependence on the Asian countries. Not only China but also ASEAN and Asian NIEs also increased trade volume.

[8] Data from Ministry of Internal Affairs and Communications (http://www.soumu.go.jp, February 14, 2010). Unemployment rate was 5.7% and a job offers-to-seeker ratio was 0.42 in July 2009; since then the ratio picked up 5.1% and became 0.4% at the end of 2009. In particular, labor market drastically worsened in the automobile company towns (Ministry of Health, Labor and Welfare, http:www.mhlw.go.jp, February 14, 2010).

Government policy also has been thrown off course. The Democratic Party of Japan (DJP) "took advantage of voter discontent with the short-term costs of liberalizing reforms by calling for a strengthened social safety net to deal with increased unemployment and inequality." This aggravated deficit spending, increasing the national debt to GDP ratio which is now the worst in the developed world, exceeds the 1944 wartime peak (204%).[9]

This makes the current economic recovery seem insecure, damping new investment. Declining wages, falling employment, diminished consumption, and social unrest are placing further downward pressure on production, just as they did in the early 2000s.[10]

The recovery continues to look like a "false dawn,"[11] battered as it is by an aging society, a declining population (i.e., labor force) and a fragile budget.

6.4. Dramatic Changes in Corporate Japan

Japan is trying to remedy the problem by reforming all aspects of its business system including industrial relations, vocational training and education, corporate governance, inter-firm relations, and employee relations.[12] The two most important aspects of the Japanese corporate system are its corporate governance and labor systems.

Japan's traditional corporate system stresses stable enterprise cross-shareholding among related companies and main banks, loyalty, and Keiretsu subcontracting, with companies attaching great importance to market share and long-term management.[13] This model (hereafter termed a "J firm") survives but has changed substantially after the collapse of the bubble economy in the 1990s.

---

[9] As more than 95% state bonds were held at home and the long-term interest is low, an increase of debts does not immediately cause sovereign crisis.

[10] Bank of Japan officially denies the deflation spiral.

[11] See note 6. The president of Bank of Japan admitted that the recovery process was not interrupted and Japan increased growth rate was towed by the high economic growth in emerging economies (December 11, 2010, *Nihonkeizai newspaper*).

[12] The various capitalism-based approaches classify corporate systems by virtue of these aspects.

[13] See Kanamori, Kousai, and Ohmori, 2004.

184 *Satoshi Mizobata*

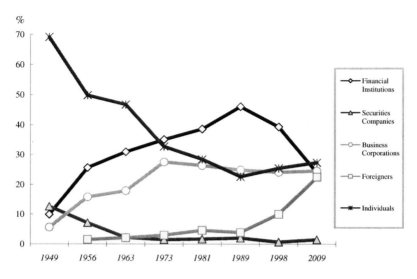

Figure 6.4. Type of shareholder.
Source: Tokyo exchange stock *et al.*, 2009.

The J firm began transforming in 1997. Shareholder authority increased. Figure 6.4 shows the distribution of unit shares held by different classes of shareholders in listed companies.

It reveals first that financial institutions sharply reduced their shares after the 1990s. The post-bubble banking crisis and the *Bank's Shareholding Restriction Law* reduced bank holdings.[14] Major commercial banks began selling corporate shares to raise funds to cover nonperforming loans and satisfy capital adequacy regulations (Jackson and Miyajima, 2007). Second, although the number of individual shareholders increased, their aggregate shareholding either remained flat or declined slightly. Third, foreigners significantly increased their holdings; their shares increased from 3.9% in 1989 to 22.1% in 2008 (25.5% in 2007), concentrated in pharmaceuticals, insurance, security, electric apparatus, real estate, and precision machinery. Foreign institutional investors own at least 30% of total capital of Sony, ROHM,

---

[14] "Major banks' shareholdings were 1.5 times Tier 1 capital in March 2001, so they were required to reduce their shareholdings by ¥10 trillion" (Miyajima and Kuroki, 2007, p. 91).

Yamanouchi Pharmaceutical Co. (Astellas Pharma after a merger with Fujisawa), Tokyo Electron, Furukawa Electric, TDK, ORIX, and Murata Manufacturing (Kagono, 2005, p. 298). Companies with high foreign ownership tend to be market oriented with American-style corporate governance.

The economic crisis diminished foreign shareholding. The largest declines occurred in: ORIX,[15] Citizen,[16] Mazda Motor Corporation,[17] and the financial institution ACOM,[18] but recovery has reversed the process.

Figure 6.5 illuminates other aspects of shareholding in Japan (i.e., listed companies in the three largest cities). Institutional and insider shareholding are on the increase at the expense of cross-shareholding.[19]

Declining cross-shareholding is attributable to reduced, "Tier 1" capital requirements,[20] set by the *Bank's Shareholding Restriction Law* in 2001.[21] Cross-shareholding fell from 18.4% in 1987[22] to just 7.6% in 2003. Likewise, stable shareholders, defined as cross-shareholdings plus shares held by long-term investors such as financial institutions or related business firms, fell from 43.1% in 1990 to just 26% in 2002. According to the

---

[15] The share decreased from 66% at the end of March 2007 to 34.3% at the end of March 2009 and returned to 50.5% at the end of March 2010 (February 20, 2010 and February 28, 2011, http://www.orix.co.jp).

[16] The shareholding of foreigners decreased from 41.2% at the end of September 2006 to 18.5% at the end of September 2009 and increased to 20% at the end of March 2010 (February 20, 2010 and February 28, 2011, http://www.citizen.co.jp).

[17] About 42.3% was owned by foreigners (foreign corporations) at the end of September 2010 (February 28, 2011, http://www.mazda.co.jp).

[18] ACOM is a member of Mitsubishi UFJ Financial Group, and the Group owns 36.88% of shares; foreigners decreased their shares to 5.0% by the end of September 2010 (from 25.8% at the end of March 2007) (February 28, 2011, http://www.acom.co.jp).

[19] Institutional investors include both domestic and foreign. Insiders include ownership of directors, domestic unlisted companies, and concerned of companies and large shareholder. See Nitta 2008, p. 9.

[20] The introduction of global accounting standards has also reduced cross-shareholding.

[21] The big banks reduced their shareholdings from around ¥30 trillion in 2001 to about ¥10 trillion in March 2009 (Bank of Japan, 2009). In January 2002, the organization for purchasing banks' shares was established, and its original operating funds were provided by 127 big banks.

[22] The peak of cross-shareholding was in 1987 because the selling of crossholding shares incurred corporate restructuring costs.

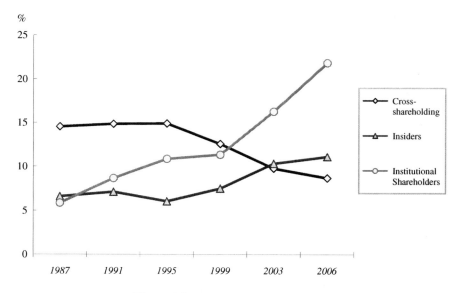

Figure 6.5. Shareholders composition.

Source: Nitta (2008).

Nisei Institute, stable shareholders decreased from 45.8% in 1987 to 24.3% in 2003. If we regard stable shareholders as insiders, the influence of Japanese type of insiders has diminished (NLI Research Institute, 2003).

J firms have been traditionally financed through external sources, with a main bank playing the key role. This changed after the collapse of the bubble economy in the 1990s. Internal funds now are primary; external funds secondary, but the change should not be overstated. While large firms reduced their links with banks, substituting debt financing; smaller firms continued borrowing from banks. Some large, listed firms depend upon capital markets; however, smaller firms continue to rely upon bank borrowing: trends unlikely to be swiftly reversed (Jackson and Miyajima, 2007; Arikawa and Miyajima, 2007).

6.5. Labor System Reform

Labor's position in J firms is distinctive, featuring lifetime employment, a seniority system, and company unions. Core workers employed by J firms are protected like their continental European counterparts (Table 6.2), but this protection is weakening around the edges (Table 6.3).

The pillars of J firm labor management are complementary. Lifetime employment is related to the seniority system; wages correlate with the length of employment, and seniority serves as "generational wage transfer" from young workers to old. Labor's share of J firms' cost (i.e.,

Table 6.2. Employment protection of core workers (late 1990s).

	France	Germany	Netherlands	UK	US	Japan
Regular procedural inconveniences	2.8	3.5	5.0	1.0	0.0	2.0
Notice and severance pay for no-fault individual dismissals	1.5	1.3	1.0	1.1	0.0	1.8
Difficulty of dismissal	2.8	3.5	3.3	0.3	0.5	4.3
Overall strictness of protection against dismissals	2.3	2.8	3.1	0.8	0.2	2.7

Note: The summary scores can range from zero to six, with higher values representing stricter regulation.
Source: OECD (1999, p. 57).

Table 6.3. Employment protection in OECD countries, 2008.

	France	Germany	Netherlands	UK	US	Japan
Protection of permanent workers against (individual) dismissal	2.60	2.85	2.73	1.17	0.56	2.05
Regulation on temporary forms of employment	3.50	1.96	1.42	0.29	0.33	1.50
Specific requirements for collective dismissal	2.13	3.75	3.00	2.88	2.88	1.50
OECD employment protection index	2.90	2.63	2.23	1.09	0.85	1.73

Note: Scale from zero (least restrictions) to six (most restrictions).
Source: OECD indicators on employment protection, February 21, 2010, http://stats.oecd.org, OECD social, employment and migration working papers, DELSA/ELSA/WD/SEM (2009) 17.

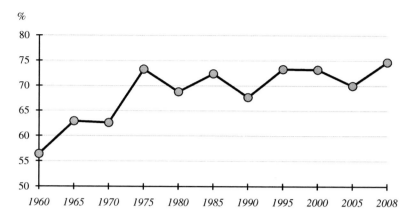

Figure 6.6. Labor share.

Source: Calculated by the author, based on Ministry of Finance, Business outlook survey (February 20, 2010, http://www.mof.go.jp).

personnel expenditure divided by the total value added), has grown with revenues (Figure 6.6), despite falling wages for those with seniority.

The Japanese labor system works best when employees are comparatively young, but as is the case now when the population ages, merit pay becomes more attractive than the competence-qualification system. The switch has caused lifetime employment to erode, reduced wages, increased labor turnover, and diminished firm-specific skills.

Legislative changes have promoted the hiring of irregular workers at lower pay with short-term contracts. The transition coincided with a Nikkeiren (the Japan Federation of Employers' Associations)[23] report entitled "Japanese Management in a New Epoch" issued in 1995. Since then regular (lifetime) workers have been gradually displaced by irregular (contract) workers, and their working hours have gotten longer

---

[23] Nippon Keidanren (Japan Business Federation) is a comprehensive economic organization that was established in May 2002 through an amalgamation of Keidanren (Japan Federation of Economic Organizations) and Nikkeiren (Japan Federation of Employers' Associations). Its membership of 1,609 comprises 1,295 companies, 129 industrial associations, and 47 regional economic organizations (as of May 28, 2009) (February 20, 2010, http://www.keidanren.or.jp).

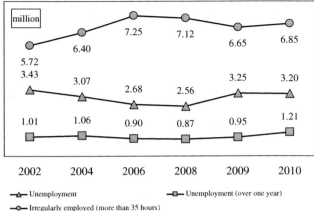

Figure 6.7. Unemployment and irregularly employed.

Source: Statistical Bureau Ministry of Internal Affairs and Communication, Japan 2010.

Table 6.4. Irregularly employed workers in Japan (%).

	1982	1987	1992	1997	2002
Male	8.3	9.1	9.9	11.2	16.5
Female	31.8	37.1	39.1	44.0	53.0

Source: Statistics Bureau Ministry of Internal Affairs and Communications, Japan, 2002.

Table 6.5. Changes in employment (thousands, %).

	Feb. 1985	Feb. 1995	2005	2009
Irregularly employed	6,550 (16.4)	10,010 (20.9)	15,910 (32.3)	17,430 (34.1)

Note: 2005 January–March average and 2009 July–September average.
Source: Ministry of Health, Labor, and Welfare, 2010.

(Figure 6.7)[24] Part-time workers accounted for 26.2% of total employment.[25] Tables 6.4 and 6.5 show a drastic increase in irregular employment. Although most irregulars are women, the share of male irregulars has been increasing. The same trend holds for older workers.

---

[24] Part-time and contract workers, as well as those with side jobs and temporary employment statuses, are included.
[25] *Monthly Labor Survey*, National Survey, Vol. 41, No. 7, January 2008.

190   *Satoshi Mizobata*

Table 6.6.   Length of service in Japan (%).

	Under 1 year	1 and under 5 years	5 and under 10 years	10 and under 20 years	20 years and over
1997 June					
Male	6.8	21.7	21.1	23.1	27.3
Female	11.0	32.8	26.5	19.5	10.3
Total	8.1	25.1	22.7	22.0	22.1
2008 June					
Male	7.8	24.9	16.8	25.1	25.3
Female	12.2	35.4	20.2	21.0	11.2
Total	9.2	28.3	17.9	23.8	20.8

Note: Sample employees are 23,605.3 thousands in 2008 and 21,455.1 thousands in 1997; and ratio in total regular employees is 49.3% and 45%, respectively.
Source: Ministry of Health, Labor, and Welfare, 1997, 2008.

In-house training and firm specific skills also have diminished in accordance with the shift from bank to equity finance (shareholder activism) (Abe and Hoshi, 2007).

Although large companies have increased their labor mobility and introduced numerous irregular workers to their production lines, they also have preserved long-term employment. Indeed, some companies are starting to reverse field moving some irregulars into regular positions. UNIQLO, for example, a clothes retailer, said in March that it would turn 5,000 of its 6,000 irregulars into lifetime employees within two years, and Canon said it would do the same for 1,000 of its 13,000 factory workers (December 1, 2007, *The Economist*, p. 13).

Table 6.6 shows that changes in the structure of employment have not significantly altered total employment. When irregular employment increases, core worker tenure does not decrease reciprocally.

METI's 2003 "Survey on the Corporate System and Employment" reports that lifetime employment persists in over 80% of Japanese firms (Jackson, 2007, p. 285). However, as Jackson and Miyajima (2007) note the following:

"Despite this continued commitment to lifetime employment, the core of employees covered under such an arrangement is shrinking. The largest 1% of firms employed nearly 23,000 people on average in 1993, but just 17,400 employees in 2002. Between 2000 and 2003, surveyed firms reduced their workforce by 15% on average, but only 4% of total exits came through outright layoffs. Thus, lifetime employment is being preserved as a norm of corporate insiders; large firms are undergoing a degree of social closure that makes it difficult for outsiders to enter." (pp. 25–26)

During the recent crisis J firms pursued a policy of "jobless growth." In the first half of 2009, large numbers of irregulars were dismissed. The process was reversed in 2010 with little impact on lifetime employers. Young and poorly educated cohorts were particularly at risk for dismissal, but the danger is mitigated by wage reductions and shortened hours of employment (Figure 6.8).

J firms prefer wage-cutting to dismissals.

6.6. Uncertain Compromise

J firms reform has been prodded by the government's harmonization (i.e., deregulation and liberalization) drive.[26] A variety of laws on company and labor were revised. Executive officers and executive committees were codified and the tasks of governance and management distinguished.

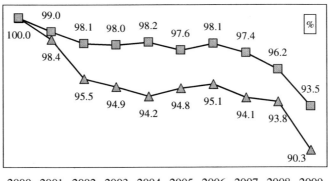

Figure 6.8. Earnings and hours worked.

Note: Monthly cash earnings in 2009 was ¥315,294. Total monthly hours worked in 2009 were 144.4.
Source: Ministry of Health, Labor, and Welfare, 2010, pp. 40, 50.

---

[26] Rosenbluth and Thies (2010) insisted changes from the view point of political change (adoption of new electoral rules in 1994). They stressed changes and conservative aspects.

192 *Satoshi Mizobata*

The main features of the change are increased outsider (including foreign) participation in corporate ownership, the introduction of a merit system, increased irregular employment, a reduction of service tenure, and increased out-house management. These changes are consonant with global trends.

Nonetheless, it is more accurate to think of J firms as hybrids rather than globalized corporate forms because insider ownership and management, team welfare provisions, insider boards and internal labor markets still dominate.[27] In short, the Japanese economic system has shown both change and continuity, and few Japanese firms have completely adopted the US model.

According to Jackson and Miyajima (2007), Japanese firms fall into three broad groups, based on cluster analysis (Figure 6.9): the traditional Japanese model, with strong relational elements on all dimensions (42% of surveyed firms, accounting for 16% of total employment); hybrid firms based on market-oriented finance and ownership characteristics (24% of surveyed firms, accounting for 67% of total employment); and an intermediate group (inverse hybrid) that has relational finance or insider boards with more market-oriented employment and incentive patterns (34% of surveyed firms, accounting for 18% of total employment).

It is 58% of J firms that have already changed into a quasi-US model according to these criteria. However, if employment and management are

	Outsider board, market employment	Insider board, relational employment
Relational finance	Inverse hybrid	J model
Market finance	US model	Hybrid

Figure 6.9. Corporate governance of J firms.

Source: Jackson and Miyajima (2007, p. 33).

---

[27] Isoya (2011) also insisted that although long-term employment has broken, it would be premature to be given up completely and emphasized the importance of path-dependent evolution (pp. 230–231).

stressed, two-thirds of those surveyed seem to have retained the J firm (Jackson and Miyajima, 2007, p. 42).[28]

The global crisis severely affected J firms, nonetheless hybridization seems to have served them well.[29] The Japan Management Association believes that the new Japanese corporate model[30]: Prioritizes employees over shareholders (75%).

1. Managers take special account of long-term gains (94.6%), employees' skills (81.6%), internal reserves (81.9%), and organizational values (78.8%).
2. More companies view lifetime employment as a key of the Japanese management system (from 0.9% in 2000 to 9.2% in 2009).

It is 80% of successful firms that have attached greater importance to regulars and life-time employees than irregulars.[31]

Nippon Keidanren (2010)[32] believes that the new labor strategy is epitomized by reduced overtime work and managerial pay cuts. It claims that companies are as sensitive to employment and seniority issues as competitiveness.

The Japan Productivity Center came to similar conclusions, finding that customers and employees are viewed by managers as primary

---

[28] *The Economist* labelled the harmonized Japanese system as "JapAnglo-Saxon capitalism" (December 1, 2007, *The Economist*, p. 19).

[29] Even the president of the Democratic Party of Japan, Yukio Hatoyama, criticized that "the recent economic crisis resulted from a way of thinking based on the idea that American-style free-market economic represents a universal and ideal economic order, and that all countries should modify the traditions and regulations governing their economies in line with the global (or rather American) standard" Hatoyama, Y (2009). A new path for Japan, Op-Ed Contributor (August 27), *The New York Times*, (http://www.nytimes.com).

[30] August 21, 2009, http://www.jma.or.jp. Questionnaire research to 299 new directors and managers of 1,504 samples during July 1–3, 2009.

[31] Respondents are 1,000 firms in September–November 2009 (February 15, 2010, http://www.jma.or.jp).

[32] Respondents are 505 firms in July–August 2010.

194 Satoshi Mizobata

stakeholders.[33] While 49.6% managers wish to preserve shareholder sovereignty, 31.6% intend to change it. Human resource management and skill formation are regarded as decisive.

Japan's Ministry of Health, Labor, and Welfare likewise favors regular and lifetime employment (Ministry of Health, Labor, and Welfare, 2009). The government believes that the Japanese management system played a stabilizing role in the global economic crisis.

Hybridized J firms thus appear to have wide support and are likely to remain essential elements of Japan's economy for the foreseeable future.[34]

6.7. Conclusion

The Japanese economy has profoundly changed since the 1970s. It is characterized today by high government debt and slow economic growth. It fared badly during the 2008 global financial crisis, and its recovery has been tepid, with limited improvement in sight.

The main obstacles to revitalization appear to be the following: (1) deficient aggregate demand caused by a "vicious circle" of cost cuts and wage declines; (2) a tepid global economic recovery, especially in the west; (3) chronic low growth, low earnings, and lack of interest in shareholders (November 21–27, 2010, *Nikkei Veritas*).

The Japanese economic system is still transitioning. It is liberalizing with pluses and minuses. Competitiveness is improving, but irregulars are bearing much of the burden. Traditional values help,[35] but the system in its entirety remains under intense international pressure. Prospects for accelerated long-term growth seem dim.

---

[33] Respondents are 117 managers in July 8–22, 2009. Tokyo Shoko Research (http://www.tsr-net.co.jp) had a high opinion of the Japanese management based on the interest of the employees.

[34] Japan Association of Corporate Executives raised the "New style of Japanese corporate management," which combines the strengths of very successful Japanese companies and those of the western models (The 16th Corporate White Paper, Creating a New Style of Japanese Management, July 3, 2009, February 15, 2010, http://www.doyukai.or.jp).

[35] Nippon Keidanren, Demanding realization of the company law contributing to enhance the competitiveness of companies, July 20, 2010.

Supplementary Notes

The Great East Japan Earthquake happened on 11 March 2011. The consequences of this disaster have considerably influenced on the Japanese economy: the sovereign crisis in Europe and a strong yen in 2011 accelerated its economic decline. In conditions of strong budget deficit, the government will become more dependent on state bonds; the trade balance will be deteriorated. Therefore, the negative impact on the economic growth is inevitable, even though special procurement measures for the disaster recovery may stimulate the domestic demand. Bank of Japan reported the minus growth in the first half of 2011 (Bank of Japan, *Financial and Economic Statistics Monthly*, September 8, 2011). Moreover, the damages of the earthquake will considerably affect on two core elements of the Japanese corporate system: keiretsu (subcontracting) and long-term employment systems. Due to a gradual recession of keiretsu and difficulties with keeping employment rates, there raises a question of its sustainable development based on the long-term employment relations.

References

Abe, M and T Hoshi (2007). Corporate finance and human resource management in Japan. In *Corporate Governance in Japan*, Aoki, M, G Jackson and H Miyajima (eds.). Oxford: Oxford University Press.

Aoki, T (2010). Disappearance and rebound of global demand. In *Global Financial Crisis and the New Order of the World Economy*, Aoki, T and K Baba (eds.). Tokyo: Nihonhyouron, pp. 30–57. (in Japanese).

Arikawa, Y and H Miyajima (2007). Relationship banking in post-bubble Japan. In *Corporate Governance in Japan*, Aoki, M, G Jackson and H Miyajima (eds.). Oxford: Oxford University Press, pp. 51–78.

Bank of Japan (2009). *Financial System Report,* August 2009 (in Japanese).

Cabinet Office (2006). *Annual Economy and Finance Report* (in Japanese).

Fujii, M (2009). *Financial Innovation and Market Crisis*, Nihonkeizai Newspaper Co., Tokyo (in Japanese).

The International Monetary Fund (2009). *World Economic Outlook Update*, July 8, 2009.

196 *Satoshi Mizobata*

Isoya, A (2011). Change and evolution of the Japanese enterprise system. In *Regulation Theory of Financial Crisis: Tasks of the Japanese Economy*, Uni, H, T Yamada, A Isoya and H Uemura (eds.). Kyoto: Showado, 188–235 (in Japanese).

Jackson, G (2007). Employment adjustment in Japanese firms. In *Corporate Governance in Japan*, Aoki, M, G Jackson and H Miyajima (eds.). Oxford: Oxford University Press, pp. 282–309.

Jackson, G and H Miyajima (2007). Introduction: The diversity and change of corporate governance in Japan. In *Corporate Governance in Japan*, Aoki, M, G Jackson and H Miyajima (eds.). Oxford: Oxford University Press, pp. 1–47.

Kagono, T (2005). Corporate governance and competitiveness. In *Japanese Firm System, Firm and Governance*, Itami, T, T Fujimoto, T Okazaki, H Ito and T Numagami (eds.). Kyoto: Yuhikaku, pp. 282–302. (in Japanese).

Kanamori, H, Y Kousai and T Ohmori (2004). *A Reader of Japanese Economy*, Tokyo: Touyoukeizaishinpousha (in Japanese).

Ministry of Health, Labor, and Welfare (1997). *Year Book of Labour Statistics* (in Japanese).

Ministry of Health, Labor, and Welfare (2008). *Year Book of Labour Statistics* (in Japanese).

Ministry of Health, Labor, and Welfare (2009). *Annual Report on Labour and Economy* (in Japanese).

Ministry of Health, Labor, and Welfare (2010). *White Paper of Labour Economics* (in Japanese).

Miyajima, H and F Kuroki (2007). The unwinding of cross-shareholding in Japan. In *Corporate Governance in Japan*, Aoki, M, G Jackson and H Miyajima (eds.). Oxford: Oxford University Press, pp. 79–124.

Nakao, T (2010). The international measures toward the global financial crisis. *Financial Review*, 3, July, pp. 22–57 (in Japanese).

Nippon, K (2010). *Top-management Survey on Personnel and Labour in 2010*, September 30 (in Japanese).

Nitta, K (2008). Change of shareholder and its influence. *NLI Research Institute Report*, 2008, p. 2 (in Japanese).

NLI Research Institute (2003). *Investigation on Mutual Shareholding in 2003* (in Japanese).

OECD (1999). *Employment Outlook*.

Rosenbluth, FM and MF Thies (2010). *Japan Transformed Political Change and Economic Restructuring*. Princeton NJ: Princeton University Press.

Statistics Bureau Ministry of Internal Affairs and Communications, Japan (2002). *Employment Structure of Japan, Summary Results and Analyses of 2002 Employment Status Survey* (in Japanese).

Statistics Bureau Ministry of Internal Affairs and Communications, Japan (2010). *Labour Force Survey: 2010* (in Japanese).

Tokyo exchange stock *et al.* (2009). *Summary of Shareownership Survey 2009.*

UN (United Nations) (2011). *World Economic Situation and Prospects.*

CHAPTER 7
CHINA

KAI KAJITANI
Kobe University, Japan

1. Chinese Economy after Crisis

The American financial crisis, triggered by Lehman Brothers bankruptcy, sent shock waves around the world in September 2008, including China. Demand for Chinese exports plummeted, exacerbating a downturn that had begun mid-2008 for purely domestic reasons. Exporters in Guandong Province were especially hard hit.

The Chinese government responded quickly by lowering interest rates in September 2008 and announcing a four trillion yuan public-spending stimulus package in November, including provisions for low income housing, infrastructure investment in inland areas, energy-related investment, investment in education, aid to victims of Sichuan's earthquake, and rural social security supplements.

The People's Bank of China simultaneously increased the money supply by repurchasing government securities and increasing interbank liquidity. As a result, interbank interest rates remained at record lows (Figure 7.1). New lending in the first quarter of 2009 was 4.6 trillion yuan, almost equal to the total for 2008. The money supply in March 2009 increased at an annual rate of 25.5%, fastest since 1999 (Figure 7.2).

Local governments also played a large role in the stimulus program. They were tasked to spend 2.8 trillion yuan: 1.6 trillion more than Beijing. Figure 7.3 shows that the stimulus promptly increased exports, but raised the specter of inflation. Much of the stimulus was derived from bonds insured by the Urban Construction Investment Group used to expand the credit base of local banks. Equity funds were created to tap private

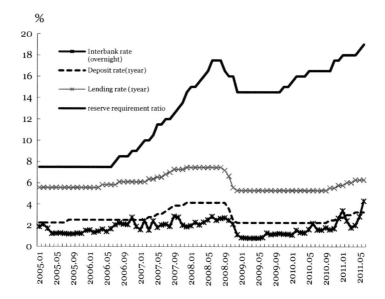

Figure 7.1. Financial policy of China.

Source: People's Bank of China; http://www.pbc.gov.cn/publish/main/index.html.

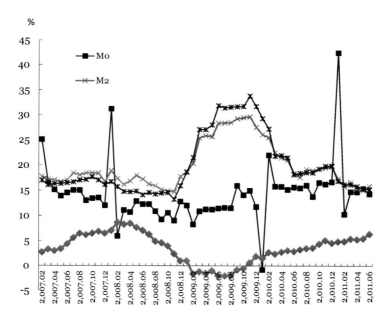

Figure 7.2. Annual growth rate of financial figures.

Source: CEIC Data, People's Bank of China.

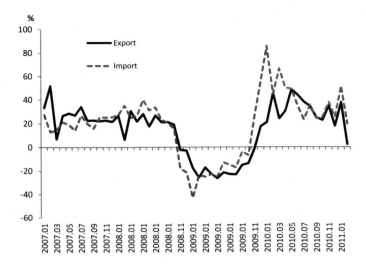

Figure 7.3. Annual growth rate of import and export.

Source: CEIC Data.

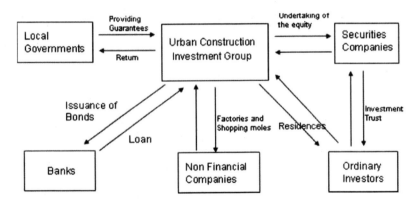

Figure 7.4. Mechanism of "loan platform."

Source: Prepared by the author.

investors as well (Figure 7.4). Both tactics were tied to anticipated real estate appreciation.

China chose to keep its renminbi (RMB) exchange rate constant during 2008–2009 to avoid diluting the stimulus package (Figure 7.5), but

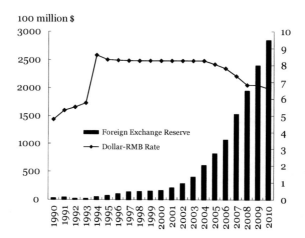

Figure 7.5. Dollar-RMB rate and foreign exchange reserve of China.
Source: CEIC data, People's Bank of China.

this entailed inflationary risks tied to the hot money "carry trade,"[1] given America's low interest rates (Figure 7.6).

The problem posed by these developments is best illuminated with a simple open-macroeconomy model, assuming fixed purchasing power parities, such that

$$S = \frac{P}{P^*}.$$

(S is long-term exchange rate; P is price level in China; and P^* is the price level in US.)

China's and America's money demand functions are:

$$\frac{M}{P} = L(i, Y)$$

---

[1] Actually, Peoples Bank of China, Chinese central bank, issued amount of PBC bills for sterilization of capital inflow. The amount of PBC bills outstanding rapidly increased from $37 billion at the end of 2003 to $538 billion in August 2007, and it peaked at $695 billion in October 2008 (Tabata, 2011). According to Ouyang *et al.* (2010), while sterilization in China was virtually complete until early 2007, it has been partial, but still high at around 0.7 between late 2007 and late 2008.

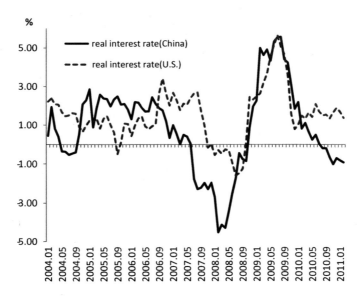

Figure 7.6. Long-term real interest rate in China and US.

Note: The figure of "real interest rate" of both countries is calculated by deducting the CPI index from the nominal Treasury bond yield with a term of 10 years.
Source: CEIC data, Bureau of Labor Statistics; http://www.bls.gov/cpi. Board of Governors of the Federal Reserve System; http://www.federalreserve.gov.

$$\frac{M^*}{P^*} = L^*(i^*, Y^*).$$

(i is nominal interest rate; Y is GDP; M is money supply; and L is money demand.)

And transforming them, we get

$$S = \frac{M/L(i,Y)}{M^*/L^*(i^*, Y^*)} = \frac{M/M^*}{L(i,Y)/L^*(i^*, Y^*)}.$$

If money demand is proportional to GDP, and the nominal exchange rate is affected by the nominal interest rate differential between China and US, we get:

$$S = \frac{M/M^*}{Y/Y^*}\alpha(i-i^*).$$

Or assuming the uncovered interest rate parity of $i - i^* = \Delta s^e$,

$$S = \frac{M/M^*}{Y/Y^*} \alpha(\Delta s^e). \quad (1).$$

Equation (1) can be used to estimate the expected rate of RMB depreciation when the dollar supply increases or American GDP growth exceeds China's. It also enables us to see how capital flows can spark inflation. During the period 2006–2008, Δs^e increased briskly, while the government restricted the rise of "S," necessitating a compensatory increase in M/M* to achieve equilibrium, which in turn compelled China to relinquish its control over domestic monetary policy.[2]

2. Global Imbalances and China-US Economic Interaction

Why did Beijing acquiesce by fixing its foreign exchange rate? Light can be shed on the matter by first considering the filial question of "global imbalances"; that is, interregional payments imbalances that have arisen between many emerging economies and the developed nations over the past decade. Figure 7.7 illustrates the changing correspondences between Japanese and Chinese current account surpluses and America's deficits

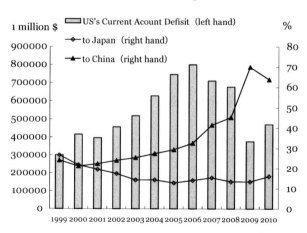

Figure 7.7. US's current account deficit and China's and Japan's surpluses.
Source: US Bureau of Economic Analysis; http://www.bea.gov/.

---

[2] See Chapter 27 of Caves, Frankel and Jones (2001).

since 2001. It shows that China has displaced Japan as the principal source of America's excess imports.

Explanations for these imbalances vary. Ben Bernanke, Chairman of the U.S. Federal Reserve Bank attributes them generically to a "global savings glut" (Bernanke, 2005). Dooley *et al.* (2003) consider them the consequences of an implicit fixed exchange rate regime (Bretton Woods II) that permits emerging economies to overexport in exchange for American monetary and fiscal independence. Others like Eichengreen-Hausmann (2004), and Ito and Hayashi (2006), while accepting the Bretton Woods II characterization, consider the bargain suboptimal and perhaps destabilizing. McKinnon (2005) stresses the danger posed to emerging nations, surrendering their control over domestic monetary policy. Others like (Caballero, *et al.*, 2008b) emphasize the adverse effect of the Bretton Woods II on emerging nations' domestic capital markets, while Prasad *et al.* (2007) highlight the perversity of capital flowing from poor to rich countries. Both urge emerging economies to improve their domestic capital markets.

This is sound advice, but gives the misleading impression that Beijing underinvests. China has not had any difficulty simultaneously holding excess dollar reserves and putting hot money to work in the construction sector and has been receptive to this because real estate development provides innumerable insider rent-granting/rent-seeking opportunities which appear to have taken precedence over inflation and inefficiency concerns (see Figure 7.8).

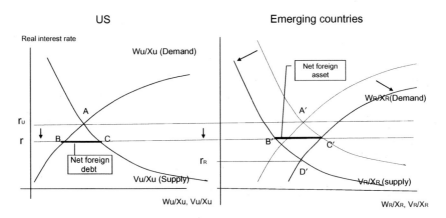

Figure 7.8. Low capital returns in the emerging countries and global imbalances.
Note: Emerging countries' current account surplus equals to the increase of net foreign asset.
Source: Caballero, *et al.* (2008a).

It seems from Beijing's perspective that its hot money abetting the real estate bubble is a growth supportive plus, which together with benefits from overexporting, warrant its implicit bargain with Washington. Consequently, it can be inferred that Chinese economic policy after the 2008 financial crisis has not and will not deviate significantly from the recent past, even though imbalances seem to be causing significant global microeconomic distortions, macroeconomic risks, and international trade tensions.

References

Abel, AB, NG Mankiw, LH Summers and RJ Zeckhauser (1989). Assessing dynamic efficiency: Theory and evidence. *Review of Economic Studies*, 56, 1–20.

Bernanke, B (2005). The global saving glut and the U.S. current account deficit. Sandridge Lecture, Virginia Association of Economics, Richmond, Virginia, Federal Reserve Board, March 2005.

Caballero, RJ, E Farhi and P-O Gourinchas (2008a). An equilibrium model of "global imbalances" and low interest rates. *American Economic Review,* 98(1), 358–393.

Caballero, RJ, E Farhi and P-O Gourinchas (2008b). Financial crash, commodity prices, and global imbalances. *Brookings Papers on Economic Activity*, Fall 1–55.

Caves, RE, JA Frankel and RW Jones (2001). *World Trade and Payments: An Introduction*, 9th Ed. New York: Addison Wesley.

Diamond, PA (1965). National debt in a Neoclassical growth model. *American Economic Review*, 55, 1126–1150.

Department of National Accounts, National Bureau of Statistics of China (1996). *Data of Gross Domestic Product of China 1952–1995*. Beijing: Zhongguo Tongji Chubanshe (Chinese).

Department of National Accounts, National Bureau of Statistics of China (2003). *Data on the Gross Domestic Product of China 1996–2002*. Beijing: Zhongguo Tongji Chubanshe (Chinese).

Department of National Accounts, National Bureau of Statistics of China (2007). *Data on the Gross Domestic Product of China 1952–2004*. Beijing: Zhongguo Tongji Chubanshe (Chinese).

Dooley, M, D Folkerts-Landau and P Garber (2003). An essay on the revived Breton Woods System. *NBER Working Paper*, No. 9971, September.

Eichengreen, B and R Hausmann (2004). *Other People's Money: Debt Denomination and Financial Instability in Emerging Market Economies*. Chicago: University of Chicago Press.

McKinnon, RI (2005). *Exchange Rates under the East Asian Dollar Standard: Living with Conflicted Virtue*. Massachusetts: MIT Press.

National Bureau of Land Resources of China. *Almanac of Chinese Land Resources*. Beijing: Zhongguo Dizhi Chubanshe (Chinese).

National Bureau of Statistics of China. *China Statistical Yearbook*. Beijing: Zhongguo Tongji Chubanshe (Chinese).

National Bureau of Statistics of China (2005). *China Compendium of Statistics 1949–2004*. Beijing: Zhongguo Tongji Chubanshe (Chinese).

Ouyang, AY, RS Rajan and TD Willett (2010). China as a reserve sink: The evidence from offset and sterilization coefficients. *Journal of International Money and Finance,* 29(5), 951–972.

Prasad, E, R Rajan and A Subramanian (2007). Foreign capital and economic growth. IZA Discussion Papers 3186, Institute for the Study of Labor.

Tabata, S (2011). Comparison of the mechanisms of the increase in international reserves in Russia, China and India. mimeo.

Ito, T and T Hayashi (2006). Inflation targeting and monetary policy. Toyo Keizai Xinposha (Japanese).

Tirol, J (1985). Asset bubbles and overlapping generations. *Econometrica*, 53(6), 1499–1528.

Tsuyuguchi, Y (2009). The recent flow of hot money in China. *Bank of Japan review*, 2009-E-3 (Japanese).

Yongding, Yu (2009). The management of cross-border capital flows and macro-economic stability in China. *TWN Global Economic Series, 14*, Third World Network.

CHAPTER 8
RUSSIA*

ERIC BRUNAT
University of Savoie, France

8.1. Introduction: The Societal Context of the Modernization in Russia

The process of transformation/modernization of the Russian economy cannot be disconnected from the deeply embedded values of Russian society and hence from the multiethnic culture of the country forged over a long period of time. This factor largely governs the success of the transformation and the progression toward a sustainable and human growth. It is this societal dimension and the attendant extreme complexity of modernization which the Center for Social and Society Observation — VtsIOM in Moscow, directed by Y. Levada — is attempting to comprehend and evaluate. A successful economic modernization in Russia is, and will be, strongly dependant on a cultural evolution which will help the country to position and locate itself in the framework of a globalized and multipolar world. The validating source of such an evolution — neglected in the first years of transformation — is found in a strong value system and a strong sense of a community's destiny. Yasin (2003) pertinently reminds us that the cultural specificity and values of the country must absolutely be taken into account in reform strategies so as not to create havoc with the identity of a nation. The question is therefore to ascertain whether a rapid convergence toward a form of "western market economy" is appropriate or simply realistic (Table 8.1).

From the point of view of human development, it appears that the traditional system of Russian sociological values presents a number of original

---

* A preliminary version of this text has been published in French in the *Annuaire Français de Relations Internationales*, Volume XI, 2010, 157–184 with the title L'économie russe. Modernisation, crise et géo-économie, La Documentation Française and Editions Bruylant, Paris-Brussels.

Table 8.1. Traditional Russian values and principal consequences.

Values	Consequences observed
Emphasis on spiritual values	Contempt for purely material interests
Propensity for team work	Effacement of the individual
"Sobornost" understood as united community of individuals and power/ strength of the State	Search for a higher messianic force
Belief that chance is a precondition of all success	Hopes for a miracle to the detriment of systematic work
Conception of work as a source of pleasure and of creativity	Possible sluggishness and relative lack of organization
Taste for ambitious plans and immediate action	Inattention and a certain irresponsibility for the medium term
Spontaneous generosity and cordiality ("poverty is a virtue")	Insufficient incentives for work, saving, business, and prosperity
Importance of sanctions through private agreement to dispense justice	System of justice above and beyond the law. Widespread system of informal relations
Importance of the emotions, of inspiration and of aesthetics	Intuition more than rationality in decision making

Source: Yasin (2003).

aspects. It has a longstanding tradition of favoring teamwork. An aesthetic and a creative sense also hold an important place in this tradition. Certain values which are strongly anchored in the Russian cultural tradition seem to be relatively in contradiction to, and even counterproductive, in a world of brutal market values whose democratic dimension is supposed to be coordinated by a legally constituted state of non-divine origins. These longstanding values which "*homo sovieticus*" has tended to reinforce rather than transform (while nonetheless adding a sense of the importance of education and a growing urbanized environment) would point perhaps toward the beginning of a specifically Russian vision and trajectory through the conception of a form of multilateralism in international relations dominated by the West. These values, even after their modification through the emerging forces of a recent and violent market regulation, are largely founded on the bases and the relationships of an archaic society which has had to compromise with a hierarchical structure dominated by a State standing above individuals and cut off from civil society. The economy was based over a long period of time on agrarian feudal relations, on varied geographic, climatic and spatial conditions which were often difficult, and which have exercised, and continue to exercise, great influence over the economic development of the country and the evolution of mentalities.

These elements are fundamental and stretch through the time of the Tsars and the Soviet period, which transferred social relationships from a rural to an urban context. They afford a better insight into the value system shared by Russians and the recent transformations in their economy as well as the way this relates to the world economy. They help us to understand the slow and distinctive process of changes in the system of shared values. Russians have remained fundamentally traditional and the radical economic transformation initiated at the beginning of the 1990s will be sustainable and take on the form of a real societal change adjusted to market and democratic mechanisms if, and only if, the principal foundations of Russian identity become the validating source of further development and the levers of institutional change. The authoritarian tensions and fears of all sorts will only dissipate when the values, proper to a Russian society in transition, will no longer be overridden when confronted with the values and the forms of power distribution of the principal western democracies. As in all forms of globalization, financial, technological, environmental, social, or fiscal, which do not proceed at the same rhythm in each field (requiring specific forms of regulations and organizations to further the cause of social justice and human development), transformation times in the case of Russia cannot simply be imposed; they vary according to the type of regulation (market or hierarchical), to the fundamental economic rules, and even to the deeper mechanisms of society and culture. At the beginning of the decade, the sociological work of Levada (2000) show that transformation times do not progress at the same rate even if a concern for individual liberty is often cited as a fundamental value, the notion of responsibility increasingly referred to, or personal work or civil rights invoked as important values. The fundamentals of Russian society have not changed radically and neglecting to respect this state of affairs in the deployment of new institutional measures, of new norms, rules or legal frameworks in general, is leaving the field wide open to contradictions and specific trading costs which in turn can lead to a very corrupt state of affairs and to a worrying spread of administrative crime.

The democratic revolution has weakened the State without paying heed to substituting another legal framework and, therefore, before it has in effect been put in place. Individual civil rights and liberties have been developed without fully integrating attendant notions of private property and responsibility. An accelerated social differentiation has not permitted a massive adherence to the rule of law and the confidence that such an adherence would induce. The massive and radical intolerance of the masses faced with corruption cannot exist alongside an increasing trust in efficiency and the probity of power and of public and private administration. Furthermore, the tyranny of the ostentatious and of the short-term must necessarily give way to a spirit of saving, investment, and economic calculation; however, here again such progress requires a self-confidence and trust in the institutional and legal environment. We put forward the hypothesis that these radical changes cannot be achieved in brutal opposition to the Russian system of shared values. In default of this, the process of global transformation loses its efficiency; civil society struggles to constitute itself, and the existing powers harden their position. Leaving aside the world financial and economic crisis, this is what we can learn from the recent pattern of economic transformation in Russia, from its socioeconomic modernization, and in a wider sense, from its principal geopolitical and geo-economic choices.

The discourse on the verticality of power and the restoration of Russian grandeur has turned in individual terms to the advantage of the supreme head (embodied in an a-typical diarchy with Dmitri Medvedev as President and Vladimir Putin as Prime Minister) whereas the social base does not, for the majority, identify with the actions of the administration or even of the government.[1] There is a clear distinction between the power of the chief "coming from heaven" whose path is cleared and the executive power with which the people do not really relate (Raviot, 2008). The supreme head speaks of Russian identity and values, whereas the executive, "in the perception of the majority of the people, applies imported

---

[1] Even in the midst of the present crisis, after a growth of unemployment which is presently about 8.5% of the working population (in International Labor Organization terms), with a drop of gross domestic product of 7.9% in 2009, the popularity of President Medvedev remains positive, according to VtsIOM, with 70% of Russians, and even more so for Vladimir Putin, as prime minister.

western measures, even measures imposed from the outside." The results from this — and in this respect the situation is very similar to that of the Soviet period — a distinct break, rather than a seamless link, between the majority of individuals and the State apparatus, the popularity of which is very feeble (economic policies in the polls of recent years generally win less than 20% of favorable opinion, and it is much the same for the army, the Church, regional and local public authorities (Condé, 2009).

The reforms have given a powerful impetus to the move toward the market economy, free enterprise and private property, with, as their underlying premise, the dissolution/rapid substitution of societal values in and through a western-style liberal capitalist model in the sense specified by Sloterdijk (Dockès *et al.*, 2009), that is to say in contrast to eastern-style authoritarian capitalism. Without following the German philosopher concerning his fear of a further reduction in Russian freedoms, it is true that one must nonetheless acknowledge and not go on denying the importance of the country's identity when promoting the positive effects which can accrue from international commerce, cooperation, and respect for plural identities. The Russian values of spirituality, solidarity, their specific way of dealing with complexity, and a certain pleasure taken in work activity can find their place in postindustrial societies and contribute to develop a complementary, if not alternative, way of thinking compared with the so-called universal values of financial capitalism. In this case, the contribution of Russia in a multipolar world could be productive and creative and not the reflex action of a defensive authoritarianism reflecting a sort of siege mentality. This is also the only way in which a responsible civil society can emerge in the Russian Federation, so that economic growth can truly be transformed into human development.

8.2. A Strong Growth After the Collapse of 1998, but Institutional and Societal Weaknesses Remain

Since the financial collapse of 1998 and up to the present world economic crisis, the Russian economy had made a lively recovery in spite of structural weaknesses. Table 8.2 shows, Russia experienced strong economic growth of its real GDP over the last 10 years in contrast to an average annual decline in GDP of 6.8% during the period 1992–1998. The positive

214   Eric Brunat

Table 8.2.   Annual percentage variation in Russian GDP.

2000	2001	2002	2003	2004	2005	2006	2007	2008	2009	2010	2011 (est.)
10,0	5,1	4,7	7,3	7,2	6,4	7,4	8,1	5,7	−7,9	4,0	4,3

Sources: IMF, World Bank, and Central Bank of the Russian Federation.

GDP trends are reflected in other measurements that point to an improved Russian standard of living throughout the period.

This result is remarkable but it must be put into perspective. The Russian economy constitutes less that 3% of the world economy; the GDP per inhabitant represents 28% and 35% of the GDP per inhabitant of the United States and of EU, respectively. It will be very difficult for Russia to attain its declared objective of 50% of the American GDP per inhabitant in 2020. To get even close to this ambitious objective, it will be necessary in the coming ten years to restore confidence and boost both domestic and international investment. The principal motors of growth will come from the resilience of the private sector but articulated around a modern and healthy public sector, in education and research, with a restored social sphere and health provision, with modernization of infrastructures and international cooperation. Apart from the effects of the world crisis, these are all fields of activity, suffering adverse effects from the hardening attitudes of the authorities, who have not succeeded in stabilizing a clear legal framework understood and respected by all or in effectively liberating the economy and society through the democratic give-and-take of true political and industrial competition. The mechanisms of a "western-type liberal market economy" have been at least partially deployed in a poorly prepared framework with the ideological conviction that assuming the "interplay of universal values" would be enough to modify the framework.

In such a context, the weight of natural resources in the economy often has a harmful effect. It has distorted investment flows and not contributed to a sufficient diversification of investment effort. It has led to a concentration of powers in a counterproductive fashion as well as to inefficient product distribution. The adaptation of market mechanisms has been brutal, unequal, and above all has contributed to an effacement of the specific solidarity reflexes of Russian society, modifying in a violent fashion attitudes to money and work. The result is very negative, pointing to a society consumed by doubt and which is henceforth prone to retreat into nationalist reflexes which are worrying. For all these reasons, one of the primary motors of growth, which is the end consumption of households, can be effectively curbed, calling into question both the recovery from the present crisis but, more seriously, the sustainable character of growth and its transformation in human development terms. To re-launch the process of a modern economic and social transformation based on the positive and specific values of Russian society, the following should be considered:

1. The principal problem of the country is its endemic problem of corruption. Many segments of public and private administration are concerned at all levels. Among the countries which are advanced on the technological level but with medium incomes — in the World Bank definition — Russia is among the most corrupt in the world, according to *Transparency International* (Russia is ranked 146 out of 180 countries in 2009). Moreover, government insiders and private owners (often under the influence of political and economic advisers — including international — used private, state, and hybrid (composite) institutions as vehicles for personal enrichment, instead of maximizing institutional and social welfare (Rosefielde, 2009). The legal framework as well as the institutions of the economy — the relations based on respected contacts between the economic agents, for example — the social sphere and a certain gradualism in the rhythm of reform process, have been neglected by the promoters of the "shock therapy" through the 1990s.
2. Russia needs to lower the transaction costs and raise its global productivity in order to offset speculative trading as well as accept integration into a more diversified world economy. This integration process is indispensable to facilitate modernization and the management of technological or financial complexities. So far, the protectionist climate,[2] in particular in the numerous industrial sectors

---

[2] For example, the custom duties on imported second-hand cars and trucks have gone up by 50% and 100%, respectively in January 2009. This measure was clearly imposed in order to protect the national industrial production.

216   *Eric Brunat*

considered as "strategic," but also in agriculture or finance, jeopardizes a rapid entry to membership of the World Trade Organization which would be a catalyst for structural and institutional reform and a supplementary source for growth which the World Bank estimates at between 0.5% and 1% per year through the next five years. However this sustainable opening to the outside world must be accomplished with proper respect for individuals, social balance, and preservation of Russian identities.

3. A monopolistic State capitalism in Russia now exists alongside a concentrated private capitalism. The share of private and public capital contributes 50% each to the GDP. The competitive mechanisms are not functioning, and this contributes to maintaining a level of inflation which exceeds 10% in recent years. Thus, this quasi-absence of competition, high transaction costs, monetary policy, and the ruble exchange-rate policy all have a negative effect on the general level of price increases. In addition, the flight of capital in the periods of declining confidence (the 1990s, the 1998 crisis, and the present financial crisis)[3] and the insufficiency of domestic and international investment (even if the latter has increased considerably from 2005 onward) have contributed to moderate the structural inflation which is therefore not fully reflected in the levels recorded in recent years.

4. In 2009, the percentage of investment was below 20% of the GDP in Russia, and the overall level of investment still remains far below the level reached in 1990. This crucial point could jeopardize the proactive policy of modernization and research and development policy announced by the central political power. In comparison, the principal developing countries of Southeast Asia and the most successful transition economies have levels of investment superior to 30% of their GDP.

5. The infrastructure of transport and communication must become a priority in order to improve competitiveness and reduce the transaction

---

[3] Geopolitical and geo-economic phenomena also have an influence on the movement of capital. Thus for example, the Russian–Georgian war and the recognition by Moscow of the secessionist republics from Georgia in August 2008 led to a major exit of capital (especially foreign capital) from Russia.

costs. This implies a capacity to develop major projects, attracting heavy financial investments and skills (including international cooperation and investors).

6. A significant investment and a political commitment are necessary in the sectors of health, education, research, and development toward a knowledge-based economy and society. The industrial surpluses in the private sector must also be in part oriented toward these strategic areas for development. Incentives to the private sector including fiscal ones could strengthen a social and desirable industrial policy.

7. The banking system is dominated by several large State banks, which have played a positive role during the world financial crisis by mastering the mechanisms of the public and private finances of an advanced economy. On the other hand, the current system generates high costs, and some private competition could prove to increase efficiency in the context of a modern economy.

8. The external accounts, registering a surplus, are very dependent on the export of natural resources and on the world oil and gas prices. The structural competitiveness of the economy is not assured. The pressure exercised on short-term resources favors a "rent economy"[4] (the future of which can only be fluctuating and inhibitive to growth), which distorts financial, technological, and human investment flows, directing them to the prospection and exploitation of natural resources to the detriment of other branches and sectors of the economy ("*Dutch disease*"). Moreover, performances based on energy saving and the

---

[4] Certain authors (Sapir, 2008; Ivanter and Sapir, 2008) consider that the economic turning point in terms of dependency on oil and natural resources has been passed during the last decade (and more so after 2005) and that Russia is today much more diversified in its industrial effort (telecommunications, nanotechnologies, chemistry, and metallurgy and so on). We consider that this diversification is in effect underway but that it is still appropriate, taking into account the financial constraints induced by the crisis, the proportion that natural resources contributes to the total budget, the absorption of investments and percentage of exports, to speak of an oil- and gas-based "rent economy" in Russia. It should be noted that we are here using the term "rent" in the sense of a "rent-seeking economy" as defined in Rosefielde (2005), Brunat and Klepach (2007) or Aslund (2007): a search for quick revenue by economic agents which is by nature at least as much sociological as economic and which puts a brake on savings and investments.

environment are not an effective priority. Having for a long time been used to the illusion of virtually free energy, both private and public economic agents must now modify their behavior toward a greater sense of responsibility for the individuals, the society, and the environment.

8.3. The Present World Crisis has Revealed Financial Vulnerability and Structural Weaknesses

The global economic crisis, which began in the United States in August 2007, has spared few countries. Russia has been seriously affected. At the beginning of the crisis, the macroeconomic situation of the country was healthy after several years of strong growth and payments balanced or even in surplus — and with a strong budget surplus of over 6% in 2007 and in the order of 4% in 2008. The public debt had reached a level in 2007 and 2008 which was lower than 10% of the GDP[5] and the currency exchange reserves were the third highest in the world. The financial crisis has had, however, a severe effect on Russia and revealed structural weaknesses.

Concerning the weight of raw materials in Russian exports, their contribution to the federal budget and their share in investments, a strong fluctuation in the oil and gas market prices (140 US$ the cost of a barrel for oil from the Urals in July 2008, 34 US$ in the beginning of January 2009, and about 75 US$ at the end of 2009, against 59 $ forecast, according to Table 8.3) has not been, in spite of an important stabilization fund (see below) without impact on public finances, company results, and household income. There is a clear correlation between the drop in prices of natural resources and the deterioration of the Russian economy (Connolly, 2009). The GDP dropped in 2009 by about 7.9%, industrial production by some 11.7%, investments by more than 15%, and the budget deficit was 6.4% (including the national well-being fund contribution).[6]

---

[5] It was 7% in 2007 according to the Russian Central Bank. This result was obtained thanks for the massive inflow of currencies from hydrocarbons and also from the State disengagement from the social sphere — health and education. Russia reimbursed in advance several debts incurred with the IMF, the United States, and European countries. Today, it is one of the least indebted countries in the world.

[6] Statement of A. Kudrin, Minister of Finances of the Russian Federation, Ria Novosti, January 13, 2010.

Table 8.3. Principal macroeconomic indicators 2006–2009.

	2007	2008	2009
GDP (% variation)	8,1	5,7	−7,9
Annual inflation rate (% variation)	11,9	13,3	11
Industrial production (% variation)	6,3	2,1	−11,7
Investments (% variation)	21,1	9,8	−15,4
National budget balance (% of GDP)	6,0	4,0	−6,4
Unemployment rate (in % definition of IL0))	6,4	6,2	8,4
Average price of barrel of oil (Ural) (in US$)	75	95,5	58
Reserves in currencies and precious metals (in billions of US$)	478,8	427,1	405

Sources: IMF — http://www.imf.org/external/pubs/ft/weo/2010/update/02/index.htm — Central Bank of the Russian Federation, National Statistics data.

The rate of exchange of the ruble has depreciated and the important exchange reserves have considerably diminished to stand at the end of year 2009 at about 400 billion dollars. The variation in the market prices of raw materials therefore introduces a specific parameter which has a distinctly erratic effect because of the world financial and economic crisis. The financial health of all sectors of the Russian economy is threatened by the structural weaknesses which remain.

The evaluation of financial vulnerability depends on the state of financial exchange reserves, the proportion of debt compared with the GDP, the type of debts, whether short- or long-term, and whether they are expressed in local money or foreign currencies. It is equally important to distinguish the financial balance sheets of the public sector (including the Central Bank) from those of the financial sector (principally the banks), and those of the private non-financial sector (households and enterprises). Similar distinctions must be made between resident agents and non-resident agents on the domestic market and between Russia and the rest of the world. It should be added that all these economic sectors are interdependent.

The impact of the present crisis on the Russian economy and society is however very different from what was observed in 1998. At that time, the population had been directly confronted with the reality of the crisis through the closure of the banks, the cessation of payments, a strong rise in prices, and the collapse of the exchange rate (Ivanter and Sapir, 2008). Today, with the exception of a minority who hold securities (the Moscow stock market remains small and capitalism is not mass capitalism — less than 1% of the population hold shares), the crisis remains much more abstract than in 1998, in spite of payment defaults which have multiplied and unemployment which is henceforth, in Russia also, a real worrying matter. All this does not mean that the present crisis is purely a virtual one, but it is clear that its effects are totally different from the traumatism of 1998 (Ivanter and Sapir, 2008).

The growth of domestic credit given to households, which increased strongly from 2000 to 2006, has begun to weaken so as only to represent 9% of the GDP in 2007. This is little compared with other emerging economies or the advanced economies. Nonetheless, debt in other currencies was about 20% of the total. Although linked to a banking system which is relatively underdeveloped, this point is important and in the final count quite positive, because while the ruble has weakened against the euro, the Swiss franc, or the dollar, householders have not been strangled by debt as has been the case in central or eastern Europe (Hungary in particular) or in the Baltic countries. On the other hand, Russian companies have been heavily indebted in other currencies in securing their natural resource assets on the international market. The banks have reinforced this tendency by themselves having recourse to the international finance markets in order to speculate or, simply, to finance companies.

Thus, the Russian State was relatively little in debt and held significant reserves at the beginning of the crisis. Households were similarly little in debt with a debt structure of 80% in local money. On the other hand, companies had increased their debt in other currencies on the world market which made them vulnerable to the fall in oil revenues and the consequent weakening of the ruble. These weaknesses were reinforced by the intervention of Russian troops in Georgia on the August 8, 2008, which worried investors, particularly foreign ones, and led to a severe loss of confidence. Outflows of capital, which had a positive effect on inflationist pressure, began as early as the spring of 2008, but it was in

September 2008 that the outflows accelerated after the collapse of the stock market in Moscow. Condé (2009) recalls that before the crisis, the Russian authorities had underestimated the degree of economic and financial integration of their country in the world economy. Yet, foreign investors held 70% of the securities quoted on the floor of the Moscow exchange.[7] The outcome of all this was a strong depreciation of the ruble whose rate of exchange went from 25 rubles for 1 U.S. dollar in July 2008 to more than 36 rubles in April 2009. Almost 200 billion dollars were used to uphold the ruble and bring in the required budgetary measures. Important sums were voted by the Duma in support of the economic activities which were most vulnerable to a lack of liquidity needed for the movement of capital, and this was notably the case in the agricultural sector, and in the defence, engineering, and the building industries. Public action was therefore very positive in preventing the development of a major internal liquidity crisis brought on by the international crisis. The resistance capacity of the Russian economy and administration was positive. However, it is nonetheless the case that the weight of debt in company currency holdings automatically increased and that real income dropped considerably with the weakening of terms of exchange.

---

[7] Ivanter and Sapir (2008) stress, however, that the financial volume in circulation and traded on the Moscow market at that time was very limited. During the session of September 16, 2008, the share price of GAZPROM dropped by 16%. In fact, the volume of trade on this share did not pass six million dollars: a derisory figure compared with the company's capitalization. Similar phenomena were observed for the great majority of other shares. This stems from the fact that companies have in reality much control over shareholders. Ivanter in Ivanter and Sapir (2008) estimates that "in the majority of cases, the 'floating' part of the shareholding does not exceed 3% to 4% of the company's capitalization, which in effect limits the role played by the Moscow stock market. Contrary to the developed capitalist countries, the stock market was not created in reply to companies' need for financing but as a 'ritual' act of affirmation in Russia as a country in transition. [...] It is a market without real depth, in which the average amount of an intervention by a resident broker is in the order of 20,000 dollars; the market has above all served as a pocket for speculation by non-resident agents."

Structural weaknesses became more glaring, and the weak competitiveness of a large part of industry led to a drop in industrial production which was concomitant to the fall in non-state investment. In the wake of these financial upheavals in 2008, households, which at first were relatively spared, now started to suffer from, on the one hand, the slowdown in economic activity (with the rise in unemployment affecting real income and as a consequence increasing defaults in debt repayments) and, on the other hand, a brutal drying up of access to credit (in particular for small enterprises). These difficulties engendered negative chain effects on demand in the property market and on general personal consumption.

The crisis also increased the vulnerability of the banking and industrial sectors dealing with the external world and holding debts in foreign currencies. The weight of this debt was commensurate with the depreciation of the ruble. In the second semester of 2008, the debt of industrial firms, according to the Russian Central Bank, reached around 295 billion dollars and that of the banking sector around 140 billion dollars with particularly severe constraints being imposed in the short term since the company sector is scheduled to pay back (barring rescheduling or a moratorium) 150 billion dollars between now and the spring of 2011 and the banking sector some 60 billion on the same schedule. Such repayment constraints are based on the supposition that the confidence needed to relaunch international financial flows will have been restored and that the central administration will be inclined and prompt to continue to uphold the local money and restimulate the economic activity of the whole range of production.[8] If this turns out not to be the case, then the reimbursement of the short-term debts of companies and of the banking sector could

---

[8] As well as being a question of political willpower, such action also depends on the raw materials market. This objective constraint automatically reduces the margin for maneuver toward the further diversification of the production and exporting structures of the Russian economy and the modernization of its infrastructures. Since, the 2010 State budget has been drawn up on the basis of a barrel of Ural oil at US$58, the consolidation of the money exchange rates, the recovery of accounts and the capacity to pay back industrial and bank debts will largely depend on the extent to which this price of oil can be higher, in a significant and durable way, at the end of 2009, in 2010, and 2011 at the minimum.

prove to be particularly difficult and will quite simply compromise household access to credit, and, as a consequence, will have a long-lasting effect on one of the motors of recent Russian growth, namely the equipment and provision of household goods and general consumption. The worst scenario would be a drying up of liquidities, leading to arrears and delays in wage payments and intermediary deliveries: in short, a certain demonetization of economic relations with a return to exchange through barter, incompatible with a strong and sustainable growth in line with the economic capacity objectives of the Russian Federation.

8.4. The Necessity for Modernization of the Russian Economy and for a Transition Toward a Post-Industrial Knowledge-Based Economy[9]

The strong dynamic of growth observed in Russia in recent years — first stimulated by the devaluation of the ruble following the financial crisis of August 1998 which restored competitiveness in prices for national production — is therefore largely explained by the favorable conjunction of circumstances in terms of real prices on the world market of oil and gas resources. The rise in gas and oil prices and world demand coupled with a very steady domestic consumer demand explains for the most part the growth in the gross domestic product which was above 6.5% on a yearly

---

[9] A knowledge-based economy is understood as being one in which production and services are based on an acceleration of the rhythm of advancement of technologies and of science, including also the acceptance of rapid obsolescence. The key element of the knowledge economy is a greater dependence on intellectual capacities and attributes rather than physical inputs and natural resources. This orientation is mainly fed by the emergence of new industries in which a range of technological progress engenders increases in productivity. A knowledge-based economy is also one which favors intellectual analysis of institutional economic factors alongside actors in its implementation and development, with value placed more and more on an environment which prioritizes new ideas, management through projects, innovative financial circuits, electronic management control, and coordination of available services. A knowledge-based economy is characterized by the recognition that knowledge (mental skills and intellectual competence leading to mastery and use of new technology) is the prime source of competitiveness, which implies giving accrued importance to scientific research, technology, and innovation in applying new creating thinking (Rooney *et al.*, 2003; UNDP, 2004; World Bank, 2006, 2009a).

average over the period 2000 to 2008 (Table 8.2). Up to 2008, the country accumulated more than 420 billion dollars in exchange reserves to which should be added, on the one hand a "stabilization fund" of about 125 billion dollars and on the other hand a "national well-being fund" of 32 billion dollars[10] (that is, together, more than 40% of the national wealth), which placed Russia in third place in the world in this respect, behind Japan and China.[11] During this prosperous period, the growth of the capitalization of Russian companies was clearly linked to the price of oil on the international market (Gref, 2006, Figure 8.1). It was also a period of renewed confidence in Russia and of a certain distancing from western countries, inclined to recognize Russia as a major economic power. This clear economic upturn therefore led to a hardening of Russia's diplomatic relations, with Russian leaders becoming convinced that Russia no long needed the West. In February 2007, the 43rd Conference

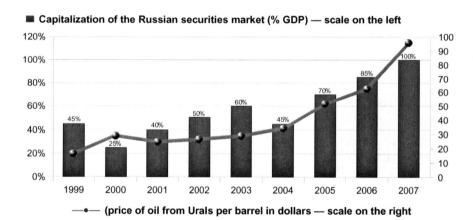

Figure 8.1. Movement in capitalization of Russian securities market (in % of GDP) and Urals oil price.

Source: Russian National Statistics.

---

[10] The "stabilization fund" is a reserve fund aiming to offset fluctuations in world gas and oil prices; the "well-being" fund exists to cushion the social effects of the current unstable economic circumstances.

[11] In January 2008, the country made its entry into the club of the 10 principal world economies, alongside Brazil, India, Mexico, and South Korea.

on World Security in Munich gave president Vladimir Putin the opportunity to express the extent of his divergences with the West and with the United States in particular (the enlargement of NATO, the Iranian nuclear question, the anti-missile shield project in eastern Europe, the militarization of space by the United States or the perception of a systematic and longstanding western interference in internal Russian affairs).

Nonetheless, the potential for the Russian economic model based on "exports of raw materials" clearly shows its limitations. It has not led to a sufficient diversification of the structure of production or to the institutional development which is indispensable for confirming and consolidating growth over a long period. Moreover, the number of Russian firms capable of playing a significant role on external world markets and in world growth sectors is quite insufficient, "except for oil and gas." So the paradox is that, in spite of results by Russian industrial and financial operators characterized by important and rapid returns on investment, the solidity of the growth is not for all that assured. Investments in innovative research and development seem to be insufficient (Figure 8.2) to position Russia on the international level yet.

This point is a fundamental one, and politicians, on the lookout for quick results, recognize the immediate potential effect of the oil market price on the economy and therefore continue to give priority to oil price in the short term. Even the brilliant economist A. Klepach, present vice-minister of Economic Development and Trade, reputed for his analyses of the impact of proactive industrial policies and structural reforms (Brunat and Klepach, 2007), seems now concentrating on the short-term constraints and expressing satisfaction that GDP growth forecasts for 2010 are convergent with those carried out by the World Bank and the European Bank for Reconstruction and Development (around +3% to + 4.3%) using as his principal argument the sustained interest of the world economy in Russian oil from the Urals at a forecast price which is well above that of 58 US$: the figure used in constructing the 2010 budget.[12] The sheer weight of exports of raw materials (Table 8.4) diverts the attention of the State, which should be turned toward a development strategy for the sectors of health, education, the knowledge-based economy, and new technologies in general.

---

[12] See the *Moscow Times* of November 16, 2009, "Klepach signals 2010 optimism."

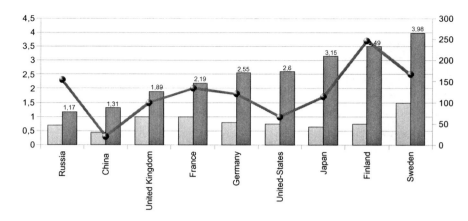

Figure 8.2. Internal expenditure on R&D in different countries (in % of GDP) — scale on left. Volume of personnel engaged in R&D — researchers and other personnel — per 10,000 employees, red curve, and scale on right (for year 2004 and following years where data available). Global internal expenditure on R&D column on right, public internal expenditure R&D column on left.

Sources: OECD and Gref (2006).

Table 8.4. Structure of Russian imports and exports in percentage 2008.

	Raw materials and energy	Agricultural products	Services and others	Manufactured products
Imports	3	12	24	61
Exports	63	4	10	23

Source: World Trade Organization: WTO and CEPII data base CHELEM.

The importance of the new economy (the knowledge economy) is still largely underestimated by the public authorities, in spite of the injunctions of President Medvedev.[13] The country's top industrialists do

---

[13] See kremlin@gov.ru. President Dmitri Medvedev, in his State-of-the-Nation address on November 12, 2009. The modernization of the Russian economy was the central point of the speech, including the importance of dedicated science parks as Skolkovo. For example (this district near Moscow has been selected as the site for a huge science park, where the government will invest billions of dollars to help boost the nation's technology industry).

not accord sufficient priority to education and research in order to make it the driving force of the market economy. With the acceleration of innovation and the sophistication and expansion of new processes, competition in the modern world more and more implies a competition in knowledge and *savoir-faire*, not only concerning conception and production, but also in the diffusion and reception of the new processes. Thus, the development of a powerful education system, of initial as well as higher education, but particularly of professional training, is absolutely necessary as an element of competitive differentiation. This means also in the Russian case, not only supporting research and development (R&D) and organizing it according to international standards, but also saving, preserving, and utilizing the technological and human skills, developed during the Soviet period. The United Nations considered that the system of initial instruction and the attainment of a general culture was one of the best assets of the Soviet Union, comparatively speaking, and this notably in the fields of aviation and astronautics, nuclear physics, and laser technology, for example (UNDP, 2004). Today, however, economic success prevails for the most part in the field of extraction and distribution of crude oil and other hydrocarbons, other raw materials, closed-circuit commercial networks, and only very partially in services in general.

On the other hand, Russia is behind, compared with European and international standards, methods, and priorities in the following fields: the development of branches such as transport infrastructure (which helps greatly to reduce the transaction costs); new and innovative production; development of technology parks or business parks linking together universities and enterprises; logistical centers for transport and other modern diversified forms of communication; application of modern technologies; and organizational methods integrating new knowledge-based expertise and management into regional and local government in the interests of creating new activities and jobs. The principal consequence of this "business skills deficit" and the lack of long-term investment in research is of a nature to render Russian products and services uncompetitive on the international market, leaving in place habits and attitudes which are only looking for a quick return on

228 *Eric Brunat*

money invested, including a "rent-seeking behavior" (Rosefielde, 2005).[14]

The consolidation of economic growth in Russia and the facilitation of its transformation in terms of human development presuppose the active creation of a modern educational system on several levels, founded on the best traditions of Russian "enlightened" ideas, while at the same time facilitating its integration into the European educational scene and university–business partnerships (Brunat *et al.*, 2007), and also incorporating the idea of developing public–private types of partnerships for certain heavy investment projects aimed at reinforcing joint responsibility (Makarov, 2003). Getting businesses involved — for example through their financial involvement — in the educational domain is a sensitive subject, and one which rapidly becomes political. But here it is more a question of promoting active cooperation in terms of applied and finalized research, taking part in the complex management procedures involved and in the production of new knowledge and outlooks which can be integrated and developed in terms of the productive process.

The economic crisis now, however, places a limit on this type of commitment by firms. Windows of opportunity were partly wasted at the beginning of the year 2000, but it should now be agreed that there is no time to lose in bringing together production processes and the production of knowledge, once the short-term financial burdens have been absorbed. Traditionally, the real economy and industrial affairs have been cut off from the world of research in Russia. There are yawning gaps between creation and application, as well as between strategic action and the short-term interests of business. It is an institutional problem as well as a question of political culture involving two different ways of looking at the world. Moreover, present financial constraints are clearly not helping to bring these two together. The very low level of interest shown by Russian business structures in study projects, case studies, and research

---

[14] See also M.A. Dmitriev's materials and notes for a report presented to a seminar of the "KalEdu" project (Kaliningrad — Education) of the European Union presented to the Kaliningrad government on May 29, 2007. E Brunat possesses this unpublished material and can make it available.

has led to a distinct break between creative activities and the application of resultant knowledge, exemplified in deficient and inefficient cooperation between science and production. The private financing of R&D in developed countries is in general markedly more important than public budgetary credits, whereas in Russia the reverse is the case (Brunat, 2010).

The relative degree of importance of intangible assets, social capital as part of global capital (global wealth) in Russia compared with produced capital or natural capital (natural resources) is represented in Figure 8.3, based on work carried out by the World Bank (2006). According to the Bank's classification, the comparison of Russia with high-income countries, intermediate-income countries and even with the poorest countries is blatant, in terms of the makeup of total wealth. Natural resources largely dominate in Russia's case, whereas capital in the form of intangible assets is clearly the most important for all three groups of countries analyzed. From this point of view, the comparison is not to the advantage of Russia, even compared with the group of low-income countries: as a percentage of global capital, Russia utilizes four times less intangible capital and almost two times more natural resources. According to this, particularly interesting approach of measuring the weight of social capital

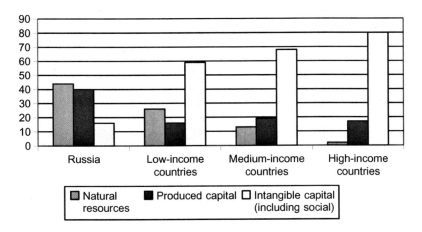

Figure 8.3. Structure of the wealth of nations in percentage.
Source: World Bank, 2006.

230   *Eric Brunat*

and the sustainable nature of growth,[15] the structure of Russian capital is not far from that of Venezuela or of Gabon (Brunat, 2010). This type of capital structure is a terrible devorer of resources and, in consequence, is not sustainable.

To the symptoms of Russia's rentier economy (rent-seeking economy) (Rosefielde, 2005; Aslund, 2007; Brunat and Klepach, 2007) and the present crisis, at least three types of specific difficulties, which heavily handicap the modernization of the economy and society, can be added:

1. the lack of large-scale national champions — leaving aside energy leaders such as Gazprom or Rosneft — capable of playing a global role or providing a driving force for research;
2. the chronic weakness of small enterprises whose total number and weight in terms of employment and their contribution to the GDP are going up but remain below the realities of the main market economies[16]; and

---

[15] The indicators used at present for measuring development level are seriously faulty. National accounting indices, such as the GDP, do not necessarily reflect the beneficial effects of education or health expenditure nor costs linked to the degradation of the environment. The World Bank (2006) proposes a new method of evaluating the total national wealth of countries, taking into account produced capital, natural resources, but also social and human capital. This new approach allows us to begin to characterize and quantify sustainable development. Thus, it points up the disparities between the different development paths chosen by countries. It appears that whole groups of countries, of whom Russia is one, are not taking a sustainable path, notably because in these countries the management of natural resources is very questionable.

[16] President Dmitry Medvedev (speech at Tobolsk on March 27, 2008 and speech to the Nation on November 12, 2009) is favorable to the suppression of barriers curbing the development of small and medium-sized enterprises (SME) and argues in favor of lightening administrative procedures. "The principal cause of the slow development of SME is the extreme heaviness of administration." D. Medvedev noted that the contribution of SME to the Russian GDP was less than 17% and that the share of knowledge-based industries is extremely low: less that 1%: these latter being virtually inexistent in informational science and technology. In order to start a company, a Russian entrepreneur has to produce a long list of documents, of which most are not mentioned in federal legislation. Besides, "numerous laws dating from the Soviet period, disconnected from reality, are still in force.

3. a falling natural demography, with emigration of the most dynamic and the best trained segment of the population.[17]

This particular situation suggests a need for a cultural and institutional evolution in the very meaning of economic development and social transformation, and as a consequence, the need for a strong political will and commitment in the short and the medium term.

Today, the growth of modern services and technologies comes up against a whole series of obstacles posed by a serious dearth of qualified manpower, the dominance of large units of production (notably the production and commercialization of energy) which distorts the employment market and wage and price formation, and a training supply which is moving away from the sciences and the fields of past excellence (technology, mathematics, theoretical and applied physics) and which need to adapt to the needs of a more competitive economy, capable of generating a more assured and sustainable growth.

The new fields of knowledge are at the heart of the required new development, which should be more economical with resources in order to merit the label "sustainable." In his messages addressed to the country's Federal Assembly in recent years, Vladimir Putin has repeatedly drawn attention to the necessity of effecting a transition toward a new

---

And the updating of technical regulations is extremely slow." In addition, inspections, aimed at the business world, are carried out for 45 reasons and by more than 30 agencies, and that is only at the federal level, with the imposition of many other "unofficial" controls. The result is that companies spend more than 10% of their turnover on all sorts of inspection and verification procedures.

[17] In most industrialized countries, the mortality rate is falling and life expectancy increasing. This is not the case in Russia. The birth rate, as in many European countries, is low (1.4 children per woman in 2007, 1.2 in 2006), but mortality is particularly high, particularly for men. One man out of three dies between 20 and 60 years old; Russian men have today a life expectancy of 61 years (73 for women) whereas it was 63.8 years in the 1960s (75 years in developed countries) (Vychnevski, 2009). In addition, the means allocated to healthcare are insufficient. In 2007, Russia spent on health 4.2% of its GDP compared with an average of 8% to 10% in Western countries. The result of this is a negative balance and a lasting fall in population, from 148.9 million inhabitants at the beginning of 1993, to 141.7 million in April 2009, according to the State Statistics Committee (Rosstat).

paradigm of development for the country and its regions. "In the conditions of strong international competition in the world in which we live, the economic expansion of the country must essentially and increasingly be conditioned by its scientific and technological advantages (...) We must take proactive and decisive steps to encourage growth of investment in the industrial infrastructure and to promote innovation to assure us of a worthy position in the international division of labor."[18] The appeal for modernization made by President Medvedev on November 12, 2009, in his annual speech to the Nation also tends in this same direction.

The major innovations required (which we term generic) as well as those which can be termed less important (those inscribed on a technological improvement path) presuppose new ways of looking at things as well as new fundamental knowledge acquisition, both with a view to accelerating the competitive transition to a knowledge-based economy (UNDP, 2004 and Brunat *et al.*, 2004). It is true that the objective of passing to a "knowledge-based economy" is officially acknowledged and also that public policy is being reinforced in this direction. On the other hand, the delay incurred is worrying and recent observed tendencies are not yet correcting the growth model, based on a "rent-seeking economy" and on immediate results or "quick returns on quick investments."

The new ambitions of Russia are collated in the report of July 2007 of the Ministry of Economic Development and Trade, entitled "The Conception of economic development of Russia up to 2020" (MEDT, 2007). It points to three possible scenarios for economic growth. The first, on the conservative side, supports the model which is still operational today, based on the dominance of dependable income (the "rent economy"); the second relates to the massive promotion of exports of natural resources the results of which could be oriented more to industrial diversification of a more voluntarist nature; and finally the third which, though a long way from current reality, has the support of recent declarations for long-term policy development, which is the model

---

[18] See in the directory of messages of the Presidency delivered to the Federal Assembly of Russia, the message of May 10, 2006 (electronic resource: http://president.kremlin.ru).

founded on innovation and knowledge, presupposing the definition of priorities and objectives as well as measuring the knowledge economy[19] (see Table 8.5).

The objectives of the third scenario are particularly ambitious, if not out-of-reach, without the adoption of policies which are radically proactive[20] and without the implementation of a truly comprehensive industrial policy (Brunat and Klepach, 2007), and these are henceforth heavily compromised by the world economic crisis. Nonetheless, according to this scenario, Russia should take an important place, of around 10% of world markets, for high technology products and services in "four to six domains." That presupposes that internal expenditure on research and development (IERD) reaches 3.5% of GDP (compared with less than 1.5% today), and no less than 5% to 6% of GDP for education (as against 3.6% in 2006) (see Table 8.6).

---

[19] Measuring the knowledge economy is about the return of investment in science which can be measured through productivity trends (the GDP per employee, for example). The Competitiveness Index of the World Economic Forum can also be an element in the calculation. The relative proportion of high technology products in exports, the external technological balance of trade, the share of world patents and product licences, and so on can also be part of the parameters of evaluation. It is however the World Bank which has set up the most advanced tool of analysis and measurement (World Bank Institute, 2008; World Bank, 2009a): their "Knowledge Economy Index" establishes a method for measuring the knowledge economy under the generic phrase "Knowledge for Development" or K4D.

K4D is based on the Knowledge Assessment Methodology — KAM — which is a model which itself is based on about 110 structural and qualitative variables taken from 146 countries and based on four chief categories: (1) institutional incentives to promote knowledge production and creation of activities; (2) the density of the network of enterprises, universities, research centers, and technological centers, that is to say the National Innovation System (NIS); (3) the educated proportion of the population, both through initial training and lifelong learning; (4) the technologies and infrastructures of information and communication — TIC (including their production and dissemination). All these are collated into the KEI — Knowledge Economy Index — emerging in a general weighted and reconstituted index of competitiveness on a scale going from 0 to 10 (see Brunat, 2009, 2010).

[20] Financial sanctions are envisaged for enterprises and prioritized branches of industry, as for Universities and Research Institutes, which do not modernize or innovate, at all, or not to a sufficient extent (Declaration in April 2007 of S. Ivanov, Deputy prime minister of Russia, quoted in Kastouéva-Jean, 2008).

234　*Eric Brunat*

Table 8.5. Comparison of the knowledge economy index of several nations. Indexes recomposed by the World Bank from 0 to 10.

Country	World ranking	Knowledge economy index	Institutional system of knowledge production	National innovation system	Education	Information technology (TIC)
Denmark	1	9,52	9,61	9,49	9,78	9,21
United States	9	9,02	9,04	9,47	8,74	8,83
Germany	12	8,96	9,06	8,94	8,36	9,47
Japan	20	8,42	7,81	9,22	8,67	8,00
France	22	8,40	7,67	8,66	9,02	8,26
Russia	60	5,55	1,76	6,88	7,19	6,38
China	81	4,47	3,90	5,44	4,20	4,33

Source: World Bank (2009a), http://info.worldbank.org/etools/kam2/KAM_page5.asp.

The improvement in quality of higher education provision, in both its initial and professional training, presupposes the highlighting of certain human factors concerning localization and technological and industrial know-how: factors which have declined in importance but which remain relevant and concern the cultivation of a qualified manpower, open to change. The development of international cooperation, incentives for developing interfaces between universities and enterprises, promotion of specific scientific zones or "technoparks,"[21] setting-up of clear legal

---

[21] See note 13. With the development of territorial structures, with public support and in cooperation with small and medium-sized enterprises, the question of the number (related to the density of small structures in order to benefit from positive externalities in a competitive context) and their proximity (short distances are advantageous for successful localization decisions) (Pecqueur, 1989; Courlet, 2008; World Bank, 2009b). It is interesting to note that the World Bank with its World Development Report in 2009, "Reshaping Economic Geography" stresses the crucial and urgent character of spatial transformations and the importance of linking distances. Three principal dimensions/arguments are advanced on three levels for favoring growth: (1) the importance of human and company density (for economies of scale and critical mass featuring as positive factors as more important than the negative factors such as congestion or "ghetto-ization" — this is the *local argument*; (2) the reduction in (physical) distances, thus facilitating human movement. This human movement reduces the distances for fulfilling economic opportunities

frameworks which are both transparent and stable at both the national and the regional level, promotion of public and private research, promotion of European formats in education and in new technologies, institutional cooperation toward the setting up of public–private partnerships are actions and recommendations which should contribute to the institutional, economic, social, and human development of Russia. In this context, work must be pursued toward establishing policies concerning patents and property rights: work which is at present in its infancy and terribly counterproductive in its effects.

To move toward a knowledge economy and reflect on a new form of development, there is a need to create synergies in terms of economic flows, analyses of regional integration, and the contribution of institutionalist economists (Williamson, 1975, 1989; North, 2005), all of which points to the importance of cooperation including the concept of "competition-cooperation" (Brunat, 2009, 2010), to the proximity and density of structures

Table 8.6. Comparison between the data for 2005–2006 and the 2020 objectives of the ministry of economic development and trade of the Russian federation (in %) — MEDT.

	Data 2005–2006	Objectives 2020
Proportion of high technology in the Russian GDP	10.5 in 2006	17 to 20
Contribution of innovative sectors in the annual growth of GDP	1.3 in 2006	2.5 to 3
Proportion of industrial enterprises involved in technological innovation	9.3 in 2005	40 to 50
Proportion of innovative products in industrial production	2.5 in 2005	25 to 35
IERD as % of GDP	1.24 in 2006	3.5 to 4
Education expenditure as % of GDP	3.6 in 2006	5 to 6

Sources: MEDT (2007); Kastouéva-Jean (2008).

(urban centers, coastal zones, building connections, and so on) — this is the *national argument*; (3), less divisions and administrative obstacles between countries and territories. Frontiers should no longer be seen as factors of divisiveness but as facilitating link-ups — this is the *international argument*.

236   *Eric Brunat*

better organized in a horizontal fashion, to the provision of local link-ups of development "from the bottom up." The synergy of these paradigms and the renewal of development presupposes a strong and committed public policy which must include the following elements:

1. a cooperative vision of development and the institutions necessary to bring it about;
2. modernized infrastructures for education and health provision;
3. cooperation between the agents of local development including the forming of networks for purposes of solidarity and exchange;
4. the emergence and then the densification of small and medium-sized enterprises over a given space;
5. the consolidation and structuring through the statement of objectives of economic intelligence in given territories as a strategic element in development;
6. the emergence of essential social infrastructures[22] as also the provision of services offered, paying as well as free (transport and overall logistical support having an impact on productivity, efficiency, and the lowering of the transaction costs);
7. facilitating access to the financing of modern technology and private research (fiscal incentives, risk capital, and so on) as well as public research (through voluntarist and proactive public policy).

A modernized Russia must go beyond short-term constraints and its "rent economy" cultural structure in order to play its full constructive role among the emerging countries (the BRIC — Brazil, Russia, India, and China) and beyond that, in the G8 and the G20. What is at stake is transforming what could be a return to economic growth in 2010 into a move forward in human development. To build a competitive knowledge-based society, breaking with a society, based on extensive exports of energy and natural resources, Russia must therefore invest massively in research and education, reinforcing its economic and legal institutions as well as the

---

[22] At the present time, social expenditure represents less than 5% of the GDP, and this should be multiplied by a factor of 4 to 5 to reach the minimum standards of modern societies.

diffusion and relative standing of its information and knowledge-based systems. However, in order to achieve this, an opening to the outside world, a balanced international cooperation together with a shared political will and a vision of the long term are necessary prerequisites.

8.5. The Importance of a Renewed External Policy: A Regional "Soft Power" Independent Policy is not Sufficient to Stimulate the Modernization Process

The international component, as much for commercial flows as concerning direct foreign investment or technological cooperation, is an essential dimension of the modernization process for the Russian economy (Garanina, 2009). Since the beginning of the new century, Russia is much more present and distinctly more on the offensive on the international scene, but this has revealed a contradictory facet which has not so far been successfully addressed. On the one hand, it is a question of defending a multipolar world, leaving room for dialogue, and pluralist expression of economic, political, cultural, and religious expression in order to humanize the asymmetric and a-rhythmic aspects of western liberal globalization (and thereby guaranteeing a place for societal, cultural, and linguistic Russian specificities in the interplay of nations); on the other hand, making use of a very firm rhetoric (itself the product of refound confidence with the macroeconomic prosperity of the years 2000) to restore a power which had been lost. On this last point, Russia, which likes to see itself as part of the "great European house,"[23] is nonetheless reticent, if not hostile, to the West and its uniform conception of the world (Foucher, 2009; Brunat, 2010).

---

[23] A recent opinion poll carried out by the VtsIOM (Ordzhonikidze, 2007) shows that, in 2006, 63% of Russians interviewed (especially the older generation and those coming from less-favored social backgrounds) thought that "western culture" had a negative influence on life in Russia. It seems also that there is confusion in people's minds between the perception of the European Union as a developing integrated economic and political entity and their conception of Europe in history and in geography. According to this study carried out by Levada and his team and produced by Ordzhonikidze, 75% of Russians in 2006 think that Russia is a Eurasian State which follows its own line of development. This "turning in on oneself" and withdrawal seems to reflect the diplomatic low points and hardening attitudes of the Russia–Western dialogue in recent years.

238 *Eric Brunat*

The energy weapon, frequently brandished, is a reflection of these tensions which are symptomatic of a hybrid foreign policy (Delcour, 2008) which tends nonetheless in the direction of adapting to the world rather than breaking with the world in an isolationist way. The tone of the Russian–Western power relationships is largely inherited from the Soviet period but is now nourished by the will to take control of its own destiny that the influence of Western expertise has largely ignored since 1992. Russian diplomacy has its underlying principles: Russia wishes to take its rightful place more than to dominate. It is probably that the gradual crumbling of its privileged sphere of influence, without dialogue or compensation, has contributed to the hardening of attitudes, once its recovered growth allowed the resentment to be expressed. The European Union has proposed little to Russia since the enlargement of the Union process begun in the 1990s (Brunat *et al.*, 2004). NATO continues to enlarge its sphere of influence as if the Cold War remained the driving force of the balance of power whereas the ideological content behind confrontation has disappeared. The United States, which is a minor economic partner compared with the European Union (Table 8.7) continues to prefer a weak Russia to a strong Russia and tends to ride roughshod over Russian sensitivities with a defence policy which was often unilateral over the recent years (for example, the planned setting up of an antimissile shield with medium and long-range missiles to be installed in Poland and in the Czech Republic).

In this context, the European Union is truly the key economic partner of the Russian Federation. Its weight in the external flows of the country is six

Table 8.7. Russia's commercial partners as percentage of total in 2005.

	Belarus	**Japan**	**United-States**	**China**	**Ukraine**	**European Union**	**Others**
Imports	6	6	7	7	8	44	22

	Switzerland	**Belarus**	**China**	**Ukraine**	**United States**	**European Union**	**Others**
Exports	4	5	5	5	7	50	24

Source: Data WTO.

to seven times greater than that of the United States, in volume and value. In fact, multilateral economic world policies cannot be realized without the existence of a mutually profitable and more peaceful framework between the two entities. This presupposes that the oil and gas provisioning of the Union is made secure and that serious thought is finally given to the integration of Russia in a sufficiently attractive European Common Economic Area which is capable of going beyond the present level of cooperation between businesses or between European and Russian institutions. At a time when Asia is emerging as a massive actor on the international economic and political stage and a new dialogue is emerging, more complex, logical and deeper, between the American and Chinese powers, it is not in Russia's interests to play the isolationist card. With the Europe–United States liaison assured both in practice and in its essence, the isolation of Russia would compromise the solidity of its growth and its development. Also, it is not in Europe's interests to have on its frontier a weakened, unstable, and protectionist Russia, wrongly convinced that it can face on its own the complexities of the 21st century (Brunat, 2006). The specificities of Russia, its vision of the world, strength in terms of energy, and human resources, (although seriously hindered in its dynamics through a catastrophic demographic distribution and evolution over its rich territory of 17 million square kilometres) constitute essential elements in European growth in its widest sense. Therefore, a strengthened dialogue and an increasingly successful integrated cooperation (notably through its joining the WTO) should facilitate the modernization of Russia, while at the same time making secure gas supplies to Europe in the framework of economically realistic supply projects.[24]

---

[24] There are three quite grandiose schemes for future gas supplies in Europe, and this is not realistic given the costs of implementation, as well as climate warming and economic growth forecasts for Europe up to 2020 and above all because of the desire to make meaningful economies in energy use. Two projects have been initiated with Russia (Gazprom) with European link-ups for France with EDF and GDF-Suez and Germany with massive commitments particularly with BASF and E.On. These concern on the one hand a Baltic project "North Stream" for supplies to northern Europe and Germany as early as 2010–2011 and on the other hand a "South Stream" project which should supply southern and central Europe (Greece, Italy, and Austria in particular) with Russia and Kazak gas from 2015–2016 onward. It seems clear that by bypassing the Ukraine and including non-Russian gas in the "South Stream" (from Kazakhstan and Turkmenistan in particular),

240 *Eric Brunat*

The modernization and diversification of the Russian economy are two keys to the dialogue of Russia with advanced market-economy countries, implying the necessary strengthened cooperation of Russia — Europe. It is worth remembering in this respect that, apart from military equipment, Russian exports of manufactured goods were weak in 2008 (hardly above 10% of exports) and very largely destined for countries in the Community of Independent States (CIS): in other words, countries with low or medium incomes in the World Bank definition. The mediocre industrial productivity and unsatisfactory product quality mean that Russian production is less attractive in the consumer markets of advanced countries.

In order to rectify this situation and favor the modernization of fixed capital, a change of strategy is needed. The present protectionist temptations of Russia must be overcome as soon as possible in order to favor organizational and technological modernization within the framework of action based on a diversified and proactive industrial policy of the State and international cooperation via the reactivation of direct foreign investments (Table 8.8).

It should, however, be pointed out that the crisis has also allowed Russia to recover a role as a relatively active regional operator. Often more affected than Russia by the socioeconomic destabilization induced by the world crisis, several countries of the CIS have appealed for help to Moscow which has replied quickly and favorably with a contribution of almost eight billion dollars to an anti-crisis fund (endowed with 10 billion) principally intended for the liquidity needs of the Eurasec countries, the Eurasian Economic Community.[25] In part, no doubt as a consequence of the financial crisis, a form of "soft power" (Condé, 2009) seems to be

---

Gazprom and Russia wish to control Europe's gas supply. It is precisely to attenuate this possible dependence that the European Commission (and the United States) envisage a third project "Nabucco" as a rival to the "South Stream" pipeline, with the aim of importing gas from Iran and Azerbaijan through Turkey and without the participation of Gazprom. The question is, beyond the geo-political and geo-economic circumstances, whether such concurrent investments are really realistic.

[25] Eurasec was set up in 2000 and includes as well as Russia, Belarus, Kazakhstan, Kirgizstan, and Tajikistan.

Table 8.8.   Direct foreign investments — DFI: comparison of Russia, Ukraine, and Poland.

	2005			2006			2007		
	Russia	**Ukraine**	**Poland**	**Russia**	**Ukraine**	**Poland**	**Russia**	**Ukraine**	**Poland**
Flow of incoming FDI (billion US$)	12,9	7,8	10,4	32,4	5,6	19,2	52,5	9,9	17,6
Stocks of FDI (billion US$)	180,3	17,2	90,7	271,6	23,1	124,5	324,1	38	142,1
Performance indicator (1) classification/141 économies	89	35	60	87	37	57	81	35	60
Number of "greenfield" investments (2)	512	125	270	386	124	323	363	104	333
Incoming FDI (as % of GFCF (3)	9,5	41,2	18,7	17,8	21,1	28,5	19,3	25,6	18,7
Stock of FDI (as % of the GDP)	23,6	20,0	29,8	27,6	21,5	36,4	25,1	27,0	33,8
Stock of FDI per inhabitant (in thousands US$)	/	/	/	/	/	/	2287,0 *(141,7 millions popul.)*	817,0 *(46,5 millions popul.)*	3730,0 *(38,1 millions popul.)*

Sources: UNCTAD (2008), http://www.unctad.org/sections/dite_dir/docs/wir08_fs_ru_en.pdf.

(1) The performance indicator of CNUCED is based on the proportion of the country's incoming FDI in the world total incoming FDI and its share in the world GDP.

(2) Investments are called "greenfield" when corresponding to the creation of new subsidiary companies *ex nihilo* by a mother company.

(3) The gross fixed capital formation (GFCF) is an indicator measuring the sum of investments carried out during a year.

replacing the more radical reactions and traditional "power-play" politics of Russia in its sphere of influence with its closest neighbors. This new diplomatic approach leans more on giving cultural, financial, and economic support (Russia being now considered as an "emerging net donor" country in United Nations terms) and confers on the country a more important regional influence. Supporting these adjacent sovereign powers (often sweetened with an effective financial aid package for its immediate neighbors, notably in Moldova and Central Asia) is often now understood as a possible alternative to pursuing a liberal Western market economy. Influence, through culture and the media, directly or indirectly, is gradually being substituted for power politics, and this has been received with much approval and has moderated hostile reactions. Restoring the euroasiatic orientation as a partial alternative to looking to the West, or even to Europe, is now explicitly under study, but this would bring greater reliance on narrow and fragile economies and regimes which are often authoritarian and would not help Russia with its road map toward a necessary economic modernization.

8.6. Conclusion: The Europe–Russia Relationship and the Potential Effects Accruing from Membership of the WTO must be the Driving Force for Modernization

The relationship between the European Union and Russia is more important and durable, tactically and strategically, that the euroasiatic orientation which is weak on the economic and institutional level. It is also more realistic than the Russia–United States axis in terms of geography, the volume of exchanges and importance of cooperative programs. The development of institutions and the clarification/stabilization of the juridical framework, the affirmation of a State based on integrity, and the rule of law as the guarantor of Russia's specific societal values, together with the renewal coming from membership of the WTO are the determining factors for the future of the country (Matelly, 2008). The integration of Russia in the world economy reinforces the imperative need for structural reforms, the modernization of industry, and the promotion of new knowledge-based ideas and production. The precise vision of a postindustrial Russia, oriented more toward production and service consumption, is still insufficient. The process of Russian application and membership to the World Trade Organization is again a laborious one, because of the transfer of power in the United States and the financial crisis. Moreover, the member-states of the WTO are preoccupied with completing the laborious cycle of the Doha negotiations. Thus, Russian membership no longer seems to have the urgent priority stamp on it which it has had in recent years and this as much from the WTO's point of view as from the reiterated Russian interest, expressed by its principal negotiator Maxim Medvedkov. Moreover, the measures taken to help banks and national industries in Europe and the United States in order to attenuate the effects of the crisis have not in themselves been a reason to slow down the negotiations with Russia, but these measures have been in fundamental contradiction with the precepts and the basic rules of the Organization which rejects any mechanism which distorts competition. This is why, through default, that the Russian membership negotiations have been put on ice. More fundamentally, although Russia has terminated its bilateral negotiations with many countries, no global agreement has yet been reached. The Russian minister of Economic Development and Trade is now talking of 2011, or even beyond, as the prospective likely date of Russian membership of the WTO: the long process of negotiations on this membership having begun way back in 1995. After long and tortuous negotiations, its membership of WTO was called into question both by Moscow and the United States in August 2008 after Russia's armed intervention in Georgia. Moreover, the recent decision of Russia to join the WTO at the same time as Belarus and of Kazakhstan, rather than on her own, reflects the disenchantment of Russian ruling élites with the Organization and shows that it does not any longer officially consider membership as a priority. In effect, the debate is the same as that of ten years ago. For certain Russians, Russia does not need the WTO to the extent that it remains essentially a raw materials exporter (metals, oil, and gas): a sector which is not regulated by the Organization. This argument is reinforced by the weak competitiveness of Russian manufactured products: entering the WTO would, in this view, have very negative effects in the short term.

Others do not share this approach, and quite rightly. The Russian economy, to modernize itself, needs stimulus through competition and direct foreign investments. The WTO would provide therefore a favorable framework, with exceptional temporary protection in a probationary

244　*Eric Brunat*

period, giving time for structural and institutional adjustment. Having said this, Russia is henceforth the last economic power not to be integrated into the multilateral commercial system.

A study by the Russian European Center for Economic Policy in Moscow sought in 2002 to measure the impact of structural changes even in the case of very disrupted sectors of the economy and identify the comparative and competitive advantages of Russia in its interaction with the international environment, and including the European Union.[26] This type of study seems to us to need to be carried out anew in relation with the re-launch of negotiations for the Russian Federation joining the WTO, with the study treating the whole question of the opening of Russia to the world economy. Joining the WTO would facilitate the definition of the contours and the content of a Common European Economic Area to include Russia, the principle of which must be studied anew; as also an agreement with the European Union on the *Acquis Communautaire* would assure an important part of the obligations required for membership of the WTO. There are a number of advantages that Russian membership of the WTO would certainly promote:

1. a stimulation of productivity both globally and by sector and a stimulation toward modernization, moving toward a knowledge-based economy and toward a production of goods and services in a context of protection of industrial and intellectual property rights;
2. easier access to markets by the extension of the most favored nation clause[27];
3. the abandonment in a progressive but programmed way of social dumping practices;
4. a lowering of trading costs and a growth in competitiveness;
5. an economy and a society more concerned with savings and long-term investment, in order to consolidate recovered growth and facilitate human development;

---

[26] See Soos *et al.* (2002) and Sharipova (2002).

[27] This argument does not convince certain Russian economists and political experts who are very opposed to joining and who consider that by proceeding through bilateral treaties Russia benefits from equivalent treatment.

6. the judgement of the concert of nations that Russia has a "normal" economy inscribed in a long-term historical process;
7. the defining of a truly coherent programme of modernization and an ordered production process: a program which should principally relate to the European economy.

References

Aslund, A (2007). *Russia's Capitalist Revolution, Why Market Reform Succeeded and Democracy Failed.* Washington, DC: Peterson Institute for International Economics, p. 356.

Attali, J (2009). *La crise et après.* Paris: Poche, Paris, p. 186.

Brunat, E (2006). Europe needs a stable Russia. *Pro Economic Journal*, 14, November 20–26 (in Russian).

Brunat, E (2009). Economie de la connaissance, réseaux de formation et dynamique territoriale en Russie. In *Compétitivité et Accumulation de Compétences dans la Mondialisation:Comparaisons Internationales*, Guerraoui, D and X Richet (eds.), *Editions ARCI et L'Harmattan*, pp. 377–402, Paris: Rabat et Paris.

Brunat, E (2010). L'économie russe: Modernisation, crise et géo-économie. *Annuaire Français de Relations Internationales*, XI, 157–184.

Brunat, E *et al.* (2004). National innovation system: The basis of Russia's knowledge economy in "Towards a knowledge based society." *Human Development Report*, Russian Federation, November 2004, UNDP.

Brunat, E *et al.* (eds) (2007). Integrated Cross-Modular Learning Programme in Business and Public Administration: Towards Oriented Regional Programme, 2 Volumes, p. 490 and p. 332, I. Kant State University of Russia Publishing House, Kaliningrad, Russia (in Russian and English).

Brunat, E, X Greffe, V Mau , V Novikov and I Samson (eds.) (2004). *Common Economic Space and the Perspectives of the EU-Russia relations* Moscow: Izdatelstvo "Delo" Publishing, p. 240.

Brunat, E and A Klepach (2007). Productivity and competitiveness: Challenges for the Russian Economy: Room for a more proactive policy? In *Globalisation in China, India and Russia*, Huchet, JF, X Richet, J Ruet (eds.), p. 364, New Delhi: Academic Foundation in association with Center de Sciences Humaines, and University of Paris III Sorbonne Nouvelle.

246 Eric Brunat

Colosimo, JF (2008). *L'Apocalypse Russe* (Dieu au pays de Dostoïevski), Paris: Fayard, p. 358.

Condé, P (2009). La crise en Russie. *La Revue Géopolitique*. www.diploweb.com/La-crise-en-Russie.html. October.

Connolly, R (2009). Financial vulnerabilities in Russia. *Russian Analytical Digest*, 65, 1–6, www.res.ethz.ch and www.laender-analysen.de.

Courlet, C (2008). *L'économie Territoriale*. Collection l'économie en plus, PUG, Grenoble, p. 135.

Delcour, L (2008).(under the direction). La Russie, entre héritages et mutations. *La Revue Internationale et Stratégique,* 68, IRIS, 2007/2008.

Dockès, P, F Fukuyama, M Guillaume and P Sloterdijk (2009). *Jours de Colère–L'esprit du Capitalisme*. Paris: Éditions Descartes & Cie, p. 160.

Entin, M (2007). Relations entre la russie et l'union européenne: Hier, aujourd'hui, et demain. *Géoéconomie*, 43, 35–57.

Fontanel, J (2005). *La Globalisation en 'Analyse', Géoéconomie et Stratégie des Acteurs*. L'Harmattan (ed.). Paris, p. 627.

Foucher, M (2009). *L'Europe et l'Avenir du Monde*. Paris: Odile Jacob, p. 142.

Garanina, O (2009). *La Russie dans l'Économie Mondiale*, L'Harmattan (ed.). Paris, p. 327.

Gauchon, P (ed.) (2008). *Le Monde. Manuel de Géopolitique et de Géoéconomie*. Paris: Collection Major, PUF, p. 914.

Grandville, B and P Oppenheimer (eds.) (2001). *Russia's Post-Communist Economy*. Oxford: Oxford University Press, p. 551.

Gref, G (2006). Rapport au Gouvernement de la Fédération de Russie du 17.08.06 [electronic resource]. http://www.economy.gov.ru/wps/portal.

Hayashi, H (2009). Social impact of the global economic crisis in Russia. *The Journal of Comparative Economic Studies*, 5, 47–60.

Ivanter, V and J Sapir (2008). La situation de l'économie russe dans le cours de la crise financière internationale. Séminaire EHESS, Paris, October 23.

Kastouéva-Jean, T (2008). *Enseignement supérieur, clé de la compétitivité russe*. Russie. Nei. Visions No. 28, IFRI, Center Russie/NEI, April.

Kuznetsov, B (2009). Russia and the global crisis. *The Journal of Comparative Economic Studies*, 5, 25–45.

Kuznetsov, OL (2005). Problèmes de la construction de la société du savoir dans la Russie contemporaine: Mythes, bases, perspectives. *EKO Économie et Organisation de la Production Industrielle,* N°8, 40–46.

Levada, Y (2000). From opinion to understanding. *Library of the Moscow School of Political Research*, Moscou (in Russian).

Makarov, VL (2003). Economie du savoir: Quelles leçons pour la Russie. *Vesti, Académie Nationale des Sciences de la Russie*, 73(5), 450–456.

Mandeville, L (2008). *La Reconquête Russe*. Paris: Grasset, p. 391.

Matelly, S (2008). La Russie et l'OMC: un intérêt réciproque mais des enjeux contradictoires. In L Delcour (ed.), La Russie, entre héritages et mutations, *La Revue Internationale et Stratégique*, No.68, IRIS, winter 2007/2008.

MEDT (2007). *Conception du Développement Économique de la Russie Jusqu'en 2020* (electronic resource).www.economy.gov.ru, Moscow, July.

North, D (2005). *Understanding the Process of Economic Change*. Princeton, NJ: Princeton University Press, p. 187.

Ordzhonikidze, M (2007). La Russie et l'Occident, une enquête d'opinion. *Géoéconomie*, 43, 89–97.

Pecqueur, B (1989). *Le Développement Local : Mode ou Modèle?* Paris: Editions Syros, p. 149.

Raviot, JR (2008). *Démocratie à la Russe*, Paris: Ellipses, p. 158.

Rooney, D, G Hearn, T Mandeville and R Joseph (2003). *Public Policy in Knowledge-Based Economies: Foundations and Frameworks*. Cheltenham, UK: Edward Elgar, p. 206.

Rosefielde, S (2005). *Russia in the 21st Century, the Prodigal Superpower*. Cambridge, UK: Cambridge University Press, p. 244.

Rosefielde, S (2009). Russia's aborted transition: 7000 days and counting, Working Paper, December, p. 23.

Rosstat (2008, 2009). Données statistiques du Comité d'Etat aux Statistiques de la Fédération de Russie.

Sapir, J (2008). La Russie en 2008. Bilan économique et social des "années Poutine," *Historiens et Géographes*, N°402.

Sharipova, E (2002). Euro-zone financial criteria: Application for CEECs and questions for Russia. *Russian European Center for Economic Policy*, Working Paper, March.

Soos, KA, E Ivleva and I Levina (2002). The Russian manufacturing industry in the mirror of its exports to the European Union. *Russian European Center for Economic Policy*, Working Paper, March.

UNCTAD (2008).World investment report, http://www.unctad.org/sections/dite_dir/docs/wir08_fs_ru_en.pdf.

UNDP (2004). *Towards a Knowledge Based Society*. Moscow: National Human Development Report, Russian Federation, UNDP, November.

Vychnevski, A (2009). *Les Enjeux de la Crise Démographique en Russie*. Paris: Institut Français des Relations Internationales (IFRI), June.

Williamson, OE (1975). *Market and Hierarchies — Analysis and Antitrust Implications*. New York: Free Press.

Williamson, OE (1989). Transaction cost economics. In *Handbook of Industrial Organization*, R Schmalensee and RD Willig (eds.), Vol. 1, 135–183. North-Holland: Elsevier Science Publishers B.V.

World Bank (2006). *Where is the Wealth of Nations: Measuring Capital for 21st Century*. Washington DC: World Bank, p. 188.

World Bank (2009a). *K4D, Knowledge for Development Programme*, www.worldbank.org.

World Bank (2009b). *World Development Report 2009 "Reshaping Economic Geography,"* www.worldbank.org.

World Bank Institute (2008). *Measuring Knowledge in the World's Economies*. Washington DC: World Bank Institute, p. 10.

Yasin, Y (2003). "Russian soul" and economic modernisation, Russia in global affairs. *Journal on Foreign Affairs and International Relations*, 4, September, http://eng.globalaffairs.ru/.

PART IV

EXPORT-LED MODERNIZATION AND DECOUPLING

CHAPTER 9

EXPORT-LED DEVELOPMENT AND DOLLAR RESERVE HOARDING

STEVEN ROSEFIELDE
University of North Carolina, Chapel Hill

9.1. Black Swan Risk

Financial crises are riveting experiences because there is always the chance that the fire this time will be catastrophic, even though history shows that "Black Swan" disasters are extremely rare.[1] At the crisis's onset, scholars diagnose symptoms, round up the usual suspects, identify novel elements, prescribe remedies, scour the past for clues about the shape of things to come,[2] and prognosticate.

The global financial crisis of 2008 was not an exception. At first, panic led many to fear the worst, but cooler heads gradually prevailed, reassured by policymakers' confident claims that their timely interventions had limited the down draft to a severe recession, averting any possibility of a Black Swan debacle. The Troubled Asset Relief Program (TARP) and quantitative easing (QE2) are said to have saved the financial system, forestalled deflation, and dampened what might otherwise have been a disastrous drop in aggregate effective demand. Moreover, world leaders contend that tomorrow's prosperity has been insured by "stress tests" that make Western financial institutions invulnerable to speculative assaults, together with a host of regulatory

---

[1] Taleb, N (2007). *The Black Swan: The Impact of the Highly Improbable*. New York: Random House.

[2] Reinhart, C and K Rogov (2009). *This Time is Different: Eight Centuries of Financial Folly*. Princeton, NJ: Princeton University Press.

252   Steven Rosefielde

reforms including better "mark to market" illiquid asset-pricing, improved US Security and Exchange Commission (SEC) fiduciary oversight against recurrent Harry Madoff type Ponzi frauds, enhanced supervision of derivatives and electronic trading, and subprime mortgage prohibitions. Also, belts have been tightened, and steps taken to repair toxic assets.

However, one crucial vulnerability has been left unattended and could prove to be the world economy's Achilles' Heel. Global policymakers have been completely stymied by Chinese dollar reserve hoarding: a novel and important aspect of the 2008 financial crisis that continues to fester and intensify. China's dollar reserve holdings have grown astronomically since it joined the WTO. Beijing held approximately 250 billion dollars in foreign reserves in 2001: a third less than Japan. Nine years later, the figure has risen to 2.6 trillion dollars, more than double Tokyo's holdings and continues to rapidly rise.[3] If this recent trend persists, China's dollar reserve holdings could increase to 24 trillion dollars. The exact number is not important.[4] What matters is that China's mounting dollar reserve hoard is a barometer of Black Swan risk that should, but is not being given adequate attention either because policymakers do not see the Black Swan connection, or believe that market forces and "rationality" will bring about an amicable compromise. Both attitudes reflect a profound misunderstanding of China's market communist economic system.

---

[3] When China joined the WTO in September 2001, it held approximately 250 billion dollars in foreign reserves: a third less than Japan. See Haymond, J (2008). Living in interesting times: The economics of a Chinese currency attack. *Strategic Studies Quarterly*, Winer, 84–105. Nine years later, the figure rose to 2.6 trillion dollars, more than double Tokyo's holdings. See Wikipedia, "Foreign Exchange Reserves". IMF currency reserve holding data are expressed in dollars, even though a portion of these "dollars" are actually held in other hard currencies. A modest and changing portion of the 2.6 trillion dollars reported for China in the text are held in euros, yen and some other currencies.

[4] Projecting last decade's dollar reserve holdings forward, Chinese stealthy protectionism could cause a 24 trillion dollar shortfall in American aggregate effective demand. See www.tradingeconomics.com. However, the benchmark may be seriously misleading. Dollar reserve accumulation in 2010 has slowed, implying a Chinese reserve hoard around five trillion dollars in 2020, assuming that 500 billion dollars of Beijing's total holdings are legitimate transactionary and precautionary reserves.

9.2. Patchwork Pragmatism

China is not a "normal" self-regulating free enterprise market economy.[5] It is a communist, state-controlled, market-assisted system. The state overrides the market and is in command, especially in foreign trade, where its actions have been driven by patchwork pragmatism rather than competitive free enterprise.

Patchwork communism has led Chinese policymakers along a path that allowed them to discover how to reconcile opposites within the new globalist liberal trade order by successfully overtrading (overexporting), underimporting, and shifting much of the resulting adjustment burden to other nations, while nimbly avoiding retaliation and receiving plaudits for improved creditworthiness. The tactics employed to achieve these outcomes look like modern surrogates for the Hawley-Smoot Tariff Act (second highest in American history, imposed June 17, 1930), complete with "beggar-thy-neighbor" unemployment effects,[6] but Beijing flatly denies any protectionist intent.

---

[5] Rosefielde, S. Russia: An abnormal country. *Journal of Comparative Economics*, 2(1), 3–16. Shleifer, A and D Treisman. A normal country. *Foreign Affairs*, 84(2), 20–38.

[6] Protectionism in the 1930s was blatant. Republicans, including presidential candidate Herbert Hoover lobbied ardently for the Hawley-Smoot Tariff. The retaliation that ensued was equally overt, as were efforts to penetrate tariff walls with competitive devaluations and export subsidies. The fundamentals were straightforward. Protectionists in the importables sector sought to increase production, employment, prices, wages and profits by erecting high tariff walls and imposing quantitative restrictions (quotas), while their counterparts in the exportables sector lobbied for production and marketing subsidies, supplemented with currency devaluations. Protectionists claimed that these strategies were win-win for the home team. All domestic constituencies it was contended would be better off at the expense of foreigners forced to curb their exports and absorb cheap American imports. Moreover, protectionism could be made partly or wholly self-financing by using tariff revenues to subsidize exports. Protectionists understood that this beggar-thy-neighbor approach to domestic prosperity was mean spirited, and could provoke trade-destroying retaliation as every nation tried to prosper at others' expense, but assured critics that benefits would exceed costs. They did not contest Adam Smith and David Ricardo, acknowledging that free trade could make every nation better off, but counterclaimed that America would prosper even more by taking advantage of foreigners.

254 *Steven Rosefielde*

Its foreign trade practices given core Keynesian assumptions,[7] willy nilly cause at least some of the West's high unemployment in the import-competing (importables) and export (exportables) sectors. Spurred by an exchange rate intentionally set to make goods artificially inexpensive (implicit subsidization), China exports more goods to the West than it should, forcing American and EU importables manufactures to reduce production and domestic employment. Free traders acknowledge these lost importable sector jobs (currently estimated for America at 2.4 million),[8] but contend that increased Chinese imports create compensating employment opportunities in America's and Europe's export sectors. On balance, trade liberals insist that all China's foreign partners, together with the Middle Kingdom itself win, despite some unavoidable losses, claiming that society's gain exceeds trade victims' pain.

This tough love judgment is realistic as long as the facts fit. Sino–Western trade, however, deviates from the script. Jobs in the exportables sector have not increased to compensate for positions lost in the importables sector because Beijing refuses to purchase Western imports with its export earnings. China today is sitting on more than two trillion dollars in hoarded foreign exchange reserves (total, less transactionary and precautionary reserves), all accumulated after it joined the WTO in 2001; a figure likely to double by 2020 at the current rate of dollar reserve growth. Consequently, as many as eight million contemporary American lost jobs can be plausibly imputed to China's dollar reserve hoarding, with millions more to come, as Beijing's excess dollar reserves mount.

---

[7] Keynes, JM (1936). *The General Theory of Employment, Interest and Money*. London: Macmillan. Keynes accepted all aspects of Adam Smith's concepts of supply and demand, but rejected the claim that markets automatically and instantaneously maintain full employment equilibrium ("Says" law) because of the difficulty of identifying equilibrium wages and price when income is falling (sticky wages). He and later economists have elaborated on these and other rigidities, without reaching a consensus other than acknowledging that rigidities are real and are responsible for involuntary unemployment that should not otherwise exist.

[8] An Economic Policy Institute report, "Unfair China Trade Costs Local Jobs," March 2010 estimates that China's excess export practices have cost American workers 2.4 million jobs since 2001, when China joined the WTO. www.epi.org.

9.3. The Conundrum

This paradox of "job destroying free trade," driven as it is by accumulating dollar reserve hoarding, is a key aspect of the Black Swan risk, flummoxing contemporary American statesmen and international policymakers. It belies liberal predictions, and Chinese denials of beggar-thy-neighbor protectionist intent,[9] and poses a treble conundrum.

1. Why do Western free traders find it so difficult to believe that Beijing might misbehave?
2. Why is not China maximizing competitive gains from trade?
3. What should be done?

The first question is easily answered. Free traders are perplexed because they never knew or forgot that communist foreign trade patterns are determined by party agendas that subordinate *laissez-faire* profit-maximizing and consumer utility-seeking to domestic and international political priorities. Chinese policymakers can and do substitute their own for outsider market preferences and have created the instruments needed to control all aspects of foreign trade. The state owns the means of production, leasing assets to "private" companies. It has the administrative authority to ban whatever foreign business activities it chooses on the mainland, prohibit export sales, bar foreign imports, subsidize, tax, set foreign exchange rates, and most important of all require exporters to surrender their dollar earnings (at the border) to the state

---

[9] Political considerations permit limited protectionism today in developed countries in a handful of sensitive sectors, especially agriculture, and there are "dirty floats," but for the most part, free trade principles are "workably" in command. Quotas are prohibited, and tariffs are a small fraction of previous levels. These principles are supposed to hold in developing nations like China, admitted to the WTO in 2001 on a concessionary basis. New entrants are permitted to protect themselves more than established advanced nations, but also are expected to eliminate quotas, reduce tariffs and subsidies, and set exchange rates to assure rough balance on the merchandise account as time goes by. All rhetorically endorse free trade and liberalization, and claim to comply with their WTO obligations, giving the misleading impression that protectionism is off the radar screen.

bank.[10] China has a communist market system, but free traders fail to appreciate that this does not make the market king.[11] It is the party, not the market that ultimately is in command. Beijing marches to its own drummer, and pretending that this comes to the same thing as maximizing private gains from trade is not enough to assure that China's foreign trade behavior, including dollar reserve hoarding, conforms with free trade expectations.

Two aspects of this free trade myopia deserve special attention. First, and foremost, it is essential to understand that the Chinese foreign exchange rate is not competitively determined by the forces of supply and demand. Exporters including Western multinational corporations, operating on the mainland, are required by law to surrender their dollar earnings to the government on terms (foreign exchange rate) fixed by the state.[12] In a competitive environment, the renminbi would appreciate as state dollar reserves increased (diminishing dollar utility), but in China the leadership can set the rate as it pleases. Beijing, at its sole discretion can even depreciate the renminbi further, despite accumulating excess dollar reserves, if it desires to increase export subsidies. There is

---

[10] West, L (1993). Reform of China's Foreign Trade System and Prospects for Freer Trade. Center for International Research, U.S. Bureau of the Census, CIR Staff Paper No. 69.

[11] The Chinese people own the means of production. The communist party as the people's custodian leases assets as it sees fit. There is no freehold property and no rule of law. As a consequence, the state controls trade directly and indirectly through its lessor, command, administrative, supervisory, and regulatory managerial powers.

[12] The Foreign Exchange Administration Regulations of the People's Republic of China provide that all payment transactions in mainland China must be settled with renminbi, the Chinese currency. However, this restrictive foreign exchange regime does not bind companies located in a special economic zone (SEZ). Subject to the required documentation, payments between a SEZ company and its offshore counterpart should in general be settled in a foreign currency. Transactions between a SEZ company and Chinese entities registered inside or outside the SEZ may be settled by using renminbi or by another foreign currency. See Chen, C (2010). Operating business in Chinese free trade zones (August). *Taylor Wessing Newsletter*. Multinational companies operating outside a SEZ must purchase renminbi with dollar export earnings FOB. These renminbi are not freely convertible, so that companies desiring to wind down their businesses must receive special permission to convert, transfer holdings to other entities, or over-invoice dollar intermediate good import purchases abroad. This could create immense problems if multinational corporations collectively seek to repatriate their Chinese assets.

Export-Led Development and Dollar Reserve Hoarding 257

no automatic foreign exchange rate mechanism that can restore foreign trade equilibrium against the party's will.[13] Second, there is no automatic market mechanism that compels the party to disgorge its dollar reserve hoard to would-be importers, including the Chinese people who are its rightful owners. Presumably, if the Chinese people were given two thousand dollars each, they would not have any difficulty finding Western goods to purchase, but their preferences cannot countervail the party's decision to hoard.[14] Clearly then, those expecting the invisible hand to set China's foreign trade pattern right, do not adequately grasp the institutional realities.

Still, foreign trade liberalizers have a point. From their perspective, China pays an exorbitantly high inefficiency price for overtrading, overexporting, underimporting and dollar reserve hoarding which rational Beijing leaders should be trying to minimize, not increase.[15]

---

[13] State controlled trading systems frequently fix their foreign exchange rates at disequilibrium levels, causing them to over or under trade, and in the process over (under) import and export. This is called forced substitution. Under such disequilibrium conditions, if the state spends its entire foreign currency receipts on imports, the foreign trade market "clears," but there is only the semblance of equilibrium, not real equilibrium because if the foreign exchange rate were permitted to competitively adjust, "market clearing" would occur at a different activity level. Persistent surpluses and deficits in general competitive regimes only can occur if one party desires to hold a portion of foreign currency receipts in foreign financial instruments, or currency reserves, and the other party accommodates. Imbalances of these kinds are "optimal," not indicators of involuntary disequilibrium. Most state trading nations like the Soviet Union of yesteryear strive for market clearing, or maintain small precautionary surpluses. China's state-controlled trading is aberrant. See Rosefielde, S (1973). *Soviet International Trade in Heckscher-Ohlin Perspective.* Lexinton, MA: Heath Lexington; Holzman, F (1963). Foreign trade. In *Economic Trends in the Soviet Union*, Bergson, A and S Kuznets (eds.). Cambridge, MA: Harvard University Press.

[14] The author vetted this idea at the People's Liberation Army Academy of Science conference, "The Economic Crisis — Implications for Global Security," Beijing, held July 13–17, 2009. The women officers conceded that they would have no difficulty spending such windfalls on their families' behalf.

[15] Free trade theory teaches that protectionism, or similar behavior, driven by other motives, has substantial microeconomic efficiency costs for China and its trading "partners," compounded by potentially severe macroeconomic losses borne mostly by China's victims. On the micro side of the ledger, resources are suboptimally allocated at home and

Overtrading and overexporting necessarily mean that China could increase its GDP and social welfare merely by reducing its trade participation, curbing its exports, and redeploying the resources saved to best use in the domestic importable sectors. Chinese foreign trade specialists appear to understand this, and the leadership recently has begun encouraging a transition from export-led to a balanced development strategy.[16] Nonetheless, by resisting substantial renminbi appreciation, policymakers also are signaling a reluctance to tamper with success. Renminbi undervaluation has made China a magnet for foreign direct investors and outsourcers seeking a low cost production platform that has expedited technology transfers and turbocharged economic growth, and many are content to leave well enough alone.[17]

Dollar reserve hoarding and the underimporting it has entailed however are zebras of very different stripe. The official position is that Beijing cannot find enough Western goods worth importing, other than weapons

---

abroad, with China suffering additionally from low returns to its "idle" dollar balances, together with sundry forms of debt and inflationary risk. China's "partners" are harmed by underemployment in both the importables and exportables sectors, and mass unemployment generally when automatic job adjustment fails as it routinely does in Keynesian models. Beijing's accumulation of idle dollar balances, moreover spurs inflationary and speculative financial behavior in China and across the globe. Excessively easy credit and subequilibrium interest rates raise the risk of 2008-type financial crises and global mass unemployment that can harm everyone including China. The path to trade-destroying rack and ruin under stealthy and overt protectionism differ, but the ultimate result is apt to be the same. Protectionism often seems to be a good idea to those who enjoy adversarial games, but more often than not, it is almost universally detrimental.

[16] Leightner, J (2012). Chinese Protectionism. In *Prevention and Crisis Management: Lessons for Asia from the 2008 Crisis*, Rosefielde, S, M Kuboniwa and S Mizobata (eds.). Singapore: World Scientific Publishers. Cf. Fisher, E (2012). Optimal Asian Dollar Surplus. In *Prevention and Crisis Management*.

[17] China employs an export-led development strategy, meaning that it overtrades compared to the competitive ideal. Beijing stresses exports over importables development because institutional rigidities in the importables sector make export profit opportunities greater abroad than at home. Capitalizing on these second best opportunities is sensible, but Beijing carries the strategy too far by undervaluing the renminbi with respect to the second best. This is difficult to prove statistically because state controls distort wages and prices, but party leaders appear to agree because they have been callings of late for the replacement of export-led with balanced modernization.

Export-Led Development and Dollar Reserve Hoarding   259

technologies the Pentagon refuses to sell.[18] The explanation is frivolous. Western exportables may appear dear to state import authorities, but this is the unavoidable consequence of Beijing's undervaluing the renminbi. Appreciate the renminbi enough under competitive market conditions, and Western exports will immediately deplete China's excess dollar holdings.

The true explanation(s) must lie elsewhere, but plausible benign justifications are hard to find. The best that can be conjectured is that the leadership believes that returns on the money it lends directly and indirectly exceed investing the funds at home.[19] Alternatively, the leadership might have an exaggerated perception of international financial and domestic political risks, driving it to accumulate excessive precautionary foreign reserves. This fear factor, ascribed by some to the trauma of the 1997 Asia financial crisis,[20] may make sense for low precautionary dollar reserve accumulations, but not for dollar reserve hoarding mounting into the trillions. Other motives are even less convincing. China leaders surely cannot be so afraid of the Chinese people that they cannot distribute a portion of the hoard to its citizens. Nor, is it plausible to claim that the leadership is so irrational that it cannot grasp the wastefulness of hoarding.

---

[18] The generals at the People's Liberation Army Academy of Science conference, "The Economic Crisis-Implications for Global Security," Beijing held during July 13–17, 2009 complained that America was responsible for China's huge dollar reserve holdings because it would not sell the PLA-sensitive military technology.

[19] Fisher, E (2012). Optimal Asian Dollar Surplus. In *Prevention and Crisis Management: Lessons for Asia from the 2008 Crisis*, Rosefielde, S, M Kuboniwa and S Mizobata (eds.). Singapore: World Scientific Publishers.

[20] Fourteen years ago, South Korea, Thailand, Malaysia, Singapore, Indonesia, and the Philippines were enjoying export-led growth spurts and strong balance of payments surpluses, just like China now, and thought that their dollar reserves were sufficient to stem foreseeable speculative assaults. Then, sentiment changed, prompting foreign investors to abruptly repatriate short-term loans. They sold local currencies for dollars (yen) at fire sale prices, contracting credit and forcing nations across the region to sharply devalue their foreign exchange rates. Policymakers burnt by capital flight and the subsequent depression, learned their lesson. Dollar reserve holdings were increased throughout the region, including China even though Beijing's state-controlled trade mechanism had saved the nation from devaluation and arrested economic growth. Asia's decision to deepen its dollar reserve holdings was prudent. Leaders everywhere vowed to prevent another financial crisis. However, Beijing's response was excessive. Although, it weathered the 1997 tempest unscathed without being forced to devalue the renminbi, China increased its dollar reserve disproportionately. Modestly bolstering reserves was wise; dollar hoarding was not so.

260 Steven Rosefielde

This brings us through the process of elimination to a set of more disreputable motives, divisible into two categories: stealthy (undeclared) protectionism and the pursuit of economic power. Stealthy underimporting logically complements aspects of Beijing's motive to overexport. The party may find it politic to indulge privileged domestic producers in both its exportables and importables sectors with subsidies and anticompetitive protection that enhance profits and rents. Stealthy protectionism here is merely a matter of insiders using their foreign trade control powers to enrich themselves and loyal supporters,[21] with little or no thought given to the policy's impact on outsiders, domestic and foreign alike. Alternatively, the party might have decided more altruistically to employ stealthy import protectionism to bolster domestic employment, with or without any further intention of beggaring its neighbors.[22] Both rationales are pragmatic and therefore plausible, but also incompatible with China's obligations as a WTO member to the international community.

Worse still, Beijing could be hoarding excess dollar reserves to enhance its economic power. China's 2.6 trillion dollar reserve conveys an impression of economic might, useful for pressuring neighbors into accommodating the regional hegemon.[23] Or, more aggressively, party

---

[21] Rosefielde, S (2011). *Asian Economic Systems*, unpublished manuscript. Rosefielde, S (2011). After Soviet communism: Authoritarian economic evolution in Russia and China. In *Pekka Sutela Festschrift*, I Korhonen (ed.). Helsinki: Bank of Finland. pp. 81–92, Cf. Abdelal, R and A Segal (2007). Has globalization passed its peak? *Foreign Affairs*, 86(1),103–114. Gaddy, C and B Ickes (2001). *Russia's Addiction: The Political Economy of Resource Dependence.* Washington, DC: Brookings. Gaddy and Ickes assert that the Russian economy is run on a mafia business model. The concept applies to China as well because both countries rely heavily on state insider rent-granting.

[22] Ken Miller contends that Chinese leaders dollar reserve-hoard not so much to make its importables sector more profitable, but to save jobs. See Miller, K (2010). Coping with China's financial power: Beijing's financial foreign policy. *Foreign Affairs*, 89(4). http://www.foreignaffairs.com/articles/66466/ken-miller/coping-with-chinas-financial-power. Cf. Aaronson, S (2010). How China's employment problems became trade problems. *Global Economy Journal*, 10(3), Article 2.

[23] China buys up the world (November 13, 2010). *The Economist*, p. 11. Sutherland, P (2008). Transforming nations. *Foreign Affairs*, 87(2),125–136. Kleine-Ahlbrandt, S and A Small (2008). China's new dictatorship diplomacy. *Foreign Affairs*, 87(1), 38–56. Kaplan, R (2010). China's grand map. *Foreign Affairs*, 89(3), 22–41.

leaders may be waging stealthy economic war by inflicting mass unemployment on the West, and otherwise destabilizing the global financial system, while denying any such intentions.

9.4. Perversity

At the end of the day, stealth protectionism seems the least implausible of the various possibilities, but there is no reason to exclude other dubious motives. Trade liberalizers are right to feel that Beijing's dollar reserve-hoarding and underimporting are injuriously to its welfare, but Western policymakers must still face the fact that China's communist leaders are tenacious.

9.5. Storm Warnings

There seems little chance that Beijing will have an epiphany any time soon. The leadership may cosmetically adjust the renminbi, but this does not come to the same thing as slowing, depleting, or reversing China's dollar reserve hoard. Therefore, our Black Swan barometer, which already is in the red zone, almost certainly will soon signal the imminent approach of a category 5 hurricane, capable of causing a Great Depression, with catastrophic mass unemployment, underproduction, financial chaos, and social turmoil.

9.6. What Should Be Done?

The best solution to China's foreign trade challenge, assuming that communist party leaders will not soon abandon state-controlled trading, foreign exchange rate-fixing, renminbi undervaluation, and dollar reserve hoarding is to improve Western macroeconomic policy management to eliminate domestic unemployment. In principle, if the Chinese are intent on holding idle cash balances, in effect refusing to accept payment for their exports, the West should thank Beijing for the gift and allow domestic wages and prices to fall until aggregate purchasing power equals aggregate full employment equilibrium supply (Say's Law).

Most economists, especially United States Federal Reserve Chairman Ben Bernanke, however, recalling the Great Depression, are unwilling to take the risk that wage and price deflation will worsen unemployment.[24] They prefer monetary and fiscal solutions like increasing the money supply(QE2), lowering interest rates, and fiscal deficit spending (Troubled Asset Relief Program [TARP]), but the stimulus to date has barely dented unemployment.[25] More recently, Western governments have started hinting that the unemployed should grin and bear it, trying to defuse the political impact of intractable double-digit unemployment. Monetary authorities also have assured the public that stern measures will be taken to control speculative bubbles, linked to excess global liquidity generated by Chinese dollar reserve hoarding and the West's accommodative monetary and fiscal policies, although, here, the evidence suggests that they are failing.[26] Muddling through in these ways no doubt is the course of least resistance, but the strategy is not failsafe. China not only can continually intensify Western unemployment by increasing its dollar reserve hoard, but attendant political pressures could easily trigger competitive devaluations, and beggar-thy-neighbor protectionist policies across the board, resurrecting the mentality that many believe caused the Great Depression. There is no evidence that China's leaders want this to happen, but it may well happen if Beijing is recalcitrant.

Perhaps, fortune will smile, and the West will be spared the worst, but for the proactive there is another option free traders abhor; fighting fire with fire. The West can prevent Beijing from increasing its dollar hoard by reciprocally restricting Chinese exports. Beijing is using a buyers strike to close its ports, and the West can respond tit for tat (blow for blow) with dollar for dollar import quotas. This Axelrod-Rapoport type disciplinary

---

[24] Bernanke, B (2004). *Essays on the Great Depression*. Princeton, NJ: Princeton University Press.

[25] Razin, A and S Rosefielde (2012). The 2008–2009 Global Crisis. In Prevention and Crisis Management: Lessons for Asia from the 2000 Crisis, Rosefielde, S, M Kuboniwa and S Mizobata,(eds.). Singapore: World Scientific Publishers.

[26] Stockman, D (2010). Banana Republic finance: Why Keynes is rolling in his grave (December 9, 2010). *Yahoo! Finance.*

Export-Led Development and Dollar Reserve Hoarding 263

sanction is surgical.[27] It targets the Sino–Western trade imbalance exclusively, without prohibiting or taxing the bulk of Chinese exports, or harming third parties. Moreover, the tactic is trade-diverting rather than trade-suppressing. Any nation willing to abide by free trade principles can substitute its goods for barred Chinese exports. Western importers will have to pay more for these third party substitutes because the Chinese are least-cost vendors, but this loss will be compensated by reduced Western unemployment. If, as assumed, third parties are competitive and do not dollar reserve hoard, they will spend their dollar export earnings on Western imports. Also, policymakers should make it clear that the West disapproves of bilateral balancing and is not interested in playing tit for tat for its own sake. It is only acting to alleviate a multitude of greater evils including beggar-thy-neighbor global economic war, hyperdepression, mass unemployment, deflation, financial ruin, and social upheaval.[28]

Tit-for-tat solutions are flexible. The basic concept can be modified with warnings, consultations, and negotiations. If this fails, tit for tat can be introduced gradually, beginning with small import ban quotas, increased as required. Gradualism might be more powerful than some suppose because as third parties begin to capture part of China's export market, outsourcing and foreign direct investment will shift in tandem. Foreign direct investment and the free technology transfer it provides are important

---

[27] For a discussion of tit-for-tat games and nuances in optimal decision making, associated with the "prisoner's dilemma," see Axelrod, R (1984). *The Evolution of Cooperation*. New York: Basic Books; Rapoport, A (1960). *Fights, Games and Debates*, Ann Arbor: University of Michigan Press.

[28] Theory teaches that protectionism is doubly bad because it impairs competition and can lead to beggar-thy-neighbor policies that partly or wholly cause mass unemployment and global depression. Postwar leaders convinced that high tariffs and competitive devaluations were responsible for the intensity and duration of the Great Depression created an array of institutions to prevent its recurrence, including the Bretton Woods accord, International Monetary Fund (IMF), International Bank for Reconstruction and Development (IBRD), the World Bank, the General Agreement on Tariffs and Trade(GATT), and the World Trade Organization(WTO). They claimed that free trade conducted under the rule of law, with equilibrium either achieved through the adjustable peg, or a competitive flexible exchange rate mechanism would optimize the global division of labor, spur economic development, and foster worldwide macroeconomic stability. Experience seems to have validated their vision; the severity of the 2008 financial crisis and its aftermath notwithstanding.

drivers of Chinese economic growth, and reducing these inflows is sure to catch party leaders' attention.[29]

Gradualism also seems in order to forestall unnecessarily heated confrontations that might divide American constituencies and adversely affect business sentiment, sparking deflationary expectations and reducing income velocities of money and Keynesian multipliers. Western exporters, outsourcers, foreign direct investors, and free trade purists can be expected to vigorously oppose any remedial policy that jeopardizes their livelihoods, and the polemics could harm business confidence, essential for full post-crisis recovery. The waters will be roiled further by hypocritical Chinese claims that the West is being provocative. The tit-for-tat solution thus, although seemingly attractive, nonetheless is not foolproof and will require delicate judgment and deft handling to bolster employment and strengthen the free trade order, with minimal collateral damage.[30]

Still, prospective benefits probably vastly outweigh expected risks. A two trillion dollar tit-for-tat jolt in aggregate effective demand generated by some combination of increased Chinese and third party imports (twice TARP and treble QE2) should produce a salutatory macroeconomic response. Western exports and employment should surge, together with business confidence, income velocities of money, and Keynesian multipliers, contributing mightily toward the reattainment of full employment GDP in the West and across the globe. This solution also should work later if the treatment is deferred, but only up to some unknown threshold when the world economy is plunged into a catastrophic free fall, impervious to simple remedies. Thus, while it may seem paradoxical, temporarily curtailing the cash hoarding aspect of Sino–West free trade today may be just the ticket for strengthening the free trade system in the long run and permanently averting a Chinese-generated Black Swan.

The Obama administration has been tiptoeing in this direction, but does not yet sufficiently comprehend the special role played by dollar reserve hoarding as distinct from renminbi undervaluation in China's underimportation of Western goods. Tim Geithner, United States Secretary

---

[29] Gilboy, G (2004). The myth behind China's miracle. *Foreign Affairs*, 83(4), 33–48.

[30] Policymakers in deliberating on this matter should not forget the microeconomic benefits of Chinese dollar reserve hoarding, including the global competitive benefits of outsourcing.

of the Treasury, recently vetted a plan addressed to G20 countries to cut trade imbalances to less than 4% of their output:[31] a suggestion which went beyond coaxing China to appreciate the renminbi on traditional microeconomic efficiency grounds, broaching the sensitive issue of quantitative targets and controls. The trial balloon was swiftly met with catcalls from numerous quarters and withdrawn before the November 2010 G20 meeting in Seoul. Bernanke followed suit shortly thereafter condemning Chinese overtrading and was accused in turn by Beijing of fomenting a new cold war.[32] These skirmishes reveal that progress toward creating a level playing field, where state-controlled trading is properly disciplined is unlikely to succeed without cogent macroeconomic and trade war-averting justifications. Nor should it be mis-supposed that Adam Smith's "invisible hand" in any of its numerous manifestations including factor productivity changes in America and China can coax Beijing roundabout into acting as free traders feel it ought. State-controlled trading regimes can flout market forces whenever the party leadership believes that it is in its interest to do so, and the West can only defend its interests by forcefully engaging them. Thus, although doing nothing other than chiding the Chinese for undervaluing the renminbi is the path of least resistance, it is apt to be ineffectual. The issue cannot be dodged as long as Beijing sticks to its guns. The West must either vigorously engage China on the twin issues of state-controlled trading and dollar reserve hoarding, or be "beggared" by accepting a degraded global trading system and mass unemployment, compounded by secondary exchange rate, monetary, and financial disorders that could reach Black Swan proportions.[33]

---

[31] US drops call for trade surplus target amid dollar spat. BBC News Business. November 8, 2010, http://www.bbc.co.uk/news/business-11708005.

[32] Ewing, J and S Chan (2010). Echoing Obama, Bernanke Press China on imbalances (November 18, 2010). *New York Times*. China knocks US plan to pump money into the system (November 8, 2010). *Yahoo Finance*. China accused the United States of creating conditions for another global financial bubble by indulging in quantitative easing; a euphemism for printing money (or monetizing the debt). Cf. China and Germany belittle U.S. actions before G20 (November 5, 2010). *Yahoo Finance*.

[33] Razin, A and S Rosefielde (2011). *Currency and Financial Crises of the 1990s and 2000s*, CESifo Economic Studies.

CHAPTER 10

CHINESE OVERTRADING

JONATHAN LEIGHTNER
Augusta State University, Georgia, USA

China's greatest loss from the 2008–2010 crisis is the death of its 1986–2007 growth model. However, like a phoenix resurrected from its funeral ashes, what China metamorphoses into has the potential to be even better than its past. Section 10.1 of this chapter explains China's 1986–2007 export-driven growth model and why the 2008–2010 crisis has killed it. Section 10.2 explains China's short-term response to the crisis — an increase in fiscal stimulus — and produces preliminary quantitative estimates of its effectiveness. Section 10.3 explains China's long-term response to the crisis — a switch to a domestic consumption-driven growth model — and why it could make China an even better economy. Section 10.4 concludes.

10.1. China's 1986–2007 Growth Model and its Recent Death[1]

China's 1986–2007 growth model was built on the promotion of exports. China promoted exports in several ways. First, China fixed its exchange rate at lower-than-market clearing levels. In order to eliminate the resulting shortage of China's currency — the yuan — China printed more yuan and exchanged it for foreign assets, primarily US dollar reserves or US treasury bonds. In order to prevent the increased world supply of yuan from fueling

---

[1] Section 10.1 of this paper is similar, but not identical, to Sections I and III of Leightner, JE (2009). How the Crisis is killing one Asian development model, while birthing another one" (in Chinese). In *Transformation of Development Models and Reforms in the Post-Crisis Period,* Fulin, C and Y Zhongyi (eds.), 134–144. Beijing: Huawen Publishing Corporation).

268   *Jonathan Leightner*

inflation in China, China imposed strong capital controls and forced Chinese banks to buy government bonds in order to remove the extra liquidity from the market (this is called sterilization and its effectiveness is subject to debate). Prima fascia evidence that China has used this strategy is China's accumulation of over US$ 2.8 trillion in foreign reserves as of December 2010[2]— the largest holding of foreign reserves in the world for all of history. Second, China promoted labor-intensive exports by suppressing wage rates and labor power. Both of these strategies cause domestic markets to develop slowly, if at all. The export promotion–wage suppression combination makes it possible for the rich owners of export industries to further enrich themselves (keep all the returns as profits) with relatively minimal improvement occurring for labor.

A major consequence of China's export promotion–wage suppression combination is an unprecedented rapid increase in inequality. The Gini coefficient is the most common measure of inequality. This coefficient would be one if a society had complete inequality (one person receives all the income of that country) and zero if a society had complete equality. Because larger countries tend to be less equal, it is especially noteworthy that China was one of the most equal countries in the world in 1983 with a Gini coefficient of only 0.28. However, by 2001, China's Gini had risen to 0.447, making China less equal than Korea (Gini = 0.32), India (Gini = 0.325), Indonesia (Gini = 0.34), the US (Gini in 2000 = 0.408), and Thailand (Gini = 0.43). Although China is not yet as unequal as Brazil (Gini = 0.59) or Mexico (Gini = 0.55), there is probably "no other case where a society's income distribution has deteriorated so much, so fast" (Naughton, 2007, pp. 217–218). Furthermore, China's Gini has continued to rise; as of 2006, it was 0.47 (Xin, 2008), and this author has heard unofficial estimates that in 2009 China's Gini was 0.50.

It is important to realize that, by suppressing wages and thus the domestic market, China must export its excess production. Furthermore, for an export promotion strategy to succeed there must be an importer. Individuals, businesses, and countries will not continue to produce if there is no one to buy what they produce. China has enticed other countries to buy its goods

---

[2] People's Bank of China. http://www.pbc.gov.cn/publish/html/2010s09.htm. Accessed on March 10, 2011.

by keeping the prices of its exports extremely low. Prices were kept low by fixing the yuan exchange rate below its market clearing level (and thus accumulating foreign reserves) and by keeping the cost of production low via suppressing wage rates. China's net "exports" (exports minus imports) is its "trade surplus" which equals the amount that China produces over and above what it consumes domestically, which equals its "excess savings." Trade surpluses can be maintained only if other countries have offsetting trade deficits. One country can have excess savings (produce more than it consumes domestically) only if other countries have offsetting excess consumption (consume more than they produce domestically). Thus the "Export Promotion" strategy underlying China's 1986–2007 Development Model could have been named the "Trade Surplus Strategy" or the "Excess Savings Strategy," and these strategies necessarily imply that there must be trade deficit countries with excess consumption (Leightner, 2010a).

Modigliani and Cao (2004, pp. 165–166) state as follows:

> By the early 90s, the Chinese personal saving rate had reached a remarkable level of nearly 30% .... This occurred despite the fact that, even with the high growth rate, the per capita income remained one of the lowest in the world. The saving rates are stunningly high in comparison with those of the United States, one of the world's richest nations. During those same years, the personal saving rate in the United States was 7.6%: and even the "private" saving rate, which is the sum of personal saving and corporate saving (profit retention), rises to only 10% .... Since then the saving rate has slipped further with the personal down to 3% and the private down to 5%.

Corporate savings (or retained profits) are also huge and rising in China due largely to the tremendous increase in profits due to the suppression of wages and labor. Furthermore, "until very recently, state-owned enterprises were not required to pay dividends to their shareholders or to the state, thereby creating an incentive for these firms to retain their profits rather than distribute them" (Prasad, 2009, p. 13).

An "Excess Savings" strategy can be maintained if and only if, year after year (forever more), a country accumulates more and more savings (i.e., if they keep accumulating more and more US dollar reserves and

270   *Jonathan Leightner*

never use them). If a previously export-promoting country would stop accumulating more savings and start spending those accumulated savings, then it would run a trade deficit. If the rest of the world is willing to ship their exports to the US and then to hold on to the dollars they are paid and never cash those dollars in, then the US has got those exports for printed paper. In this type of deal, the US is the big winner. The big losers are the Chinese consumer and worker. The winners in China are the rich who own the companies that export — they get to keep the profits which are artificially high due to the suppression of labor and wages.

The Asian financial crisis of 1997–1998, which started in Thailand (see Leightner, 1999, 2007), caused China (and many other countries) to redouble its efforts at export promotion. From 1986 to 1995, Thailand, which had an exchange rate fixed below market clearing rates, was one of the fastest growing countries in the world, and the IMF had lauded it as a model to be emulated by other developing countries. After a massive speculative attack against Thailand's currency (the baht) in the spring of 1997, Thailand was forced to float its currency on July 2, 1997. The exchange rate was 25 baht for US$1.00 on July 1, 1997, but, by January 1998, the baht was trading at 54 baht per dollar. Furthermore, Thailand accepted an IMF loan (complete with normal IMF conditionality) of 17.2 billion in August 1997. Thailand's crisis spread throughout Asia and the world. Between August 1997 and November 1998, Thailand, Indonesia, South Korea, Brazil, and Russia accepted IMF loans and IMF conditionality. The world was shocked. If Thailand, which was lauded by the IMF as a model for the world, could fall so hard and so fast, then what country was safe?[3] Furthermore, if problems in Thailand could start a panic,

---

[3] The author of this paper had an interesting conversation with one of the leaders of CIRD (China Institute for Reform and Development) on November 1, 2009. This leader explained that George Soros, who led the speculative attack against the Thai baht, was denied a visa to China. George then contacted CIRD and asked for its help getting a visa. CIRD contacted the Chinese government and successfully argued that George should be given a visa so that the Chinese could ask him to never have a speculative attack against the Chinese yuan and ask him how to defeat an attack if one was ever launched against the yuan. China then gave George a visa, and CIRD leaders met with him for several hours to discuss speculative attacks.

forcing four other countries to such desperation that they would accept IMF loans and conditionality, then what country was safe? Moreover, before the start of Thailand's crisis, its foreign reserves of 39 billion US dollars were viewed as more than adequate to handle any problems Thailand could face. When the events of 1997–1998 showed that these reserves were inadequate, many countries started to accumulate as many dollars as they could. These countries did this either out of the fear of facing a similar fate as Thailand and/or out of a desire to keep their exchange rates artificially low in order to promote exports.

Evidence for the connection between the Thai crisis of 1997 and the worldwide accumulation of foreign reserves includes total reserves (minus gold) for all countries in the world grew 3.23-fold from 1,265 billion SDRs in 1997 to 4,080 billion in 2007. For just developing countries, total reserves grew 4.55-fold from 683 billion SDRs in 1997 to 3,107 billion in 2007. For just Asian countries, total reserves grew 4.92-fold from 384 billion SDRs in 1997 to 1,891 billion in 2007. For just China, total reserves grew 9.13-fold from 106 billion SDRs in 1997 to 968 billion SDRs in 2007 (International Monetary Fund, 2008). Much, but not all, of these increases in foreign reserves were held in US dollars or US treasury bills.

Between 1997 and 2007, the US gained tremendously from the world's increased appetite for US dollar reserves. However, this appetite also set up the US for the current crisis. If we assume that two trillion of the increase in foreign reserves for the world between 1997 and 2007 was US dollars (which is a conservative estimate), then this means that the US received two trillion dollars of foreign goods or physical assets in exchange for other countries that accept printed US paper in the form of US dollar bills, treasury bonds, and so on. If the world would never cash in these US dollar bills or treasury bonds, then the US has received two trillion dollars of goods and physical assets for free.

This US gain is compounded when nations fix their exchange rates below market clearing levels. Lindsey (2006), focusing on just China's fixed exchange rate, explains:

> The Chinese clearly undervalue their exchange rate. This means American consumers are able to buy goods at an artificially low price, making them winners. In order to maintain this arrangement, the

> People's Bank of China must buy excess dollars, and has accumulated nearly $1 trillion of reserves [this is now over $2 trillion]. Since it has no domestic use for them, it turns around and lends them back to America in our Treasury, corporate and housing loan markets. This means that both Treasury borrowing costs and mortgage interest rates are lower than they otherwise would be. American homeowners and tax-payers are winners as a result.

Lindsey recognizes that US producers who compete with Chinese imports lose from China's fixed exchange rate; however, he insists that the US consumer, tax payer, and homeowners gain more than what US producers lose. What Lindsey (2006) did not consider is that China and the rest of the world accumulating US dollar reserves would fund a speculative bubble in the US that would lead to the worse recession the US has suffered since the great depression. Nor did Lindsey consider the possibility that China might someday cash in their US dollar reserves.

The deceptive actions of certain corporate leaders in the US and confusion about the true risks from financial derivatives compounded the US bubble. Once this bubble burst, the US greatly reduced its imports, which created a crisis for China's Export Promotion Development Model. Recall that in order to have an export promotion strategy, you must have someone who is willing to import your goods. It is very important to realize that I am NOT blaming China for the current world financial crisis. China (in conjunction with many other countries) did "finance" the bubble that caused the crisis, but the core of the problem (and thus where blame should be placed) is with the deceptive actions of American business leaders.

The only way that China could return to its export promotion model after the crisis is if countries like the US would return to their excess consumption, and China would return to its perpetual accumulation of US dollar reserves. It is unlikely that Americans will return to the same level of excess consumption in the near future because this crisis has scared many Americans into saving more than before. The memory of this crisis will fade slowly, meaning that a return to excess consumption will return slowly, if ever.

It is also unlikely that China will continue its perpetual accumulate US dollars after the crisis in the volumes that have been accumulated in the last decade. Already, with both actions and words, China has threatened selling some of its US dollar assets. On March 13, 2009, Wen Jiabao (premier of the State Council of the PRC), "spoke in unusually blunt terms ... about the 'safety' of China's $1 trillion investment in American government debt, the world's largest such holding and urged the Obama administration to offer assurances that the securities would maintain their value" (Wines *et al.*, 2009). In response, the US Treasury and the White House made reassuring statements. Even before Premier Wen Jiabao expressed his concern so publicly and bluntly, the US Secretary of State (Hillary Clinton) personally reassured China when she visited China in February 2009 (Wines *et al.,* 2009).

Moreover, Zhou Xiaochuan (the governor of China's central bank) has urged the world to stop using the US dollar as the world's reserve currency and instead use an IMF-issued currency, like Special Drawing Rights (Wang, 2009). At the G20 meetings of November 2008, Hu Jintao (China's President, General Secretary of the Chinese Communist Party and Chairman of China's Central Military Commission) proposed a complete reform of the international financial system (Wang and Xin, 2008). Although President Hu did not explicitly say it, such a reform would entail replacing the US dollar as the world's reserve currency.

Not only are Chinese officials making strong statements about abandoning the US dollar as the world's reserve currency, they are making these statements with the full knowledge that their words are likely to cause the value of the US dollar to fall. On November 7, 2007, Cheng Siwei, who serves on an advisory board for China's parliament, said "foreign reserves should take into account the strength of currencies, as strong currencies such as the euro could offset weak ones such as the U.S. dollar" (Molinski, 2007). Within one day of Cheng Siwei's statement the euro surged 1.2% to a new record high against the US dollar. If Cheng Siwei's statement implying that China should increase the percentage of its reserves held in euros gets such a strong reaction, then what does China expect to happen when Hu Jintao and Wen Jiabao suggest a worldwide abandonment of the US dollar as the world's reserve currency?

Even more disturbing than these words and their expected impact on the value of the US dollar is the fact that China has already experimented with selling relatively small amounts of dollars in recent months. From

274   *Jonathan Leightner*

January 2000 to June 2010 (a total of 126 months) China's foreign reserves fell in only five months — December 2003, October 2008, January 2009, February 2009, and May 2010 (Leightner, 2010b). It is significant that of these five months, four of them occurred after the beginning of the crisis. China's holdings of US Treasuries were 939.9 billion in July 2009 and only 843.7 billion in June 2010 for a reduction of 96.2 billion dollars — a more than 10% fall (http://www.ustreas.gov/tic/mfh.txt). Furthermore, we know that China continues to diversify their foreign reserves — buying fewer dollar assets and more Japanese, Euro, and South Korean assets. China will not continue to finance the US's excess consumption forever — this has been made very clear by both words and actions.

Some experts argue that China will not sell its US dollar assets because selling part of their US assets would drive down the value of the rest of their US dollar assets (Wines *et al.*, 2009). Using a new analytical technique (Leightner and Inoue, 2007) that solves the omitted variables problem, Leightner (2010b, p. 35) finds that the value of the US dollar would fall in Europe and Asia by 4.42% if China sold 10% of its foreign reserves.

> [Thus] if 1.27 trillion of China's reserves are in US dollar assets (or 65% of the total reserves as estimated by Molinski, 2007), then China selling 10% of its reserves (for 195.4 billion dollars) could cause the value of China's remaining reserves to fall by 50.5 billion dollars ($1.27 \times 0.90 \times 0.0442$), greatly diminishing China's return. Given this large effect, China has the incentive to either sell none of its US dollar reserves or to sell all of its US dollar reserves. If China was convinced that the value of the US dollar would fall by a significant amount, no matter what China did, then it would be rational for China to sell as many of its US dollar assets as possible and as quickly as possible. If China sold all of its US dollar reserves then the value of the US dollar would plummet by at least 44% which would cause the value of US exports to fall by 44% (as measured in other currencies) and the dollar price the US pays for imports to increase by 44%. Such changes in exports and imports would drive the US economy much further into recession.

Some scholars in China have argued that China's currency, the yuan, should ultimately move "from the periphery to the center where it belongs." It is possible that the yuan reforms that China is now implementing (Blumenstein *et al.*, 2010) are a preparation for the yuan to make a bid to replace the dollar as the world's reserve currency in the future (LeVine, 2009). If China wants the yuan to replace the dollar as the world's reserve currency, then China might want to orchestrate a massive fall in the value of the dollar once the yuan is ready. Whether or not China wants the yuan to replace the dollar and whether or not China would actually sell its holdings of US dollar assets is controversial. However, it is a fact that China, in 2010, is shifting its purchases of foreign assets away from US dollars assets which means that China is already reducing its financing of the over-consumption of US.

10.2. China's Short-Term Response to the Crisis

As a short-term response to the crisis, the Chinese government pledged to spend two trillion yuan (292 million US dollars) between 2009 and 2010. For modern day China, this is an unprecedented large stimulus package. In contrast, during the 1997–1998 Asian financial crisis, the Chinese government spent only 0.9 trillion yuan over a six-year time period. This large planned increase in Chinese government spending alarmed this researcher because he had found that, whenever the US drastically increased government spending, the US government spending multiplier plummeted (Leightner, 2010d). Thus, Leightner (2010d) used Bi-Directional Reiterative Truncated Projected Least Squares (BD-RTPLS), to estimate the effect of government spending (G) in China's 31 provinces on Gross Provincial Product (GPP) between 1996 and 2006. He found that $\partial GPP/\partial G$ was highest in 1996 while China was drastically cutting government spending to curb inflation and lowest in 1997 when China increased spending to counteract the Asian Financial crisis; $\partial GPP/\partial G$ slowly rose between 1998 and 2004 and then declined some in 2005 and 2006 when the Chinese yuan was slowly appreciating. These results implied that, if China proceeded with its huge planned increase in government spending, China's government spending multiplier would likely plummet.

276   *Jonathan Leightner*

In contrast to China's publicized plans to increase spending by two trillion yuan between 2009 and 2010, the Chinese government actually increased spending in 2009 by a mere 0.266 trillion yuan (according to Asian Development Bank data). To see how China's actual short-term response to the crisis affected GDP, BD-RTPLS was applied to data from the Asian Development Bank on 20 Asian countries (including China) between 1990 and 2009. BD-RTPLS, and its predecessor RTPLS, produce a separate $\partial GPP/\partial G$ estimate for each observation. Thus, BD-RTPLS can be used to show how omitted variables affect $\partial GPP/\partial G$ over time.

BD-RTPLS is designed to handle cases where the assumptions underlying more traditional techniques do not hold. Traditional techniques, like Ordinary Least Squares (OLS), assume that there are no omitted variables that can change the estimated relationship between different observations. As a result of this assumption, traditional techniques produce only one estimate for the entire data series.

There are many reasons why the assumption of no omitted variables (which is necessary for OLS) is invalid for China during the time period that is studied. In 1994, China underwent massive changes in the way it collects taxes and in the way it spends tax revenues. For example, prior to 1994, most taxes were collected by the local government; after 1994, most taxes were collected by the central government (Naughton, 2007, pp. 430–442). The changes due to the 1994 fiscal reform did not occur immediately; indeed, they probably stretched over several years. Furthermore, in 1989 (just before my data begins), 1994–1996, and in 2004, China was suffering from severe inflation; but in the middle of my data set, China fought against two episodes of deflation. Moreover, the Chinese government's stated goal has shifted from increasing total output (GPP) to increasing harmony during the time period studied. The provinces in which the government is spending money has also shifted — at the beginning of my data, the Chinese government primarily focused on the coastal provinces of China, whereas at the end of my data, the Chinese government has begun to address the problems of the interior provinces. The last two years of my data correspond to the beginning of the current global crisis. Furthermore, the items that the government buys with its spending have changed over time and the purchase of different items would stimulate investment and consumption to varying degrees and thus would have differing effects on gross domestic product. All of these factors affect the true relationship between government spending and gross domestic product ($\partial GDP/\partial G$). In order to correctly use traditional analytical techniques, all of these factors would have to be adequately modeled and measured.[4] Such a task is not feasible. Fortunately, Leightner (2002) introduced Reiterative Truncated Projected Least Squares (RTPLS) — a technique that produces estimates that include the influence of omitted variables without having to know, model, measure or find proxies for the omitted variables. Leightner and Inoue (2007) prove theoretically that RTPLS produces less bias than OLS when there are omitted variables that interact with the included variables. Leightner and Inoue (2007) also run 90,000 simulation tests which show that RTPLS produces (on average) less than half the error of OLS when there are omitted variables that interact with the included variables. They show that this result is robust — the results were confirmed when the omitted variable makes a 1,000% or 100% difference to the real slope, to when 10%, 1%, or 0% measurement and rounding error is included, and to when sample sizes of 500 or 100 observations were used. Leightner (2007a) proposed improvements in RTPLS to create BD-RTPLS (bidirectional RTPLS).

BD-RTPLS estimates are reduced from estimates that capture all the ways that Y and X are correlated. Thus, complicated systems of equations do not have to be created, justified, and solved to use BD-RTPLS. In other words, I do not have to build and justify an entire macroeconomic model in order to use BD-RTPLS to estimate $\partial GDP/\partial G$. However, the resulting $\partial GDP/\partial G$ estimates would capture all the ways that GDP and G are correlated. Thus if, when faced with high inflation, governments cut spending and reduce the money supply and they do the opposite when fighting unemployment, then the BD-RTPLS estimates of $\partial GDP/\partial G$ would include the combined effects of the coordinated fiscal and monetary policies.

Additional information on exactly how BD-RTPLS captures the effects of omitted variables can be found in Leightner and Inoue (2007) and in Leightner (2007a). Peer reviewed journal publications that contain

---

[4] To apply traditional regression techniques to this paper's data set, which includes data from 20 different countries, similar considerations would have to be modeled for every country.

278   *Jonathan Leightner*

applications of RTPLS or BD-RTPLS include Leightner (2005a, 2005b, 2007a, 2008b, 2010d and 2011) and Leightner and Inoue (2007, 2008a, 2008b, and 2009).

This chapter's analysis used annual data, downloaded from the Asian Development Bank's web page (http://www.adb.org/documents/Books/ Key_Indicators/2010/Country.asp) on real gross domestic product (GDP) and real government spending in Australia, Bangladesh, Bhutan, Cambodia, China, Hong Kong, India, Indonesia, Japan, South Korea, Malaysia, Nepal, New Zealand, Pakistan, Philippines, Singapore, Sri Lanka, Taipei, Thailand, and Vietnam between 1990 and 2009. For each country, I used the maximum number of years available that utilized a single base year for its GDP deflator. The Asian Development Bank's Chinese data between 1990 and 2009 utilized three different base years for its GDP deflator. Translations between each base year's deflator for China were derived from data found on the 2008 Statistical Yearbook of China's web page (http://www.stats.gov.cn/ tjsj/ndsj/2009/html/C0203e.htm) which made it possible to include data for China from 1990 to 2009.

All data was normalized by adding one to the percentage change in that data. For example, China's real gross domestic product (GDP) using 2000 as a base year was 3,702 billion yuan in 1990 and 4,014 billion yuan in 1991. The percentage change in China's GDP from 1990 to 1991 was [4,014 − 3,702]/3,702 or 0.084. Thus, the normalized value for China's real GDP in 1991 was 1 + 0.084 = 1.084 (see China row of Table 10.1). This normalized value means that China's GDP in 1991 was 108.4% of its 1990 GDP. Normalized values for government spending in each country and in each year were calculated in the same fashion. By normalizing the data, I make sure that my BD-RTPLS estimates capture the effects of just this year's spending on this year's GDP.[5]

---

[5] If I did not normalize the data and if last year's spending was correlated with this year's spending, then the reduced form estimates produced by BD-RTPLS would capture the influence on GDP of (1) this year's spending and (2) of last year's spending multiplied by a factor showing how last year's spending was correlated with this year's spending. By normalizing the data, I prevent this problem. Furthermore, by normalizing the data, I eliminate problems due to different countries having different base years for their GDP deflators and different currency units.

Table 10.1. The normalized GDP data.

	1991	1992	1993	1994	1995	1996	1997	1998	1999	2000	2001	2002	2003	2004	2005	2006	2007	2008	2009	Mean
Australia	0.994	1.002	1.036	1.040	1.044	1.042	1.039	1.044	1.052	1.040	1.020	1.038	1.032	1.041	1.028	1.031	1.038	1.037	1.011	1.032
Bangladesh	1.033	1.050	1.046	1.040	1.050	1.046	1.054	1.053	1.048	1.060	1.053	1.044	1.052	1.063	1.060	1.066	1.064	1.061	1.058	1.053
Bhutan	0.996	1.046	1.020	1.050	1.071	1.056	1.054	1.059	1.080	1.069	1.088	1.109	1.072	1.040	1.070	1.064	1.197	1.050		1.066
Cambodia				1.093	1.064	1.053	1.057	1.050	1.125	1.084	1.077	1.070	1.086	1.103	1.133	1.108	1.102	1.067		1.085
China	1.084	1.143	1.140	1.130	1.110	1.100	1.093	1.079	1.076	1.084	1.082	1.091	1.101	1.101	1.114	1.127	1.142	1.096	1.091	1.104
Hongkong	1.057	1.061	1.060	1.060	1.023	1.042	1.051	0.940	1.026	1.080	1.005	1.018	1.030	1.085	1.071	1.070	1.064	1.022	0.972	1.039
India															1.095	1.097	1.092	1.067	1.074	1.085
Indonesia											1.036	1.045	1.048	1.050	1.057	1.055	1.063	1.060	1.045	1.051
Japan	1.033	1.008	1.002	1.009	1.019	1.026	1.016	0.980	0.999	1.029	1.002	1.003	1.014	1.027	1.019	1.020	1.024	0.988	0.948	1.009
Korea	1.097	1.058	1.063	1.088	1.089	1.072	1.058	0.943	1.107	1.088	1.040	1.071	1.028	1.046	1.040	1.052	1.051	1.023	1.002	1.053
Malaysia											1.005	1.054	1.058	1.068	1.053	1.058	1.065	1.047	0.983	1.043
Nepal												1.001	1.039	1.047	1.035	1.034	1.034	1.061	1.049	1.037
New Zealand	0.987	1.011	1.064	1.053	1.042	1.034	1.017	1.005	1.053	1.024	1.035	1.049	1.043	1.037	1.031	1.008	1.029	0.985	0.996	1.026
Pakistan											1.020	1.031	1.047	1.075	1.090	1.058	1.068	1.037	1.012	1.049
Philippines											1.017	1.045	1.049	1.064	1.053	1.053	1.071	1.037	1.011	1.044
Singapore															1.086		1.085	1.018	0.987	1.044
SriLanka													1.059	1.054	1.062	1.077	1.068	1.060	1.035	1.059
Taipei	1.079	1.076	1.067	1.076	1.064	1.055	1.055	1.035	1.060	1.058	0.983	1.053	1.037	1.062	1.047	1.054	1.060	1.007	0.981	1.048
Thailand	1.086	1.081	1.082	1.090	1.092	1.059	0.986	0.895	1.044	1.047	1.022	1.053	1.071	1.063	1.046	1.051	1.049	1.025	0.978	1.043
Vietnam						1.093	1.082	1.058	1.048	1.068	1.069	1.071	1.073	1.078	1.084	1.082	1.085	1.063	1.053	1.072
Mean	1.045	1.054	1.058	1.066	1.061	1.057	1.047	1.012	1.060	1.061	1.035	1.050	1.052	1.061	1.062	1.063	1.073	1.041	1.016	1.051

Table 10.2.　The normalized government spending data.

	1991	1992	1993	1994	1995	1996	1997	1998	1999	2000	2001	2002	2003	2004	2005	2006	2007	2008	2009	Mean
Australia	1.084	1.067	1.043	1.019	1.045	1.058	1.033	1.057	1.077	1.059	1.063	1.061	1.064	1.065	1.078	1.067	1.083	1.085	1.068	1.062
Bangladesh	0.956	1.076	1.116	0.995	0.953	0.951	1.002	1.076	0.961	0.991	1.029	1.154	1.083	1.063	1.025	1.008	0.996	0.952	0.995	1.020
Bhutan	0.804	1.065	1.145	0.990	1.275	1.215	1.181	0.931	1.251	1.000	1.081	1.087	1.076	1.074	1.130	1.039	1.040	1.103		1.083
Cambodia				1.686	0.751	1.238	1.002	0.924	1.155	1.150	1.094	1.531	1.040	0.958	1.039	1.008	1.197	0.948		1.115
China	1.183	1.156	1.134	1.117	0.996	1.117	1.109	1.112	1.124	1.119	1.105	1.076	1.052	1.013	1.139	1.114	1.093	1.079	1.070	1.100
Hongkong	1.077	1.132	1.021	1.038	1.030	1.037	1.022	1.005	1.031	1.020	1.060	1.024	1.018	1.007	0.968	1.003	1.030	1.018	1.024	1.030
India															1.083	1.038	1.097	1.167	1.105	1.098
Indonesia											1.076	1.130	1.100	1.040	1.066	1.096	1.039	1.104	1.157	1.090
Japan	1.022	1.021	1.010	1.023	1.019	1.025	1.007	0.991	1.010	1.007	1.016	1.011	1.004	1.016	1.013	1.015	1.016	0.993	0.990	1.011
Korea	1.056	1.065	1.050	1.036	1.038	1.073	1.027	1.022	1.030	1.018	1.050	1.049	1.044	1.038	1.043	1.066	1.054	1.043	1.050	1.045
Malaysia											1.157	1.119	1.086	1.076	1.065	1.050	1.066	1.107	1.031	1.084
Nepal											1.078	1.105	1.088	1.012	1.008	1.072	1.033	1.097		1.062
New Zealand	0.995	1.010	1.014	1.009	1.049	1.014	1.074	0.996	1.058	0.979	1.041	1.013	1.049	1.041	1.049	1.045	1.049	1.042	1.014	1.029
Pakistan											0.944	1.150	1.072	1.014	1.017	1.483	0.904	1.389	0.685	1.073
Philippines											0.947	0.962	1.026	1.015	1.023	1.104	1.066	1.004	1.110	1.028
Singapore																1.073	1.030	1.084	1.082	1.067
SriLanka															1.048	1.093	1.120	1.096	1.074	1.098
Taipei	1.081	1.023	1.014	0.996	1.042	1.072	1.058	1.036	0.961	1.012	1.019	1.015	0.988	1.006	1.002	0.993	1.021	1.007	1.036	1.020
Thailand	1.062	1.064	1.051	1.082	1.053	1.120	0.972	1.039	1.030	1.023	1.025	1.007	1.024	1.057	1.113	1.022	1.097	1.046	1.059	1.050
Vietnam						1.074	1.040	1.032	0.943	1.050	1.066	1.054	1.072	1.078	1.082	1.085	1.089	1.075	1.076	1.058
Mean	1.032	1.068	1.060	1.090	1.023	1.083	1.044	1.019	1.053	1.036	1.048	1.090	1.053	1.041	1.056	1.071	1.056	1.069	1.045	

Table 10.3. $\partial GDP/\partial G$ BD-RTPLS estimates.

	1991	1992	1993	1994	1995	1996	1997	1998	1999	2000	2001	2002	2003	2004	2005	2006	2007	2008	2009	Mean
Australia	3.260	2.939	2.693	2.710	2.715	2.692	2.696	2.661	2.561	2.574	2.573	2.424	2.385	2.287	2.261	2.159	2.050	1.963	1.951	2.503
Bangladesh	6.151	6.190	5.892	6.047	6.661	7.269	7.716	7.525	8.209	8.828	9.000	8.433	7.894	7.730	8.130	8.623	9.266	10.504	10.990	7.950
Bhutan	1.254	2.306	2.312	2.152	1.545	1.529	1.383	1.626	1.101	1.470	1.337	1.268	1.428	1.499	1.277	1.391	1.299	1.556		1.541
Cambodia				1.906	7.580	5.522	5.911	6.693	4.285	5.239	5.611	3.294	4.222	5.494	4.965	6.012	4.003	6.524		5.151
China	1.718	1.182	1.319	1.494	2.352	1.892	1.949	1.993	1.908	1.796	1.831	1.944	2.254	1.654	1.669	1.746	2.148	2.251		1.837
Hongkong	3.035	2.771	2.977	3.027	3.132	3.091	3.140	3.005	3.002	3.026	3.200	2.994	2.986	3.140	3.586	3.735	3.818	3.958	3.932	3.240
India															2.402	2.702	2.501	2.411	2.351	2.473
Indonesia											4.936	4.514	4.239	4.242	4.146	3.994	4.069	3.855	3.685	4.187
Japan	0.599	0.602	0.590	0.590	0.583	0.584	0.582	0.559	0.574	0.578	0.583	0.573	0.571	0.582	0.586	0.590	0.594	0.574	0.539	0.581
Korea	1.759	1.887	1.898	1.943	2.028	2.027	2.184	2.201	2.049	2.274	2.350	2.275	2.399	2.351	2.368	2.294	2.291	2.340	2.321	2.170
Malaysia											3.358	2.573	2.484	2.407	2.473	2.473	2.426	2.397	2.422	2.557
Nepal												4.170	3.614	3.388	3.448	3.529	3.523	3.440	3.353	3.558
New Zealand	1.705	1.746	1.790	1.880	1.896	1.923	1.955	1.815	1.807	1.859	1.926	1.953	1.966	1.970	1.960	1.951	1.863	1.859	1.715	1.870
Pakistan											3.522	3.675	3.321	3.443	3.650	2.455	3.343	2.677	1.331	3.046
Philippines											3.973	4.566	4.717	4.902	5.074	4.801	4.652	5.031	5.209	4.769
Singapore																2.854	3.166	3.362	3.292	3.169
SriLanka													2.533	2.453	2.251	2.129	2.202	2.158	2.127	2.265
Taipei	1.469	1.631	1.738	1.898	1.898	1.885	1.885	1.934	2.115	2.179	2.207	2.186	2.284	2.418	2.535	2.692	2.775	2.830	2.877	2.181
Thailand	3.469	3.555	3.697	3.532	3.788	3.748	3.677	4.086	3.446	3.515	3.586	3.651	3.753	3.752	3.677	3.715	3.575	3.627	3.678	3.659
Vietnam						3.609	4.009	4.255	4.729	4.705	4.667	4.759	4.682	4.607	4.515	4.519	4.450	4.722	4.738	4.498
Mean	2.442	2.481	2.491	2.471	3.107	2.981	3.091	3.196	2.982	3.170	3.414	3.243	3.190	3.273	3.208	3.214	3.181	3.397	3.265	3.265

282   *Jonathan Leightner*

The normalized data is shown in Tables 10.1 and 10.2.[6] BD-RTPLS estimates[7] for $\partial GDP/\partial G$ are given in Table 10.3 and presented in Figures 10.1 through 10.4. Figure 10.1 shows how the Chinese data and $\partial GDP/\partial G$ results changed over time. Notice that in 1995, when actual government spending slightly decreased in China, and in 2004, when the annual rate of increase in government spending slowed noticeably (both cases causing the normalized G line to fall), the estimated $\partial GDP/\partial G$ results spiked upward (see Figure 10.1). Thus, in China, smaller increases in government spending are associated with larger multiplier effects and relatively large increases in government spending are associated with much smaller multiplier effects. Estimated $\partial GDP/\partial G$ for China was 2.35 in 1995 and 2.25 in 2004 in contrast to 1.65 in 2005 (see Table 10.3). This means that the last yuan increase in government spending in 2004 caused GDP to increase by 2.25 yuan in 2004 but only by 1.65 yuan in 2005. This result mirrors what Leightner (2011) found for the US, and what Leightner and Inoue (2009) found for Japan.

Table 10.2 (row 5) shows that Chinese government spending did not increase by an unusually large amount in either 2008 or 2009, and Figure 10.1 shows that the government spending multiplier increased noticeably in those years. Thus, China's short-term strategy for the global

---

[6] The data downloaded from the Asian development Bank's web page was for the years shown in Tables 10.1 and 10.2 and also the year before the first year, shown in these tables for each country. The first year's data is always lost when the data is normalized. It might surprise the reader to notice that I only had very recent data for several important countries, like India. Even though the Asian Development Bank reported many more years of data for India than 2004–2009, I had to start the India data at 2004 because the Asian Development Bank switched GDP deflators between 2003 and 2004 without giving any years of overlap between subsequent deflators which would have made a translation possible.

[7] The slope estimates, produced when using normalized data, are equal to elasticities of the original data $[\partial (\%y) / \partial (\%x)]$ because the normalized y and x are the %y and %x of the original data. Finding an elasticity of 0.34, for example, implies that a change in x of 1% is correlated with a 0.34% change in y. In this paper, I first estimate $\partial [\%GPP] / \partial [\%G]$, using the normalized data. I then change these elasticities into slope estimates by multiplying them by GDP/G. $\partial [\%GDP]/\partial [\%G] = [\partial GDP/GDP]/[\partial G/G]$. Thus, $[\partial GDP/GDP]/[\partial G/G]*GDP/G$ causes the G and GDP to cancel producing $\partial GDP / \partial G$, which is a fiscal multiplier. A fiscal multiplier of 1.72 means that a one yuan increase in government spending would cause GDP to increase by 1.72 yuan.

Chinese Overtrading 283

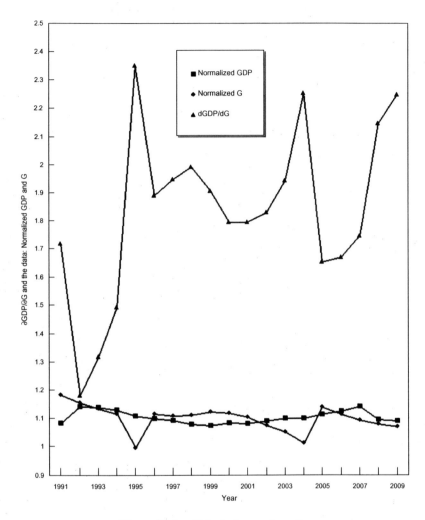

Figure 10.1. China's data and results.

crisis of increasing spending at a normal pace served China well. This contrasts to what happened in Australia, India, Indonesia, Singapore, and Sri Lanka (see Figure 10.2).[8] The government of these five countries increased

---

[8] Bhutan was added to Figure 10.3 because it increased spending by 10.3% in 2008; however, the Asian Development Bank did not have data for Bhutan in 2009.

284 *Jonathan Leightner*

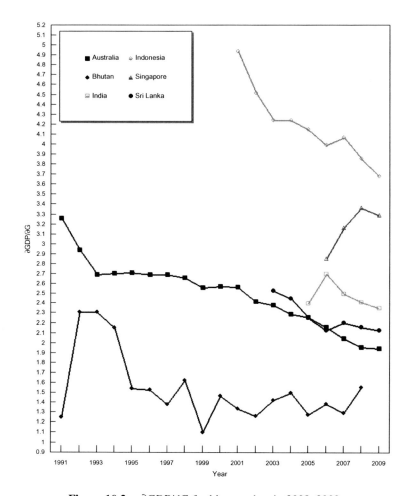

Figure 10.2. ∂GDP/dG for big spenders in 2008–2009.

spending in 2008 and 2009 by relatively large amounts in both 2008 and 2009 (see Table 10.2). Of this group, Australia increased spending the least with 8.5% followed by a 6.8% increase in 2008–2009 (notice that those percentage increases would compound), and India increased spending the most with a 16.7% increase followed by a 10.5% increase. Figure 10.2 shows that the estimated ∂GDP/∂G did not rise in 2009 for any of these countries.

Figure 10.2 reveals an unexpected pattern — many of the countries that increased spending for the crisis the most were the countries that had suffered declining government spending multipliers for many years — compare the negatively sloped lines of Australia, Indonesia, and Sri Lanka in Figure 10.2 with the many positively sloped lines in Figure 10.3. Figure 10.3 shows what happened to $\partial GDP/\partial G$ in countries that increased government spending in 2008 and 2009 by relatively normal amounts. In

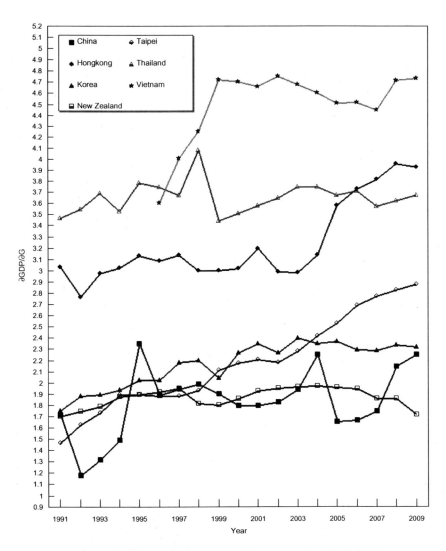

Figure 10.3. $\partial GDP/\partial G$ for more steady spenders in 2008–2009.

286   *Jonathan Leightner*

all of these countries (with the possible exception of New Zealand) $\partial GDP/\partial G$ stayed relatively constant or rose for 2008 and 2009. A close examination of Tables 10.1–10.3 and Figures 10.2–10.3 imply that normal increases in government spending during a crisis may be helpful, but that relatively huge increases in government spending may be counterproductive because of declining multiplier effects.

Figure 10.4 depicts the results for countries that neither spent big nor spent steadily (notice that the scale for the y-axis of Figure 10.4 is double of what it was for Figures 10.2 and 10.3). Bangladesh's $\partial GDP/\partial G$ line shows an increase in 2008 and 2009 and that is not good news because Bangladesh actually decreased spending in those two years.[9] Thus, the rise in $\partial GDP/\partial G$ for Bangladesh in 2008 and 2009 imply that the *negative* effects of the cuts in government spending were bigger than they were in 2007. Cambodia's fiscal multiplier was the most unstable in my data set (see Figure 10.4); however, every time that Cambodia increased the rate of their spending increase, the Cambodian fiscal multiplier fell, and every year that Cambodia decreased the rate of their spending increase, Cambodia's fiscal multiplier rose (compare rows 4 of Table's 10.2 and 10.3). Leightner and Inoue (2009) found a similar result for Japan in the 1990s; they found that decreases in government spending caused larger changes in Japanese GDP than equal increases in government spending.[10] If results from Japan, Cambodia, and Bangladesh can be generalized, then they imply that governments that try to balance the budget during crises by cutting spending will probably cause GDP to fall more than increases in government spending cause GDP to rise.

---

[9] Bangladesh and Japan are the only countries in my data set that cut real spending for both 2008 and 2009. Japan will be discussed later in the text. Cambodia also cut spending in 2008, but the Asia Development Bank did not have data on Cambodia for 2009. Like Bangladesh's multiplier, Cambodia's fiscal multiplier also rose in 2008 (relative to its 2007 level) which means that the negative effects of a cut in real government spending were amplified.

[10] Leightner and Inoue (2009) used Japanese data in current prices, and they found nominal government spending multipliers in the range of 8.5 to 14. In contrast, the paper you are reading now used data corrected for inflation and found real Japanese government spending multipliers in the range of 0.539 and 0.602. In this paper, no other country had a fiscal multiplier lower than 1.

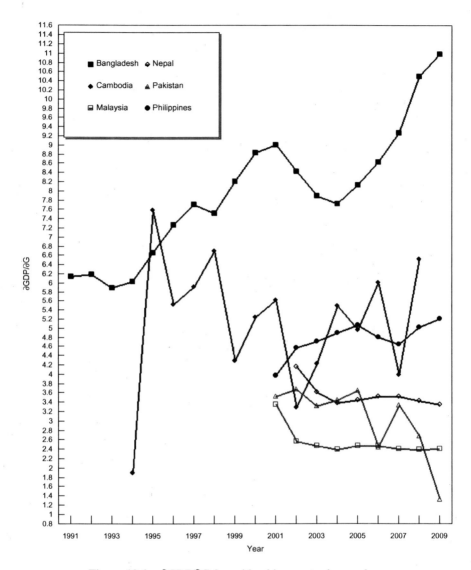

Figure 10.4. $\partial GDP/\partial G$ for neither big nor steady spenders.

Malaysia, Nepal, and the Philippines increased spending dramatically in either 2008 or 2009, but not in both of those years. These countries did not suffer the declines in $\partial GDP/\partial G$ in 2008 and 2009 that Australia, Indonesia, and India (countries that increased spending dramatically in both

288   *Jonathan Leightner*

2008 and 2009) suffered (compare Figures 10.2 and 10.4). Japan was the only country in my data set that had real government spending multipliers less than one (see row 9 of Table 10.3). Let us hope that Japan's problems, of the last two decades, are not a foreshadowing of the world's future. In their efforts to prevent that future, the results of this chapter imply that governments should not follow the two extremes of decreasing spending to balance the budget or of dramatically increasing spending for several years in a row. The empirical results of this chapter (and of Leightner, 2010d and 2011) imply that a perpetual fiscal stimulus from increasing government spending is not a viable long run response to this crisis.

10.3. China's Long-Term Response to the Crisis

China's excess savings (export promotion) model of 1986–2007 is dead — China is no longer willing to finance US over consumption, and the current crisis has caused Americans to save more and consume less. China needs a new buyer for its goods — China cannot return to export promotion, and perpetually increasing government spending is not a viable option. There is no greater potential source of buyers on this earth than the relatively underdeveloped domestic market of China. Hu Jintao is actively promoting China's switch from an export-driven growth model to a domestic consumption-driven growth model.[11] In order to use a domestic consumption-driven growth model, China will have to redistribute income from the rich to the poor and from the owners of businesses to the workers. The National People's Congress, China's top legislature, has proposed a major reform in income distribution to "be launched as soon as possible," which aims to increase incomes, reduce the wealth gap, and make the middle class the largest sector of society ("Legislature", 2010). These proposals will be included in the 12th Five-Year Plan (2011–2015).

---

[11] When the author of this paper went to a conference on "Can emerging economies return to the same growth model after the crisis" in Hainan, China, October 31, 2009–November 1, 2009, every single scholar from China talked about how a domestic consumption growth model was the best plan for China's future. However, one Chinese provincial leader proudly declared that income had risen in his province by 10% last year and savings by 16%. He claimed that those percentages prove that his province was following Hu Jintao's consumption-driven growth model.

Furthermore, Wen Jiabao recently told a visiting Japanese delegation that "Labor disputes are occurring at some foreign companies [located in China], where there is a problem of relatively low wages. We would like (Japan) to address this issue" (Chang, 2010). Moreover, China is allowing labor strikes and slowdowns to occur in foreign-owned factories located on Chinese land. This is a major shift, because, in the recent past, any efforts to organize strikes or labor unions (that were not officially set up and controlled by the government) were harshly suppressed.

The policy shifts already discussed aim at increasing disposable income for China's relatively poor masses.[12] However, China needs to do more than just increase disposable income. China needs to fix the major problems that plague its health care and pension systems. People can either save or consume their disposable income. Chinese households save almost 30% of their disposable income out of fear of major health care problems and/or pension funds-failing (Prasad, 2009; Leightner, 2010a). Solving these problems would free up Chinese disposable income for a consumption-driven growth model.

China also needs to fix the exploitation of rural migrants in cities and the taking of land by local governments (Leightner, 2010c). Most importantly, China must solve its corruption problem. In this author's opinion, corruption (rent seeking) is the single biggest obstacle to economic development. Allowing democracy to spread upward in the political system to the provincial level would help reduce corruption. Establishing a well-functioning and fair judiciary that holds all citizens (including government officials) equally accountable under the law is the key. Allowing a totally free press (that would be severely prosecuted if it accepted bribes) would help. Finally, China needs to solve problems with the safety of its products. Repeated cases of Melamine in milk, lead paint on toys, and Lyme in flour reduce consumer confidence and consumption of domestically produced goods.

---

[12] China began making policy shifts to help the poor even before the crisis. Most importantly, China's new labor law took effect in January 2008. This law requires that all employees be given written contracts and that an employee can be given a maximum of two temporary labor contracts. At the end of the second temporary contract, the employee must either be fired or given a permanent labor contract. Under a permanent labor contract, the worker can only be fired if the worker breaks his obligations as outlined in the written contract.

If these problems were solved, then increased consumption could lead to several waves of domestic investment and growth. This type of phenomenon has happened before in Japan and in the US. Ozawa (1985) describes how a large increase in the real income of Japan's working class led to several waves of domestic demand-driven investment during the 1960s. At first, Japan's working class spent part of its increased real income on washing machines, automatic rice cookers, TVs, air conditioners, and automobiles. In response to this increased demand, Japanese companies built new factories and expanded old factories in order to increase their production of these consumer items. Japanese housewives who acquired these goods discovered that they had an increase in their leisure time. The average Japanese housewife spent 11 hours per day on household chores before the war, but less than eight hours every day by 1969. This increase in leisure time produced increased demand for, and investment in, domestically produced leisure goods and services.

The US in the 1920s also enjoyed several successive waves of demand-driven growth. Rosenberg (2003, p. 4) explains:

> Though invented earlier, the full impact of the automobile on the US economy was not felt until the 1920s. Car production increased three-fold during this decade. This generated strong demand for investment in the automobile industry as well as in other industries dependent on car production such as tires, auto parts, plate glass and steel. Roads and traffic lights needed to be built and gas stations soon followed. The automobile fostered the growth of the suburb. With suburbanization came increased spending on new housing. Many of the new homes would be electrified and have telephones and radios. Thus, investment spending in the electric power, telephone and communications industries took off.

President Hu Jin Tao is promoting China's shift to a domestic consumption growth model. This type of growth model has successfully been used in the past. Furthermore, the policy changes needed to implement a consumption-driven growth model would also result in a more harmonious society.

Please note that neither Hu Jintao nor I are advocating a turning of our backs on trade. We are advocating a redistribution of income from profits to wages and from rich to poor. Such redistribution would, without any direct government control of trade, cause China to import more and export less. Thus, such a redistribution would cause self-sustaining growth and much more balanced trade. China would no longer be so dependent on the US and Europe buying its goods. Furthermore, shifting to a domestic consumption-driven growth model will change the government spending multipliers estimated in Section 10.2. If China solves its problems with health care, pensions, exploited migrants, land taking, and corruption, then China's marginal propensity to consume (MPC) will rise, causing the government spending multiplier to increase significantly.

10.4. Conclusions

China's greatest loss from the current global crisis is the death of its 1986–2007 growth model: a model that emphasized exports, savings, and trade surpluses. China's long run response to this crisis is to shift from an export-driven growth model to a domestic consumption-driven model. Such a shift will produce a China that is more equal, more harmonious, and less vulnerable to external shocks.[13] Empirical estimates of the effectiveness of China's short run response to the crisis — an 8% increase in government spending in 2008 followed by a 7% increase in 2009 — indicate that it has worked well. Countries that cut spending in 2008 and 2009 (perhaps to balance the budget), like Bangladesh, and countries that increased spending by more than 8% for both 2008 and 2009 did not do as well as China.

The economics profession needs to learn several things from China and the crisis. Economists for decades have advocated increasing savings which will fund investment which drives growth. The current crisis has

---

[13] I do not want to imply that China does not face significant risks. For example, the current Chinese government is very concerned (with good cause) about a speculative bubble in China's real estate market and about inflation. Moreover, if China ultimately wants the yuan to replace the US dollar as the world's reserve currency, it might some day in the future dump its dollar holdings in order to encourage the world to switch to yuan. This could blow up in China's face if it excessively destabilizes international currency markets.

revealed flaws in this argument. The current crisis has shown that countries with relatively high savings rates can enjoy greater investment and growth only if there is a buyer for what their investment produces (Leightner, 2000, 2010a). When that buyer goes into crisis, he will pull the seller into it with him. A much better (but admittedly more complex) strategy is to correctly balance savings with consumption. Savings provides the funds for investment, but consumption provides the reason for the investment. Both are needed. Furthermore, if consumption and savings are correctly balanced, then speculative bubbles will not occur (Leightner, 2008a).

A corollary to the above conclusion is that a correct balance needs to be found between profits and wages. Mr. Deng Xiaoping is famous for saying that "Whatever makes profits is good for China." However, the current crisis has revealed that profits, at the expense of wages, results in a "trade surplus growth strategy" which makes a country vulnerable.

Finally, governments need to realize that increasing fiscal spending is just a short-term response to this crisis — it is not a viable permanent fix. Free, competitive markets that function under fair, effective, and impartial laws which are efficiently and consistently enforced by an unbribable judiciary and a government that works for the people without seeking rents are keys to a long run solution to this crisis.

References

Blumenstein, R, A Browne and D McMahon (2010). China deflects pressure for yuan rise (September 1, 2010). *Wall Street Journal*, pp. A9, 1–6.

Chang, A (2010). China Premier Wen Jiabao says Japanese companies' wages too low (August 29, 2010). *Huffington Post*, available at http://www.huffingtonpost.com/2010/08/29/wen-jiabao-china-wages-japanese-companies_n_698297.html. [accessed September 1, 2010].

International Monetary Fund (2008). *International Financial Statistics Yearbook.*

Legislature proposes narrowing the gap in wealth (2010). *China Daily On Line*, August 24.

Leightner, JE (1999). Globalization and Thailand's financial crisis. *Journal of Economic Issues*, 33(2), 367–373.

Leightner, JE (2000). Asia's financial crisis, speculative bubbles, and underconsumption theory. *Journal of Economic Issues,* 34(2), 385–392.

Leightner, JE (2002). *The changing effectiveness of key policy tools in Thailand.* Institute of Southeast Asian Studies for East Asian Development Network, EADN Working Paper # 19(2002) x0219–6417.

Leightner, JE (2005a). Fight deflation with deflation, not with monetary policy. *The Japanese Economy: Translations and Studies,* 33(2), 67–93.

Leightner, JE (2005b). The productivity of government spending in Asia: 1983–2000. *Journal of Productivity Analysis,* 23, 33–46.

Leightner, JE (2007a). Omitted variables, confidence intervals, and the productivity of exchange rates. *Pacific Economic Review,* 12(1),15–45.

Leightner, JE (2008a). Bubbles. *International Encyclopedia of the Social Sciences.* Darity, W, Jr (ed.), 1, 2nd Ed. Detroit: Macmillan Reference USA, 78–379.

Leightner, JE (2008b). Omitted variables and how the Chinese yuan affects other Asian currencies. *International Journal of Contemporary Mathematical Sciences,* 3(14), 645–666.

Leightner, JE (2010a). Are the forces that cause China's trade surplus with the USA good? *Journal of Chinese Economic and Foreign Trade Studies,* 3(1), 43–53.

Leightner, JE (2010b). How China's holdings of foreign reserves affect the value of the US dollar in Europe and Asia. *China & World Economy,* 18(3), 24–39.

Leightner, JE (2010c). Alternative property systems for China. *China: An International Journal,* 8(2), 346–359.

Leightner, JE (2010d). China's fiscal stimulus package for the current international crisis, what does 1996–2006 tell us? *Frontiers of Economics in China,* 5(1), 1–24. Available online at http://www.springerlink.com/openurl.asp?genre=article& id=doi:10.1007/s11459–010–0001–8.

Leightner, JE (2011). Fiscal stimulus for the USA in the current financial crisis: What does 1930–2008 tell us? *Applied Economic Letters,* 18(6), 539–549.

Leightner, JE and T Inoue (2007). Tackling the omitted variables problem without the strong assumptions of proxies. *European Journal of Operational Research,* 178(3), 819–840.

Leightner, JE and T Inoue (2008a). Capturing climate's effect on pollution abatement with an improved solution to the omitted variables problem. *European Journal of Operational Research,* 191(2), 539–556.

Leightner, JE and T Inoue (2008b). The effect of the Chinese yuan on other Asian currencies during the 1997–1998 Asian Crisis. *International Journal of Economic Issues,* 1(1), 11–24.

Leightner, JE and T Inoue (2009). Negative fiscal multipliers exceed positive multipliers during Japanese deflation. *Applied Economic Letters,* 16(15), 1523–1527.

LeVine, S (2009). China's yuan: The next reserve currency? *BusinessWeek, May 26,* available online at http://www.businessweek.com/globalbiz/content/may2009/gb20090522_665312.htm. [accessed October 14, 2009].

Lindsey, LB (2006). Yuan compromise? (April 6, 2006) *Wall Street Journal,* p. A14.

Modigliani, F and SL Cao (2004). The Chinese saving puzzle and the life-cycle hypothesis. *Journal of Economic Literature,* 42(1), 145–170.

Molinski, D (2007). Dollar pummeled on report by China over its reserves (November 8, 2007). *Wall Street Journal,* p. C5.

Naughton, B (2007). *The Chinese Economy: Transitions and Growth.* Cambridge, Massachusetts: MIT Press.

Ozawa, T (1985). Macroeconomic factors affecting Japan's technology inflows and outflows: The postwar experience. In *International Technology Transfer: Concepts, Measures, and Comparisons*, Rosenberg, N and C Frischtak (eds.), pp. 233–234. New York: Praeger.

Prasad, ES (2009). Rebalancing growth in Asia. Manuscript available at http://www.fullermoney.com/content/2009–07–17/RebalGrowthinAsia.July09.pdf. [accessed August 3, 2009]. An earlier version of the paper was presented at the NIPFP-DEA conference in New Delhi in March of 2009.

Rosenberg, S (2003). *American Economic Development Since 1945: Growth, Decline, and Rejuvenation.* New York: Palgrave Macmillan.

Wang, X (2009). Call for global currency wins int'l backing (March 28–29, 2009). *China Daily,* p. 1, Col. 3–6.

Wang, X and X Zhiming (2008). Hu urges revamp of financial system (November 17, 2008). *China Daily,* p. 1, Col. 1–2.

Wines, M, K Bradsher and M Landler (2009). China's leader says he is "worried" over U.S. Treasuries (March 14, 2009). *The New York Times On-Line,* http://www.nytimes.com/2009/03/14/world/asia/14china.html?_r=1& page-wanted=print. Assessed on May 1, 2009.

Xin, Z (2008). Transfer payments set to rise (April 17, 2008). *China Daily,* p. 13.

CHAPTER 11

COUNTER-CRISIS TRADE EXPANSION*

MIA MIKIC
*Trade and Investment Division of the UN Economic
and Social Commission for Asia and the Pacific*

11.1. Export-Led Growth and its Role in the Current Imbalances

Export-led growth has been always associated with the successful development experience of many East Asian economies. If anything, the East Asian experiences have been put forward as a model of how to apply export-led growth policies and strategies in countries in other (sub) regions which were slower in opening up their trade. It is widely recognized that export-led growth enabled countries such as the Republic of Korea, Singapore, and Thailand, not only to spur their development and reduce poverty in the first place but also to quickly recover from the financial crisis that hit these countries in the period 1997–1998. In the current crisis, however, the situation is not the same. The center of the crisis was not in the Asia-Pacific region, and the region did not trigger the global economic slowdown. While in the late 1990s, the world was worried about contagion spreading from Asia, this time around, Asia not only was on the receiving end of the contagion (which started with the subprime mortgage crisis in the United States in mid-2007 and spread globally), but also may be providing steam to the locomotive, pulling economies out of crisis.

---

* Sections from this chapter were used as inputs into the ESCAP Economic and Social Survey of Asia and the Pacific 2008 and ESCAP Asia-Pacific Trade and Investment Report 2009. The author is grateful to Ors Penzes, Chorthip Utoktham, Wei Cai and Jon Rosseland for excellent research assistance. None of those people should bear any responsibility for any remaining errors. The opinions, figures and estimations in this chapter are the responsibility of the author and should not necessarily be considered as reflecting the views or carrying the endorsement of the United Nations.

11.1.1. *Advantages and disadvantages of export-led growth*

Advantages of export-led growth arise from export being fully based on comparative advantage of a country (such as labor-intensive manufactures or resource-intensive commodities), and by allowing domestic producers to use overseas market to utilize economies of scale. An important aspect (as well as an advantage) of this strategy is the presence of low and transparent trade barriers which enable domestic firms to improve their competitiveness in both domestic and overseas markets.

However, there are disadvantages of the export-led growth too. These disadvantages date back to the original export-pessimism argument of Nurkse (1959) who emphasized the need for sufficient absorption capacity in developed countries for products as the most serious limitation to export-led growth for developing economies. The fear was that if all developing countries start exporting goods at the same time and exports were mostly directed to the developed economies of the time, sooner or later these import markets would need to undergo structural changes to accommodate increasing imports, and, therefore, there would be a limit to amount of exports from the developing countries. This restructuring need would push the developed countries toward protectionist policies targeting imported manufactures, which would curtail the development efforts of developing countries. Fortunately, further elaborations of export-led growth such as the "stages approach to comparative advantage" (Balassa, 1979) and "flying-geese model" (Akamatsu, 1962) were able to show that developing countries would enter and graduate from manufacturing exports over longer period of time, leaving enough time for adjustments in developed countries. Over time, developing countries themselves would become importers of some type of manufacturing goods. Advantages and disadvantages of the export-led growth model are shown in Table 11.1.

Another disadvantage of export-led growth is less related to structural changes and more to regular economic cycles and sudden crises in the importing markets, destabilizing growth. Perhaps, Lewis put it best in his Nobel Prize Lecture in 1979: "For the past hundred years the rate of growth of output in the developing world has depended on the rate of growth of output in the developed world. When the developed grow fast, the developing grow fast, and when the developed slow down, the developing slow down."

Table 11.1. Advantages and disadvantages of export-led growth.

Export-led growth	
Advantages	**Disadvantages**
• based on comparative advantage	• sensitive to business cycles and recessions
• utilization of economies of scale	• may result in increasing protectionism in importing markets
• anchoring nonprotectionists trade regime in exporting countries	• may have adverse environmental impacts

11.1.2. *Transmission of impacts and decoupling*

So what happens when the importing economy faces an economic slowdown or recession? A slowdown in growth leads to reduced demand for consumer goods as well as intermediate products, commodities, services, and factors. As the absorption capacity of the domestic market declines, governments are tempted to favor domestic products to imports, through trade protectionism and exchange rate manipulations. Initially foreign suppliers will try to compete and maintain their share in the market by reducing export prices (though they may risk encountering antidumping allegations). This will cause a drop in profitability, which is exacerbated as a result of reduced production runs, rising costs as a result of efforts to search for alternative markets and costs of idle capacity, among other costs. Unless the domestic market can compensate for falling export market demand (e.g., as a result of stimulus packages or similar "New Deal" policies), business profitability will continue to decline, pushing national economies into a probable recession. In short, reduced import demand in overseas markets leads to reduced export sales which lead to reduced domestic production, rising unemployment, and a fall in GDP growth rates in national economies.

Transmission, of course, is not instantaneous, and the intensity of impacts along the causality transmission chain from one economy to the next may either increase or decrease in the process of transmission. For policymakers in exporting developing countries, the principal question is how to break (or even better, prevent) this contagion of recession into their economy. Weakening the link between a country's GDP growth and the principal factors that lead to such growth (i.e., exports or, more precisely, overseas demand in developed countries for exports from developing countries), has become known as decoupling or de-linking.[1] Lewis suggests that de-linking can be made possible only by a sharp acceleration in trade among developing countries. No other crisis in modern times has tested the need and possibility for such acceleration in trade among developing countries more than the current crisis.

Another important transmission channel of recession is financial in nature. Financial linkages among countries are based not only on the capital flows that normally cross national borders in search of higher returns, but also on financial market integration in general. For many developing countries, for instance, reduced flows of remittances as a result of recession abroad significantly affect the level of investment capital at home, and, hence, domestic investment and economic growth as well. Typically, both trade and financial linkages will operate at the same time even though they may have seemingly different manifestations and/or effects.

In order to formulate appropriate policies in support of decoupling, policymakers need to understand the main factors which will influence the intensity by which a shock in one economy will be transmitted into their own economy. The literature on this topic includes studies which claim that the more integrated countries are through trade and financial market linkages the more they tend to share correlated business cycles.[2] On the other hand, some argue (e.g., Krugman, 1993) that countries trading on the basis of comparative advantage will have fewer synchronized fluctuations. This is based on the assumption that comparative advantage supports interindustry trade (thus, each country developing dominantly different industries) and that the shock particular to one industry is less likely to be transmitted into other (different) industries.

---

[1] Decoupling in an economic sense implies weakened linkages rather than completely breaking them. However, note that older literature uses term "linkage" (e.g., Lewis, 1979). Note also that economics borrows a number of terms from physics; "Decoupling" is one of them. In physics, decoupling means phenomenon in which the interactions between some physical objects cease to exist. See also Akin and Kose, 2008.

[2] Empirical studies seem to go along with this claim. See for example "Asia's Growth and Financial Cycles: Are they Synchronized with the United States?" In "Asia and Pacific" *Regional Economic Outlook*, International Monetary Fund, April 2008.

However, in today's globalized world, production locations tend to be spread across several countries in a number of suitable centers (most often, special zones within countries) and are connected through complex supply (or value) chains. Since these supply chains are mostly organized along intraindustry linkages, it is expected that countries which are engaged more extensively in intraindustry trade would be affected to a larger extent. This is because the industries producing similar products are technologically more similar, and thus shocks are more easily transmitted across border into the "same" industry. On the other hand, an important characteristic of the globally integrated world is that shocks are not industry specific and do not discriminate among industries.[3]

In 2008, it appeared that there were two major problems associated with the world economy: (1) excess demand for commodities such as energy, food, and metals, pushing their prices to historical highs, and (2) excess supply of financial services, such as short-term capital, hedge funds, and other derivatives, pushing up prices of assets and creating bubbles.[4] At the beginning of 2009, the world economy looked very different, with many commodity prices falling to lower levels, many bubbles already burst, and credit crunches paralyzing production and trade, especially in small developing countries and for small and medium-sized enterprises (SMEs) (cf. Lamy, 2008).

11.1.3. *Global imbalances are part of the export-led growth mechanism*

Many try to pin the 2008 financial crisis on global imbalances, as represented by the sizable deficits in the current account and government budget of the United States which are mirrored by current account surpluses in other (mostly developing) countries which followed the

---

[3] Apart from technology differentiation, there are other reasons why a financial crisis may have different impacts on different industries.

[4] See Kenneth Rogoff's "The world cannot grow its way out of this slowdown," published on July 29, 2008 at www.voxeu.org.

"export-led growth" strategy. There have even been calls for an end to globalization, free trade and free movement of capital, the "wicked trinity" believed to be causing the current troubles.

While the current macroeconomic imbalances are indeed uniquely high and will require special international coordinated action, especially with regard to financial regulation (see the G20 reports of November 15, 2008 and April 2, 2009), it is not the first time in the postindustrial revolution economic history that imbalances in one major economy are financed by the savings in other economies. As Alesina and Giavazzi show, the deficit of the United Kingdom at the end of the 19th century was financed from savings in other Commonwealth countries, while "negative" savings in the United States were financed from excess savings first in Germany, later in Japan, and today in China[5] (and some other Asian countries).

The enormity of the problems today is more related to the scale of the imbalances and concomitant financial flows, rather than their existence per se. After all, if surplus savings in one country could **not** be invested in another country where they would earn the highest returns, the growth of both countries would certainly be adversely affected. Therefore, to allow these beneficial flows to continue in a sustainable manner, there is a need for reasonable and prudential regulation and supervision of international financial transactions, not their elimination.

On the other end of the spectrum, some argue that the model of export-led growth contains some self-corrective mechanisms that would automatically fix the imbalance problems (albeit in the longer term and probably not without any help from policy makers). This argument rises from the fact that export-led growth is typically driven (at least in the early stages) by policies causing (1) higher rates of export growth than economic (i.e., GDP) growth; (2) disequilibrium real exchange rates (requiring an appreciation of home currency); (3) current account surpluses; (4) a limited control of capital movements; and, (5) a relatively high savings rate. As those imbalances start to get corrected, domestic currencies appreciate, current account surpluses are expected to decline, and

---

[5] See Alesina and F Giavazzi (2008).

domestic demand will play an increased role in sustaining economic growth.[6]

11.2. The Pattern of Asia-Pacific Integration into the Global Economy Sets: These Economies' Future

11.2.1. *Recent trends in exports and imports*

Despite robust trade growth (surpassing the GDP growth) for much of the period since the Asian financial crisis, exports and imports dwindled as the recession took hold in the major importing developed markets in the later part of 2008 and early 2009. Figures 11.1 and 11.2 track year-on-year changes of monthly values of export and imports of selected Asian economies, respectively, for longer period of time to reflect on the severity of the contraction of trade in the current crisis. As shown in Figure 11.1, exports started to fall in August 2008 and continued to decline through early 2009. For most of the depicted economies, the exports plunged in two stages, first during October and November of 2008 by around 20% and in January 2009 when rates of decline reached 40%. It should be noted that these contractions in exports were almost twice as sharp as those experienced in the aftermath of the Asian financial crisis during 1997–1998 and the dot.com recession in 2001.[7] Nominal monthly exports in US dollars in the early months of 2009 declined to the values, prevailing in 2005 and 2006. These are significantly lower than nominal export values in the 2007 and early 2008 which saw the most dynamic growth of exports from this region.

---

[6] However, there are problems with switching from an export-led to a domestic demand–led growth (which arguably is the whole art of decoupling). Recently, a former chief economic adviser to the Government of Thailand was quoted to have said "We have had export-led growth for more than 30 years. We have not geared ourselves toward investment in domestic-led growth" quoted in Fuller (2008). In addition, the level of domestic demand depends on the size of the population and income level, which cannot be easily manipulated, certainly not in the short run.

[7] This also applies to a contraction of trade at global level. Furthermore, global nominal trade has fallen in 2008 more sharply than during the Great Depression in 1930s (see Eichengreen and O'Rourke, 2009).

302 Mia Mikic

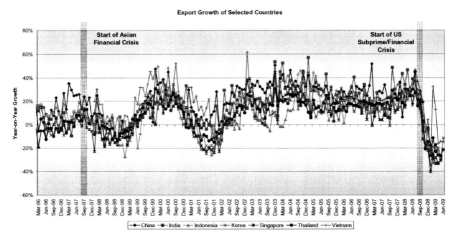

Figure 11.1. Trends in exports of selected Asian economies, February 1996–June 2009.
Source: ESCAP calculation based on data downloaded from CEIC database.

From Figure 11.2, it appears that imports of these economies slowed down in the second half of 2008 and that from October 2008 until the end of June 2009, it remained at the significantly lower level compared to the previous year. Rates of import contraction on the year-on-year basis are also in double digits, and they shadow closely the rates of export contraction. The magnitude of imports contraction at between 20% and 40% in the current crisis is larger than contraction recorded in the Asian crisis and certainly deeper than in the dot.com crisis.

From June 2009 there are signs of exports and imports rebound, as well as return to positive changes in real GDP and industrial production in a number of countries in the region, including its giants, China and India. This, however, should not be taken as an indication of a return of dynamic economic and trade growth as experienced during 2006–2008.[8] The changes in real economies, as deep as they have been in the current crisis, cannot be simply and quickly, if ever, inverted.

---

[8] Pascal Lamy stated that "…the trade contraction…seems to (have begun) bottoming out, it is unclear how and how long it will take us to exit the crisis" (WTO, 2009). See also ADB, 2009 (July).

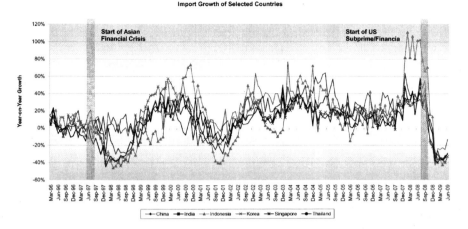

Figure 11.2. Trends in imports of selected Asian economies, February 1996–June 2009.
Source: ESCAP calculation based on data downloaded from CEIC database.

11.2.2. Developments in trade orientation and trade dependence prior the current crisis

Let us first explore regional orientation. Table 11.2 summarizes changes that have taken place in export orientation of Asia-Pacific economies[9] between 1995 and 2007. Increased reliance on export to emerging markets in Asia is obvious as the share of those markets in total exports of Asia-Pacific more than doubled from 1995 to 2007. At the same time, the share of three developed market destinations dropped by almost eight percentage points to less than 40%. The Figures 11.3 and 11.4 show the changes in orientation to the developed and emerging markets for the individual Asia-Pacific economies. Only Vietnam and countries from North and Central Asia register increase in share of developed markets in their overall exports. Since these countries started exporting to the developed countries only after the changes in political regimes of the early 1990s, this is not a surprising result.

---

[9] Asia-Pacific economies refer to the members and associate members of ESCAP. There are 58 regional members and associate members, three of which are classified as developed (Australia, Japan, and New Zealand). However trade data is not available for most of the associate members and for some of the members — in total, 29 developing members and associate members and the three developed members are included in the analysis here unless specified otherwise.

304 Mia Mikic

Table 11.2. Geographical reorientation of Asia-Pacific exports, 1995–2007.

As a percentage of total Asia Pacific exports	1995*	2007*	Change 2007–1995**
Export to all selected markets (EU, Japan, US, ASEAN, China, and India)	57.4	61.6	4.2
Export to three developed markets (EU, Japan, and US)	45.9	38.0	−7.9
Export to three emerging markets (ASEAN, China, and India)	11.5	23.6	12.2

*Simple averages of national export shares; ** Percentage point differences.
Source: IMF, Direction of Trade Statistics, September 2008.

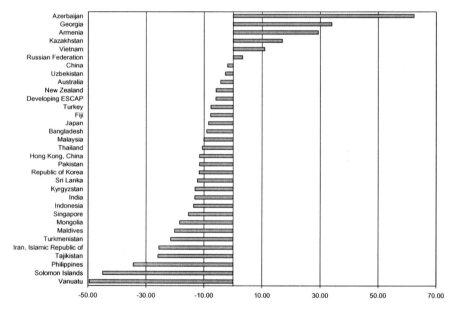

Figure 11.3. Export to US, EU, and Japan in total exports (percentage point differences, 1995–2007).

Indicators of export dependence (percentage contribution of export to GDP) support the claim of the increased importance of the three emerging markets for the Asia-Pacific economies as a whole. Table 11.3 shows the changes in export dependence on all the selected markets (US, EU,

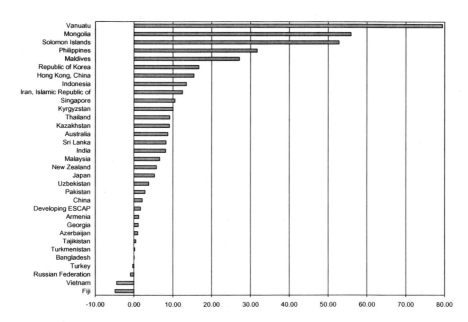

Figure 11.4. Export to China, India, and ASEAN in total exports (percentage point differences, 1995–2007).

Japan, China, India, and ASEAN), as percentage points differences (see also APTIR 2009 Statistical Appendix).

The Figures 11.5 and 11.6 focus on four individual economies that show more dramatic changes with respect to exports to these markets. Figure 11.5 contrast changes in export dependence indicators for selected economies with respect to exporting to the US and China. As is clear from the figure, more than half of the Asia Pacific economies are still experiencing increasing export dependence on the US market. This is particularly true for economies which are more involved in the vertical supply chains (Thailand, China, and Japan), and depend on the US market for one group of products (textile and commodities). Countries like China, record slightly larger increase in export dependence than rise in share of export to the US in its total export. However, number of countries which now belong to a group of more mature exporters (such as Singapore, Hong Kong, China, Malaysia, Republic of Korea, and Turkey) record reduced export dependence on the US market.

306   *Mia Mikic*

Table 11.3. Export dependence of ESCAP countries, 1995–2007, percentage point difference.

	Japan	EU	US	China	India	ASEAN
East (and North Asia)						
China	−0.8	4.6	3.7	0.0	0.6	1.43
Hong Kong, China	0.1	4.0	−3.4	40.9	1.6	1.88
Mongolia	−2.9	−2.4	0.2	25.4	0.0	−0.10
Republic of Korea	−0.7	1.6	−0.1	8.0	0.4	0.16
Southeast Asia						
Indonesia	0.0	0.0	−0.1	1.5	1.0	2.25
Malaysia	−1.6	0.3	−2.2	6.2	2.2	1.74
Philippines	1.9	0.8	−2.0	14.3	0.1	4.26
Singapore	−2.0	0.5	−9.1	14.7	4.0	16.40
Thailand	1.7	3.1	1.8	5.1	0.9	6.16
Vietnam	0.8	10.2	13.8	2.4	0.2	5.35
South and South-West Asia						
Bangladesh	−0.1	4.5	1.5	0.1	0.2	0.05
India	−0.3	0.6	0.6	1.1	0.0	0.44
Iran, Islamic Republic of	1.0	−2.5	−0.8	4.0	−0.3	0.53
Maldives	0.3	0.9	−2.1	0.0	0.1	4.40
Pakistan	−0.6	−0.4	0.8	0.5	0.3	−0.29
Sri Lanka	−0.9	0.2	−3.9	0.1	2.4	−0.49
Turkey	0.0	3.0	0.0	0.1	0.0	−0.06
North and Central Asia						
Armenia	0.1	−0.6	0.8	0.1	0.0	0.04
Azerbaijan	0.5	25.1	5.6	−0.1	0.0	0.56
Georgia	0.0	3.9	1.6	0.1	0.1	0.04
Kazakhstan	0.1	6.3	0.9	3.8	0.0	−0.26
Kyrgyzstan	0.0	−4.5	−0.1	2.2	0.1	0.02
Russian Federation	−0.3	2.2	−0.3	0.3	0.0	−0.40
Tajikistan	−1.4	−62.2	−2.6	−0.7	0.0	0.04
Turkmenistan	0.0	−7.3	0.3	0.1	0.0	−0.03
Uzbekistan	−0.3	−0.8	0.5	0.8	0.1	0.11
Pacific Island Economies						
Fiji	−0.6	−3.8	1.6	−0.2	0.0	−1.35
Solomon Islands	−20.6	0.6	−0.9	43.7	0.8	5.36
Vanuatu	3.1	−3.8	0.2	0.1	10.2	33.10

(Continued)

Counter-Crisis Trade Expansion   307

Table 11.3. (*Continued*)

	Japan	EU	US	China	India	ASEAN
Developed ESCAP						
Australia	−0.3	0.2	0.0	1.6	0.6	−0.60
Japan	0.0	1.1	1.0	2.1	0.1	0.51
New Zealand	−1.8	−0.3	0.2	0.5	0.1	0.40

Source: IMF, Direction of Trade Statistics, September 2008.

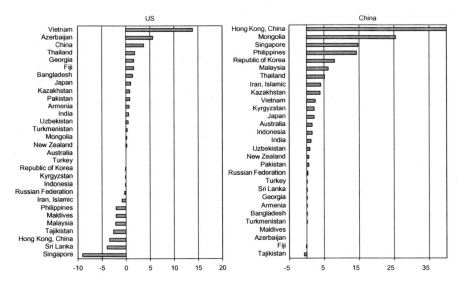

Figure 11.5. Export dependence on US and Chinese markets, 1995–2007, percentage point differences.

In case of dependence on exporting to Chinese market, only Fiji and Tajikistan record negative values, while for all other observed economies in the sample export to China contributes an increasing portion of their GDPs. At the top of the list are Hong Kong, China, Mongolia, Singapore, and other members of ASEAN. We will offer some explanations for this increased dependence on Chinese market for this group of countries, based on their ability to integrate into vertical supply chains and engage in fragmented production later in the text.

308 *Mia Mikic*

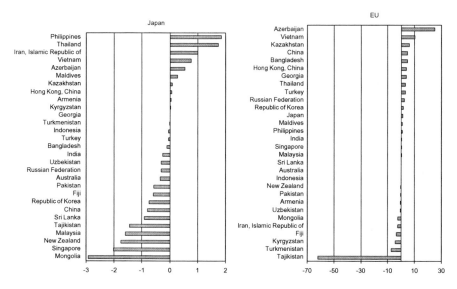

Figure 11.6. Export dependence on Japanese and the EU markets, 1995–2007, percentage point differences.

Figure 11.6 offers pictorial description of export dependence changes with respect to Japanese and European market. More than half of the observed ESCAP economies are becoming less dependent on exporting to Japan. There are some exceptions, however. Some countries (e.g., Philippines and Thailand) have recently signed the free trade agreements with Japan, and thus increased export dependence on Japan is to be expected. It is at the same time encouraging that such countries do not engage in trade diversion and are also increasing dependence on export to other markets, such as China in the region. It is necessary to note that scale of increased dependence to Japanese market range up to two percentage points, while the changes in export dependence on Chinese market for about half of the countries are above that range (Figure 11.4). Also in Figure 11.5 are the changes of export dependence indicators for the EU market. The changes here are regionally split with most of Central Asian economies recording weakened dependence, as well as traditional exporters to the EU such as New Zealand or Australia. On the other hand, South Asian and Southeast Asian countries, with few exceptions still note increasing export dependence *vis-à-vis* the EU market.

11.2.3. *"Factory Asia" phenomenon*

The Table 11.3 and Figures 11.3–11.6 provided information on developments in indicators of export dependence, based on direct export flows. However, as the IMF (2008) study shows, direct export dependence indicators do not provide the complete picture on export dependence. Thus, to get better idea on if and by how much Asia Pacific economies are decoupling from the US economy, it is also necessary to explore indirect export linkages. The IMF study estimates the total export exposure which takes into account the flows of intermediate and capital exports used as inputs to produce goods in all third countries and then reexport them to the US and the EU for the final consumption. These total export dependence indices are important to take into account when exploring impacts of the recession in the US and EU. Changes in both direct and total indices are shown in Figure 11.7 (calculated from IMF results) for selected economies in ESCAP region. First of all, there is no reduction in either direct or total export dependence on EU market, while some economies do witness reduced direct export exposure to the US

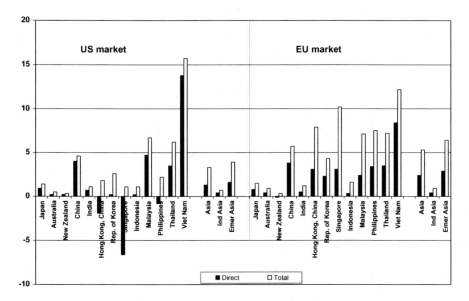

Figure 11.7. Direct and total export exposure changes (1995–2007) in US and EU markets.
Source: Based on data from IMF (2008, Table 2.1, p. 28).

(Hong Kong, China; Singapore, and Philippines). Although direct export dependence for Singapore shows weakening exposure to the US economy, when total dependence is taken into account, Singapore remains almost equally dependent on US economy and is much more dependent on EU economies, in 2006 than it was in 1994. Similarly, while Korean or Thai direct dependence is weakening or growing slowly, total dependence is increasing. With respect to the EU market, total export dependence has lower variance and therefore may signal deeper connection between the exporting and the EU economies. One thing is certain, when exploring decoupling possibilities, it is not sufficient to look only on direct export or capital flows. One must take into account indirect linkages which are increasingly getting more influence.

The indirect dependence on developed, in particular the US economy, arises because of way the manufacturing goods are produced using fragmented production and vertical supply chains. Many factors contributed to this state of affairs, including declining transport costs (until mid-2000s), reduction of trade barriers, and impact on declining service link costs necessary for the establishment of international production networks. These networks have flourished in automobile, electronics, office equipment, and in general parts and components sectors and are the main reason why we now refer to this region as "Factory Asia": this is a phenomenon of production networks being used to produce final goods destined for consumption outside the region, mostly in the US and the EU.[10]

---

[10] Athukorala, P-C (2007, pp. 18–19) concluded: "The data clearly reflect China's evolving role as an assembly center within the East Asian region. The share of East Asia in total parts and component imports to China has increased sharply. By 2004/5 over two-thirds of total components imports to China originated in the region. By contrast, China's final goods exports are heavily concentrated in extra-regional markets, particularly in industrialized countries in Europe and North America. Between 1992/3 and 2004/5, the share of Chinese exports to East Asia in total final goods exports declined from 49.5% in 1992/3 to 26.5% while exports to OECD countries (excluding Japan and Korea) increased from 29.3% to 50.1%. There is a close similarity between the country composition of China's components imports and exports, with East Asia accounting for the lion's share on both sides. This reflects the multiple border-crossing of components between China and the other countries in the region at different stages of the production process."

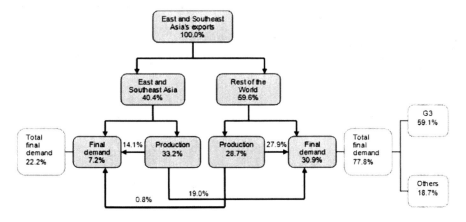

Figure 11.8. Breakdown of emerging Asian exports.

Source: Kim *et al*. (2009).

These production networks, which are based on the import of parts and components from low-cost regional producers for further processing in more advanced developing countries, and for final assembly and export of final goods out of the region, are concentrated across the region but mostly in China and Southeast Asia. Figure 11.8 shows the conclusion that about 60% of all Asian exports are eventually consumed by the United States, European Union, and Japan (instead of about 32% of total exports if only direct exports are taken into account). The results suggest that developed countries still "remain the main export destination for final goods departing from Asian ports when taking into account the share of intermediate goods that are traded for assembly and production within the region before being shipped out of the region." (Kim *et al*., 2009, p. 8).

Looking at the direction of import flows from the region to China, one can get a stylized evidence of the above described process. Figure 11.9 shows the net changes in import flows as shares of total China imports between 1995 and 2007. Share of imports from ASEAN, Republic of Korea, South Asia, and the Rest of the World (ROW) have risen,[11] while share of imports from the United States, EU, and Japan have declined for more than five percentage points over the period.

---

[11] Reflecting higher dependence on energy and other primary commodities from outside the region.

312 *Mia Mikic*

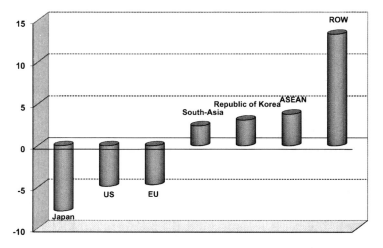

Figure 11.9. Change in sourcing of Chinese imports, 1995–2007 (percentage point differences).
Source: IMF, Direction of Trade Statistics, September 2008.

This is also the reason why there is a strong correlation between Chinese exports to the United States and the European Union and imports of China from the rest of emerging Asia (as shown in Figure 11.10).[12]

11.2.4. *Intraregional trade grows asymetrically*

With the rapid increase in total exports and imports of developing economies in Asia and the Pacific, the current dollar value of their intraregional trade has also grown rapidly. Since Asian financial crisis the total trade of Asian developing countries tripled, while their intraregional trade rose 3.2 times. That allowed for only a small increase in the share of intraregional trade. Figure 11.11 shows how the total and intraregional trade annual growth rates shadow each other closely and leave almost no space for an increase in share of intraregional trade for the Asia-Pacific

---

[12] "This is consistent with the large role of China as an assembly hub for final products in the Asian production networks — as shown by the steady increase of parts and components in China's imports from emerging Asia during the recent past. The collapse of exports to China helps explain why economies like Hong Kong, China, and Taiwan Province of China have been severely affected — exports to China account for about 20% and 45% of their total exports, respectively, compared with 10% on average for the other economies in the region." (IMF, 2009, pp. 3–4).

Counter-Crisis Trade Expansion 313

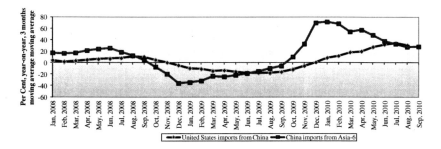

Figure 11.10. Are Chinese exports to US and Asian exports to China associated?

Note: Asia 8 comprises Indonesia, Malaysia, Philippines, Republic of Korea, Thailand, Taiwan Province of China, Singapore and Hong Kong, China. Monthly raw export data in Hong Kong, China, Malaysia, Singapore, and Thailand are only available in their local currency. Average spot exchange rates were used to convert into US dollars.
Source: ESCAP calculation based on data from the CEIC Database.

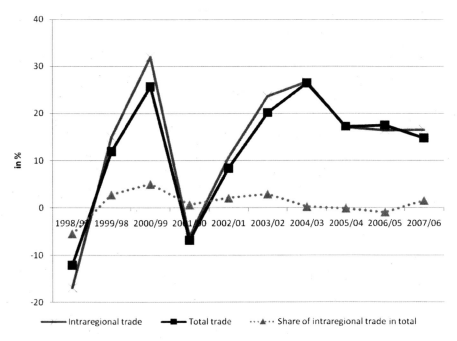

Figure 11.11. Growth of total and intraregional trade of developing Asia Pacific economies.

Source: Calculated based on Comtrade data downloaded from WITS.

314   *Mia Mikic*

economies. This absence of stronger reliance on the regional trade explains why Asia-Pacific economies suffered such a sharp reduction of trade when demand for imports in the developed market economies collapsed with the financial crisis.

The question then remains why intraregional trade among Asia Pacific economies did not become more important and whether that may remain an obstacle in further development of Asia and the Pacific. Some elements for the answer are provided here, based on descriptive statistics, while other developmental issues are discussed at length in ESCAP (2009). It has been already established that developing Asia Pacific countries have not increased their intraregional trade at the expense of the rest of the world. This means that the increasing intraregional trade of developing Asia-Pacific economies does not divert trade from other countries, at least not in a noticeable way. Two other important features of this intraregional trade are identified.

First, the main driver of intraregional trade is the ASEAN+3 group and within that group, it is China. China's trade with ASEAN+3 (ASEAN + China, Japan and Republic of Korea) has contributed the most to the rise of intraregional trade value. As depicted in Table 11.4, from 1997 to 2007, China's contribution in intraregional trade almost doubled, while the share of ASEAN countries, Japan, and Republic or Korea either dropped or did not change over that decade. Tracking the shares of intra-ASEAN+3 in total export and imports of the group on a monthly basis since year 2000, shows an inverted U shape for both exports and imports. Figure 11.12 shows that up to mid-2004, intraregional exports and imports relative to total export and imports increase and then take a mild downward trend. However, since August 2008, these shares have been moving in opposite direction: intraregional export continued to fall, while imports from the region as a share of imports from the world shot up to reach almost 50%.[13]

---

[13] This surge is due to much sharper decline in imports from the world to the decline of intraregional imports. There are several possible explanations for this. Spread of recession and crisis obviously halted importation of nonnecessities, most of which were sourced from outside the region. On the other hand, some inputs and intermediates. Furthermore, imports from the region has been encouraged by initiatives such as currency swaps and payments in local currency within ASEAN + 3, but it remains difficult to assess contribution of those to this trend in Figure 11.12.

Table 11.4. Who are the major players in the Asia-Pacific intraregional trade? (%).

	1997			2007		
	Export	Import	Trade	Export	Import	Trade
Intra-ASEAN+3/ASEAN+3 to ESCAP	71.0	81.8	**76.1**	65.8	82.5	**73.5**
of which:						
ASEAN	41.2	44.7	**43.0**	38.5	35.1	**36.7**
China	14.3	14.6	**14.5**	23.9	30.3	**27.2**
Japan	31.4	27.6	**29.5**	23.7	21.2	**22.4**
Republic of Korea	13.0	13.1	**13.0**	13.9	13.3	**13.6**

Source: Calculated from Comtrade data downloaded by WITS.

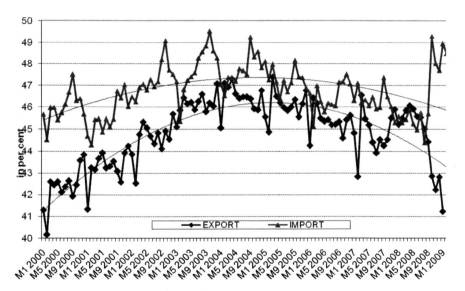

Figure 11.12. Intraregional exports and imports as share in total exports and imports of ASEAN+3 (monthly).

Source: Calculated from data downloaded from DOTS, IMF.

The second distinguishing feature is that this intraregional trade was driven by a need to obtain intermediates, parts, and components from the region for further processing of the products destined to be exported to major developed markets of the United States and the EU. As already mentioned, and evidenced in the ADB report (July 2009), more than half of total intraregional trade in East Asia[14] consisted of intermediate inputs, while intraregional trade of final goods accounted for only 22% of exports. This feature of intraregional trade is the one that differentiates Asian integration the most from the European and North American integration because in the latter area, intraregional trade has been driven by higher than proportional increase in intraindustry trade of final goods.

11.3. Helping the (New) Engine to Run

It is true that Asia of the early 2000s is not any more on the map. As it was shown, trade flows and characteristics of fragmented production are pointing toward stronger, although asymmetric, intraregional dependency, even if exporters are still not weaned off the American market for the sales of final goods. In other words, decoupling of Asia is indeed not a theoretical construct, even though it is far from established in reality. To help with decoupling process, it seems other export-led Asian economies will be able to lean on the large countries of the region (India, China, and Indonesia) where the domestic demand still contributes the lavish part of the GDP creation. The region has the largest share in the global foreign exchange reserves and is making efforts toward a coordinated approach on how best to use these reserves for developmental purposes of the region. Some of the governments have already started to implement New Deal type of policies aimed at boosting demand (see for example Chinese 2008–2009 package). All these measures require China and other larger economies to move into a position of a locomotive for regional exports.

11.3.1. *Fiscal policy and, stimulus packages*

According to the United Nations (2009, p. 65) the key response to declining external demand however has been fiscal policy. While expansionary fiscal policy suggests a possibility of combining a reduction in taxes with an increase in spending, most countries of the region have opted to increase spending and apply tax reductions only selectively. On the spending side,

---

[14] Which is the same as ASEAN + 3 in terms of country coverage.

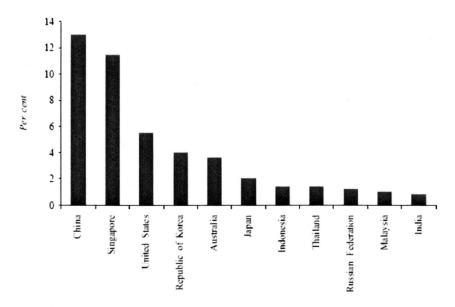

Figure 11.13. Selected stimulus packages as share in economy's GDP.
Source: UN, 2009, p. 65, Figures IV–V.

a number of countries have adopted stimulus packages with the objectives of providing support to (selected) industries, maintain jobs, build domestic demand, and protect individuals. These packages vary substantially in terms of absolute amount and as share in GDP (see Figure 11.13).

In relative terms, China adopted the largest stimulus package in the region, of over 12% of GDP (based on this measure, this is the largest stimulus package undertaken by any of the countries).[15] Figure 11.14 illustrates the breakdown of the stimulus packages in several countries of the Asia-Pacific region with respect to the use of increased public spending. Not all spending will be equally effective in boosting demand and the modalities are wide-ranging from stimulating private consumption through transfers to households/individuals or by providing them with public goods, to investing in physical and social infrastructure, or assisting

---

[15] The 2009 stimulus packages in China and in the Asian region in general are larger than the stimulus in the USA, Germany (and the Eurozone in total), and Japan, although most countries in developing East Asia have more limited fiscal space (World Bank, April 2009, p. 24).

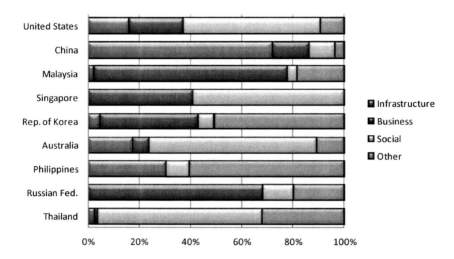

Figure 11.14. Stimulus breakdown by use.

Source: World Bank (2009, Appendix Table 14), various World Bank country quarterly economic reports and EIU county reports.

selected sectors, industries or producer groups such as small and medium-size enterprises. Interestingly, the countries of the region vary in focus for their programs, with China spending approximately 70% of its stimulus package on infrastructure, while Thailand is investing over 60% of its program on provision of public goods such as health, schools, and households. According to an assessment provided by the UN (2009), fiscal stimulus packages in the region may pay insufficient attention to social protection, as the spending is more biased toward boosting consumption rather than on improving protection of those who work, but may not have adequate health or pension coverage.

In general, there is a feeling that while the stimulus seems to be necessary and apparently has been working in a number of countries to provide relief from the global recession, there should be no complacency in terms of designing policies that will deal with repayments of these packages in the future. There is a concern that an easy monetary policy combined with expansionary fiscal spending will lead to inflationary pressures that may have serious adverse impacts on the long-run competitiveness of smaller developing countries. These impacts can be made worse by trade, investment and exchange rate policies which will be based on protecting selected sectors or groups in the economy or society. Section (11.3.2.) provides some evidence that Asia Pacific countries as yet have not opted to pursue such a policy direction.

11.3.2. *Trade, investment, and exchange rate policies*

The level of tariff protection in the Asia Pacific region varies from applied tariffs equal to zero (in economies such as Singapore, Hong Kong, China) to very high tariffs for specific products (so-called tariff peaks). Most of the countries that are members of the WTO accepted to bind their tariffs, though for many the bound rates are much higher than the applied levels (see Figure 11.15), while the coverage of binding is rarely 100%. Though it is encouraging to note that on average no subregion has an applied MFN tariff higher than 20%, one needs to consider that (1) the difference between applied and bound tariffs is quite high in most countries, and (2) protectionist policies in trade in current times are determined as much as or more by nontariff measures (NTMs) such as standards, antidumping measures, safeguard measures, and non-trade measures than tariffs.

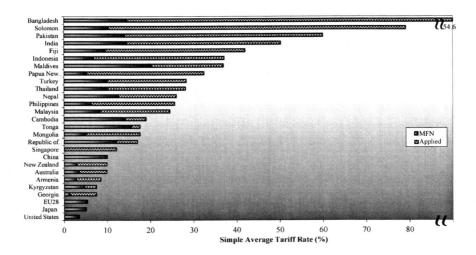

Figure 11.15. Difference between applied and bound tariffs.

Source: Trade profiles 2008, WTO 2008.

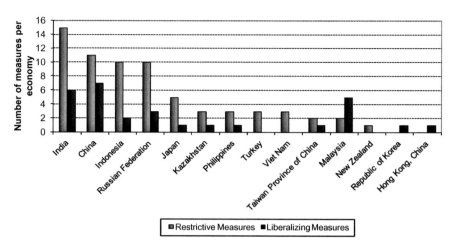

Figure 11.16. Trade measures enacted by Asia Pacific countries from October 2008 to June 2009.

Source: Part I, Annex Table 1, ESCAP, APTIR 2009.

Countries in the region have enacted many trade measures since they started to feel the bite of the recession. According to data collected by the World Trade Organization (WTO), which started tracking and reporting such measures in the second half of 2008, a total of 62 measures have been enacted in the region, of which 42 are restrictive measures, and 20 are liberalizing measures, with China adopting the largest number of liberalizing measures, and India adopting the largest number of restrictive measures. Figure 11.16 summarizes the measures taken by countries of the Asia Pacific region from October 2008 until June 2009.[16]

In addition to trade measures, countries have adopted measures to boost liquidity in foreign currency especially for export financing. A number of countries have negotiated credits from international financial bodies to support trade finance but also for more general purposes.

---

[16] The website www.globalalertontrade.org was created to enable traders and other stakeholders to report such restrictive or liberalizing trade measures.

With respect to policies related to capital flows, given that many countries are faced with a decline in FDI from developed countries in 2009, a concern has been that countries might use policies to attract capital away from other destinations. Fortunately, as already described, an upward trend in intraregional investment has been observed during the last few years. Furthermore, there are expectations that this trend will continue through 2010 and beyond. However, this is subject to improvements made in three important areas. First, intraregional cooperation within Asia should be supported further by governments as this may accelerate the recovery of financial flows into the respective countries. Second, protectionist policies intended to ease the effects of the crisis may well lead to other adverse effects and hinder recovery. Third, governments are urged to continue their efforts to improve the investment climate of their countries in order to keep attracting FDI from within the Asian region as well as other countries enabling an early recovery from the impact of the current crisis.

Finally, trade policies are often complemented by exchange rate manipulations to increase relative export competitiveness. While prior to 2008 many Asian governments were pressured into allowing an appreciation of their currencies *vis-à-vis* the major global reserve currency, i.e., the US dollar, not much movement in that direction has taken place since the transmission of the crisis on real economies started in earnest in mid-2008. The only exceptions were the Japanese yen and, to some extent, the Chinese yuan (see Figure 11.17 and IMF, 2009). In contrast, regional currencies' movements against the euro have been less volatile and generally showed an upward trend (Figure 11.18).

11.4. Way Forward

Liberalized trade in goods and services and easier movements of capital and financial flows has made the world economy even more interdependent. Tracking economic developments since the last global downturn in 2001, points to the growing dependency of regional economies on the Chinese economic growth and the lesser dependence on sound US growth. Nevertheless, the recession in the US that has already spread to Europe and Japan, will definitely have an impact on Asia-Pacific

Figure 11.17. Regional currencies movements against US$.

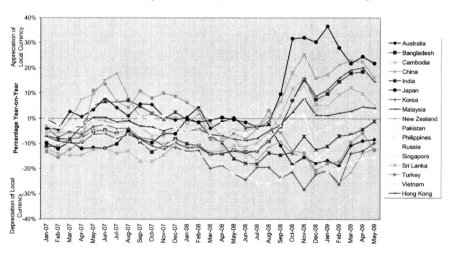

Figure 11.18. Regional currencies movements against the euro.

economies. Therefore, Asia Pacific, especially its smaller economies, cannot be complacent and wait for the solution to the problem to arrive from the global meetings. There are number of actions that each country can do independently, but the fact remains that no country can ride this crisis out on its own.

The recommended actions include actions and measures that are meant to further facilitate South–South trade in the region and strengthen their capacities to decouple.

1. First, do no harm.[17] By this it is meant that governments should not resort to nationalistic economic policies of protectionism and harm trading partners by forcing terms of trade against them (as would, for example, export restrictions on rice cause for rice net-importing countries). This also applies to using the real challenges of climate change or food crisis to obscure protectionist policies.

2. As part of the actions on trade policies, there should be a revitalization of efforts for pushing through with the agreed commitments under the Doha Development Agenda. Majority of WTO members from this region still have big differences between their bound and applied tariff rates, and many still too often use nontariff protection and contingent protection not in line with principles of the WTO. Thus, an agreement of the Doha Round would strengthen the case for applicability of multilateral rules. Due policy space should be given to developing countries as envisaged, *inter alia*, by the Doha Declaration.[18]

3. Special attention to be put on trade agreements that at present fragment the regional market by imposing rules of origin that are costly to comply with and other trade procedures that increase cost of trading. A conscious effort should be made when negotiating trade agreements within the region to make such agreements trade and development

---

[17] These points were discussed in ESCAP 2008. Schott published his opinion on the topic of Global financial crisis under the title "First, Do No Harm" on November 3, 2008 on the Peterson Institute for international Economics webpage available at http://www.petersoninstitute.org/realtime/?p=210.

[18] Strengthened multilateral rules are obviously not needed only in trade area, but most importantly for monitoring and regulating international financial flows. This means better international financial architecture. This region should not miss this opportunity to contribute new ideas and solutions that would put forward the interests of developing countries and the need for removing inherent asymmetries of the multilateral monetary system.

324   *Mia Mikic*

friendly and preferences possible to be utilized by small traders which in many cases include women entrepreneurs and farmers.

4. Supporting South–South investment by removing biases on FDI from other developing countries. Active encouragement of such flows as well as South–South transfer of technology and knowledge is overdue.

5. Aid for Trade should be promoted and channelled particularly into building the supply-side responses of developing countries so that they can make more effective use of the market access opportunities that will arise in future. Investments to tackle bottlenecks in transit, transport and trade facilitation continue to be most effective ways to assist developing countries in using trade as an engine of growth.

6. Finally, policies in support of domestic demand, including infrastructure investment should not be ignored. Financial resources for such policies are to be easily found in the region.

References

ADB (2009). *Asia Economic Monitor*, July, available at http://www.aric.adb.org/asia-economic-monitor/.

Akamatsu, K (1962). A historical pattern of economic growth in developing countries. *The Developing Economies*, 1, 7–13.

Akin, C and MA Kose (2007). Changing nature of North–South linkages: Stylized facts and explanations. IMF Work in progress, WP/07/280.

Alesina, A and F Giavazzi (2008). Globalization is not our enemy (October 30, 2008). The Economists' Forum in *Financial Times,* accessed at http://blogs.ft.com/wolfforum/2008/10/globalisation-is-not-our-enemy/.

Athukorala, P-C (2007). The rise of China and East Asian export performance: Is the crowding-out fear warranted? The Australian National University, Working papers in trade and development, No 2007/10, September.

Balassa, B (1979). A "stages approach" to comparative advantage. In *Economic Growth and Resources*, I Adelman (ed.), pp.121–56. London: Macmillan.

Eichengreen, B. and K.H. O'Rourke (2009). A Tale of Two Depressions. Vox.eu column. originally published on April 6, 2009, available from http://www.voxeu.org/index.php?q=node/3421#jun09

ESCAP (2008). Macroeconomic policy brief: Financial crisis. 1(2), December. Accessed from http://www.unescap.org/pdd/publications/me_brief/mepb_2.pdf

ESCAP (2009). *Asia-Pacific Trade and Investment Report 2009: Trade-led recovery and Beyond.* ESCAP Bangkok.

Fuller, T (2008). This time, Southeast Asia is not at center of the crisis (November 11, 2008). *The New York Times*, printed version appeared on November 12, 2008 on page A8 of the New York edition. Online version accessed at http://www.nytimes.com/2008/11/12/world/asia/12thailand.html

IMF (2008). Asia's growth and financial cycles: Are they synchronized with the United States? In Asia and Pacific, *Regional Economic Outlook*, International Monetary Fund, April 2008.

IMF (2009). *Regional Economic Outlook: Asia and Pacific — Global Crisis: The Asian Context* (Washington, D.C.) May.

Kose, MA, C Otrok and E Prasad (2008). How much decoupling? How much converging? *Finance and Development*, 45(2), June. Available at http://www.imf.org/external/pubs/ft/fandd/2008/06/kose.htm

Krugman, P (1993). Lessons of Massachusetts for EMU. In *The Transition to Economic and Monetary Union in Europe*, Giavazzi, F and F Torres (eds.) pp. 241–269. New York: Cambridge University Press.

Lamy, P (2008). Lamy warns trade finance situation "deteriorating". Speaking notes for the informal meeting of heads of delegations, general council, WTO, November 12, [accessed November 13], at http://www.wto.org/english/news_e/news08_e/gc_dg_stat_12nov08_e.htm

Lewis, A. (1979) The Slowing Down of the Engine of Growth. Lecture to the memory of Alfred Nobel, Prize lecture delivered on December 8, 1979, accessed November 24, 2011 from http://www.nobelprize.org/nobel_prizes/economics/laureates/1979/lewis-lecture.html

Rogoff, K (2008). The world cannot grow its way out of this slowdown, published on July 29, 2008 at www.voxeu.org.

UN (2009). The Global Economic and Financial Crisis: Regional Impacts, Responses and Solutions, United Nations, New York.

World Bank (2009). *Battling the Forces of Global Recession*, East Asia and Pacific Update, April (Washington, DC).

WTO (2009). Lamy presents road map for the autumn negotiations. Statement by Director-General to the Trade Negotiations Committee on July 24, 2009, available from http://www.wto.org/english/news_e/news09_e/tnc_dg_stat_24jul09_e.htm

CHAPTER 12

COLLAPSE, CONSEQUENCES, AND PROSPECTS OF JAPAN'S TRADE

RYUHEI WAKASUGI
Kyoto University, Japan

12.1. Introduction

The financial crisis initially triggered in 2007 by defaults among subprime mortgage borrowers and the resulting accumulation of bad loans deteriorated to the point where it caused an acute credit crunch following the failure of Lehman Brothers in 2008. The US-initiated financial crisis quickly spread to the world. The world GDP, which grew at 3.2% in 2008, shrank negatively by 1.3% in 2009 and remained low in 2010.[1] Japan's economic recession was acute. Table 12.1 shows its severity. Japan's GDP fell 0.6% in 2008 and fell 6.2% in 2009. By contrast, America's GDP fell 2.8% in 2009 after growing 1.1% in 2008.

It is noted that not only the growth rate of Japan but also the export from Japan shrank. The decline in US demand sent shockwaves through export-dependent countries. However, we find that the impact of the reduction of US demand hit Japan more than other countries. We find that the impact of the reduction of US demand on trade varies among countries because of different structures of comparative advantage. It is important to investigate why Japan was affected so seriously by the change in US demand and what feature of Japanese exports caused the severe decline after the financial crisis. The seriousness of the Japanese recession stemmed from three reasons: a reduction of the world demand, a specific feature of Japan's exportable goods, and a change of the structure of Japan's triad trade with the US and China.

---

[1] World Economic Outlook, IMF.

328 Ryuhei Wakasugi

Table 12.1. Growth rates of GDP.

	2005	2006	2007	2008	2009	2010	2011e
World	4.5	5.1	5.2	3.2	−1.3	1.9	4.3
U.S.	2.9	2.8	2.0	1.1	−2.8	0.0	3.5
EU	2.2	3.4	3.1	1.1	−4.0	−0.3	1.7
United Kingdom	2.1	2.8	3.0	0.7	−4.1	−0.4	2.1
Japan	1.9	2.0	2.4	−0.6	−6.2	0.5	2.2
China	10.4	11.6	13.0	9.0	6.5	7.5	10.2
NIES-4	4.7	5.6	5.7	1.6	−5.6	0.8	4.4
ASEAN-5	5.5	5.7	6.3	4.9	0.0	2.3	4.3
India	9.2	9.8	9.3	7.3	4.5	5.6	6.9

Source: World Economic Outlook, IMF.

The US government and other Western countries including Japan were bold in their policy responses to the crisis. In addition to providing $700 billion in public funds for financial institutions to facilitate the disposal of bad assets, the US government made emergency bridge loans available for the three big US automobile manufacturers to help them stave off imminent bankruptcy. Further, it laid out plans for huge fiscal expenditures. The US Federal Reserve also adopted a zero interest rate policy by lowering its target for the benchmark federal funds rate to 0%–0.25%. Those tonics helped the US economy recover from the crisis in a short term. Although the US government launched an immense economic stimulus package, it is obvious that the government cannot afford to continue the expansionary fiscal and monetary policies forever. The resulting fiscal deficit in the US will bring problems to both the US and world economies. Few policy options are available for the Federal Reserve. Meanwhile, the emerging economies including China, India, and Brazil are recording high post-crisis growth. Domestic demand has been increasing steadily because of a rising income level, stimulating expanded world trade. The development of emerging economies is crucial for the prospects of the world economy.

The chapter aims to discuss the causes and consequences of Japan's trade collapse and the prospect of Japanese export. In the following section, paying attention to the change in US imports, we discuss the reasons why the impact on Japanese exports was more serious than other nations.

Section 12.2 describes how the development of a trade triad between the USA, China, and Japan, which was accelerated by the growing offshore outsourcing of Japanese multinational corporations (MNCs), caused a change in specialization of Japanese exports to high-end goods. Specialization had a major effect on the reduction of the Japanese exports to the USA. In Section 12.3, by decomposing the Japanese export value to the number of products (extensive margin) and exports per product,(intensive margin), the chapter statistically examines how they have changed since 1990 and estimates what factors have contributed to these changes. In particular, we find that the long-term trend of the extensive margin differs between the exports for China and the US. In Section 12.4, it examines the degree to which the number of products and exports per product changed after the financial crisis. In comparing the two margins, the drop in the intensive margin of Japanese exports to the US far exceeds expectations and is a primary reason for the sharp reduction in Japanese exports. Section 12.5 discusses the development of emerging economies as a driving force of the growth of world trade. The last section concludes.

12.2. Comparative Advantage and Import Variation

As Figure 12.1 demonstrates, the US economy increased its imports by almost 10% every year since 2002 after recovering from the recession caused by the crash of the IT bubble. However, US import demand fell sharply after the financial crisis as shown in Figure 12.1.

Note however that an import reduction after the financial crisis did not have the same effect on every exporting country across the world. In fact, as shown in Table 12.2, while imports from Japan decreased by 40% in the first quarter of 2009 when compared to the rate for the same quarter in the previous year, imports from China decreased only 10%. Imports from both Japan and Canada decreased most sharply after the financial crisis.

We also find that the reduction of US imports differed among products. As shown in Table 12.2, the reduction in US import-demand for automotive vehicles, parts, and engines, industrial supplies, and materials was very large — over 40% in the first quarter in 2009. The contraction of US automobile loans, provoked by the financial crisis, resulted in a sharp fall in car demand in the US. The reduction in imports of food,

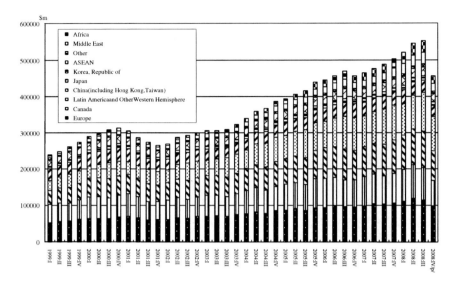

Figure 12.1. Changing US imports by country and region.
Source: Statistics of International Trade, US Department of Commerce.

consumer durables, and nondurables was smaller. The export specialization pattern explains the difference.

The US was Japan's largest importer. It absorbed one-fifth of Japan's exports in 2008. As Figure 12.2 shows, Japan specialized in the export of automobile, electronics and electric goods, and machinery industries to the US in 2008. The share of automobiles and parts was 33.3%, electronics and electric machinery 16%, general machinery 20% of the total exports to the US. In total, exports in these three product categories amounted to over 70% of total exports. The sharp reduction in US demand of industrial supplies and materials, automotive vehicles, parts, and engines in which Japan has a comparative advantage with other countries hit Japanese exports to the US more seriously than the export from other countries to the US.

As Table 12.2 reveals, Canada, concentrating its exports to automotive vehicles, parts, and engines, also experienced a sharp drop in imports of 38% at the first quarter of 2009, while US imports from China fell far less.

Table 12.3 shows that Japanese exports to the US declined significantly more than the exports to all countries. The figures also confirm that the drop in auto trade is the largest. While the average drop was 47% in

Table 12.2. Changing rates of the US imports by country and product.

	2008:I	2008:II	2008:III	2008:3IV	2009:I/p/
All countries	0.12	0.15	0.13	−0.09	−0.30
Europe	0.13	0.14	0.10	−0.07	−0.27
Canada	0.12	0.15	0.16	−0.14	−0.38
Mexico	0.08	0.10	0.04	−0.11	−0.26
China	0.02	0.07	0.10	0.01	−0.10
Japan	0.03	0.03	−0.07	−0.16	−0.41
Petroleum and products	0.60	0.60	0.59	−0.15	−0.54
Foods, feeds, and beverages	0.08	0.12	0.10	0.06	−0.05
Industrial supplies and materials	0.34	0.35	0.37	−0.10	−0.45
Capital goods, except automotive	0.05	0.07	0.03	−0.06	−0.20
Automotive vehicles, parts, and engines	0.00	−0.02	−0.12	−0.24	−0.49
Consumer goods (nonfood)	0.01	0.05	0.05	−0.06	−0.13

Source: Statistics of International Trade, US Department of Commerce.

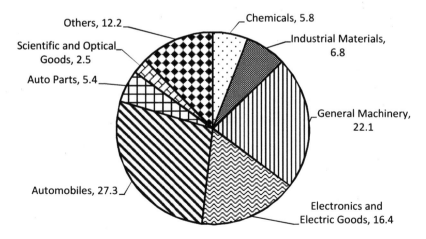

Figure 12.2. Japan's export to US by commodity (2008).
Source: Statistics of International Trade, Japanese Ministry of Finance.

332 Ryuhei Wakasugi

Table 12.3. Changes of Japanese export by country and goods.

	2008:I	2008:II	2008:III	2008:IV	2009:I
Japanese exports by regions/countries					
All countries	6%	2%	3%	−23%	−47%
US	−7%	−11%	−15%	−30%	−54%
Europe	7%	−4%	−3%	−30%	−53%
ASEAN	14%	9%	11%	−14%	−46%
China (including Hong Kong, Taiwan)	5%	4%	4%	−25%	−44%
Korea	3%	1%	13%	−28%	−42%
Japanese exports by goods					
Automotive vehicles, parts, and engines	10%	3%	1%	−26%	−57%
Capital goods, except automotive	0%	−2%	−1%	−22%	−47%
Consumer goods (nonfood)	2%	0%	−2%	−28%	−44%
Industrial supplies and materials	7%	2%	9%	−20%	−39%
Foods, feeds, and beverages	−1%	−3%	8%	−15%	−20%

Source: Statistics of International Trade, Japanese Ministry of Finance.

2009Q1, it was almost 57% in autos and parts. Capital goods more generally fell in line with the average, but the fall off was less severe in consumer goods and industrial supplies.

12.3. Shifting Sources of US Import and Japan's Offshore Sourcing

The goods which Japanese multinational firms export to the USA as the final destination consist of two types: those produced in Japan and exported to the US; parts and components produced in Japan and exported to China, then reprocessed in China before being exported as final products to the US. The former type is high-end knowledge-intense goods requiring skilled labor, and the latter is low-end goods that require unskilled labor. The fall of both direct exports and reexports seriously hurt the Japanese economy.

The sourcing countries for US imports from Asia changed after 2000, while the total remained stable at 34% until 2007. Figure 12.3 and Table 12.4

Collapse, Consequences, and Prospects of Japan's Trade 333

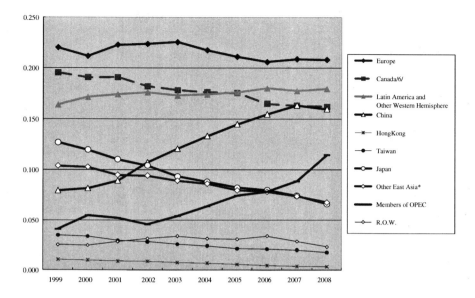

Figure 12.3. Shifting sources of US imports: China's rise and decline of Japan and other East Asia.

Source: Statistics of International Trade, US Department of Commerce.

Table 12.4. Shifting sources of US imports.

	2000	2007
Europe	0.212	0.209
Canada	0.191	0.163
Latin America and Other Western Hemisphere	0.171	0.177
East Asia	0.347	0.334
China	0.082	0.163
Hong Kong	0.010	0.004
Taiwan	0.033	0.020
Japan	0.120	0.074
Other East Asia*	0.103	0.074
Members of OPEC	0.055	0.089
R.O.W.	0.024	0.028

Note: Other East Asia* includes Indonesia, Korea, Malaysia, Philippines, Singapore, and Thailand.

Source: Statistics of International Transaction, Department of Commerce, US.

334 *Ryuhei Wakasugi*

Table 12.5. Shifting destination of Japanese export (%).

	2000	2007	2008	2009
US	29.7	20.1	17.5	16.1
China	6.3	15.3	16.0	18.5

Source: Statistics of International Trade, Japanese Ministry of Finance.

show that in 2000, the import share from Japan was 12%, Asian NIEs-ASEAN (except for Hong Kong and Taiwan) 10%, and China 8%, respectively. In 2007, just before the financial crisis, the import share from Japan dropped to 7%, Asian NIEs-ASEAN (except for Hong Kong and Taiwan) fell to 7%, while the import share from China rose to 16%. The import share from China has increased significantly, while the import shares from Japan and Asian Newly Industrialized Economies (NIEs) and ASEAN have fallen.

During the same period, the destination of Japanese exports also shifted. As shown in Table 12.5, the share of Japanese exports was 30% to the US and 6% to China in 2000. In 2007, the share of Japanese exports to the US dropped to 20% while its share to China increased to 15%. The share of Japanese export to China has continued to increase. In 2009, China became the largest destination for Japanese exports. The formation of the trade triad between the US, China, and Japan caused to shift the source of US imports from Japan to China.[2] Some of products directly exported to the US replaced products made in China, using parts and intermediate goods made in Japan and exported to China. In other words, the fall in Japan's share of US imports, the rise of China's share, and the rise of China's share of Japanese exports and imports reflect the development of Japanese value-added chains.

Ito *et al.* (2009), in collaboration with RIETI, surveyed the offshore outsourcing of Japanese manufacturing firms. The results demonstrate the extent to which the division of Japanese enterprise labor is evolving domestically and in the overseas markets. It is 21% of Japanese firms that optimize the division of labor transnationally, while 42% do so solely within the domestic economy. The number of firms engaged in offshore

---

[2] As for the triad trade between the US, China, and Japan, see Dean *et al.* (2009).

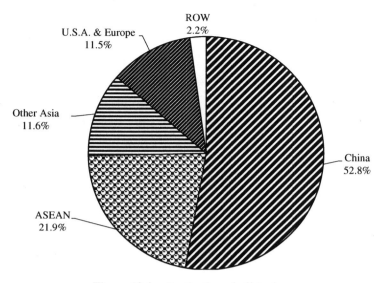

Figure 12.4. Destination of offshoring.

Note: The figure presents that offshoring to China is 52.8%, ASEAN countries, 21.9%, other Asian countries, 11.6%, US and EU, 11.5%. ROW means rest of the world.
Source: Ito *et al.* (2007).

tasking increased from 15% to 21% during the five years from 2001 to 2006. Figure 12.4 shows that offshoring to China (53%) and ASEAN countries (22%) represents three-fourths of the total while the United States and EU comprise only 11%.

This type of trade triad formed by Japanese MNCs' offshore sourcing which facilitated the concentration of Japan's exports to a handful of high-end products clarifies why the crisis hit the nation so hard.

12.4. Changes of Japanese Exports: Extensive and Intensive Margins

Export values can be decomposed into two margins: the number of products exported (extensive margin) and exports per product (intensive margin). The decomposition further illuminates changes in Japan's trade. Recent theoretical and empirical studies of international trade stress extensive margins, highlighting both the number of goods exported and countries of destination. Please refer to the following: Melitz (2003);

336   *Ryuhei Wakasugi*

Bernard *et al.* (2003); Bernard *et al.* (2006); and Chaney (2008). Bernard, *et al.* (2009), however, also studied the intensive margin of average import or export value per firm-products. Bernard *et al.* (2009) decomposed the volume of trade x_c with country c as follows:

$$x_c = [f_c] [p_c] \left[\frac{x_c}{f_c p_c} \right] \tag{12.1}$$

where f_c is the number of firms which export to country c, p_c the number of the goods per firm, $\left[\frac{x_c}{f_c p_c} \right]$ the average trade volume. f_c and p_c express the extensive margin and the intensive margin, respectively.

Bernard *et al.* (2009) investigated the nominal export growth of US from 1993 to 2003 and also examined the behavior of US exports around 1997, at the time of the Asian financial crisis.[3] Their calculations revealed that the intensive margin accounted for the majority of export declines, even though there were substantial changes in extensive margins around the crisis. Since the prior literature had shown that extensive margins of trade can account for a large share of the variation in exports across countries, the new results obtained by Bernard, Jensen, Redding, and Schott should be noted.

This section employs statistical analysis to investigate changes in Japan's trade pattern further. Wakasugi (2009), using "gravity relationships" between partner size and trade flows, studied how the extensive margin and the intensive margin contributed to variations in Japanese exports between 1990 and 2007 just before the financial crisis. Data for the number of exporting firms per destination country and the number of products per firm are not available in Japan. Therefore, instead of using Equation (12.1), Wakasugi (2009) decomposed the trade volume $V_{i,t}$ to the number of products $N_{i,t}$ as the extensive margin and the average trade value $\left[\frac{V_{i,t}}{N_{i,t}} \right]$ as the intensive margin, as follows:

$$V_{i,t} = N_{i,t} \times \left[\frac{V_{i,t}}{N_{i,t}} \right] \tag{12.2}$$

where t expresses the year.

---

[3] Trade density used in Bernard *et al.* (2009) is omitted here.

Collapse, Consequences, and Prospects of Japan's Trade   337

The coefficients are estimated on the basis of the gravity equation in which the size of trade partners determines the trade volume. For the estimation, the extensive margin and the intensive margin are dependent variables, and the GDP size of trade partners, the exchange rate, and the accession of WTO, are included as explanatory variables in Equations (12.3)–(12.5)

$$\ln V_{i,t} = \alpha_0 + \alpha_1 \ln \text{GDP}_{i,t} + \alpha_2 \ln \text{GDP}_{J,t} + \alpha_3 \ln EX_t$$
$$+ \alpha_4 \text{WTO dummy}_i + \varepsilon_t \qquad (12.3)$$

$$\ln N_{i,t} = \beta_0 + \beta_1 \ln \text{GDP}_{i,t} + \beta_2 \ln \text{GDP}_{J,t} + \beta_3 \ln EX_t$$
$$+ \beta_4 \text{WTO dummy}_i + \mu_t \qquad (12.4)$$

$$\ln \left[V_{i,t} / N_{i,t} \right] = \gamma_0 + \gamma_1 \ln \text{GDP}_{i,t} + \gamma_2 \ln \text{GDP}_{J,t}$$
$$+ \gamma_3 \ln EX_t + \gamma_4 \text{WTO dummy}_i + v_t \qquad (12.5)$$

where $V_{i,t}$ is the Japanese export to country i in the year t, $N_{i,t}$ is the number of exported goods from Japan to the country i which are counted on the basis of HS 6 digits product categories, $\text{GDP}_{i,t}$ is GDP of country i in the year t, $\text{GDP}_{J,t}$ is the GDP of Japan in the year t, EX_t is the exchange rate expressed by yen per dollar or yuan, WTO dummy is the dummy variable of China's WTO accession, taking one if China is the member of WTO in the year t. As the estimation is on the time series data, the country pair-specific factors such as language and distance are subsumed in the constant term. The estimation is conducted for Japanese exports to the US and China, respectively based on the data of 18 years from 1990 to 2007.[4]

Table 12.6 shows the estimation results for the trade between the US and Japan. According to the estimation for Japanese export to the US, the income elasticity to the extensive margin was negative, while the income elasticity to the intensive margin was positive.[5]The negative trend of the extensive margin of Japanese exports to the US implies that the number of exported goods from Japan decreased along with the increase of the US demand during the years from 1990 to 2007. Meanwhile, the income elasticity to the intensive margin showed a positive coefficient. This result

---

[4] Cited from Wakasugi (2009).
[5] The source of estimation results is Wakasugi (2009).

338 *Ryuhei Wakasugi*

Table 12.6. Estimation of extensive and intensive margins: export to the US.

	Total value of export	Extensive margin (No. of products)	Intensive margin (exports per product)
GDP of US	0.645**	−0.069**	0.714**
	(8.60)	(−4.32)	(9.14)
GDP of Japan	0.340*	0.110*	0.230*
	(1.96)	(2.99)	(1.28)
Exchange rate (yen/$)	0.867**	0.199**	0.668*
	(4.10)	(4.44)	(3.03)
Constant	3.453	4.912**	−1.458
	(0.58)	(3.92)	(−0.24)
Number of observations	18	18	18
Adjusted R^2	0.817	0.727	0.823

Note: The figures in parenthesis are t-statistics; * and ** indicate 5% and 1% significance. * and ** present 5% and 1% statistics of significance, respectively.
Source: Wakasugi (2009)

suggests that Japanese firms narrowed the product range of exported goods and concentrated on the high-value-added products. As for the effects of exchange rate changes on extensive and intensive margins, the results showed that the yen depreciation had a positive effect, increasing both extensive and intensive margins at a high statistical significance.

The estimated results of Japanese exports to China show a different trend from the exports to the USA. Table 12.7 shows that both the extensive and intensive margins of Japanese exports to China increased with Chinese income with a high statistical significance. Japanese exporters increased the number of exported goods and also raised the average export value as market demand expanded in China. The yen depreciation to the yuan has a negative effect on the extensive, but a positive effect on intensive margin.

These results show Japan's trade structure from 1990 to 2007 shifting as follows:

1. The increase in US demand narrowed product range of Japan's exports to the USA and increased their average value, and the yen depreciation pushed Japanese exporters to expand both the product range of exported goods and the exports per product.

Collapse, Consequences, and Prospects of Japan's Trade 339

Table 12.7. Estimation of extensive and intensive margins: export to China.

	Total value of export	Extensive margin (No. of products)	Intensive margin (exports per product)
GDP of China	0.922**	0.078**	0.844**
	(9.95)	(4.76)	(9.45)
GDP of Japan	2.328**	−0.185	2.512**
	(4.18)	(−1.86)	(4.69)
Exchange rate (yen/yuan)	1.022**	−0.201**	1.224**
	(3.46)	(−3.83)	(4.30)
WTO dummy	0.394**	0.008	0.386**
	(3.76)	(0.43)	(3.82)
Constant	−74.214**	12.203**	−86.418**
	(−4.28)	(3.95)	(−5.17)
Number of observations	18	18	18
Adjusted R^2	0.978	0.941	0.975

Note: The figures in parenthesis are t-statistics; * and ** indicate 5% and 1% significance. * and ** present 5% and 1% statistics of significance, respectively.
Source: Wakasugi (2009).

2. Rising China's demand pushed Japanese exporters to expand the product range and raise the average value of exported goods to China. The depreciation of yen pushed Japanese exporters to raise the exports per product.

3. The reduction of the product range of exports to the USA with the expansion of the product range of exports to China epitomizes the development of the outsourcing-driven trade triad by Japanese multinationals.

12.5. Changes of Japanese Exports after the Financial Crisis

The estimated results of the variation of Japanese exports after 1990 provide a benchmark for predicting changes in Japanese exports after the financial crisis. Table 12.8 shows actual and predicted values for the extensive and intensive margins of Japanese exports to the US during the period from 1990 to 2008. Predicted values are calculated from the estimated coefficients of Equations (12.4) and (12.5).

After 2003, the actual extensive margin of exports to the US shows a downward trend. In particular, it fell sharply in 2008. Meanwhile, the

340   *Ryuhei Wakasugi*

Table 12.8.   Extensive and intensive margins of Japanese exports to the US.

	US					
	Extensive margin			**Intensive margin**		
	Actual (A)	**Predicted (B)**	**Difference (A)–(B)**	**Actual (A)**	**Predicted (B)**	**Difference (A)–(B)**
1990	8.46	8.45	0.01	14.83	14.82	0.01
1991	8.44	8.45	−0.01	14.79	14.79	0.00
1992	8.44	8.45	−0.01	14.78	14.79	−0.02
1993	8.43	8.44	−0.01	14.76	14.78	−0.02
1994	8.42	8.43	0.00	14.79	14.78	0.00
1995	8.42	8.42	0.00	14.73	14.78	−0.05
1996	8.43	8.43	0.00	14.79	14.83	−0.04
1997	8.44	8.44	0.00	14.94	14.88	0.06
1998	8.44	8.44	0.00	15.02	14.93	0.09
1999	8.43	8.43	0.01	14.97	14.93	0.04
2000	8.43	8.42	0.01	15.02	14.94	0.08
2001	8.43	8.43	0.01	14.98	14.98	0.00
2002	8.44	8.43	0.01	14.98	15.00	−0.02
2003	8.43	8.42	0.00	14.89	15.00	−0.10
2004	8.42	8.41	0.01	14.92	15.00	−0.08
2005	8.41	8.41	0.00	15.01	15.03	−0.02
2006	8.42	8.42	0.00	15.14	15.05	0.08
2007	8.39	8.42	−0.03	15.16	15.07	0.09
2008	8.37	8.37	−0.01	15.01	15.12	−0.11

actual intensive margin of exports began to show an upward trend after the year of 2004 in which the US economy recovered from the recession caused by the crash of IT bubble and sharply dropped after the financial crisis. In comparison of the difference of actual and predicted values between extensive and intensive margins, the downturn of intensive margin of Japanese exports to the US was far larger than the downturn of extensive margin. This implies that a sudden drop of the intensive margin mainly caused the contraction of Japan's exports to the US after the financial crisis.

Table 12.9 shows the comparison of actual and predicted values for the extensive and intensive margins of Japanese exports to China. Both extensive and intensive margins kept an upward trend during the period

Table 12.9. Extensive and intensive margins of Japanese exports to China.

	China					
	Extensive margin			Intensive margin		
	Actual	Predicted	Difference	Actual	Predicted	Difference
	(A)	(B)	(A)–(B)	(A)	(B)	(A)–(B)
1990	8.28	8.29	−0.02	12.32	12.43	−0.11
1991	8.30	8.33	−0.03	12.57	12.50	0.07
1992	8.34	8.35	−0.01	12.79	12.61	0.18
1993	8.37	8.38	−0.01	13.00	12.70	0.30
1994	8.41	8.41	0.00	12.96	12.93	0.04
1995	8.44	8.45	−0.01	13.01	13.17	−0.16
1996	8.48	8.45	0.02	13.11	13.21	−0.09
1997	8.48	8.46	0.02	13.21	13.22	−0.02
1998	8.48	8.45	0.03	13.20	13.23	−0.03
1999	8.47	8.47	0.00	13.23	13.36	−0.13
2000	8.48	8.49	0.00	13.43	13.47	−0.04
2001	8.50	8.48	0.01	13.55	13.88	−0.33
2002	8.52	8.49	0.04	13.81	13.93	−0.13
2003	8.53	8.51	0.02	14.08	14.06	0.02
2004	8.54	8.53	0.01	14.26	14.23	0.03
2005	8.55	8.55	0.00	14.36	14.33	0.03
2006	8.53	8.56	−0.04	14.58	14.42	0.15
2007	8.53	8.58	−0.06	14.75	14.55	0.20
2008	8.50	8.49	0.01	14.78	14.76	0.02

from 1990 to 2008. The number of exported goods from Japan has kept expanding as MNCs sought to profit from the international division of labor with China. We find no significant difference between actual and predicted values for both extensive and intensive margins. This contrasts with the sharp drop of the actual intensive margin for exports to the US and suggests that the financial crisis did not seriously harm Japanese exports to China.

12.6. Sustainable Growth of World Trade

From a long-run perspective, we observe two features of the world economy: global imbalance and the growth of middle-income countries.

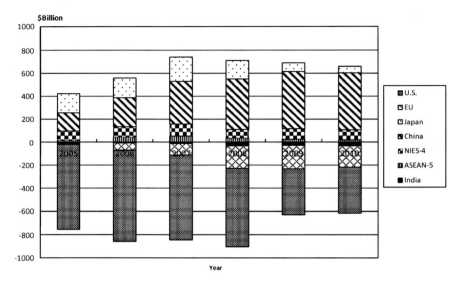

Figure 12.5. Current balance of major countries.

Source: World Economic Outlook, IMF.

Figure 12.5 depicts the current surplus and deficit of major economies including the US and China. After the mid-2000s, China accumulated current account surplus, while the US recorded huge current deficits. Even after the financial crisis, the US still is expanding deficit fiscal expenditure to stimulate the domestic economy. China is also accumulating the trade surplus. These two big imbalances jeopardize the development of world trade. To avoid another economic crisis, both countries should discipline themselves. The reduction of fiscal deficit is essential for a healthy US economy. The appreciation of yuan will adjust the huge trade surplus. The appreciation of yuan also will be beneficial to the development of industrial basis and domestic economy.

Second, we note the significant changes of the world distribution of purchasing power. The share of nations with per capita GDPs ranging from $2,000 to $10,000 has dramatically increased from 16% in 1996 to 40% in 2006 (Table 12.10). The high rate of economic growth in these countries including China and East Asia is likely to be one of the engines that will help world trade to recover, especially given the huge current

Table 12.10. Growth of middle-income countries.

	GDP share		Population share	
Per capita GDP	1996	2006	1996	2006
$\leqq 2,000$	0.08	0.05	0.68	0.45
$2,000 \leqq 5,000$	0.06	0.08	0.11	0.28
$5,000 \leqq 20,000$	0.11	0.15	0.07	0.14
$20,000 \leqq 30,000$	0.56	0.04	0.11	0.01
$30,000 \leqq$	0.19	0.68	0.03	0.13

account deficit of the US. The trade expansion between OECD and middle-income countries is essential for the sustainable development of international trade and the recovery of the world economy. In this sense, the inclusion of middle-income countries into the talks for multilateral trade liberalization is more important than ever.

12.7. Conclusion

The financial crisis affected Japanese exports more seriously than other countries. The sharp decline in American demand for precisely the goods Japan exports explains why the global financial crisis hit Japan harder than most developed OECD countries.

The relationship between the trade structure and macroeconomic shock revealed by the current recession prompted an investigation of Japan's export structure before the financial crisis and the finding that Japanese exporters have narrowed the range of export goods and concentrated their export in high-end goods with high-income elasticity like automobiles and capital goods. A trade triad among the US, China, and Japan has emerged in the process, widening the range of goods exported to China. The structural change of Japanese exports has sharply decreased Japanese exports to the US. Before the crisis, reflecting a rising American preference for high-end Japanese products, exports per product increased but was hit by a sharp fall in income after the financial crisis. In the analysis of post-crisis US exports to Asian countries, Bernard *et al.* (2009) discovered that the intensive margin was strongly affected by diminished demand. This chapter confirms the finding and is consistent with Bernard *et al.* (2009).

Global interdependencies and couplings have increased after 2008 in both real and monetary terms among nations. A huge American current account deficit and a reciprocal Chinese surplus threaten to jeopardize a sustainable international trade growth. Both problems are solvable with proper macroeconomic policies and exchange rate adjustments, and it is essential for Asia's continued development that America and China act responsibly. The rapid growth of emerging economies, particularly Asian countries, is becoming the driving force behind the world's future development and must not be derailed.

References

Bernard, A, I Eaton, B Jensen and S Kortum (2003). Plants and productivity in international trade. *American Economic Review*, 93(4), 1268–1290.

Bernard, A, S Redding and P Schott (2006). Multi-product firms and product switching. NBER Working Paper, 12293.

Bernard, A, B Jensen, S Redding and P Schott (2009). The margins of US trade. NBER Working Paper, 14662.

Chaney, T (2008). Distorted gravity: The intensive and extensive margins of international trade. *American Economic Review*, 98(4), 1707–1721.

Dean, J, M Lovely and J Mora (2009). Decomposing China–Japan–U.S. trade: Vertical specialization, ownership, and organizational form. A paper presented at conference on *the PRC, Japan and the United States: Deeper Integration*, Asian Development Bank Institute, Tokyo.

Ito, B, E Tmomiura and R Wakasugi (2009). Offshoring by Japanese firms: A comparison of destinations. *Harvard Asia Quarterly*, 12(1), 14–19.

Melitz, M (2003). The impact of trade on intra-industry reallocations and aggregate industry productivity. *Econometrica*, 71, 1695–1725.

Wakasugi, R (2009). Why was Japan's trade hit so much harder? In *The Great Trade Collapse: Causes, Consequences and Prospects,* R Baldwin (ed.), VoxEU.org, pp. 209–221.

CHAPTER 13

BUSINESS CYCLE DECOUPLING

IIKKA KORHONEN
Institute for Economies in Transition, Bank of Finland (BOFIT)

JARKO FIDRMUC
Zeppelin University, Friedrichshafen, Germany

IVANA BÁTOROVÁ
Comenius University in Bratislava, Slovakia

13.1. Introduction

The past two decades have witnessed very strong growth in the global economic integration. While total output was growing quite rapidly, volume of international trade grew at pace which was often almost three times as fast. Trade integration has been accompanied and sometimes preceded by financial integration because capital flows have also grown in size. The geographical area, where the economic growth has been strongest and which has also progressed more than the others in economic integration, is Asia. Therefore, in this chapter, we concentrate on the financial integration of two largest Asian emerging market countries, China and India. We measure financial integration by the degree of co-movement in stock market returns. We look at the co-movement first with simple rolling correlations, which are already quite informative. Then, we turn to dynamic correlation analysis, which is a more robust methodology than the ordinary static correlation. Our main aim is to assess how much financial integration, as measured by stock return co-movements, has changed during the recent economic crisis.

Our main results are the following. First, stock market co-movements clearly increased during the crisis, even for countries like China and India, which otherwise were relatively less affected by the crisis. This offers further proof on the nature of the recent crisis. Second, for the two large

Asian countries, their dynamic correlation increased more with the other countries in Asia and around the Pacific. Moreover, correlation of India seems to be much higher than of China, which is somewhat surprising given the fact that India is a much more closed economy than China when measured by foreign trade. To our knowledge, this result is new to the literature.

The chapter is structured as follows. In the Section 13.1, we provide short literature survey on the topic of stock market correlation especially as it relates to emerging market countries. Section 13.2 describes the data and methodology used, while Section 13.3 discusses the results. Section 13.4 concludes.

13.2. Literature Survey

There is a large literature on financial integration investigating co-movements of stock markets, including emerging markets. However, so far only a handful of papers have looked at the Chinese case, and India is still almost uncharted territory. There are two basic approaches to financial integration of stock markets. Some papers look co-movement in first moments, e.g., returns, and some look at co-movement in second moments, e.g., variance. Many different methodologies are used, ranging from simple or conditional correlations, to dynamic correlation, VAR and multivariate GARCH models, and so on. Corsetti *et al.* (2005) provide a critical overview of the empirical work in this area.

For our purposes, we can note some papers which assess the degree of stock market correlation in East Asia. Kozluk (2008) looks at the effects of global and regional shocks on price movements on stock movements in individual countries or stock exchanges. This is done by regressing stock market returns on a number of orthogonal common factors and an idiosyncratic component. For example, if a single common factor can explain a large share of price variation in many different stock markets, it can be called "global factor." In addition, stock market returns can be explained by several regional or sectoral factors.

Kozluk finds that a global factor can explain much of the stock market movements around the world, which implies large degree of integration between different markets. However, between 1996 and 2007, the Chinese stock markets seem to have a specific position, and the global factor plays almost no role in explaining changes in Chinese stock market prices. Moreover, integration between the Chinese markets and the rest of the world did not seem to increase during the sample period. Bae (2011) utilizes similar methodology to assess the stock market integration between several Asian and other stock markets for somewhat longer time period. While correlation between stock market price movements has increased in many regions, including Europe and East Asia, Chinese stock markets are again surprisingly isolated from the rest of the world. By contrast, India is much better integrated with the rest of the world.

However, Johansson and Ljungwall (2009) find that the stock markets in Mainland China are strongly correlated with the other stock markets in the so-called Greater China, i.e., the area consisting also of Hong Kong and Taiwan. Despite the correlation in day-to-day price changes, it should be noted that the markets do not share long-run trends.

From the literature reviewed before we can see that Chinese stock markets have been very little integrated with the other markets, at least during the pre-crisis period.

13.3. Data and Empirical Methodology

13.3.1. *Data*

We assess the degree of financial integration between countries with the dynamic correlation of high-frequency stock prices. For this purpose, we have gathered daily share index data for all selected countries in our data sample from Bloomberg. We have striven to use the most widely used/representative price index for each market. Stock market data starts from January 5, 1999, and ends on March 30, 2010. As our main variable we use the log-differenced indices, which are, of course, very close to percentage changes. Table 13.A1 lists the stock market indices used in the work. Our main emphasis is on two large Asian countries, China and India, and we report dynamic correlation of their stock market indices against other countries. As an example, Figure 13.1 shows the daily price

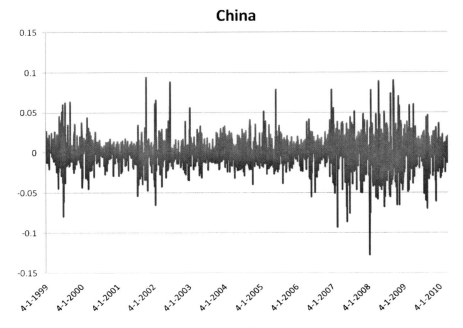

Figure 13.1. Log difference of Shanghai Composite Index.

changes (as log differences) of the Chinese Shanghai Composite Index which tracks the prices of both A and B shares.

While in the empirical part of this chapter we utilize more advanced methods, it is instructive to start examination of the data by looking at ordinary rolling correlations of price changes. Figure 13.2 shows correlation for one-year rolling window[1] between the Chinese stock market and selected major markets in developed and emerging economies. We can see that before the crisis hit, the average correlation of Chinese stock markets with the outside world was relatively low, averaging roughly at 0.1. When the crisis hit, correlation jumped much higher for most countries and regions. It is especially interesting to see that correlation with India and Japan are equally strong, while the US market seems to have very little

---

[1] The data points are quarterly to make the presentation of the data easier. For example, correlation for the third quarter of 2007 refers to the correlation of stock index changes from the beginning of October 2006 (i.e., fourth quarter of 2006) to the end of September 2007 (i.e., third quarter of 2007).

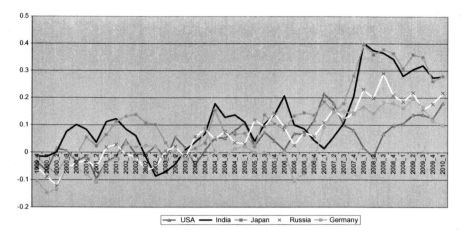

Figure 13.2. Moving correlation of Chinese stock market (one-year window).

co-movement. Looking at the correlation coefficients for the whole period, correlation of the Shanghai index is highest with Hong Kong (0.31), which is not surprising. Correlation is 0.21 with both Singapore and Australia, underlining the regional links around the Pacific Ocean. For practically all European and American stock markets, the correlation is under 0.1.

For India, the correlations are generally much higher, even although India is a much more closed economy in terms of foreign trade than China.[2] India also has higher correlation with almost all countries than China. In Figure 13.3, we can see that during the crisis the correlation of Indian stock market price changes with Japan and Germany both rises to over 0.5. For India the highest correlation coefficients for the entire data sample are with Hong Kong (0.46) and Singapore (0.45). One should remember that the Chinese market also was very much correlated with these two markets. Table 13.1 shows the correlation coefficients for the entire 1999–2010 period for the Chinese and Indian stock market returns with various countries.

---

[2] During the 2000s, the average share of exports and imports in the Chinese GDP was 57.6%, while for India, this ratio was 38.2%.

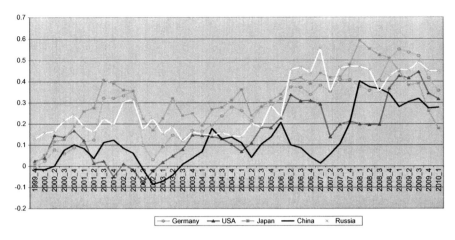

Figure 13.3. Moving correlation of Indian stock market (one-year window).

13.3.2. Empirical methodology

We employ spectral analysis, especially the so-called dynamic correlation, to study integration of selected stock market indices. The most common measure of co-movement between time series is classical correlation, which is also commonly used in business cycle correlation. Unfortunately, classical correlation does not allow for a separation of idiosyncratic components and common co-movements. It is also basically a static analysis, so it fails to capture dynamics in co-movement. For our purposes here, we prefer the alternative measure of synchronization of business cycles, namely dynamic correlation, as proposed by Croux *et al.* (2001).[3] Bátorova *et al.* (2008) and Fidrmuc and Korhonen (2010) apply dynamic correlation for analysis of business cycles of emerging economies.

Similarly to correlation analysis, we consider two stationary variables for output in countries i and j, y_i and y_j. The spectral density functions for

---

[3] Messina *et al.* (2009) discuss dynamic correlation for discussion of wage developments over the business cycle. De Haan *et al.* (2008) discuss alternative measures of synchronization of business cycles.

Business Cycle Decoupling 351

Table 13.1. Correlation of Chinese and Indian stock market returns.

	China	**India**
UK	0.06	0.28
France	0.06	0.29
Germany	0.06	0.27
Austria	0.12	0.33
Belgium	0.09	0.29
Denmark	0.09	0.32
Finland	0.04	0.23
Portugal	0.08	0.32
Spain	0.06	0.29
Sweden	0.05	0.28
Switzerland	0.05	0.27
Norway	0.05	0.27
Poland	0.08	0.33
Netherlands	0.06	0.29
Italy	0.14	0.40
USA	0.07	0.23
Canada	0.07	0.23
Mexico	0.07	0.24
Brazil	0.10	0.23
Chile	0.10	0.24
Argentina	0.06	0.20
India	0.17	1.00
Australia	0.21	0.38
Japan	0.19	0.33
Hong Kong	0.31	0.46
Singapore	0.21	0.45
Taiwan	0.15	0.29
Russia	0.09	0.31
China	1.00	0.17

these variables are denoted by $S_i(\lambda)$ and $S_j(\lambda)$ and their the co-spectrum is $C_{ij}(\lambda)$, where frequency λ is defined between zero and π. Then, the dynamic correlation, ρ_{xy}, equals

$$\rho_{ij}(\lambda) = \frac{C_{ij}(\lambda)}{\sqrt{S_i(\lambda)S_j(\lambda)}} \ . \tag{13.1}$$

The dynamic correlation lies between -1 and 1. Moreover, it is interesting to analyze the average dynamic correlations over a given interval of frequencies. If we define such interval as $\Lambda = [\lambda_1, \lambda_2)$, then the dynamic correlation within the frequency band Λ is defined as

$$\rho_{ij}(\Lambda) = \frac{\int_\Lambda C_{ij}(\lambda)d\lambda}{\sqrt{\int_\Lambda S_i(\lambda)d\lambda \int_\Lambda S_j(\lambda)d\lambda}} \tag{13.2}$$

Particularly, if $\lambda_1 = 0$ and $\lambda_2 = \pi$, the $\rho_{xy}(\Lambda)$ is reduced to the static correlation between y_i and y_j, corr (y_i, y_j). The dynamic correlation within the frequency band, defined in (2), can be used, for example, to measure the co-movement of business cycles of two countries as we can select the frequency band of interest (one-day frequency, or longer) and evaluate the dynamic correlation within this frequency band. In practice, the results are reported in charts, where the right hand of the vertical axis shows the very short-run correlation, in our case one day. Moving to left indicates that more and more days (as well as the indices' own autocorrelation) are taken into account.

We estimate the dynamic correlation for three different periods 1999–2002, 2003–2006 and 2007–2010. This allows us to discern changes in the dynamic correlation over time.

13.4. Results

In this section, we briefly sketch the results obtained from dynamic correlation analysis. In Figure 13.3, we see the dynamic correlation of the Chinese stock market against all the countries in the sample. We can see that for practically all countries the dynamic correlation is higher during the last period, i.e., during the crisis. Moreover, correlations are higher for Asian and other countries around the Pacific (e.g., Australia). This shows the importance of regional integration. Interestingly, for many European countries the dynamic correlations seem to increase when we move away from the very short-run developments. This could mean that especially the intraday and weekly dynamics of analyzed stock markets is different. For Asian countries, there is no such effect. This reflects, for example, similarities in the regulations, habits, and general investor behavior among Asian capital markets.

Business Cycle Decoupling 353

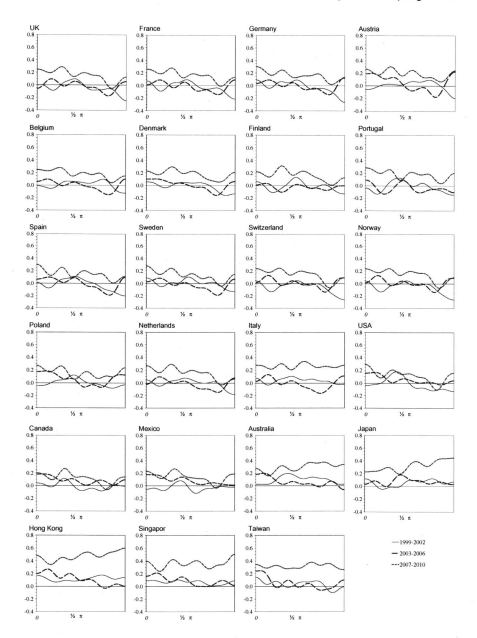

Figure 13.4. Dynamic correlation of stock market returns between China and selected countries.

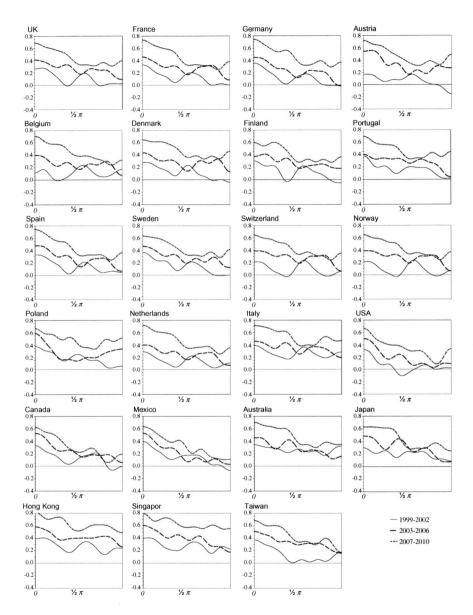

Figure 13.5. Dynamic correlation of stock market returns between India and selected countries.

For India, dynamic correlations are generally higher than for China, even for the pre-crisis period. Nevertheless, they did increase during the crisis. Interestingly, India seems to be highly correlated also with European stock markets. Dynamic correlation is the lowest — for China — for the very short-run movements and increases then steadily for longer-run frequencies. For India, Asian countries behave in the same manner as all the others.

The most important feature documented by Figures 13.4 and 13.5 is that there was a structural change in integration of stock markets around the world. Dynamic correlations for the most recent period, 2007–2010, increased both in China and India. Moreover, the increases are especially important for the long-run frequencies. The intraday dynamic remained nearly unchanged in comparison to nonAsian economies, but it increased among China (to a lesser degree also for India) and Asian economies as well.

In India, the increases of integration of stock markets continued the previous convergence of stock performance since 1999. By contrast, integration of Chinese financial markets was low before 2006. It will be interesting to observe whether integration of China will continue also in future.

13.5. Conclusions

In this chapter, we have assessed the integration of Chinese and Indian stock markets with the markets elsewhere in the world. Our focus has been on the correlation of stock market returns across different countries. The recent economic crisis — the Great Recession — provides a very interesting test case for integration of financial markets. We can see that in normal times most of the stock markets in our data sample are quite highly correlated, regardless whether we use the traditional correlation measures or more advanced dynamic correlations. However, China is the most noticeable outlier, despite it becoming a major economic power during this period. Correlation of its main stock market, Shanghai, with the other markets of the world is essentially zero for most of the 2000s, despite China's rapid integration with the rest of the world through foreign trade and inward foreign direct investment.

However, the special nature of the recent financial crisis is revealed when we look at the estimations for 2007–2010. Correlations for all markets jump up, and even the Chinese market registers correlation coefficients of well over 0.5 with different countries. Nevertheless, it is noteworthy that even during the crisis the highest dynamic correlation coefficients were registered with other Asian and Pacific countries. Even if day-to-day correlation of different markets becomes less as the crisis passes, it is clear that integration of Chinese markets with the other markets in the region will increase.

Appendix

Table 13.A1. Stock indices used.

Country	Stock index
UK	FTSE 100
France	CAC 40
Germany	DAX
Austria	ATX
Belgium	Bel20
Denmark	OMX 20
Finland	OMXH
Portugal	PSI 20
Spain	IBEX 35
Sweden	OMXS 30
Switzerland	SSMI
Norway	OSE
Poland	WIG 20
Netherlands	AEX
Italy	S&P/MIB
Ireland	ISEQ
US	NASDAQ
Canada	S&P/TSX
Mexico	IPC
Brazil	BOVESPA
Chile	IGPA
Argentina	MERVAL
India	S&P CNX Nifty
Australia	S&P/ASX 200
Japan	TOPIX
Singapore	TSI
Taiwan	TAIEX
Russia	RTSI
China	SSEC

Source: Bloomberg.

References

Bae, K-H (2011). Stock market integration and financial contagion. In *The Dynamics of Asian Financial Integration*, Devereux, MB, PR Lane, C-Y Park and S-J Wei (eds.), pp. 135–173. Routledge, London.

Bátorová, I, J Fidrmuc and I Korhonen (2008). China in the world economy: Dynamic correlation analysis of business cycles. BOFIT Discussion Paper July 2008, Bank of Finland, Helsinki.

Corsetti, G, M Pericoli and M Sbracia (2005). "Some contagion, some interdependence": More pitfalls in tests of financial contagion. *Journal of International Money and Finance*, 24, 1177–1199.

Croux, C, M Forni and L Reichlin (2001). A measure of co-movement for economic variables: Theory and empirics. *Review of Economics and Statistics*, 83, 232–241.

de Haan, J, R Inklaar and R Jong-A-Pin (2008). Will business cycles in the euro area converge? A critical survey of empirical research. *Journal of Economic Surveys*, 22, 234–273, 04.

Fidrmuc, J and I Korhonen (2010). The impact of the global financial crisis on business cycles in the emerging economies in Asia. *Journal of Asian Economics*, 21, 293–303.

Johansson, AC and C Ljungwall (2009). Spillover effects among the Greater China stock markets. *World Development*, 37, 839–851.

Kozluk, T (2008). Global and regional links between stock markets — the case of Russia and China. BOFIT Discussion Paper, April 2008, Bank of Finland, Helsinki.

Messina, J, C Strozzi and J Turunen (2009). Real wages over the business cycle: OECD evidence from the time and frequency domains. *Journal of Economic Dynamics and Control*, 33, 1183–1200.

PART V

PETRO SHOCK

CHAPTER 14
LESSONS FROM BRICS

MASAAKI KUBONIWA
Hitotsubashi University, Tokyo

14.1. Introduction

Brazil, Russia, India, and China (BRIC)[1] account for 37% of the planet's land and 40% of its population. Their efforts at catching up with the advanced economies has been described in detail by O'Neill (2001), and Wilson and Purushothaman (2003) using a conventional growth accounting [total factor productivity (TFP)].

As they predicted over the past decade, the weight of the BRICs (Brazil, Russia, India, and China) in the world GDP at a current US$ basis markedly grew from 8% in 2000 to 18% in 2010, and China contributed half the advance.[2] In 2010, BRIC GDP in US$ on a PPP basis was 25% of the global total. The share of the BRIC countries in the G6 GDP at a current US$ basis increased from 13% in 2000 to 37% in 2010. The BRICs accounted for 15% of world exports. China's GDP exceeded Japan's by eight percentage points at the end of 2010 measured in current dollars, and it hopes to overtake US soon.

In 2009, the global financial crisis caused a 2% drop in world GDP, but the BRICs expanded by 4.3% despite Russia's 7.8% contraction. China and India were the pacesetters. In 2010, the BRICs GDP surged by 8.8%.

---

[1] BRIC excludes South Africa. See BRICs *Joint statistical Publication, 2011* available at the website of National Bureau of Statistics of China.

[2] The figures in this section are based on IMF, *The World Economic Outlook Database*, April 2011, IFS and the websites of the statistics authorities of the BRICs. For India during 2008–2010, the data of the press release of the Indian Central Statistics Office dated February 7, 2011 are employed.

362   *Masaaki Kuboniwa*

In this chapter, we analyze the determinants of BRIC economic growth by comparing the dynamics of real GDI (gross domestic income) with GDP for 1995–2010 including the period of the global financial crisis. Real GDI measures the purchasing power of a country's total income generated by its domestic production (SNA 2008, Section 15.188). Real GDI is defined as "command-basis GDP" by the US Bureau of Economic Analysis (OECD, 2006); in an open economy the real GDI is real GDP *plus* the trading gain (or loss) including currency appreciation and depreciation. Accordingly, the trading gain is defined as the difference between the real GDI and GDP. It arises from changes in the terms of trade, defined as the ratio of the export price P^e to the import price P^m, namely P^e/P^m. In general, if imports and exports are large, relative to GDP, and if the terms of trade markedly change due to a large increase in export prices relative to import prices or a decrease in import prices relative to export prices, the magnitude of potential trading gains or losses would be large, as will be shown was the case for Russia 2008–2010.

The big finding of this econometric inquiry is that the Asian BRICs, China and India were hardly affected by oil price shocks and associated changes in terms of trade, even during the global depression during 2008–2010. *Ceteris paribus*, they appear well positioned to withstand future external shocks, whereas Russia's prospects appear to hinge decisively on natural resource price-driven "command GDP."

14.2. An Overview of Economic Growth in the BRICs

Figure 14.1 shows the GDP growth of the BRICs for 2000–2010.[3] As can be seen, China grew fastest, followed by India, Russia, and Brazil. The average annual growth rates of China, India, Russia, and Brazil for 2000–2010 were 10.5%, 7.8%, 4.8%, and 3.6% respectively. Russia's growth paced India's before the global financial crisis. In 2009, however

---

[3] Here, in addition to the data mentioned in the footnote 2, we employ the United Nations online database of the main aggregates (the 2011 version released in December, 2010) for 1990–2009 and the CEIC online database for 2005–2010. Russia's data are based on the updated GDP series provided on the website of its statistics office named Rosstat on April 1, 2011.

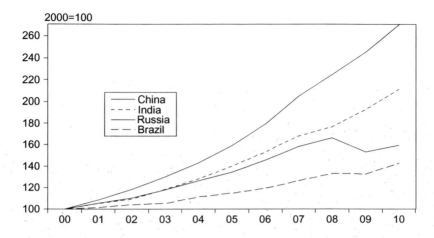

Figure 14.1. GDP growth in BRICs in the 2000s.

Russian GDP contracted, whereas India continued to grow rapidly. Thereafter, Russia's growth path followed Brazil's lead.

Figure 14.2 shows BRIC growth for the extended period 1990–2010. China and India grew fastest over this interval with the average 10.4% and 6.6% respectively. Brazil showed steady growth at the average growth rate of 3.1%. In contrast, Russia's GDP in 2010 was 1.07 times its level in 1990 due to the post-Soviet economic collapse in the early 1990s. Russia's average growth rate was only 0.34% for 1990–2000. This rate was less than Japan's low rate of 0.94% for the same period. Even though the composition of Russia's GDP became more consumer-oriented, growth point to point is negligible.[4] Russia's per capita GDP at a current US$ is about 10,000 US$, well below the level of the advanced countries.

GDP at a current US$ basis is important from the point of view of a country's collective and individual purchasing power for tradable goods

---

[4] Let us index the GDP level (Russia's peak) in 1989 as 100. Using the official, updated data, Russia's GDP level accounts for 99.9 in 2009 and 103.9 in 2010. Using our estimate of the growth rate of *minus* 0.6% for 1990 (Kuboniwa and Ponomarenko, 2000; Rosefielde and Kuboniwa, 2003) and the official data for 1991–2010, it accounts for 102.4 in 2009 and 106.5 in 2010. Anyway, in our estimation, during the global financial crisis Russia's GDP was slightly over its peak level.

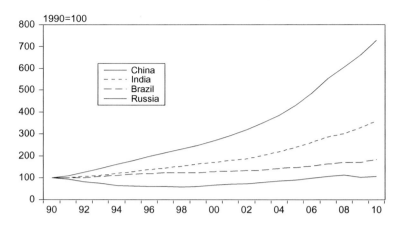

Figure 14.2. GDP growth in BRICs for 1990–2010.

and services. In particular, it is important for a country such as Russia with a free FOREX market and strong demand for imports.

Figure 14.3 shows BRIC GDP in billions of current US$. It shows that China overtook Japan in 2010. The US GDP was still 2.5 times larger than the Chinese GDP in 2010. However, China seems poised to close the gap. Its GDP in 2010 was 145 times the figure in 1990. The Soviet dream of overtaking US, voiced by Nikita Khrushchev 50 years ago, might come true in China.

Brazil's GDP decreased during 1995–2002 and then steadily rose until 2008. It fell slightly again during the global financial crisis, but rapidly recovered in 2010. Brazil's GDP is the second highest in the BRIC hierarchy.

Russia's GDP plummeted after August 1998 financial crisis, finally reaching rock bottom in 1999. It recovered steadily until 2008, catching up with Brazil. Thereafter, Russia's GDP in 2008 was 8.5 times that in 1999, due mostly to currency appreciation. China's GDP in 2008 was only four times that in 1999 on the same basis. This marked growth of Russia's current GDP contributed to a large improvement in the living standard of Russians for the same period. Russia's current and real GDP however, contracted sharply during the 2008 global financial crisis, even though ruble depreciation remained within a very limited range. Russia also

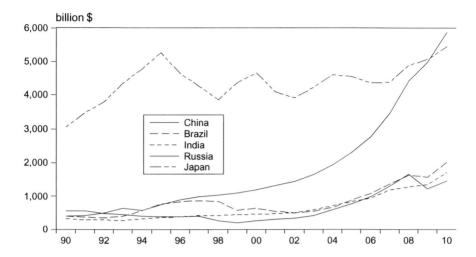

Figure 14.3. GDP at a current US$ basis in BRICs and Japan (in billions).

showed a rapid recovery in 2010, but its GDP level was still lowest in the BRICs.

India's GDP also is catching up with Brazil. Its GDP growth slowed during the global financial crisis, but it did not decline. Its GDP is the second smallest of the BRICs.

14.3. From Dutch to Russian Disease

Kuboniwa (2010) showed the followings. First, there is a strong positive relationship between the changes in real GDP and oil prices. Second, there is a strong positive impact of the changes in oil prices on Russian manufacturing, which differs markedly from the Dutch Disease (slower growth of manufacturing). Third, the increase in imports due to real appreciation of rubles, in turn, contributed to GDP growth in the trade sector, which is a major source of the overall Russian growth. These correlations make Russia sensitive to petroleum price fluctuations and vulnerable to the "Russian disease" whenever global growth slackens.

Figure 14.4 shows Russian GDP, manufacturing output, and international oil price (Urals) movements for 1995–2010, based on the official data (website of Rosstat and the oil price data of Bloomberg). As can be

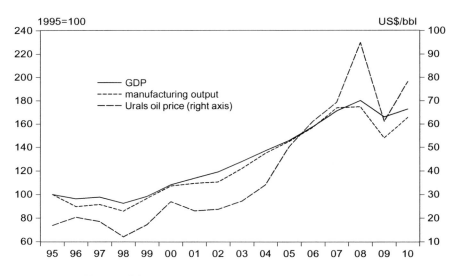

Figure 14.4. GDP, manufacturing and oil prices in Russia.

seen, GDP and manufacturing output grew and contracted along with rises and falls in oil prices.

By using an OLS regression (log-log type with trend), we have the following result with all coefficients at the 1% significance level (adj. $R^2 = 0.977$):

$$gdp = 0.217 * oil\ price + 2.16\%\ (trend), \tag{14.1}$$

in which an italic lower case x denotes the growth rate of the variable x (dx/x). Since the elasticity of GDP with respect to oil prices is 0.22, a 10% increase in oil prices induces a 2.2% increase in GDP. Equation (14.1) also suggests that the overall growth of GDP is supported by the exogenous trend of 2.2% (a technical progress, catch-up efforts and so on) which corresponds to total factor productivity (TFP) in growth accounting. In this chapter, we call this trend growth factor "quasi-TFP."

The average growth rates of GDP and international oil price (Urals) for 1995–2010 were 3.7% and 10.8% respectively. It follows from Equation (14.1) that the oil price contribution to growth (2.34% points) explains 63% of the overall growth. The residual 37% consists of the quasi-TFP (58%) and statistical error (21%). About one-half of the growth can be explained by the oil price impact. The quasi-TFP explains another half of the Russian growth. It is the growth trend; oil price fluctuation is a cyclical factor.

It is noteworthy that Russia's growth during 1995–2010 — the global financial crisis — and the present recovery are explained by a simple equation such as Equation (14.1). This was not the case 1960–1990 in the Soviet era.

We also have the following regression result (adj. $R^2 = 0.948$)[5]:

$$manufacturing\ output = 0.282*oil\ price + 1.39\%\ (trend). \quad (14.2)$$

The elasticity of manufacturing output with respect to oil prices is 0.282 much higher than the GDP elasticity whereas the quasi-TFP for manufacturing is much less than that for overall growth.

Since the average growth rate of manufacturing output during 1995–2010 was 3.4%, the oil price contribution to the manufacturing growth (3.03% points) explains 89% of the overall growth. The residual 11% consists of the quasi-TFP (41%) and statistical error (−29%). The Russian manufacturing output heavily depends on the oil price factor, without a trace of Dutch Disease in the Russian manufacturing.

14.4. The Impact of Trading Gains on Economic Growth in the BRICs

All of the BRICs are oil producers, but Russia has been the sole oil exporter since 1993 when China became an oil importer. A broader measure of the terms of trade effect is needed for Brazil, India, and China. This can be accomplished by computing changes in the trading gains defined as the changes in real GDI to real GDP, that is, current net exports, deflated by the import price *minus* real net exports (OECD, 2006). When E and M denote

---

[5] The coefficient of the oil price is significant at 1% level whereas that of the trend with the standard error of 0.8% is significant at 11% level (>10%). This problem can be avoided using monthly or quarterly data of manufacturing output for 1995 M01–2010M12. When we omit the trend factor, we have the following regression at all coefficients with the 1% significance level (adj. $R^2 = 0.941$): *manufacturing output = 0.378*oil price.*

exports and imports in current prices respectively, and P^e and P^m denote export and import prices (deflators) respectively, the real trading gain T is defined as:

$$T = (E - M)/P^m - (E/P^e - M/P^m) = (1/P^m - 1/P^e)E = (P^e/P^m - 1)E/P^e.$$

T is only meaningful in real terms if $P^e = P^m = 1$ and $T = 0$.

The real GDI is defined as

$$GDI = GDP + T.$$

The real growth of the trading gain cannot directly be defined. Instead, we measure the change in the trading gain as the change in $F = GDI/GDP$; f equals the difference between changes in GDI and GDP, that is to say, $f = gdi - gdp$.

I used the following data for the BRICs. For Russia, the official data on the website (as of May 1, 2010 and April 1, 2011) were employed. Real growth rates of GDP, exports, imports, and GDI for the period 1995–2000, the period 2000–2003 and the period 2004–2010 were based on 1995 constant prices, 2000 constant prices, and chain method (annually changing base previous year prices) respectively. For Brazil, the official data in the CEIC and IFS-WEO databases for 2005–2010 were used. The United Nations database for 1995–2009 was also used. Real of GDP, export, import, and GDI growth rates were calculated by using the chain method (changing the base year annually). For India, in addition to IFS, UN, and CEIC databases, the official press release for 2008–2010 on the website the Indian statistics office were employed. Real growth rates are calculated as in Brazil.

China's official GDP statistics on the expenditure side may be soft because most of its GDP data are based on the production side. Supplementary data on exports and imports in current prices as well as constant prices are not available. Only data on net exports in current prices are published. We employ China's data on exports and imports in current prices in IFS for 1990–2009 and CEIC for 2010. These data in US\$ are converted to those in RMB (Yuan) through the annual average exchange rates in IFS. Net exports calculated from these data in RMB are consistent with the official data on the official website except for 2010. These data for 2007–2010 are shown in Table 14.1. As is seen from this table, the data in current prices of IFS are quite different from those of UN for 2008–2009. This may be attributable to two errors in the United Nations database (main aggregates of national accounts) for China's foreign trade data in current prices during 2008–2009.[6] Although the UN data in current prices are not reliable, we employ them for real growth export and import rates of exports and imports during 1995–2009 because they are consistent with the framework of the national accounts. For 2010, we employ percentage changes of exports and imports estimated in the WEO database. Following the official methodology, our estimations of China for 1996–2000, 2001–2005, and 2006–2010 are made in 1990 constant prices, 2000 constant prices, and 2005 constant prices respectively.

Now we are in a position to present our estimations of real GDP, GDI and trading gains. Figure 14.5 summarizes real GDP and GDI (command-basis GDP) movements in the BRICs. As was stated, differences between percentages changes in GDI and GDP show changes in the trading gains (f).

In Russia, large trading gains were observed for 2000 when the oil prices showed a sharp increase. Russia also showed large trading losses in 2009 due to an adverse oil shock. The favorable growth for 2003–2007 was coupled with relatively large trading gains. The recovery in 2010 accompanied rising trading gains.

Brazil suffered from relatively small trading losses for 1997–2001 and positive trading gains thereafter. In particular, Brazil's trading gains rose 3.1% in 2008, despite oil price rises. The improvement of terms of trade was due to an increase in export prices against oil prices and a decrease in oil imports. It should be noted that Brazil showed a marked decrease in crude oil imports from 28.4 to 4.0 million tons for 2000–2009, whereas it showed a remarkable increase in crude oil extraction from 63.2 to 100.4 million tons for the same period (BP, *Statistical Review of World Energy, 2010*). The recession in 2009 was associated with trading losses. The recovery in 2010 was coupled with positive trading gains.

---

[6] As can be seen in Table 14.1, there are some similarities between figures in foreign trade of IFS in US$ and UN in RMB. The United Nations might misconstrue the data in US$ as RMB. The United Nations also might convert these erroneous figures to US$ by using IFS exchange rates.

370 *Masaaki Kuboniwa*

Table 14.1. Foreign trade data of China.

		2007	2008	2009	2010
In current prices					
	Data of IFS for 2007–9 and CEIC for 2010				
Exports	bln US$	1,342	1,582	1,333	1,753
Imports	bln US$	1,035	1,233	1,113	1,521
Net exports	bln US$	307	349	220	232
	Calculated from data of IFS and CEIC				
Exports	bln RMB	10,211	10.991	9.109	11,866
Imports	bln RMB	7,872	8.567	7.605	10,294
Net exports	bln RMB	2,339	2.424	1,504	1,571
	Data of the United Nations (as of April 1, 2011)				
Exports	bln US$	1,342	2,276	1.952	
Imports	bln US$	1,034	1.774	1,528	
Net exports	bln US$	307	502	424	
Exports	bln RMB	10,206	15,817	13,332	
Imports	bln RMB	7,868	12,328	10,435	
Net exports	bln RMB	2,338	3,489	2,897	
	Official data of NBSC				
Net exports	bln RMB	2.338	2.423	1.503	997
	Data of IFS				
Exchange rate	RMB/US$	7.608	6.949	6.831	6,770
Real percent change					
	Data of IMF(WEO) based on CEIC				
Exports	%	18.1	8.5	−10.3	34.6
Imports (cif)	%	8.0	3.8	3.7	17.7
	Data of the United Nations				
Exports	%	15.7	7.7	−10.3	
Imports	%	12.1	7.6	−2.1	

Notes: Exports and imports includes both goods and services.
Sources: Websites of IFS, WEO, CEIC, UN and NBSC (National Bureau of Statistics of China).

India also experienced relatively small trading losses during 1999–2002. The impact of trading gains on the Indian growth appeared to be negligible for 2003–2010. In 2008, India's GDP growth rate fell despite positive trading gains.

Lessons from BRICs 371

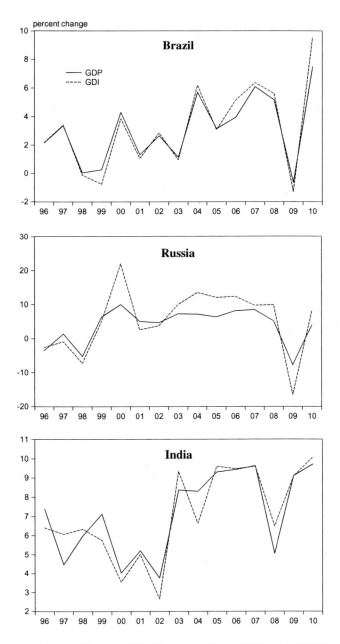

Figure 14.5. GDP and GDI (Command-Basis GDP) in the BRICs.

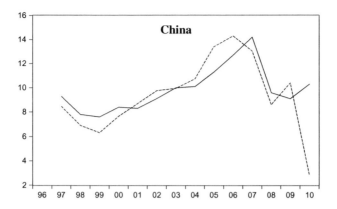

Figure 14.5. (*Continued*).

Along with Brazil and India, China too experienced relatively small trading losses during 1997–2000. China's high growth for 2001–2006 was coupled with trading gains. In particular, China experienced relatively large trading gains for 2005–2006 in spite of continuous increases in oil prices. However, it incurred trading losses during 2007–2008. The change in trading gains of *minus* 1% in 2008 was relatively small. The change in trading gains in 2008 however was about 3%, employing the WEO data on percentage changes in exports and imports for the year. This result may be more plausible taking the 2008 oil shock into account. The sharp fall in trading gains of 7.5% in 2010 is rather surprising. If we project China's GDP growth based on the past relationship between GDP and GDI as will be shown below, China's GDP growth rate should be negative. However, the official preliminary growth rate was over 10%. So the situation in 2010 is unclear. Preliminary data on exports and imports in current and/or constant prices for 2010 might distort the gap between GDI and GDP. If the data are right, the Chinese government might have taken special measures to offset the great trading loss shock. Alternatively, the 2010 GDP growth rate may be overestimated. Anyway, we need further investigation for China's large trading losses in 2010. The National Bureau of Statistics of China as well as the Statistics Division of the United States should improve China's GDP statistics on the expenditure side.

Using a log-log type regression with trend similar to Equation (14.1) we have the following results of regressions:

For Brazil: adj. $R^2 = 0.990$

$$gdp = 1.789*f + 2.6\% \text{ (trend)} \qquad (14.3)$$

All coefficients are significant at 1% level.
For Russia: adj. $R^2 = 0.981$

$$gdp = 1.255*f + 2.6\% \text{ (trend)} \qquad (14.4)$$

All coefficients are significant at 1% level.
For India: adj. $R^2 = 0.990$

$$gdp = 2.001*f + 7.0\% \text{ (trend)} \qquad (14.5)$$

All coefficients except for f are significant at 1% level. The coefficient of f is significant at 10% level (the p-value is 0.0546).

For China[7] adj. $R^2 = 0.997$

$$gdp = 1.679*f + 9.2\% \text{ (trend)} \qquad (14.6)$$

All coefficients including the dummy variable are significant at 1% level.

Russia's elasticity of GDP with respect to trading gains is the smallest in the BRICs. This can be explained by large magnitude of changes in trading gains in Russia which were in the range between 12% in 2000 and −8.8% in 2009 (the gap of 21%). Those in Brazil were in the range between 3.1% and −0.8 (the gap of 3.9%). The values of changes in trading gains in India were in the range between 1.6% and −1.7% (the gap of 3.3%). Those in China for 1996–2009 were in the range between 2.1% and −1.3% (the gap of 3.4%).

Russia and Brazil show rather low values of exogenous trend factor whereas China and India show large values of exogenous trend factor. This reflects the large differences in GDP growth trends of two groups of Brazil–Russia and India–China. For Russia, the quasi-TFP of 2.6% in Equation (14.3) is very close to the TFP of 2.5% derived from the

---

[7] A dummy variable for 2010 is introduced into the regression. The value of coefficient of the dummy variable is 0.140 (14%).

374   *Masaaki Kuboniwa*

Table 14.2.   Average growth of GDP and trading gains in the BRICs: 1995–2010.

		Brazil	**Russia**	**India**	**China**
a	GDP (percent change)	3.1	3.7	7.1	9.8
b	Trading gain (percent change)	0.28	1.30	−0.02	0.05
c	Elasticity of GDP to trading gain	1.8	1.3	2.0	1.7
d	Impact of trading gain change (b*c)	0.5	1.63	−0.04	0.1
e	quasi TFP (Trend) (percent)	2.6	2.6	7.0	9.2
f	Residual (a-d-e) (percent)	−0.1	−0.5	0.1	0.5
g	Contribution of trading gain (d/a percent)	16.5	43.9	−0.6	0.9

Notes: China's calculations are made for 1995–2009.
Source: Author's calculations.

production function (Kuboniwa, 2011). For China and India, the coefficient of the trends is much greater than their TFP in the conventional growth accounting.

Table 14.2 provides an accounting of the sources of BRICs growth, based on Equations (14.3)–(14.6) during 1995–2010. Russia showed the largest total impact of trading gains on its GDP growth (1.6% points), followed by Brazil (0.5% points). The share of contribution of trading gains to average growth, which shows a country's dependency on trading gains or terms of trade, was 44% in Russia and 16.5% in Brazil. On the other hand, the total impact of trading gains on GDP growth in India and China was statistically meaningful but almost negligible although China's great trading gains contraction in 2010 remains puzzling.

14.5. Summary

As O'Neill predicted, the BRICs countries grew relatively fast in the 2000s despite the global financial shock. Surprisingly, Russia was unscathed by the Dutch disease. Some BRICs countries were strongly affected by trading gains. About one-half of the Russian growth can be explained by this impact. About 20% of the Brazilian growth can also be explained in the same way. India and China showed large impacts *per unit* of changes in trading gains on their growth as is shown by the values of elasticity of GDP with respect to changes in trading gains. However, the *total* impacts in India and China were almost negligible. It seems that if these correlations persist, Asia's BRICs will be relatively immune to recurrent global financial crises.

References

Kuboniwa (2010). Diagnosing the "Russian Disease": Growth and structure of the Russian economy then and now. Working Paper No. 28, Russian Research Center, Institute of Economic Research, Hitotsubashi University.

Kuboniwa (2011). Russian growth path and TFP changes in light of the estimation of production function using quarterly data. *Post-Communist Economies*, 23(3), pp. 311–325.

Kuboniwa, M and A Ponomarenko (2000). Revised and enlarged GDP estimates for Russia, 1961–1990. In *Constructing a Historical Macroeconomic Database for Trans-Asian Regions*, K Odaka, Y Kiyokawa and M Kuboniwa (eds.), pp. 109–127. Institute of Economic Research, Hitotsubashi University.

OECD (2006). *Economic Surveys: Russian Federation*. Paris: OECD.

O'Neill, J (2001). Building Better Global Economic BRICs. Goldman and Sachs Global Economic Paper No. 66.

Rosefielde, S and M Kuboniwa (2003). Russian growth retardation then and now. *Eurasian Geography and Economics*, 44(2), 87–101.

Wilson, D and R Purushothaman (2003). Dreaming with BRICs: The path to 2050. Goldman and Sachs Global Economics Paper No. 99.

PART VI

WESTERN ECONOMIC FATIGUE

CHAPTER 15

EUROZONE AND GLOBAL FINANCIAL IMBALANCES

BRUNO DALLAGO AND CHIARA GUGLIELMETTI
University of Trento, Italy

The international crisis has hit hard the Eurozone (EZ) and shows remarkably distinct patterns among its countries. The EZ, and hence the Euro, has shown to be highly vulnerable to external shocks, suffering of deep-seated as well as new structural and financial imbalances. At the same time, the EZ's ability to cope with its economic vulnerability has been weak, revealing rigid decisional procedures. Coordinated policy responses have been slow. However, the crisis has given an important push to coordination of economic policies and instruments.

The unfolding of the crisis in the EZ can be explained by the interaction of institutional features and policy failures, and by their interconnection with real and financial imbalances. The aim of this chapter is to analyze those factors that opened the way to the diffusion of the external shock wave in the EZ and triggered the systemic crisis of the euro in the frame of a wider context of rising inequalities, polarization of living standards, excess demand, and increasing economic and social imbalances. It also aims at discussing the structural consequences of these events and critically analyzing the institutional and political reforms which the EZ is facing in order to enhance its capability to cope with external shocks.

The crisis has shown that internal divergence in the EZ is based on important structural components which are unsustainable in the long run. Indeed, the crisis has magnified the gap between the vulnerable peripheral member countries and a more resilient core. Increasingly accepted within the current debt crisis setting, the need for real convergence has never been really pursued in the EZ. Not at the national level, at which a short-term national view has often outweighed more structural programs, and not even at the European level, where the process stopped whenever there was a strong political obstacle to overcome, regardless how problematic was the stopping point. In this context, severe are the risks of tinkering with existing institutions slightly adjusted.

Section 15.1 briefly frames the wider context, focusing on the economic implications of the mounting polarization and inequality. Section 15.2 deals with the unfolding of the crisis in the EZ, discussing (1) the fundamental linkages among the United States and the EZ, which constituted the channels of transmission of external shocks to the EZ; (2) the common weaknesses which fueled synchronized shocks in the United States and in the EZ; (3) those idiosyncratic factors that let the Greek crisis open the way to a systemic crisis of the euro. Section 15.3 analyzes those aspects which are critical in shaping EZ vulnerability and its response to external shocks: the distinctive features of European capitalisms, the institutional architecture which leads to differential shocks in different countries, and the divergent economic situation of individual countries. Section 15.4 discusses the dilemma confronting the EZ and concludes.

15.1. The Context

The inevitability of the crisis was indeed embedded in the most dramatic structural changes that took place in the last three decades: the booming inequalities that significantly changed the economic and social landscape of the postwar period and created a critical political problem for policy makers and the policy consequences of jobless recoveries that appeared in early Nineties.

By 2007, inequalities were substantially higher than two or three decades earlier and impressively similar to the disparities existing in 1928 (Piketty and Saez, 2006; Reich, 2010). The increase of inequality has been impressive, but neither uniform nor universal in countries. Being particularly evident in the United States (Figure 15.1), this pattern, albeit with some time and quantity variation, characterized most of the developed and emerging economies.

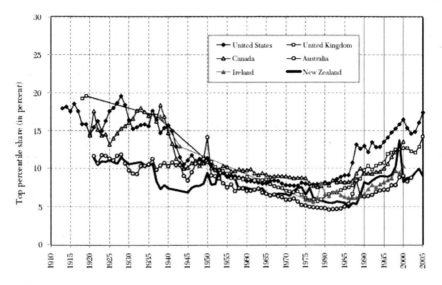

Figure 15.1. Top 1 Percent Share in English Speaking Countries (U-Shaped), 1910–2005.
Source: Atkinson and Piketty (2007, 2010).

The effect of rapidly increasing inequalities has been financially and economically destabilizing, leading to shrinking private savings as well as mounting consumer debts and mortgage loans. At the same time, inequality decreases social mobility and is inversely related to innovation (Wilkinson and Pickett, 2009), hampering in this way fundamental components of sustainable economic growth.

The rising openness and international integration of markets, as well as the dramatically increased mobility of some crucial resources (in particular, financial resources and top managerial capabilities), opened the way to the rise of inequality and polarization of the standard of living (Rodrik, 1996) also under the pressure of shareholder value policies. However, these events would not have been sufficient to increase inequalities if institutions, norms, politics, and policies had not provided the ground for that outcome in both the United States (Krugman, 2009) and elsewhere (Wilkinson and Pickett, 2009). This they did through weakening governments and trade unions, changes in taxes and benefits, policies used to fight stagflation in the 1970s and, more in general, based on the idea of efficient markets. All this led to the end of the postwar capital–labor bargain that was at the basis of the postwar economic expansion (Reich, 2007). As a consequence, the remuneration of financial organizations and their managers boomed, although even many industrial organizations and their managers did well. People at the bottom of the distributive scale lost ground during the last three decades and some of them slipped into plain poverty, but it was the middle class which suffered most, more through the loss of high salaries and related fringe benefits than through the loss of jobs. Indeed, although it is possible to speak of jobless recoveries in the short-medium run (Schreft *et al.*, 2005), perhaps more outstanding in the long run is that new jobs were often less well paid than old jobs (Reich, 2010).

Jobless recoveries appeared during the last 20 years, the first one being the recovery following the 1990–1991 recession: output grew rapidly, while jobs lagged behind. While generous welfare systems made continental European countries politically and socially more resilient to unemployment, the lack of a strong safety net for the unemployed in the United States created a strong case for policy intervention. In particular, when the jobless recovery jeopardized the middle class (usually meant to include the large part of the US population with the exception of the poor and the top decile) and its way of life, policy makers felt the political pressure to implement expansionary fiscal and monetary policies, strongly supported by private companies and investors. There are important structural and microeconomic reasons for different attitudes between the United States and large part of Europe (Rajan, 2010, pp. 89–97) that make the former more reactive to policy stimuli than the latter. Yet, these different attitudes fostered a kind of European opportunism in waiting for US expansionary policies (Rajan, 2010, pp. 98–100). Therefore, the propensity to cyclical excess demand is greater in the United States than in Europe, which makes the former the hotbed of crises, but also of recovery. An indirect effect of this is that US policies support European export propensity.

It is important to notice that the excess demand that generated bubbles is caused jointly by companies, consumers, and governments as an attempt to alleviate the consequences of a major structural breakdown in the working of Western economies and capture opportunities for profit. Easing factors of this breakdown were the rise of the knowledge economy and the fall of the Soviet Union. The latter, in particular, dismantled an important, although weakening, external political anchor for equity. The fading-away of systemic competition nearly cancelled inequalities from the political agenda. Both these facts strongly undermined the position, hence, the bargaining power, of labor, particularly the less skilled one.[1]

The worsening of the middle-class position was in some cases absolute, but more important is their loss compared to the economic élites. The critical relevance of inequality and polarization within a social context has been recently shown by the fundamental study of Wilkinson and Piketty (2009). People typically compare their situation and well-being to others and are particularly sensitive to the lifestyle of those who are ahead of them in terms of income and wealth. Although the importance of social influence on consumption decisions — the demonstration effect — was emphasized in the past by economists (Duesenberry, 1949; Frank, 1985, 1997; Veblen, 1899a, 1909), the relevance of this kind of behavior was recently proved experimentally by behavioral psychologists, who also proved its significance for economic decision making (Kahneman *et al.*, 1991; Kahneman and Tversky, 2000). Behavioral and cognitive scholars have convincingly shown that losses are more painful than gains are pleasurable, and consequently losers are more willing to take risks.

Based on these psychological and social mechanisms, one would expect that absolute and relative losers would try their best, even at the cost of extraordinary risks, to keep up with their traditional life-style and with that of those who are better off. This is even more understandable in an age of leisure-class dominance and conspicuous consumption (Veblen, 1899b) as the most evident social sign of economic success.

The middle class is politically crucial, and their consumption is particularly important for the revival of the economy. Governments have thus been more than willing to support the consumption attitude of the middle class, whose relative weight in overall income has been steadily declining in the most recent decades (Reich, 2010), in order to support a prolonged

---

[1] These phenomena were particularly relevant in the United States. However, they characterized many other countries, also in Europe.

economic boom. Therefore, risk prone attitudes by middle-class families in financing consumption, policy management by governments, financial organizations, and industrial enterprises initiative to exploit business and profit opportunities counteracted the unfavorable economic and social effects of increasing disparities. The housing sector was perhaps the most sensitive one to soft credit and excess demand (Rajan, 2010, pp. 32–43). These dynamics have been favored by the growing weight of finance relative to production in mature economies, the so-called financialization (van Treek, 2009; Lapavitsas, 2009). Households have come to significantly rely on financial markets both for assets, as pension and insurance, and for liabilities. At the same time, banks started to evolve seeking profits through intermediation in the form of commissions and fees and through own trading (Lapavitsas *et al.*, 2010). Indeed, these forces added to the booming speculative demand of financial assets (in particular, through the stock exchange, but also in other fields) and conspicuous consumption (of luxury real estate and cars) by the financial and economic élites.

Thus, the growing demand for high consumption standards by a relatively impoverished middle class added to the booming consumption by the élites and the public hand and led — also thanks to financial innovation, deregulation of financial institutions and markets, soft monitoring and control, and high liquidity from a prolonged boom — to growing and riskier credit largely supported by the state and financial organizations.

Debt was obviously not the only form of adaptation used by the losers. Among other coping mechanisms there have been the rapid decrease of savings rates,[2] the use of accumulated savings, and the increase in the number of hours worked, together with the general increase of the number of women entering the labor market (Reich, 2010).[3] However, it has been particularly the credit lever and the use of accumulated savings that created the force leading to the crisis, namely excess demand.

---

[2] The saving rates of families decreased dramatically in nearly all developed countries, while household debt exploded. See Reich (2010, pp. 62–63).

[3] On the participation of women in the labor market and the number of hours worked, see Reich (2010, pp. 61–62).

Although there was real purchasing power behind consumption and other kinds of demand by the élite, demand by the impoverished middle class was in substantial part fictitious in economic terms, i.e., not supported by real present or future income and production. Excess demand thus generated bubbles, particularly in the real estate, and also in financial markets and in various consumption markets (e.g., car markets). Bubbles stretched the economy to an unbearable situation: at that point they inevitably exploded.

15.2. The Global Crisis and the EZ: External Shocks, Global Weaknesses, and Domestic Vulnerability

If in the United States the crisis unfolded from a prolonged period of excess credit, the outcome of accommodating monetary, and fiscal policies (Quinn Mills, 2010; Razin and Rosefielde, 2011), in the EZ the moving cause has been mostly external, i.e., imported from the United States through financial, real, political, and psychological linkages. The international transmission of the US financial and economic crisis is thus often understood as a contagion process. No shared definition has yet been reached by the literature on the controversial notion of contagion, which encounters serious problems across theory and empirical work. The question which is useful to briefly recall here is the fundamental distinction, upheld by most of the literature on financial contagion (Calvo and Reinhart, 1996; Kaminsky and Reinhart, 2000; and Eichengreen *et al.,* 1996), between the following: (1) the development of synchronized shocks in different countries, which are due to similar structural vulnerabilities rather than to the presence of channel of contagion and (2) the cross-country transmission of shocks.[4] As to the latter, this literature further distinguishes between fundamentals-based contagion, which occurs when the infected country is linked to others via trade or finance, and true contagion which takes place when common shocks and all channels of potential interconnection are absent (Calvo and Reinhart, 1996).

---

[4] In line with the restrictive definition of the World Bank which depicts contagion as the transmission of shocks to other countries beyond any fundamental link among the countries and beyond common shocks.

Many EZ banks were in fragile state when entering the sudden financial arrest (Caballero, 2009) and then the Irish and Greek crises, due to easy credit and massive adoption of financial innovation, high leverage ratios, circumvention of financial regulation, and high risk investments. Moreover, the house-price bubble burst was not the mere consequence of the US subprime mortgage crisis, but rather the burst of homegrown bubbles. In the unfolding of the crisis in the EZ, the asymmetric presence of the aforementioned elements among different countries, and the interconnection of these aspects with institutional idiosyncrasies and policy failures both at the national and at the European level, are critical. Domestic imbalances and other forms of structural and policy vulnerability (e.g., accumulated public and private debt stocks, markets rigidity, unemployment structure, demography, inequalities, fiscal policies, and the differential domestic effect of the common monetary policy) have played an important role in explaining the differential vulnerability and resilience, and hence performance of distinct European countries.

From this standpoint, it is important to single out the following: (1) the fundamental linkages among the US and EU, which constituted the channels of transmission of external shocks to the EZ; (2) the common weaknesses which fueled synchronized shocks in the US and in the EU; (3) those idiosyncratic factors that let the Greek crisis open the way to a systemic crisis of the euro, and how those aspects interact.

Both financial and real linkages between the US and the EU were important. The money market sudden arrest (Caballero, 2009), the fact that European financial institutions held a large share of assets based on US residential mortgage and thus shared in the losses that arose once the US housing bubble burst, the sequence of falls in the stock market, all led to a substantial shrinking of bank credit. Export to the US market, which counted for 23.2% of total EU exports in 2006, started decreasing in 2007 at an annual average rate of 5.1% between 2005 and 2009 (Table 15.1).

The strong real appreciation of the euro before 2008 significantly hampered export. At the same time, the increasing volatility of other currencies and the price of commodities had an adverse impact on the European economy. The economic slowdown activated automatic stabilizers, increasing social spending, and decreasing, at the same time, government's fiscal revenues.

However, as aforementioned, common excesses characterized the US and the EU and fueled synchronized shocks: the housing bubble, massive

Table 15.1. EU trade with the US (millions of euro; %).

Period	Imports	Variation (%, y-o-y)	Share of total EU imports (%)	Exports	Variation (%, y-o-y)	Share of total EU exports (%)	EU trade balance with the US
2004	159,374			235,499			76,124
2005	163,511	2.6	13.9	252,683	7.3	24.0	89,172
2006	175,547	7.4	13.0	269,144	6.5	23.2	93,598
2007	181,739	3.5	12.7	261,477	−2.8	21.1	79,738
2008	186,772	2.8	11.9	250,124	−4.3	19.1	63,352
2009	159,705	−14.5	13.3	204,574	−18.2	18.7	44,869
Average annual growth (2005–2009)		−0.6			−5.1		

Source: Data DG trade, September 15, 2010.

circumvention of poor financial regulation, high financial leverage, risky financial innovation, and investments in high-risk assets. These factors show different trends in the different member countries, testifying of a composite scenario.

The burst of the housing price bubble (Figure 15.2) played an important role in the EZ crisis.

In Spain, Ireland, Britain, Iceland, Estonia, and Lithuania house prices had been steadily and sharply growing from the end of the 1990s to 2006,[5] as shown by the house price indices published by the Economist since 2002. The journal, in a telling article titled "The worldwide rise in house prices is the biggest bubble in history. Prepare for the economic pain when it pops" (June 16, 2005), reported that since 1997, home prices in most countries rose by much more in real terms than during any previous boom. Between 2004 and 2005, the prices of the houses grew at a rate of

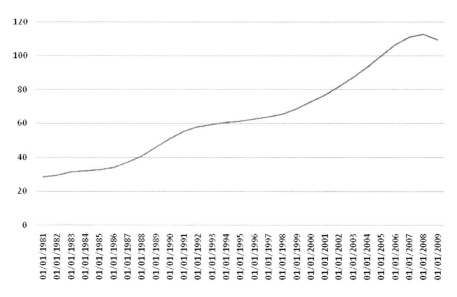

Figure 15.2. Residential property price index, EU 16 (new and existing dwelling).
Source: European Central Bank, data 2011.

---

[5] House-price inflation slowed significantly in 2004 in Ireland, having anyway reached impressively high levels throughout the observed period.

Eurozone and Global Financial Imbalances 389

9% or more in Italy, Belgium, Denmark, and Sweden, reaching in Spain and France annual growth rates of over 15%: a much faster pace than those in the rest of Europe and in the US. The growing house prices-rents ratio is a compelling evidence of the general overvaluation in the housing market. The trend was reversed in Germany, where house prices had steadily declined between 1997 and 2010 (Table 15.2). The Economist's measure of fair value in housing, which compares the ratio of house prices to rents in a country to its long-run average, shows a ratio in Germany well below its long-run average in the first quarter of 2010.

In the context of the single monetary policy and thereby of uniform interest rate policy, the uneven inflation rates which have characterized EZ member countries (Table 15.8) lead to different real interest rates which might have fueled different borrowing-based investments in housing among the member states. This might have encouraged the substantial surge in private and foreign debts experienced in Eastern and Southern European countries before the crisis onset. Germany shows a different trend, with declining private debt.

Table 15.2. The Economist house-price indicators (% change).

	1997–2005	Q1 2005	Q1 2010	Q4 2008	1997–2010	Under (-)/over (+) valued, Q1 2010
		on a year earlier	on a year earlier			
Britain	154	5.5	9.0	−14.9	180	31.2
Sweden	84	10.0	5.6	−2.0	159	37.0
Germany	−0.2	−1.3*	−0.4	1.1	na	−14.6
Netherlands	76	1.9	−2.0	−5.4	86	20.4
Belgium	71	9.4	−3.0	2.7	149	30.9
Italy	69	9.7	−4.1	1.1	96	13.1
France	87	15.0	−4.3	−3.0	133	39.7
Spain	145	15.5	−6.3	−3.2	166	53.4
Denmark	58	11.3	−13.1	−10.9	91	17.5
Ireland	192	6.5	−18.5	−9.7	142	24.5

Note: *average 2004.
Source: Authors' compilation, data *The Economist*.

As Reinhart and Rogoff (2010) empirically test on data spanning over two centuries for more than 70 countries, private debt increase, fueled by both domestic banking credit growth and external borrowing, is a recurrent antecedent to domestic banking crises, which, in turn, tend to precede or accompany sovereign debt crisis. The sequence of the events in the EZ is not an exception. What is peculiar is the unfolding of these trends within the EZ system.

In the EZ households, debt increased from 52% to 70% of GDP from 1999 to 2007, while financial institutions increased their debt from less than 200% of GDP to more than 250% (De Grauwe, 2010; Figure 15.3).

These aggregates cover intercountry diverging trends. Across the peripheral member countries households' debt increased at an unsustainable path, while in so-called EZ core — Germany, France, Austria, Belgium, and the Netherlands — households have been fiscally more solid (Table 15.3).

Less clear-cut a divide between core and periphery EZ countries can be identified in the financial sector, which shows in some way a reversed situation. Table 15.4 shows the banking exposure of Germany, France, Great Britain, Italy, and Spain toward the so-called PIGS (Portugal, Ireland, Greece, and Spain). Banks in the EZ core have massively invested in periphery countries. Large German current account surpluses *vis-à-vis* current account deficits of the PIGS, along with the latter's low interest rates following the creation of the currency block, all lead to a massive interconnectedness in the EZ (Baldwin and Gros, 2010). This, in turn, increased the vulnerability of the EZ banking system. This is one of the critical reasons why the refinancing crisis in Greece, which counts for less than 2% of the EZ GDP, opened the way to a systemic crisis of the euro.

Not only were the European banks heavily interconnected, they were also aggressively expanding lending and overleveraged.[6] In the last

---

[6] The high exposition of European banks toward Eastern European markets risked to erode their capital buffer, shrinking further their credit possibilities. Unicredit, Raiffeisen group, Erste Group, and OTP started to report startling rises in loan losses in early August, due to the substantial amount of bad loans in foreign currencies (e.g., the Swiss franc) both to corporate and household borrowers.

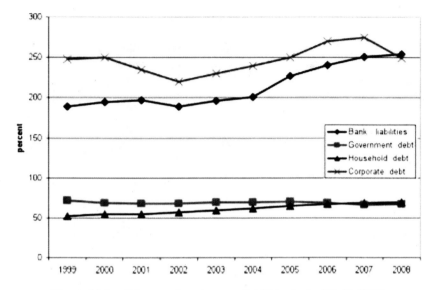

Figure 15.3. Private and government liabilities in the EZ (% GDP).
Source: De Grauwe (2010).

Table 15.3. Households' net saving rate (1995, 2000, and 2008).

	1995		2000		2008	
	Households' net saving rate	Public debt	Households' net saving rate	Public debt	Households' net saving rate	Public debt
Belgium	16.4	130.4	12.3	107.9	11.5	89.9
Denmark	0.2	72.6	−4.0	52.4	−2.4	34.2
Germany	11.0	55.6	9.2	59.7	11.2	66
Ireland		82.1		37.8	4.0	43.9
Greece	11.4	97.0	−4.5	103.4	−12.1	99.2
Spain	10.0	63.3	5.9	59.3	6.1	39.7
France	12.7	55.5	11.8	57.3	11.6	67.5
Italy	17.0	121.5	8.4	109.2	8.6	106.1
Netherlands	14.3	76.1	6.9	53.8	7.0	58.2
Austria	11.8	68.3	9.2	66.5	12.0	62.6
Portugal	6.9	61.0	3.8	50.5	−0.9	66.3
UK	6.7	51.2	0.1	41.0	−4.6	52.0

Source: AMECO; net savings as % of disposable income; public debt as percentage GDP.

392 Bruno Dallago and Chiara Guglielmetti

Table 15.4. Eurozone banking exposure, Eurozone core bank's holding of PIGS, UK, and US Debts (millions of US$).

	Bank nationality					
Exposure to	Germany	France	Great Britain	Italy	Spain	Other EZ countries
Greece	51.0	111.6	16.5	8.8	1.6	47.9
Ireland	205.8	85.7	222.4	28.6	16.2	92.5
Portugal	46.6	49.7	32.4	9.4	108	29.1
Spain	217.9	244.2	141.7	42.5		200.6

Source: Bank for International Settlements, consolidated banking statistics, end March 2010 (billions of US$).

decade, the expansion of bank lending was massive: Irish, French, Spanish, and Italian banks increased their exposition at an unprecedented pace,[7] as shown by Table 15.5. A default in the US derivatives market could thus have dangerous consequences within the EU mainly through banks: strongly exposed and highly leveraged banks, which financed weak countries (both governments and private operators), when confronted with the danger of externally caused default, would put their domestic debtors under pressure. When these events set EZ weak countries in a difficult financial situation, the euro credibility and stability could suffer consequently. This is what actually happened in 2009–2010.

The gap between leverage ratios (shareholder equity to total assets) and regulatory ratios was huge (Gros and Micossi, 2008). The 13 largest European banks average leverage ratios was 35, versus an average of 20 in the US. The average covers big national differences, with French, German, and British banks more exposed than Italian and Spanish ones, which had been subject to a more prudential domestic regulation (Table 15.6). Moreover, the lack of intra-EZ coordinated banking policy worsened already existing imbalances, contributing to the financial vulnerability of the largest economies (Baldwin and Gros, 2010) as a result of different

---

[7] In Ireland, total bank assets as a percentage of GDP rose from 360% in 2001 to 705% in 2007; in France from 229% to 373%, in Italy from 148% to 220%, and in Spain from 177% to 280%.

Eurozone and Global Financial Imbalances   393

Table 15.5.   Intra-Eurozone banking exposure, EZ core banks' holding of PIGS Debt.

	1999, 4th Quarter	2009, 4th Quarter	Percentage change 1999–2009
Portugal	26	110	320
Ireland	60	348	481
Italy	259	822	217
Greece	24	141	491
Spain	94	613	554
Total	463	2033	340

Source: Bank for International Settlements, consolidated banking statistics, end March 2010 and Gros and Baldwin (2010).

Table 15.6.   European banks' leverage ratio.

		2007	2008	2009
Hypo Real Estate Holding	DE	113	n.a.	78.35
Dexia	BE	44.1	189.4	58.7
ING Group	NL	55.8	128.5	51
Dresdner Bank *	DE	41.8	101.2	
Deutsche Bank	DE	69.1	99.5	53.6
Landesbank-Badn-Wuerttemberg	DE	43	90.4	43.6
Westleb	DE	66.9	78.6	67.7
UBS	CH	80.7	71.8	35.3
Barclays	CB	50.4	55.2	27.6
BNP Paribas	FR	35.4	44.6	30.4
The Royal Bank of Scotland Group	GB	43.1	39.4	21.9
Commerzbank	DE	41.4	33.6	36
HSBC Holdings	GB	23.8	33.5	21.8
Unicredit	IT	26.5	32.1	24.4
Credit Suisse Group	CH	27.8	31	26.4
KBC Group	BE	23.5	30.5	41.24
Banco Bilbao Vizcaya Argentaria	ES	24.4	28.3	22.4
Intesa Sanpaolo	IT	20.5	26.6	21.4
Banco Santander	ES	21.6	26.1	21.3

* taken over by Commerzbank in 2009.

government responses to the problem of toxic assets. For example, French, German, and Italian governments' intervention at this regard was very mild.

In this context of pre-crisis financial institutions' expansionary trend, the circumvention of regulatory requirements by European financial institutions has been substantial. Along with the massive amount of derivatives owned with the aim of alleviating regulatory capital obligations, the types of capital assets revealed structural weaknesses. It is worth mentioning the 527 billion US dollars of notional exposure of AIGFP's super senior credit swap portfolio (as December 31, 2007). Over 300 billion US dollars of credit insurance had been issued for European banks. AIG itself in the K-10 annex of the 2007 annual report defines those financial instruments as "derivatives written for financial institutions, principally in Europe, for the purpose of providing them with regulatory capital relief rather than risk mitigation." The immediate consequence was that AIG's crisis caused shock waves through the share prices of EU banks, as AIG's default would have exposed the European banks' gap of regulatory capital, with dramatic effects on their ratings and on the market confidence.[8]

The failure of financial and banking regulation in the EZ opened the way to the high fragility of the financial system. As Spaventa (2010) highlights, Basel II favored the undercapitalization of the banking system and contributed to the unfolding of the financial crisis through four devices: low capital coefficients; admission of hybrid capital; lax criteria for risk evaluation; and wide possibilities for circumventing the rules. A brief

---

[8] As to the structure of EU banks capital, the problems raised in the summer 2010 in Germany by the decision of Commerzbank to start halting interest payments on hybrid capital in case of losses are a clear demonstration of the confusion at stake as well as of the debt rather than risk nature of this sort of participatory instruments. The "profit-participation certificates" foresee payment of fixed interest only if the bank is profitable. This notwithstanding, Commerzbank had been paying interest on notes issued by Eurohypo even in case of losses. Moreover, as suspending interest payments was a necessary condition for receiving state bailouts, problems arose with KBC, which considered payments on its hybrid securities mandatory, and RBS, which suspended payments only on some of its hybrids.

Table 15.7. Interventions (governments and central banks) in favor of the banking system in Europe during the current crisis (billions of euros).

Country	Capital	Guarantee	Other	Total amount	Banks involved
Austria	7.3	20.2		27.6	8
Belgium	16.2	20.0	0.2	36.4	6
Denmark	6.5	14.2	1.0	21.6	23
France	25.3		0.5	25.8	8
Germany	40.8	314.4	7.3	362.5	13
UK	85.6	704.2	2.6	792.5	16
Greece	2.8	0.5	0.1	3.4	9
Ireland	10.8	84.2		95.0	6
Iceland	0.8			0.8	3
Italy	4.1			4.1	4
Luxemburg	2.9		0.2	3.1	4
Netherlands	27.6	52.1	7.5	87.2	13
Portugal		6.2		6.2	7
Spain			9.0	9.0	1
Switzerland	43.7			43.7	1
Total	274.4	1,216.0	28.3	1,518.7	115

Source: ECB, European Commission, national governments.

review of the European governments and central banks interventions in favor of the banking system (Table 15.7) shows the massive core EZ countries' interventions toward their — highly overleveraged — institutions.

15.3. Diverging Europe?

The factors discussed in the previous section need to be understood in the frame of the peculiarities of the EZ, which lead to differential impact of the crisis as well as to an uneven economic recovery within the currency block and fueled a systemic crisis.

The following three aspects are critical in shaping EZ vulnerability and response to external shocks: (1) the distinctive features of European capitalisms; (2) the institutional architecture of the EZ which leads to differential shocks in different countries; and (3) the divergent economic situation of individual countries, which refers particularly to the condition of public and private finance and the structure of the economy.

The distinct features of European capitalisms have been only marginally affected by the European integration which, together with globalization, has made the different systems mutually compatible through a set of shared rules and standards, but not through clearly converging institutions. The basic institutional features of the EZ can be summarized as follows:

- economic and commercial integration and flow of financial resources (freedoms and integrated markets);
- common fiscal parameters (Maastricht criteria);
- common currency (euro);
- institutionally separated, open financial markets (with differential rules and taxation);
- unintegrated labor markets: rules in the labor market remained national — in spite of the will of European institutional architects — due to political and cultural factors and real constrains, such as the rigidity of the housing market in many countries. The EU role is basically to grant freedom of migration and equal rights of migrants.

As a matter of fact, the main differences between European forms of capitalism concern the financial systems and the labor markets, which remained national competences.

As far as the financial system is concerned, such variables as the capitalization and liquidity of stock markets and the ratio between risk and debt capital are much higher in the US and UK than in continental European markets such as Germany, France, and Italy. In the latter, banks are relatively more important in financing firms than in the former countries; they have a universal nature, and their monitoring of and control over firms is stronger (Dietl, 1998; Rajan, 2010), in spite of significant changes in the last two decades. In such a way they are often able to detect early risky situations in firms and push them to rescue, thus avoiding default. Although capital reallocation is slowed down, the rapid contagion by financial crises can also be hindered. In this kind of economic system, though, the risk of private gain from control, entrenched management and side dealings between banks and firms may be a serious problem and may slow down post-crisis recovery.[9] As a matter of fact, European progress toward truly unified financial markets and taxation has been bumpy to say the least: the most important European instrument so far has been periodical cross-controls by the national authorities with some support from the European Union on so-called fiscal paradises within the Union and the control that taxpayers pay taxes in the country where they reside.

As to the labor markets, entry and exit flexibility are usually higher in such countries as the US, UK, and Ireland, and seniority relations and firm specific investments are more important in continental Europe. Due to these features, European labor markets are usually less reactive to financial shocks, thus hindering the contagion of the real economy, although at the price of slower labor reallocation, youth, and long-term structural unemployment.

The institutional architecture of the EZ is intended to create opportunities for European countries and increase systemic resilience through an enlarged market and greater financial discipline. However, it also introduced new elements of vulnerability, in particular, through the decoupling between fiscal and monetary policies and the asymmetry of mobility and flexibility between financial and labor markets. The common currency exacerbated both outcomes.

The institutional asymmetry has to be seen in conjunction with the inherited and new structural imbalances, i.e., the imbalances which derive from the economic history of the member countries: in particular, productivity differentials and the relation between public and private finance. Given the institutional architecture, these imbalances have prepared the scene for problematic and asymmetric adaptation to the global crisis.

To work properly as it was designed, the EZ should have complied with a number of requirements. Among the most important are the following: (1) European integration and globalization should have been compatible: this

---

[9] According to Joseph Lutton at JP Morgan (quoted in Rajan, 2010, p. 238), "the U.S. Federal Reserve started raising rates 20 months after peak unemployment in the 1990–1991 recession and 12 months after peak unemployment in the 2001 recession. By contrast, the euro area not only cut rates less but also was quicker to raise rates, doing so seven months after peak unemployment on average in the 1991 recession and nine months after peak unemployment in the 2001 recession."

aim was largely implemented; (2) a common monetary policy should have accompanied monetary integration: a goal that was implemented successfully, the ECB having kept inflation around 2%; (3) common criteria for fiscal policies should have been identified and enforced upon member countries: the Stabilization and Growth Pact (SGP) has been repeatedly broken by some of its members, even though the EZ16 as a whole exceeded the limit of 3% target only once; (4) resources should have flown from strong to weak countries for supporting microeconomic convergence: this was a major failure of the integration process, also because the EU concentrated on macroeconomic issues; and (5) domestic microeconomic adaptation and transformation should have been pursued with the support of national governments: another major failure. Overall, and in spite of important successes, the integration process was asymmetric to the disadvantage of the microeconomic side as compared to the macroeconomic one, thus generating an unbalanced integration. This asymmetry is the most critical element of EZ vulnerability, particularly in the long run.

There is an interrelation among the above successes and failures that contributes to explain the external and internal vulnerability of the EZ in front of the international crisis. The monetary integration has strengthened the European monetary system, limiting the aggregate vulnerability to exogenous shocks of Member States. Smaller states with limited capacity to manage their currency could rely on the credibility of the euro and the common monetary policy, while financially weaker economies gained reputation by giving discipline and credibility to their budgets, anchored to European shared rules. The monetary integration and the introduction of a common currency thus led to enlargement of markets, easier and smother internal flow of resources, elimination of exchange rate risk and uncertainty, and reduction of transaction costs. Since monetary integration increased the domestic effect of asymmetric shocks, due to the lack of the monetary lever, national sovereignty of fiscal policy was conceived as the main institutional device for national adaptation along with EU budget transfers. The entire system was conceived to strengthen national and European resilience to external shocks.

This process of integration and the EZ creation, together with globalization, exposed productivity differentials and made their sustainability hard, at least in the long run. Indeed, traditional coping mechanisms (in particular, the depreciation of the national currency) disappeared. In order to overcome these differentials, policy makers promoted pro-market policies in favor of profits since the 1970s, thus causing growing distributive disparities which obtained additional peculiar drivers within the EZ. They were intended to provide incentives to investment for fostering productivity convergence. Growing employment and income should have resulted through trickle-down mechanisms, thus boosting demand and production.

However, this standpoint disregarded important effects, thus meeting with unforeseen events. Indeed, increasing inequalities have reduced the importance of domestic markets, particularly of domestically produced commodities consumed by the middle-income population and have hampered opportunities for people in general and potential entrepreneurs in particular (e.g., through the polarization of savings that dried up an important source of diffused, small-scale investment). This resulted in segmentation of the economy, the society, and finally the EZ. This outcome had particularly disadvantageous effects in laggard countries. Segmentation within countries in turn depressed demand, production, and savings and fostered public and private debt. Since segmentation was primarily to the disadvantage of the middle class — a politically and economically sensitive domain — policies tried to foster the trickle-down mechanisms by supporting the middle-class consumption through different channels (easy credit, particularly for consumers and housing). Such policies increased the vulnerability of the countries and economies. Vulnerability, together with nonconvergent fiscal rules at the European level, created the conditions for microeconomic failures hampering macroeconomic convergence and stability.

In this frame, the crisis has indeed magnified the gap between the vulnerable peripheral EZ member countries and a more resilient core, made up of economies with high private savings, low public debt, strong current account surplus, low disparities, high productivity, and low unemployment. These economies, whose prototype is Germany, are competitive internationally and internally and capable of affording microeconomic reforms which further increase their competitiveness. They can thus implement and sustain financial constraints. On the other hand, EZ periphery is undergoing a remarkably severe downturn, which is urgently calling at the time of writing for resolute intervention spanning from "internal devaluation," mainly through wage adjustments (Baldwin and Gros, 2010), to credible fiscal action and structural reforms (Draghi, 2010), to sovereign default (Rodrik, 2010) and debt restructuring (Eichengreen, 2011).

At a general level of analysis, peripheral economies suffer from low or negative savings, low productivity (Figure 15.4) and activity rates (mostly to the disadvantage of women), high disparities (Figure 15.5) and unemployment (with remarkably elevated youth unemployment), rapidly rising ratios of debt to gross domestic product, high fiscal and current account deficits, and elevated interest rates. The specifics differ among Greece, which meets all the aforementioned features, Portugal, which has low public and high private debt, Spain, which has low savings and low public debt, Ireland, experiencing a bank and financial system crisis hampering financial stability, and Italy, which has elevated private savings but suffers from high public debt (Table 15.8).

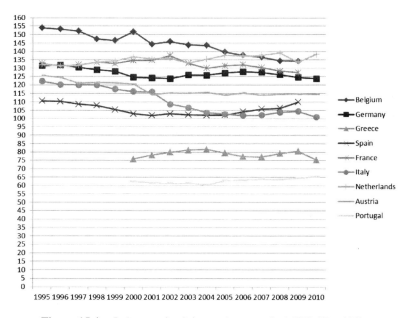

Figure 15.4. Labor productivity per hour worked (EU–27 = 100).

Source: Eurostat.

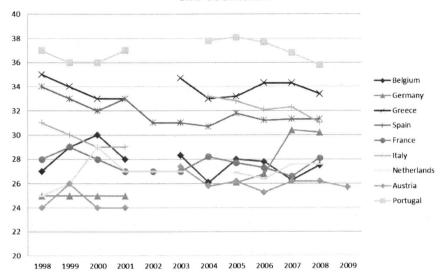

Figure 15.5. Gini index.

Source: AMECO.

All of them have been unable to comply with structural and microeconomic reforms and implement and sustain financial constraints and are consequently uncompetitive both externally and internally.

When the euro has been introduced in 1999 (2001 in Greece), member countries differed remarkably in fundamentals as well as in the structure and the dynamism of the economy. The working of the EZ has reinforced previous patterns, amplifying divergences rather than easing structural convergence. The common currency and monetary policy prevented unbalances to be solved through currency depreciation. At the same time, common fiscal parameters to be complied with limited significantly the members' freedom to set fiscal policies. Indeed, in an integrated area with common currency, only microeconomic reforms are possible and effective to improve the performance and competitiveness of individual economies. In particular, economic adjustments were meant to be obtained *via* labor market reform, aimed at increasing flexibility and lowering real wages.

402 *Bruno Dallago and Chiara Guglielmetti*

Table 15.8. Deficit, current account, inflation, and growth in the EZ: 2000–2007.

	Cumulative deficit, % GDP	Cumulative current account, % GDP	Cumulative inflation above EZ16 rate, percentage points	Cumulative growth above EZ average, percentage points
Austria	11.8	13	−4.1	1.014
Belgium	2.7	26	−1.0	0.002
Finland	−32.4	50	−5.3	10.5
France	21.7	4	−3.3	−0.3
Germany	17.7	26	−4.2	−5.3
Greece	40.0	−67	8.1	16.6
Ireland	−11.9	−15	10.0	31.0
Italy	22.9	−10	1.0	−5.5
Luxembourg	−18.6	83	4.1	21.2
Netherlands	4.7	45	2.4	0.2
Portugal	28.9	−71	6.3	−5.6
Spain	−2.3	−46	7.6	11.7

Source: Baldwin and Gros (2010).

In this context, the idea behind free circulation of capital — the risk of countries default being equalized thanks to the EU guarantee — is that capital should flow from strong countries to weak countries, where interest rates are higher (positive spread). The flow of capital to weak countries should re-establish equilibrium and even out interest rates. To this end the EU has established the Maastricht criteria to avoid governments' free-ridings in public finance.[10] These criteria include a set of controls and also the possibility of punishment for non-complying countries.

As aforementioned, however, the equilibrating mechanisms foreseen in the EU build-up did not work properly (in particular because of the lack of control over fiscal policies to balance asymmetric shocks and the failure of microeconomic reforms). Yet, it turned to be to the advantage of

---

[10] Compared to a fixed exchange rate system, the common currency area has to solve the critical and potentially dangerous problem of avoiding free-riding among member countries to the disadvantage of virtuous ones.

strong countries, in particular Germany, and to the disadvantage of weak countries.

Weak countries suffered higher price increases which had effects similar to real exchange rate appreciation and led to export discouragement. If labor market reforms had worked as expected, compression of wages could have counterbalanced this effect. However, this kind of reforms encounter two serious problems which make them easier to be pursued and more successful in stronger economies as Germany than in EZ peripheral member countries. These problems are related to the structure of the economy and the welfare state provisions. First, the scope of these reforms is narrower in the periphery, where real wages are lower and social services are worst. Compression of wages would exacerbate the negative consequences of increasing inequalities and jeopardize labor incentives and productivity. Second, the consequences of focusing on downward wage flexibility rather than on investment in infrastructure, research, innovation, and human capital in rather static economies with low level of technology are serious for competitiveness in the long run, pushing them to choose labor intensive and low productivity technologies. Relative costs in the periphery have thus risen for a decade, leading to loss of competitiveness in the rather closed EZ real economy where the bulk of trade takes place among member countries (Table 15.9). This situation favored strong countries, particularly German producers: their traditional competitors could not take advantage by depreciating their currency. Moreover, the euro has been much more conducive to additional EZ exports than a strong Deutsche mark would have been. Strong countries accumulated increasing current account surpluses with weaker member countries (Figure 15.6).

They kept balance of payment equilibrium by exporting capital to weak countries where returns were higher, although riskier. The high growth rate in Ireland and Spain has been fueled by this inflow of capital, which, however, went mainly into non tradable activities as construction. The gains of the periphery were, as Wolf puts it, transitory, if not illusory (Wolf, 2010). Strong countries' advantage came at the cost of the weak countries' inability to comply with common fiscal rules, thus increasing systemic risk that, in turn, hit particularly

Table 15.9. Intra EZ export (% of total export).

	2005	2008
Belgium	76.4	77.0
Czech Rep.	84.2	99.4
Denmark	70.5	69.9
Germany	63.4	63.7
Ireland	63.4	68.3
Greece	52.9	64.0
Spain	71.8	68.2
France	62.6	63.0
Italy	58.6	58.5
Luxemburg	89.4	89.0
Netherlands	79.2	78.7
Austria	69.3	72.3
Portugal	79.8	73.7
Finland	56.0	55.9
Slovenia	66.4	68.1
UK	56.9	56.9

Source: EUROSTAT.

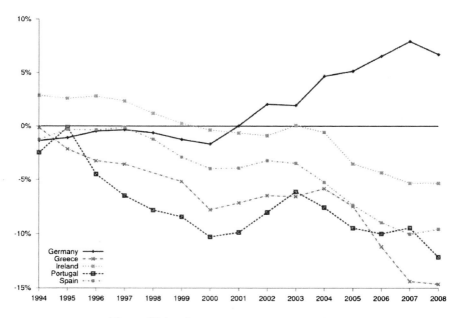

Figure 15.6. Current account balance (% GDP).

Source: IMF BOF, in Lapavitsas *et al.* (2010).

the credibility of strong countries. If the EZ economy proved to be rather stable in the short run, it nevertheless progressively accumulated tensions. At the basis there was the inability to implement micro economic reforms.

15.4. European Sovereign Debt and Euro Crises: The Fork in the Road of the EZ and the Risks of Muddling Through

In *A Euro Rescue Plan*, a public appeal to the German Federal Government, Franz, Fuest, Hellwig, and Sinn, four leading German economists directly committed in policy advisory at the Federal level, stated that "What Europe needs is not an economic government but political and economic mechanisms that effectively limit public and private indebtedness in the member states." In their interpretation the EZ crisis is ascribable "to the debt and financing problems of some euro member states" (Franz *et al.*, 2010, p. 101), and the crisis of the euro was a "danger to very specific countries rather than a systemic danger of the euro system as such" (Sinn, 2010, p. 7).[11] They moreover identify 10 fiscal policy rules for strengthening national individual responsibility, defined in the document as a *conditio sine qua non* for the survival of the European Monetary Union. It is worth recalling rules 9 and 10 here: a majority of the EZ members may ask an insolvent country to leave the EZ, and a voluntary exit from the EZ must be possible at any time.

The main points of this analysis are the following: the EZ has always been suffering from economic imbalances which burdened its development. In particular, the irresponsible fiscal policies of peripheral countries led to unsustainable level of public — and private — debts and fiscal deficit and had pernicious economic spillovers to

---

[11] The starting point of their analysis of the EZ crisis is the integration of capital markets which followed the EMU and led to a convergence of interest rates in the EZ, regardless the underlying different country risks. This, in turn, caused a massive capital flow toward the southwest periphery of Europe. The consequences were threefold: a boom in construction and investments in these countries, which ended up in bubbles whose busting is now threatening solvency of banks and public finance; the unsustainable level of government deficit.

virtuous countries. Irresponsible policies overheated these economies, leading to a huge flow of investments toward these countries which inflated bubbles whose bursting hampered EZ sustainability. While the EU was ineffective in imposing the respect of the rules designed for avoiding negative spillovers, fiscal stabilization is now deemed as badly needed.

The authors' position epitomizes a widespread vision of the dynamics underlying the crisis in the EZ. The unprecedented depth and magnitude of the crisis has put the sustainability of the EZ institutional and political framework into question. If the urgency of a comprehensive reform is widely acknowledged, the direction that this reform should take is question of debate. The necessity of a clear leap forward toward integration is recognized in part of the academic debate. Far less clear on this issue are even those policy makers most committed with the European project. On the other side, the focus on national interests has sensibly risen since the onset of the Greek refinancing crisis. The bulk of European policy makers appear more concerned with the reaction of their domestic constituencies than with an EZ coordinated strategy. The discussion is shifting toward the evaluation of how costs are allocated and gains are distributed among members in a sort of zero-sum-game logic. The public debt crisis in the periphery of EZ, the ECB securities market program, the bailout of Greece worth 110 billion euros, and the Special Purpose Vehicle worth 750 billion euros, the bailout of Ireland worth 85 billion euros, all gave rise to a harsh political and scientific debate on the working of the EZ and the reform of its institutions, giving fuel to what has been labeled as a new German question.

In a context of shrinking budgetary revenues, fiscal consolidation, and common monetary policy, deflation — in particular the cut of wages, pensions and other costs — is addressed as the unique, and necessary, adjustment mechanism for deficit countries. There is widespread agreement, as well, in identifying differentials in downward rigidity of labor cost as the critical determinant of inflation and competitiveness differentials among member states. Therefore, the pillars of post-crisis recovery are identified as fiscal austerity, wage flexibility, and regulation. If the

Eurozone and Global Financial Imbalances 407

scientific and policy debate over fiscal austerity is getting more and more momentum in US and Europe,[12] far less momentum seems to have gained in Europe the question of real convergence. Yet, two of the more risky countries, Ireland and Spain, have been remarkably disciplined in containing their debt. Much more than countries as Germany and France, which broke the "Stability and Growth Pact" four and three times respectively, from 2000 to 2007. The problems do not lie in the fiscal behavior of a group of peripheral members, but rather in the different starting conditions of the members. Greece is the only peripheral country which was fiscally irresponsible, hiding the actual amount of her public debt and deficit. The sovereign debt crises of the others are mainly the effect of the public rescue of the financial sector (Figures 15.7 and 15.8). Governments and central banks interventions in terms of capital and guarantees toward the financial sector absorbed respectively the 13% and the 30% of EU GDP as to December 2009. This happened in a context of high pressure on public finance due to the working of automatic stabilizers.

This notwithstanding, if ECB engaged since 2008 in massive liquidity provision in order to allow overleveraged European banks to adjust their balance sheets, the support to member countries suffering speculative attacks on public debt has been slow, encountering fierce opposition by Germany. This poses a weighty responsibility to the EZ decision makers, especially in consideration of the credit crunch under which peripheral members were seeking extra funds in the financial markets. The collapsing of lending put upward pressure on yields. Irish,

---

[12] Testified by the extreme position of the so-called generational accountants, a strand of research developed since the early 1990s, for example, by Kotlikoff of the Boston University. In this line was the article by Hagist of the Freiburg University on Britain fiscal position published by the Financial Times in July 2010. Fiercely faulted by Galbraith, who defined them 'not only wrongheaded, but also dangerous' as well as inconsistent in their analysis, generational accountants calculate fiscal gap as the difference between the amount the government will be able to collect by present and future generations, and the amount it is expected to spend. The figures are therefore much higher than those calculated through standard measures.

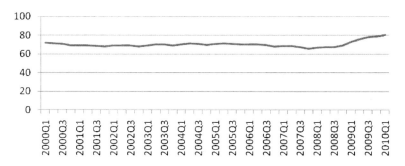

Figure 15.7. Average government debt as a percentage of GDP in the Eurozone.
Source: OECD.

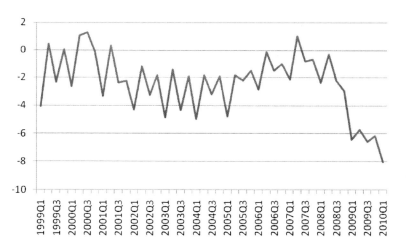

Figure 15.8. Average government deficit as a percentage of GDP in the Eurozone.
Source: OECD, data neither seasonally nor working days adjusted.

Greek, Portuguese, and Italian bond yield spreads *vis-à-vis* the German bond rose to unprecedented high levels (Figure 15.9). Moreover, as Krugman highlights, a likely reason of the loss of lenders' confidence has been the very existence of the euro, which implies that troubled countries "have to deflate their way back to competitiveness, with all the pain that implies" (Krugman, 2011).

Eurozone and Global Financial Imbalances 409

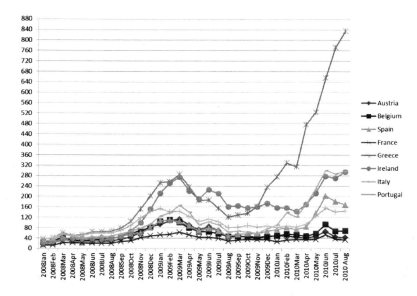

Figure 15.9. Interest rates spread in Europe.

Source: OECD.

Moreover, only two years after Lehman Brothers' default, European institutions have started the reform of financial regulation.[13] However, the deadlines set, and the lack of any provision for the shadow bank system, will leave the financial system highly exposed for long, allowing capital migration toward countries with milder regulation and thus hampering efforts of more rigorous countries. If the USA asks for more rigorous regulations than Europe, Germany maintains the necessity of a longer timeframe in order to sustain her public banks which needed the second biggest public rescue plan (both in terms of capital and guarantee) in Europe after UK.[14]

---

[13] The roadmap is made up of four pillars: (1) Capital ratios, defined within Basel III in September 2010 and analyzed in the subsequent G20 in Seoul, which anyway are to be implemented since 2013–2014 and to be fully accomplished by 2019; (2) Regulation over derivatives, CDS and short sells, presented on September 15, which will have to be discussed and approved by European and national parliaments and be into force by 2012; (3) The institutions too big to fail; and (4) The shadow bank system. Moreover, minimum standards of leverage ratios and short-term liquidity will be defined respectively in 2018 and 2015.

[14] The German banking association foresees that, following Basel III standards, the 10 biggest banks could need 105 billion euros of recapitalization.

A substantial leap forward in financial market supervision has been made with the establishment of European Systemic Risk Board (ESRB),[15] an independent body responsible for the surveillance of the financial system within the Union, and three European supervisory authorities (EBA, EIOPA, and ESMA) which are to ensure an improved prudential supervision of banks, insurances, and investment firms.[16] These innovations add room for coordination to the still very nationally oriented financial supervision. However, banking and finance regulation could have been dealt with in stricter connection with the reform of the economic governance, being the vulnerability of sovereigns unavoidably related with that of banks.

As to the economic governance, the European Council endorsed in October 2010 the Report of the Task Force, chaired by Van Rompuy, established to devise proposals for better budgetary discipline and an improved crisis resolution framework (European Council, 2010). Even though the Council and the European Parliament intend to reach agreement on the Commission's legislative proposals by the summer of 2011,[17] it is nevertheless useful to briefly recall here the main features tabled so far.

The report focuses on five domains: greater fiscal discipline, new economic surveillance mechanism, enhanced coordination, robust framework for crisis management, and stronger institutions for more effective economic governance (Task Force, 2010).

The main focus remains fiscal discipline further enhanced, with broader criteria for the assessment of public finance stability and a wider range of sanctions and measures of financial,[18] reputational, and political nature in

---

[15] Regulation (EU) No 1092/2010 of the European Parliament and the Council of November 24, 2010 on European Union macro-prudential oversight of the financial system and the establishment of a *European Systemic Risk Board.*

[16] The European System of Financial Supervision (ESFS) comprises — along with the ESRB, the European Banking Authority (EBA), the European Insurance and Occupational Pensions Authority (EIOPA), and the European Securities and Markets Authority (ESMA) — the Joint Committee of the European Supervisory Authorities (ESAs) and competent authorities in the member states.

[17] COM (2010) 522; COM (2010) 523; COM (2010) 524; COM (2010) 525; COM (2010) 526; COM (2010) 527; all adopted on September 29, 2010.

[18] These are interest-bearing deposits and fines.

both the preventive and corrective phases of surveillance (Task Force, 2010).[19] A greater importance is given to public debt and to the interplay between the latter and deficit. Debt surveillance is threefold: (1) all countries which do not meet the target — 60% of GDP — need to reduce the debt every year at a rate of one-twentieth of the excess part; (2) in the frame of the preventive phase, member countries which exceed the target of public debt are to define and implement medium-term budget objectives even if the deficit target is met; and (3) the level and the dynamic of the debt will play a substantial role in the deficit infringement procedures. A reverse majority rule for the adoption of enforcement measures is proposed, in order to limit bargaining processes and make the operation of the GSP more "technical." Moreover, with the aim of strengthening institutions, public bodies providing independent analysis, assessments, and forecasts on domestic fiscal policy matters are recommended. The coordination among member countries is enforced through the European Semester, started in January 2011 with the aim of simultaneous assessment of both budgetary measures and structural reforms fostering growth and employment (Task Force, 2010).

The provision of a permanent crisis management, the European Stability Mechanism (ESM), has been foreseen by the Report, agreed by the Euro Area Ministers of Finance in November 2010 and endorsed by the European Council in December 2010. ESM will be operational as of mid-2013 following the expiry of the existing European Financial Stability Fund (EFSF) and the European Financial Stability Mechanism (EFSM), with the aim of supporting countries in financial distress. Private sector involvement will be decided on a case-by-case basis, in line with the IMF practice.

The need for broadening macroeconomic convergence beyond the budget focus of SGP has been recognized through the provision of vulnerability indicators to be monitored. A first assessment of a scoreboard made up of indicators as private debt, competitiveness, current account, credit expansion, level of prices, and productivity growth would be followed by in-depth analysis in case of actual or potential excessive imbalances.

---

[19] These are enhanced reporting requirements, ad hoc reporting to the European Council and enhanced surveillance, eventually followed by a public report.

412 *Bruno Dallago and Chiara Guglielmetti*

However, recent literature has questioned the use of scoreboards (Manasse and Roubini, 2009) and pointed out that some of the areas specified should be addressed by European regulation and supervision (Manasse, 2010; Spaventa, 2010). The Report foresees that "in particularly serious cases, an 'excessive imbalance position' should be launched by the Council, with a deadline to take a set of policy measures to address the problem. Euro area Member States may ultimately face sanctions in case of repeated noncompliance" (Task Force, 2010, p. 2). The infringement procedure appears unlikely to be put into practice for a number of reasons, the time lag which reforms encounters to produce effects, the difficulty of establishing targets in these areas, and the lack of competences of the Commission in a substantial number of areas being the most relevant.

To date the institutional framework of the EZ has been focused on monetary integration and common fiscal parameters, depending on loosely coordinated national initiatives banking and finance regulation as well as structural reforms. The latter were however recognized important for the smooth working of common monetary policy and should have been harmonized via the Lisbon Strategy. Competitiveness policies and current account imbalances were instead completely left to the national level. The enhancement of labor flexibility and the adjustment of nominal and real wages in order to help absorbing shocks — as long as the increase of retirement age, the decrease of average and marginal tax rates and unemployment benefits — have been for long considered the only way ahead (Trichet, 2007) for fostering productivity and labor utilization while maintaining stable macroeconomic conditions. The pressure of the EZ at this regard has been high, exerting a deep influence on national attitudes toward labor policy. Yet, this influence has been much wider than the actual European competences would suggest. On the other side, the commitment of the EZ toward social protection has been poor to say the least.[20] Notwithstanding intense debate on growth and convergence, this structuring does not seem to be substantially changed in the reform proposals so far.

---

[20] For example, the management of the flagship European Globalization Adjustment Fund has been since its creation in 2007 unsatisfactory, leading to an embarrassing actual disbursement of euros 140 m out of nearly €2 bn available (just over 5% of total capacity) due to sclerotic bureaucratic procedures, as highlighted by Pignal (2010).

France and Germany are upholding a pact of economic convergence to strengthen the competitiveness of European economies. This pact, which is a highly disputed issue at the time of writing, foresees the removal of automatic indexation of wages to prices, the delay of the age of retirement according to demographic developments, the leveling of taxation, development instead of binding caps deficit, mutual recognition of diplomas and professional qualifications, a common corporate tax base, national crisis management regime for banks, debt-alert mechanisms into their constitutions, and the provision of infringement procedures. The bulk of these proposals magnifies rather than mitigate pro-cyclical adjustments and are tailored according to a "German model" of development. As Manasse reminds, fiscal policy should be mildly countercyclical in order to minimize tax distortions over time and maximize welfare, while "tougher budget cuts, the deeper the recession" (Manasse, 2010). As aforementioned, moreover, high pressure on downward flexibility in the labor market, as the only way ahead for growth and competitiveness, encounters risks of increased segmentation and negative effects on the quality of the human capital, along with deterioration of standards of living and social unrest. Strong is the need of tackling the real roots of high productivity differentials among member states, and not only fiscal consolidation. Not only is convergence of productivity essential for the stabilization of the euro in the long run, it is also a necessary condition for the sustainability of a European institutional framework.

The EZ is a highly interconnected monetary union in which the links between members are both real and financial. Fiscal policies in each of the countries have systemic implications. Therefore, both surplus and deficit countries, to recall Eichengreen and Temin (2010), "have the responsibility for contributing for its stability and smooth operation." Yet, the Monetary Union, being an extreme case of fixed exchange rate schemes, relies only on deficit countries for addressing trade imbalances, thus showing a bias toward deflation. If deficit countries are expected to cut prices and wages to curtail trade imbalances, surplus countries are not required to countervail them by boosting internal spending. It is the very rationality of EZ institutional setting (institutional and policy "dualism"), together with diverging interests and the national governments' myopia, which is at the heart — together with the weakness of the European

414   *Bruno Dallago and Chiara Guglielmetti*

Commission — of the lack of a concerted European fiscal response to asymmetric shocks, and namely to the current crisis. This fact, being the EU a productively integrated area, hampers the effectiveness of national fiscal strategies, and weakens the resilience of the Member states in coping with the global financial crisis and depression. It also undermines the influence exerted by the EU response at the monetary level.

It seems that the EU has to return urgently to the old spirit of a positive sum game in a radically new context which has now jeopardized mutual trust. What EZ needs are institutional reforms and policies based on the acknowledgment of the Member State's interdependence, and coordinated adjustments toward higher balance among members. In this perspective, critically important is a new credible pact whereby strong member countries finance growth in weak countries in exchange for fair returns and the right of inspection of correct financial management through European authorities. This would require, on the one side, to pursue the long-term aims of tackling productivity differentials, supporting investments in infrastructure and intangible assets, savings and a more balanced pattern of consumption, thus decreasing disparities. On the other side, this would entail less formal and static fiscal criteria, which could foster long-term investments and punish acritical public spending.

References

Atkinson, AB and T Piketty (2007). *Top Incomes over the Twentieth Century: A Contrast between Continental European and English-Speaking Countries.* Oxford and New York: Oxford University Press.

Atkinson, AB and T Piketty (2010). *Top Incomes: A Global Perspective.* Oxford and New York: Oxford University Press.

Baldwin, R and D Gros (2010). Introduction: The euro in crisis — What to do? In *Completing the EZ Rescue: What More Needs to Be Done*? R Baldwin, D Gros and L Laeven (eds.). VoxEU.org.

Caballero, R (2009). Sudden financial arrest. VoxEU.org, November 17.

Calvo, S and CM Reinhart (1996). Capital flows to Latin America: Is There Evidence of Contagion Effects? Policy Research Working Paper Series 1619, The World Bank.

Dietl, HM (1998). *Capital Markets and Corporate Goverance in Japan Germany and the United States. Organizational Response to Market Inefficiencies.* London: Routledge.

Frank, RH (1985). *Choosing the Right Pond: Human Behavior and the Quest for Status.* New York: Oxford University Press.

Frank, RH (1997). The frame of reference as a public good. *Economic Journal,* 107 (November), 1832–1847.

Gros, D and S Micossi (2008). The beginning of the end game. VoxEU.org, September 20.

De Grauwe, P (2010). Fighting the wrong enemy. VoxEU.org, May 19.

Draghi, M (2010). Trade, competitiveness and Europe. European Firms in the Global Economy (EFIGE) Scientific Workshop and Policy Conference, June 18. Rome.

Duesenberry, JS (1949). *Income, Saving and the Theory of Consumer Behavior.* Cambridge, Mass: Harvard University Press.

Eichengreen, B, A Rose and C Wyplosz (1996). Contagious currency crises. National Bureau of Economic Research Working Paper No. 5681.

Eichengreen, B and P Temin (2010). Fetters of gold and paper. VoxEU.org, July 30.

Eichengreen, B (2011). Europe's inevitable haircut. Project Syndicate, www. project-syndicate.org.

European Council (2010). *Background European Council Thursday and Friday 28 and 29 October in Brussels.*

Franz, W, C Fuest, M Hellwig and HW Sinn (2010). A Euro rescue plan. *CESifo Forum,* 11(2), 101–104.

Kahneman, D, JL Knecht and RH Thaler (1991). Anomalies: The endowment effect, loss aversion, and status quo bias. *Journal of Economic Perspectives,* 5(1), 193–206.

Kahneman, D and A Tversky (2000). *Choices, Values and Frames.* Cambridge: Cambridge University Press.

Kaminsky, GL and CM Reinhart (2000). On crises, contagion, and confusion. *Journal of International* Economics, 51(1), 145–168.

Krugman, P (2009). *The conscience of a liberal: Reclaiming America from the right.* London: Penguin Books.

Krugman, P (2011). Can Europe be saved? (January 12, 2011) *The New York Times.*

Lapavitsas, C (2009). Financialised capitalism: Crisis and financial expropriation. *Historical Materialism,* 17(2), 114–148.

Lapavitsas, C, A Kaltenbrunner, D Lindo, J Michell, JP Painceira, E Pires, J Powell, A Stenfors and N Teles (2010). *EZ Crisis: Beggar Thyself and Thy Neighbour*, Research on Money and Finance Occasional Report, March, www.researchonmoneyandfinance.org.

Manasse, P (2010). Stability and growth pact: Counterproductive proposals. VoxEU.org, October 7.

Manasse, P and N Roubini (2009). Rules of thumb for sovereign debt crises. *Journal of International Economics*, 78(2), 192–205.

Piketty, T and E Saez (2006). The evolution of top incomes: A historical and international perspective. *The American Economic Review Papers and Proceedings*, 96(2), 200–205.

Pignal, S (2010). EU workers aid fund failing to pay out (September 6, 2010). *Financial Times*.

Quinn Mills, D (2010). *The World Financial Crisis 2008–2010*. Lexington, KY.

Rajan, RG (2010). *Fault Lines. How Hidden Fractures Still Threaten the World Economy*. Princeton: Princeton University Press.

Razin, A and S Rosefielde (forthcoming 2011).The currency and financial crises of the 1990s and 2000s. In *Handbook of Major Events in Economic History*, Parker, R and R Whaples (eds.). New York: Routledge.

Reich, R (2007). *Supercapitalism. The Battle for Democracy in an Age of Big Business*. London: Icon Books.

Reich, R (2010). *Aftershock. The Next Economy and America's Future*. New York: Alfred A. Knopff.

Reinhart, CM and K Rogoff (2010). Debt and growth revisited. VoxEU.org, August 11.

Rodrik, D (1996). Understanding economic policy reform. *Journal of Economic Literature*, 34(1) (March), 9–41.

Rodrik, D (2010). Thinking the unthinkable in Europe. Project Syndicate, www.project-syndicate.org, December 10.

Spaventa, L (2010). How to prevent excessive current account imbalances. Eurointelligence.

Schreft, S, A Singh and A Hodgson (2005). Jobless recoveries and the wait-and-see hypothesis. *Economic Review*, Federal Reserve Bank of Kansas City, 81–99.

Sinn, HW (2010). Rescuing Europe. *CESifo* Forum, 11(Special Issue): 1–22.

Task Force (2010). Strengthening economic governance in the EU. Report of the task force to the European Council, Brussels, October 21, http://www.consilium.europa.eu.

Trichet, JC (2007). Governance and convergence: The state of play in the Euro area. Speech at the conference *Euro zone — Converging or Drifting Apart?*, organized by the European Parliament (Committee of economic and monetary affairs), open debate with national parliaments, Brussels, February 28.

Van Treek, T (2009). The political economy debate on "financialization" — A macroeconomic perspective. *Review of International Political Economy*, 16(5), 907–944.

Veblen, T (1899a). *Conspicuous Consumption*. London: Penguin Books.

Veblen, T (1899b). *The Theory of the Leisure Class*. New York: Macmillan.

Veblen, T (1909). The limitations of marginal utility. *Journal of Political Economy*, 17 (November), 151–175.

Wilkinson, R and K Pickett (2009). *The Spirit Level. Why Equality is better for Everyone*. London: Penguin Books.

Wolf, M (2010). Germans are wrong: The EZ is good for them (September 7, 2010). *Financial Times*.

PART VII

TWO ASIAS

CHAPTER 16

EAST–WEST CONVERGENCE AND INTRA-ASIAN STRATIFICATION

STEVEN ROSEFIELDE
University of North Carolina, Chapel Hill

MASAAKI KUBONIWA
Hitotsubashi University, Tokyo

SATOSHI MIZOBATA
University of Kyoto, Japan

Modernization, enlightenment, liberalization, and democratization allowed the West to surpass Asian economic achievements from 1500 to 1945. After World War II, Japan, building on its Meiji, Taisho and Showa era successes, together with Taiwan, South Korea, Singapore, and Hong Kong began rapidly converging to the West's high per capita income frontier. Market communist China and Vietnam followed on their heels with a 40-year lag.[1] All these countries adopted export-led development strategies and liberalized in accordance with neoclassical microeconomic theory. All embraced the nostrums of Western macroeconomic and monetary theory and joined the World Trade Organization (WTO), International Monetary Fund (IMF), and World Bank. All pursued rapid modernization policies, including gender-neutral mass education, and increased female labor-force participation. They acquired superior technologies and skills through outsourcing and technology transfer. All marketized, liberalized, and promoted entrepreneurship.

Many construe these developments as the inevitable consequence of westernization and predict that it is only a matter of time before oriental living standards fully converge to the occident's high frontier. However, the evidence points to a more complex reality, conditioned by systemic,

---

[1] See Chapter 1 in this volume.

epochal, conjunctural, evolutionary, and demographic factors.[2] The heart of the matter is whether generic modernization is enough, or is it also necessary to properly modernize and westernize so that technologies, culture, and institutions yield neoclassical results. The postwar Asian experience has revealed that modernization with selective westernization was sufficient to narrow the East–West living standard gap, propelled by export-led development strategies, but the jury is still out about full convergence and intra-Asian leveling because Japan, and perhaps Taiwan and South Korea, are beginning to falter; Asian export-led development is causing micro and macroeconomic problems in the West, and East–West cultural, systemic, and institutional forces remain deep-seated.

The 2008 financial crisis and its aftermath have brought all these latent issues to the surface. Mia Mikic, Ryuhei Wakasugi, and others have shown that export-led development still appears to tie Asia to Western macroeconomic fortunes,[3] but post-crisis prospects are not alike. Mature Asia, specifically Japan, Taiwan, and South Korea seem to face a sluggish environment with growth prospects at or below the Western norm (despite the China connection), while market communist Asia, Thailand, and perhaps Laos and Cambodia have better outlooks due to untapped catch-up possibilities. North Korea and Myanmar also should flourish if they shed their command communist/socialist systems. The precise rates of advance (and/or decline) will depend on whether Asia and the West are entering new micro and macroeconomic development epochs. There are signs to this effect suggesting that 25 years later, full East–West convergence and intra-Asian leveling will not materialize unless the East breaks more radically than it has with critical aspects of its cultural legacy, or the West succumbs to various degenerative tendencies. Instead, after a turbulent period of adjustment to depleting advantages of economic backwardness and the macroeconomic reverberations of the 2008 global financial crisis, the Orient still seems likely to find itself lagging behind the West: stratified into "Two Asias," with one cluster of nations distinctly more productive than the other. In 2030, per capita income in Japan, Taiwan,

---

[2] Eberstadt, N (2010). What population growth and decline means for the global economy. *Foreign Affairs*, 89(6), 54–64.

[3] See this volume, Part IV.

South Korea, and Singapore probably will substantially exceed levels found in market communist Asia, Thailand, Myanmar, and North Korea, once the current surge in Chinese and Vietnamese growth has run its course.

These inferences are predicated on the judgment that Asian development will remain coupled to the West, that there will be diminishing returns to export-led growth, and that systemically embedded domestic barriers will prevent some countries in the East from overtaking the West no matter what strategies are tried, including replacing the dollar with a multi-reserve currency system (unless the West hogties its markets). The unifying assumption here is the neoinstitutionalist perception that institutions and systems matter as much as Heckscher-Ohlin axioms[4]; that while export-led development may be second best given anticompetitive aspects of Asian systems, it provides an inadequate platform for keeping pace with unfettered competition on a sustained basis as soon as peak catch-up possibilities are exhausted.

This outlook is a new twist on the old debate over the comparative merit of command and market economic systems. According to the "duality theorem" there was an exact theoretical correspondence between perfect planning and perfect competition[5]; that all systems at an engineering level were fundamentally alike and were capable of achieving the same ideal performance regardless of their mechanisms (markets versus plans) or cultures. Therefore, the only critical issue during the "cold war" was how these contending approaches would fare in practice. In the same way, one easily can imagine how anticompetitive aspects of the Japanese, Taiwanese, South Korean, Thai, Myanmar and market communist systems could be transcended through "perfect systems protocols," without believing that systems engineering actually could yield consistently good results.

The historical record is clear. Command communist mechanisms were fundamental, not subsidiary determinants of the USSR's real economic

---

[4] Rosefielde, S (1973). *Soviet International Trade in Heckscher-Ohlin Perspective.* Lexington MA: Heath-Lexington.

[5] Dorfman, R, P Samuelson and R Solow (1958). *Linear Programming and Economic Analysis.* New York: McGraw-Hill.

performance. Just as the Soviet Union's demise proves that the Kremlin's post-Stalin brand of terror-free economic command was a dead end, we now know that Japan's export-led, and Asian command communist modernizations failed to bridge the East–West living standard gap. Borrowing occidental technologies, skills, institutions, and management proved insufficient, despite hopeful beginnings.

Japan was Asia's pioneer. Although, it demonstrated beyond a shadow of a doubt from the 1868 Meiji Ishin (renewal) to 1945, and then in the postwar era until 1990 that it was possible to recover lost economic ground without abandoning its shame-based communalist culture[6]; systemic inefficiencies gradually outweighed the gains from emulation, indigenization, incremental technological improvement, and domestic innovation. Angus Maddison has shown that Japanese per capita income managed to pull within hailing distance of the American benchmark (81%) by 1990, but then went into reverse, falling to 73% by 2008.[7] After more than 100 years of export-led catch-up, Japan's miracle degenerated into two lost decades, with no relief in sight.

The experiments of Mao Tsetung and Ho Chi Minh with autarkic, seige-mobilized terror command communism (widespread forced labor, Great Leap Forward, Cultural Revolution) seemingly fared better,[8] but the successes claimed were a mirage. Although, command communism could modernize, innovate, transfer some foreign technologies, capital deepen, capital widen, educate, and improve labor skills, outcomes were distorted by ineffectual planning, coerced labor, and forced substitution. Physical productivity and material growth happened, but were disconnected from values, resulting in growth without prosperity and a rapidly accumulating capital stock with little or no competitive market worth [East Germany's industrial capital stock had to be almost entirely scrapped after the DDR merged with West Germany]. Worse still, statistics were treated as instruments of class war and freely invented. A single example exposes

---

[6] See Rosefielde, S (2010). *Asian Economic Systems*, unpublished manuscript. Cf. Mizobata, Chapter 6, this compendium,

[7] www.ggdc.net/MADDISON/oriindex.htmwww.ggdc.net/MADDISON/oriindex.htm; Russia, China 1991–228(EU benchmark).xls.

[8] Rosefielde, S (2010). *Red Holocaust*. New York: Routledge.

the larger deception. Although it is now conclusively proven that Pol Pot's terror-driven experiment in agro-industrial communism killed approximately 20% of the Cambodian nation during 1975–1979, official Kampuchean statistics still accepted by the OECD report that Cambodia's GDP miraculously grew 6.8% per annum.[9] The Khmer Rouge wanted the world to believe that a catastrophe was a triumph and cooked the data to substantiate it.

It is impossible to accurately calibrate the dimensions of Asian command communism's failure from politically malleable statistics, but their leaders' summary judgments can be inferred from their actions. Deng Xiaoping and Ho Chi Minh's successors must have concluded that command communist modernizations were irreversible failures because they scuttled command for market communism, despite the immense political risks of being branded Marxist-Leninist renegades. Japan's export-led development by contrast disappointed, but not enough to induce leaders to discard communalist principles for individualistic free enterprise.

Any hope therefore that modernization can make the East equally or more productive than the West rests with the "tiger," and market communist models. The Taiwanese, South Korean, and Singaporean experiences are the most encouraging because their export-led modernizations have allowed them to steadily narrow the East–West per capita income divide for more than 50 years and catch up to the EU, while preserving vital aspects of their Japanese communalist and Sino-Confucian legacies. Nonetheless, Maddison's data indicate that their growth rates have decelerated in the new millennium raising the specter that Taiwan and South Korea are approaching the limits of modernization like the Japanese before them and may be vulnerable to falling back.[10]

Taiwanese and South Korean growth retardation is especially worrisome because the Chinese and Vietnamese economic "miracles" have expanded their export markets, allowing them to enjoy augmented economies of scale, while simultaneously bolstering aggregate effective demand and consumer utility (through inexpensive imports). However, the potency of these special factors must wane as the advantages of

---

[9] Rosefielde, S. *Red Holocaust*, Tables 15.6 and 15.7, pp. 167–68.

[10] See Chapter 1 in this volume.

Chinese and Vietnamese catch-up are depleted, and when they do, the odds favor Taiwan and South Korea following the Japanese precedent: losing ground *vis-à-vis* the West.

Of course, as some seem to believe Chinese and Vietnamese market communists may have stumbled upon a modernization formula that allows them to surpass the West without decriminalizing freehold property, adopting the rule of contract law, abandoning communist party insider rent-granting, creating universally competitive domestic markets, permitting unfettered capital outflows and inflows, establishing competitive renminbi (RMB) exchange rates, shunning government overregulation, installing effective multiparty democracy, and promoting civic empowerment.[11] Should this come to pass, China and Vietnam could pull the tigers along by their coattails, but it would be foolish to bet on miracles. There are no magic wands as the Soviets discovered to their dismay that can make anticompetitive systems superior in the long run. Market communist, Taiwanese and South Korean modernizations may seem to be substitutes for westernization rather than complements, but are not so. The more their systems constrain and/or warp competition, the lower their ultimate potentials, implying not only that market communism cannot be the solution to depleted advantages of relative economic backwardness; also, in the not too distant future, the intrinsic inferiority of market communism will become manifest, like command communism before it.

In the interim, while market communism probes the limits of its export-led modernization strategy, Asia's future is being shaped more by the seldom considered phenomenon of "post-modernization" than by mechanical catch-up possibilities. The most sobering aspect of Japan's two lost decades is not that convergence ceased, but that instead of plateauing, living standards have fallen against America and the EU. This is surprising because catch-up is a relative concept. When laggards fall back, the pool of beneficial technology transfers should automatically

---

[11] Rosefielde, *Comparative Economic Systems*; This volume, Chapter 9 . Halper, S (2010). *The Beijing Consensus: How China's Authoritarian Model Will Dominate the Twenty-First Century.* New York: Basic Books. Nathan, AJ (2010). A review of Stefan Halper. The Beijing consensus: How China's authoritarian model will dominate the twenty-first century. *Foreign Affairs*, May–June, p. 150.

increase placing a floor under further declines. This may still happen, but if it does not happen, Asia could succumb to postmodern catch-up fatigue and disorientation, where prior successes erode the system's potential. For example, Japan's celebrated work ethic and communality made it easier to seize the benefits of technology transfer shortly after the war than today when affluence encourages leisure, and creeping American style individualism diminishes team effort. Likewise, while North Korea kept pace with its southern twin from 1947–1990, it swooned thereafter, widening the per capita income gap to 15-fold where living standards once had been identical across the peninsula.[12] Apparently, systems and evolutionary systems change matter in ways few economists other than Douglass North and Oliver Williamson adequately appreciate.[13]

They imply that Asia's futures not only depend on core epochal, micro and macroeconomic forces (including White and Black Swan cyclical factors),[14] but hinge as well on intrinsic patterns of cultural potentials and their evolutionary adaptations. In this expanded perspective, if Asia's potentials are immutable and support Heckscher-Ohlin convergence, then East–West living standards will eventually merge, and intra-Asian disparities will be leveled, regardless of White and Black Swan cyclical oscillations, or epochal shifts in the rate of sustainable growth. The only uncertainties are the pace of eastern catch-up and leveling amid fluctuating global cyclical and epochal currents.

However, if core cultural factors and subsequent adaptations are incompatible with East–West per capita income equalization and intra-Asian leveling, then neither global nor intra-regional convergence are assured. Likewise, the 2008 financial crisis's feedbacks may be more complicated than those implied by neoclassical and Heckscher-Ohlin theories. This is the conceptual space where the "Two Asias" conjecture

---

[12] See Chapter 1 in this volume.

[13] North, D (1990. *Institutions, Institutional Change and Economic Performance.* Cambridge: Cambridge University Press; North, D and R Thomas (1973). *The Rise of the Western World: A New Economic History.* Cambridge: Cambridge University Press; Williamson, O (1996). *Mechanisms of governance.* Oxford: Oxford University Press.

[14] Taleb, N (2007). *Black Swan: The Impact of the Highly Improbable.* New York: Random House.

becomes interesting; where the widely supposed certainty of convergence and leveling is replaced by the prospect of an East, rigidly divided into clusters of superior and inferior core systems with oscillating living standards mostly below the Western benchmark.

The superior systems today are Japan, Taiwan, South Korea, and Singapore, judged by their per capita incomes and technological prowess, rather than their growth rates. The inferior systems are the market communist quartet, China, Vietnam, Laos, and Cambodia, together with command communist North Korea, Myanmar, and Thailand. China and Vietnam alone in both clusters seem to be displaying vigorous catch-up momentum; the rest are falling back, pacing, or converging at a modest rate.[15] The big question marks for the future hierarchy of East's per capita income are Japan, China, and Vietnam, assuming systems (and culture-based institutions) matter. Will Japan fall from the high to the low living standard cluster? And/or will China and Vietnam join the tigers?

The trend as well as the immediate postcrisis environment, envisioned by the IMF, suggest that Japan will lose ground to the tigers in Asia's rich men club,[16] but its living standard should remain comfortably above Thailand's at the top of the poor men cluster for the next 25 years. Japan's postmodernization fatigue is not mysterious, although it has some subtle aspects. All the easy gains from catch-up have long since been exhausted. Its labor force is graying and population declining. Asia is no longer Japan's hinterland as had been the case during the cold war, forcing domestic exporters to compete for market share with market communists and the tigers. Yen appreciation, attributable to persistent current account surpluses and negligible foreign debt, has compounded the problem by transforming Japan into a high-cost producer, reliant on cheap outsourcing abroad. The tactic helps the bottom line, and Japanese GNP, but not per capita GDP because outsourcing productivity gains accrue to less developed Asian countries, supplying intermediate inputs and assembly services. Japanese authorities had hoped to offset this loss to GDP growth

---

[15] Myanmar claims that its GDP is growing at double digits, but the author believes that these statistics are freely invented.

[16] See Chapter 1 in this volume.

with a series of "big bang" liberalization initiatives,[17] but the benefits were disappointing. Dreams of a macroeconomic consumption-driven surge also went unrealized, even though savings as a share of personal disposable income fell sharply. Japanese culture appears to be adapting to a steady state mentality where it seems wiser to reduce effort (including the pursuit of innovation and technology diffusion), rather than strive for elusive productivity gains. Security and stability have become more important than risk-taking, despite persistent efforts promoting the virtues of individual self-seeking, entrepreneurship, competition, and free trade alliances.

The 2008 global financial crisis and its aftermath have seriously exacerbated these adverse tendencies by sharply appreciating the yen (Asian safe haven effect), creating expectations of further dollar depreciation, and dampening demand for Japan's mass market exports. Higher yen foreign exchange rates, other things being equal, mean that Japan's export competitiveness must decline. Domestic exporters either will have to absorb yen appreciation by cutting wages and other costs, or accept a smaller market share. Either way, GDP growth is apt to be impaired. Lackluster prospects for the West's middle class further aggravate Japan's woes. The West's wealthy appear to have escaped relatively unscathed from the 2008 financial crisis thanks to bailouts and expansive monetary policy, while the middle class has borne the brunt of high involuntary unemployment, weak wage growth, and ballooning public debt. This could change temporarily if the American government succeeds in engineering new bubbles in the housing, derivatives, stock and commodities markets as its current QE2 (quantitative easing) policy suggests,[18] but the

---

[17] Prime Minister Hashimoto announced a "big bang" (quick, large-scale liberalization) of the Japanese financial industry in 1996, modeled after the 1986 British initiative. The concept was then extended to other types of deregulation, particularly in the retail sector. A major educational reform thrust, begun in 2004, also is often described as a "big bang."

[18] QE2 is an acronym for "quantitative" "easing"; that is printing money and making life easier for bankers who have increased loanable reserves, and gift interest income from the United States Treasury. Ben Bernanke advocates the policy as an unemployment fighting tactic, but as is widely understood on Wall Street, expanding the money supply increases the likelihood (risk) of excess asset price appreciation.

430 Steven Rosefielde, Masaaki Kuboniwa, and Satoshi Mizobata

transcyclical effect probably will be detrimental. At the end of the day, Japan is likely to be hardest hit by America's middle class trading down to Chinese substitutes. Nor should one expect China's emerging middle class to save the day. Its demand grew rapidly during Japan's two lost decades without spurring revival.

None of these postcrisis disadvantages would matter from the standpoint of sustainable per capita GDP growth, if Japan were able to capitalize on the untapped productivity potential of its importables and nontradables sectors, implied by its relative economic backwardness. The problem here is Japan's dim prospects for further westernization. If it were able to transcend the productivity constraints imposed by anticompetitive communalism, including allowing foreign investors to do it, Japan would have done so long ago.[19] Perhaps, someday it will. Until then, however, deteriorating postcrisis export conditions (including the possibility of rising protectionism, exchange rate wars, and global financial instability) are likely to prevent Japan from converging to America's high frontier, and are apt to erode its position in Asia's rich men club.

China is better situated. It still is in the throes of fast-track modernization that shows few signs of fatigue. The 2008 financial crisis and subsequent global depression hit Beijing's exports hard, but 2009 per capita GDP somehow managed to barrel ahead at a 8.6% per annum clip,[20] before accelerating into the low double digits. The government attributes the "miracle" to deprioritizing export-led modernization (rather than false statistics) in favor of importables and nontradables (abetted by protectionist dollar reserve hoarding). On its telling, the new policy was an instant success. Falling exports had little immediate impact on technology transfer, and government-driven domestic projects expedited technology diffusion. In China's comparatively full employment economy,[21] resources were deftly shunted out of exports and into other more productive sectors. Henceforth, Beijing will optimize its growth by

---

[19] Ahearn, R (2005). Japan's Free Trade Agreement Program. CRS Report for Congress, Order Code RL33044, August 22. Rosefielde, *Asian Economic Systems*, Japan chapter.

[20] CIA, *World Factbook: China*, 2010.

[21] Unemployment hovers in a narrow range around 4% of the labor force. See CIA, *World Factbook: China*, 2010.

funneling domestic resources to best dynamic use in accordance with shifting opportunities.

If it succeeds, then consonant with the logic of perfect mixed market-command planning and the official GDP growth trend, China will quickstep to the world's highest living standard by 2040. No one, of course, believes that Beijing can perfectly manage market communism, or that official Chinese growth rates are accurate, but perhaps second best will be good enough. Is it plausible that Chinese market communism is potentially as efficient as its Western rivals? Have the internal barriers that warped Mao's modernization efforts and prompted Deng's experiment with export-led development been surmounted sufficiently to make market communism equal or superior to its Japanese and tiger rivals now or in the foreseeable future? China's prospects for ascending from Asia's low to its high productivity cluster depend on the answers. Unless it can be shown that China has not only marketized, but that its system is as competitive as the frontrunners, it cannot be convincingly maintained that it will join the rich men club, or more ambitiously attain Western living standards.

The evidence points entirely the other way. First, and foremost, China proscribes freehold property on Marxist principle. Productive assets are wholly owned and directed by the state, or leased (fixed term) in part or in their entirety. The term state-owned enterprise should be applied to all Chinese productive assets because the state (people) is the ultimate proprietor. By convention however, the term state-owned enterprises (STO) designates wholly or mostly state-owned property under direct government supervision, with the misnomer "private" applied to state leaseholds of other sorts. The vast preponderance of private productive wealth in the middle kingdom is leasehold property of both the STO (mostly state-owned) and "private" sort that inadequately rewards lessees for efficient management and legitimate risk-taking, while simultaneously opening the door to rent-seeking and moral hazard, judged from the neoclassical benchmark. Lessees are disincentivized, receive unearned benefices, and have a license to speculate and plunder. Misbehavior, sternly repressed under Mao's command communism, is now tolerated as a necessary evil. Beijing has recently begun encouraging STOs and lesser state-owned enterprises (not directly government-supervised) to sell minority shares with "quasi freehold aspects" on various stock exchanges and through direct placements, openly to foreigners and informally to nationals, including STO insiders. This should be beneficial if China were a freehold competitive regime, but is prone to abuse under market communism.

Leases are allocated by the communist party on a prioritized insider basis. Properties with high rental (unearned monopoly income) components are granted (also rescinded and re-assigned) opportunistically to high officials, their families and networks without regard for efficiency, as instruments of party power and rewards for loyal service. Rent-granting has a Beijing party-centered aspect, but regional and local party officials operate on the same principle with central oversight. Rent-grantees of all sorts are permitted to participate when they wish in competitive marketplaces, but also can augment receipts through privileged intra-state contracting and subsidies; practices Clifford Gaddy and Barry Ickes characterize as a "mafia" business style.[22]

What the Soviets used to call the economy's commanding heights are firmly and anticompetitively controlled by party rent-granters and rent-seekers on satisficing rather than optimizing principles, although this is publically denied. It constitutes the upper tier of a two level "planned" management mechanism that is complemented below with a competitive leasing regime where small proprietors of various descriptions acquire leases at auction or through administrative means. These second tier businesses too might prefer the luxury of rentier satisficing, but lacking "godfathers," are compelled to behave more or less like neoclassical profit-seekers. They are the "market" heart of Chinese market communism; party privilege seekers are its brain.

This flawed systems architecture is compounded by a host of other deficiencies. Chinese market communism in its entirety operates under the rule of men, as distinct from the rule of (contract) law. The communist party is superior to the nation's constitution and judiciary. In the West, injured transactors can redress their grievances (contract disputes) through the mediation of independent judicial authorities: a right that

---

[22] Gaddy, C and B Ickes (2011). *Russia's Addiction: The Political Economy of Resource Dependence.*Washington, DC: Brookings. Gaddy and Ickes assert that the Russian economy is run on mafia business model. The application of the term is extended here to China because both countries rely heavily on state insider rent-granting.

greatly diminishes business risk and expands the scope of rational profit-seeking. China's rent-seekers, competitive leaseholders, and foreigners are denied this recourse[23] and consequently are compelled to forego legitimate profit-augmenting opportunities including gains from innovation and modernization.

The system also preserves numerous command aspects. The state dominates international commerce and finance formally and informally. It fixes the renminbi exchange rate, compels most exporters (STOs, leasing enterprises, foreign joint venturers and direct foreign investors outside the special foreign trade zones [SEZs]) to transfer dollar earnings to the state in return for renminbi.[24] This has enabled the government to amass more than 2.6 trillion dollars, much of it in excess reserves that protect China's domestic economy by effectively closing its ports to foreign exporters; at the same time, it acquired an impressive inventory of natural resource companies abroad.[25] The state restricts financial institutions, labor mobility, and hampers collective bargaining. Its research and development institutions adhere to the command paradigm, with state bank credit-financed anti-recessionary construction projects (offsetting plummeting

---

[23] China has a court system and so claims that it has the rule of law. The system may well adjudicate minor disputes fairly but is obedient to the party when insiders choose to rule.

[24] The Foreign Exchange Administration Regulations of the People's Republic of China provide that all payment transactions in mainland China must be settled with renminbi, the Chinese currency. However, this restrictive foreign exchange regime does not bind companies, located in special economic zone (SEZ). Subject to the required documentation, payments between a SEZ company and its offshore counterpart should, in general, be settled in a foreign currency. Transactions between a SEZ company and Chinese entities registered inside or outside the SEZ may be settled by using renminbi or by another foreign currency. See Cody Chen, "Operating Business in Chinese Free Trade Zones," *Taylor Wessing Newsletter*, August 2010. Multinational companies operating outside a SEZ must purchase renminbi with dollar export earnings FOB. These renminbi are not freely convertible, so that companies desiring to wind down their businesses must receive special permission to convert, transfer holdings to other entities, or over-invoice dollar intermediate good import purchases abroad. This could create immense problems if multinational corporations collectively seek to repatriate their Chinese assets.

[25] China buys up the world (November 13, 2010). *The Economist*, p. 11. Sutherland, P (2008). Transforming nations. *Foreign Affairs*, 87(2), 125–36; Kleine-Ahlbrandt, S and A Small (2008). China's new dictatorship diplomacy. *Foreign Affairs*, 87(1), 38–56.

exports), and limited market guidance.[26] Public programs at the central, regional, and local levels are determined by rulers, not democratic consumer sovereignty. They are devised by the party/state for the party, with perfunctory civic participation.

Just as in Mao's regime, state programs, allocations, distributions, controls, supervision, and management are pervasively distorted by the rule of men causing immense waste, fraud, and abuse, concealed by China's aggregate GDP statistics. Partial marketization and export-led development mitigate these inefficiencies by allowing domestic and foreign consumers to influence aspects of the party's rent-granting, control, regulatory and management systems; however, in the final analysis, long-term inefficiency prospects in the importables and nontradables sectors seem closer to those of command than tiger and Japanese communalist systems. This is contrary to Beijing's claims that if market communism is maintained, the party can achieve its development goals by switching from export-led to optimal growth, and that in the fullness of time its comparative productivity will put it near or at the top of Asia's rich men club. This is wishful thinking. China's living standard is more likely to plateau at levels below Japan and the tigers, or at the bottom rung of the affluent cluster. Its exact position in the hierarchy ultimately may depend on whether it can avert the sort of evolutionary degeneration bedeviling Muscovite Russia, where corruption and satisficing privilege have become paralytic.[27] Communism's autocratic and rent-granting proclivities make it inferior in practice, with or without markets. Market communism can advance from its present stage of development, but it cannot converge to the neoclassical high frontier, or equal the welfare achievements of Japan and the tigers.

The 2008 financial crisis and its immediate aftermath conceal these fundamentals because state financial and foreign exchange controls protected China from Western derivatives speculation, hot money flows, and a depressionary credit crunch. These factors together with the

---

[26] Gilboy, G (2004). The myth behind China's miracle. *Foreign Affairs*, 83, 4,33–48. Li, Y (2010). *Imitation to Innovation in China*. North Hampton, MA: Edward Elgar.

[27] Rosefielde, S (2010). Russia's aborted transition: 7000 days and counting. *Institutional'naya Ekonomika Razvitie*. Rosefielde, S (2001). After Soviet communism: Authoritarian economic evolution in Russia and China. In *Pekka Sutela Festschrift*, I Korhonen (ed.). Helsinki: Bank of Finland, pp. 81–92.

prospect of continued high profits and a shift in Western import demand to lower-priced goods prevented a steep growth recession, making China's advance seem unstoppable. The illusion will fade as catch-up depletion and retarded Western growth erode China's vitality.

The inflection point may be closer than some suppose because Beijing's stealth protectionism is beginning to roil the postwar liberal international trading order.[28] Globalists had pressed for China's admission into the WTO hoping that once inside, Beijing would gradually reduce implicit export subsidies (via renminbi undervaluation) and import barriers, sharing the benefits of Chinese outsourcing and export expansion equitably. The renminbi has appreciated modestly both in real and nominal terms, but not enough to halt overexporting. On the import side, Beijing curbed quotas, cut tariffs, and slapped the wrists of copyright and patent violators. These positives however have been more than offset by dollar reserve hoarding, which among other things has proven to be an effective form of importables protection. The WTO does not require nations to buy goods and services with its export proceeds and assumes that these revenues will be used to competitively maximize transactors' utilities without protectionist distortion. This makes sense for individuals and companies, but not for countries with state-controlled trading regimes, where leaders can protect home industries, case by case, or generically merely by refusing to buy foreign goods. Perhaps, someday the WTO will recognize its error; however, until the loophole is closed, China can have its cake and eat it with backdoor quotas masquerading as precautionary foreign currency reserves. From a protectionist standpoint, Beijing is in the blissful position of simultaneously overexporting and underimporting,[29]

---

[28] Rosefielde, S. Export-led Development and Dollar Reserve Hoarding. Chapter 9 in this volume.

[29] An undervalued renminbi makes imports more expensive than they would be under optimal or second best equilibrium. This imparts a protectionist element. However, this is only a partial equilibrium effect. If government export receipts are higher than equilibrium (as they should be if policymakers are rational), then Beijing's imports likewise will be above the optimal and second best levels, making the import element of renminbi undervaluation antiprotectionist on balance. This should be the result: absent dollar reserve hoarding, and it provides some protectionist insight into why Chinese foreign trade policymakers have chosen to prevent the importation of foreign goods by simply refusing to buy them.

allowing workers to be overemployed in both the exportables and importables sectors.[30]

Unfortunately, what is good for Chinese employment is bad for America's because Beijing's stealth protectionism reduces US jobs across the tradable economy, transforming what was supposed to be a free trade regime into an unsustainable, state trade-controlled "beggar-thy-neighbor" system.[31] The true nature of Chinese protectionism is just beginning to crystalize because, before the 2008 financial crisis, analysts fixated on renmimbi undervaluation, China's funding of American deficit spending, and the rapid growth of international commerce, said to raise all boats.

Persistent American and EU double digit unemployment, however, are prompting many to point fingers at unfair Chinese trading practices. Secretary of the US Treasury Tim Geithner and US Federal Reserve Chairman, Ben Bernanke have started taking potshots at China pressing helter-skelter for redress, and there is considerable chatter about impending currency devaluation and trade wars.[32] The situation does not have to spiral out of control. China's leadership can pare its dollar reserve hoard to tolerable limits, or let the Chinese public spend the money. Nonetheless, should it persist for protectionist or other reasons, preserving or increasing its current 2.6 trillion dollar hoard (current account trade surplus), support for free trade underpinning globalization could abruptly end, bringing the epoch of extraordinarily rapid economic growth that began in 1990 to an unceremonious conclusion.

Most economists agree that a return to 1930s-style protectionism would depress global economic activity and alter the fortunes of various nations in complex ways. China doubtlessly would be a principle victim

---

[30] Chinese unemployment today is around 4.3%, close to what would be the Keynesian full employment rate, allowing for transitory unemployment. If a portion of China's unemployment qualifies as Keynesian involuntary unemployment, it should be attributable to the usual Keynesian cause and amenable to further monetary, fiscal, and protectionist stimulus.

[31] Rosefielde, S (2011). China's perplexing foreign trade policy: Causes, consequences and solutions. *American Foreign Policy Interests*.

[32] Ewing, J and S Chan (2010). Echoing Obama, Bernanke Presses China on imbalances (November 18, 2010). *New York Times*.

of its own recalcitrance, as diminished trade, outsourcing, and technology transfer retard its economic progress, but other Asian nations also would suffer. The near-term impact of the 2008 financial crisis in this way could be more adverse than expected, propelling the globe on an evolutionary collision course no one desires.[33] Although East–West living standard asymmetries and intra-Asian performance orderings ultimately might still correspond with underlying systemic potentials, wellbeing everywhere could be severely repressed. The invisible hand it seems may not be able to stop "rational" leaders from playing with matches, turning dull endings into something far worse.

---

[33] Cf. Mahbubani, K (2008). The case against the West. *Foreign Affairs*, 87(3),111–124. Some statistical sources make it appear as if Singapore's and Hong Kong's per capita GDP already surpass America's. This is the misleading consequence of failing to distinguish indigenous from total per capital income. See Steven Rosefielde, *Asian Economic Systems*, Chapter 7.

CONCLUSION

Asia is a modernizing, heterogeneous region of diverse economic systems and cultures at different stages of development that could share a common destiny. Mikic and Ryuhei Wakasugi demonstrate in Chapters 11 and 12 that Asian nations are linked together through the intermediate input trade and coupled with the West through the exchange of final goods and services.

Korhonen, Fidrmuc, and Batorova (Chapter 13) however have discovered that trade coupling is only part of the story. Their econometric tests reveal that China (and perhaps the tigers and Vietnam) have successfully decoupled from the global business cycle, while other Asian states like Japan and North Korea have not done so. Consequently, China, the tigers, and other market communist states that flourished during the past two decades seem poised to surpass their rivals east and west, while Japan, North Korea, and probably Myanmar underperform.

This surmise is supported by country studies which reveal that some Asian nations weathered the 2008 financial crisis better than others, with internals that suggest winners will continue to excel. China, the tigers, and Vietnam have not faltered, while North Korea remains zombified, and Japan appears headed for its third "lost decade" in succession, regardless of whether China, the tigers, Thailand, Vietnam, Laos, Cambodia, Myanmar, Malaysia, Indonesia, India, Russia, and North Korea prosper.

Postcrisis Asian economic performance therefore seems destined to proceed along two divergent trajectories: one that will allow China and the tigers to substantially catch up with and perhaps overtake the West; the other causing Japan, North Korea, and Myanmar to fall back.

This duality is perplexing because the Japanese, Taiwanese and South Korean systems share many common traits, and market communism suffers from numerous debilitating inefficiencies including the criminalization of freehold property, state-controlled foreign trade, rent-granting and the "rule of men" as opposed to "rule of law." Parts of the mystery are explicable. China has the advantage of acute economic backwardness, and Singapore's GDP drastically overstates its per capita indigenous income, but Japan's lethargy still remains puzzling. If a solution is not found, then the partitioning of Asia into two disparate performance groups will endure, even if market communist and tiger economic growth rates revert to the mean as China's catch-up epoch draws to a close.

Regional growth rates in this scenario must slow as the catch-up stimulus depletes in Asia and abroad: a phenomenon compounded by the depressive effects of exorbitant Western debt. Any recurrence or intensification of worldwide financial instability will make matters worse. Consequently, it seems unlikely that the exuberant economic successes of 1990s and 2000s will be repeated in the decades ahead.

Competitive theory implies that Japan and the tigers should outshine China in the long run because their markets are more efficient. Japan and the tigers should be on top of any ultimate two Asian hierarchy; China, Vietnam, Laos, Cambodia, and Myanmar on the bottom. A restoration of the status quo ante thus is thinkable, but Japan's two lost decades and the possibility of contagion in Taiwan and South Korea suggest that the wisest course is to keep an open mind.

INDEX

Aid for Trade 324
Applied tariffs 319
Article IV consultation 172
ASEAN 328, 332, 334, 335
ASEAN+3 168–171, 174
ASEAN+3 Macroeconomic Research Office (AMRO) 171
Asian crisis 155, 160, 161, 163, 166–170, 172–174
Asian economic performance 9, 439
Asian Monetary Fund (AMF) 168
Asian Newly Industrialized Economies (NIEs) 328, 334

balance-of-payment crisis 160, 172, 174
beggar-thy-neighbor protectionism 75
big bang liberalization 429
bilateral currency swaps (BSAs) 168, 169
Black Swan 76, 251, 252, 255, 261, 264, 265, 427
Bound tariffs 319
Bretton Woods II 205
BRIC 361–364

capital control 173, 175
catch-up 13, 15–17, 73, 422–424, 426–428, 435, 440
Chiang Mai Initiative (CMI) 155, 156, 167–171, 174
China 81–83, 88, 94, 98–100, 267–276, 278–283, 288–292, 345–347, 349, 351
CMI multilateralization (CMIM) 169, 170
command communism 14, 19, 20, 424–426, 431
command-basis GDP 362, 371
common fiscal parameters 396, 401, 412
communalism 13, 430
communist growth 11, 13, 14
Comparative Advantage 327, 329, 330
confucian systems 13, 17
consumption driven growth 267, 288–291
convergence 14–20, 61–65, 71, 421, 422, 426–428
corporate governance 183, 185, 192
Current account surplus 342

de facto dollar pegs 161
decoupling 156, 249, 297, 298, 301, 309, 310, 316

442 *Index*

deflation 71–73, 251, 262, 263
divergence 14–20, 61–65
divine coincidence 71
dollar reserve hoarding 251, 252, 254–259, 261, 262, 264, 265, 430, 435
double dip recession 72
dynamic correlation analysis 345, 352

economic crisis 185, 193, 194
Economic Review and Policy Dialogue (ERPD) 171
economic system 177, 179, 192, 194
Emerging economies 328, 329, 344
epochs 422
euro 379, 380, 386, 387, 390, 392, 396–398, 401, 403, 405, 408, 411–413
euro area 82, 83, 85, 89–92, 97
European Monetary Union 405
European Union 397, 410
Eurozone 379, 392, 393, 408
excess savings 269, 288
Exchange rate 81, 82, 91, 92, 95–97, 267, 269–272, 337–339, 344
Exchange rate manipulations 297, 321
Export dependence 304–310
export driven growth 267, 288, 291
Export pessimism 296
export-led development 251, 258, 421–423, 425, 431, 434, 435
Export-led growth 295–297, 299–301
Extensive margin 329, 335–341

Factory Asia 309, 310
Financial and Economic Crisis in Russia 212, 219
financial crisis 199, 206, 327, 329, 334, 336, 339–343
financial integration 345–347
fiscal stimulus 267, 288
Flying-geese model 296
foreign reserves 268, 269, 271, 273, 274

GDI (gross domestic income) 362, 367–369, 372
global financial crisis 69, 70, 155, 156, 160, 161, 173, 251, 422, 429
Global imbalance 74, 204, 205, 341
global saving glut 205
global trade 86, 87
golden age economic growth 71
government spending 275, 277, 278, 280, 282, 285, 286, 288, 291
Gravity relationships 336
Great Recession 70, 77, 78, 82

Heckscher-Ohlin 257, 423, 427
High-end 329, 332, 343
IMF 270, 271, 273
IMF link 168, 169, 171, 174
IMF program 163, 168, 170, 174
Impossible Trinity 161
Income elasticity 337, 343
India 345–349, 351
inequality 268, 380, 381, 383
Innovation Process 227
Institutional Economics 223, 235
institutional run on bank 73
intensive margin 329, 335–341, 343
intra-Asian stratification 421

Index 443

Intraregional trade 312–316
IT bubble 329, 340

Japan 177–183, 185, 187–190, 193–195
Japan's lost decade 424, 426, 430, 114

Knowledge-Based Economy 217, 223, 225, 232, 244

labor market 182, 192, 384, 396, 397, 401, 403, 413
Labor suppression 269, 270
leasehold property 431
Lehman Shock 158, 161, 167
leveraging 79
liberalization 191
loan platform 201
local governments 199
Low-end 332

mark to market 69, 252
market communism 9, 18, 425, 426, 431, 432, 434, 439
mobilization 10, 17
modernization 10, 13–15, 209, 212, 214–216, 222, 223, 226, 230, 232, 237, 239, 240, 242, 244, 245, 249, 258, 421, 422, 424–426, 428, 430, 431, 433
Multilateral trade liberalization 343
Multinational Corporations 329

New-Keynesian-Perfect Arbitrage 75
noncommunist growth 13

Offshore outsourcing 329, 334
Offshoring 335
overtrading 253, 257, 258, 265

post-modernization 426
pre-crisis consensus 70
Product range 338, 339
Production networks 310–312
productivity 397–400, 403, 411–414
Purchasing power 342

QE2(quantitative easing) 73, 75, 79, 251, 262, 264, 265, 429

real convergence 379, 407
real estate bubble 206
Regional Soft Power 237
rent-granting 260, 426, 432, 434, 439
Ricardian equivalence 71
RMB 201, 202, 204
rule of law 256, 263, 433, 440
rule of men 432, 434, 440
Russia 209, 211–221, 223–225, 227–245
Russian Federation 213, 214, 218, 219, 223, 235, 238, 244

self-insurance 167, 169, 174
Stages approach to comparative advantage 296
state trading 257
stealthy protectionism 252, 260
stimulus package 199, 201, 297, 316–318
Structural Reform 225, 242

444 Index

subprime mortgage securities 155, 158

surveillance 156, 169, 171–174

TARP 75, 251, 262, 264

terms of trade 362, 367, 369, 374

Thailand 268, 270, 271, 278–281

tigers 9, 13, 17, 426, 428, 434, 439, 440

tit-for-tat 263, 264

total factor productivity (TFP) 361, 366, 367, 373, 374

Trade structure 338, 343

trading gain 362, 367–369, 370, 372–374

Transaction Costs 215, 216, 227, 236

Transmission 297, 298, 321

Triad trade 327, 334

twin crises 172

underimporting 75, 253, 257–261, 435

Unskilled labor 332

US 267–275, 282, 288, 290, 291

USA 83–85, 87–89, 95, 96, 98, 99

US government 328

vector autoregression (VAR) 156, 163–165, 167, 173

White Swan 75

WTO 226, 238, 239, 242–244, 337, 339